GLOBAL TRADE AND COMMERCIAL NETWORKS: EIGHTEENTH-CENTURY DIAMOND MERCHANTS

Perspectives in Economic and Social History

Series Editor: *Robert E. Wright*

Titles in this Series

1 Migrants and Urban Change: Newcomers to Antwerp, 1760–1860
Anne Winter

2 Female Entrepreneurs in Nineteenth-Century Russia
Galina Ulianova

3 Barriers to Competition: The Evolution of the Debate
Ana Rosado Cubero

4 Rural Unwed Mothers: An American Experience, 1870–1950
Mazie Hough

5 English Catholics and the Education of the Poor, 1847–1902
Eric G. Tenbus

6 The World of Carolus Clusius: Natural History in the Making, 1550–1610
Florike Egmond

7 The Determinants of Entrepreneurship: Leadership, Culture, Institutions
José L. García-Ruiz and Pierangelo Toninelli (eds)

8 London Clerical Workers, 1880–1914: Development of the Labour Market
Michael Heller

9 The Decline of Jute: Managing Industrial Change
Jim Tomlinson, Carlo Morelli and Valerie Wright

10 Mining and the State in Brazilian Development
Gail D. Triner

Forthcoming Titles

The Clothing Trade in Provincial England, 1800–1850
Alison Toplis

Sex in Japan's Globalization, 1870–1930: Prostitutes, Emigration and Nation Building
Bill Mihalopoulos

Energy, Trade and Finance in Asia: A Political and Economic Analysis
Justin Dargin and Tai Wei Lim

Welfare and Old Age in Europe and North America: The Development of Social Insurance
Bernard Harris (ed.)

Financing India's Imperial Railways, 1875–1914
Stuart Sweeney

GLOBAL TRADE AND COMMERCIAL NETWORKS: EIGHTEENTH-CENTURY DIAMOND MERCHANTS

BY

Tijl Vanneste

LONDON AND NEW YORK

First published 2011 by Pickering & Chatto (Publishers) Limited

Published 2016 by Routledge
2 Park Square, Milton Park, Abingdon, Oxfordshire OX14 4RN
711 Third Avenue, New York, NY 10017, USA

First issued in paperback 2015

Routledge is an imprint of the Taylor & Francis Group, an informa business

BRITISH LIBRARY CATALOGUING IN PUBLICATION DATA

Vanneste, Tijl.
Global trade and commercial networks: eighteenth-century diamond merchants.
–(Perspectives in economic and social history)
1. Diamond industry and trade – Europe – History – 18th century. 2. Merchants – Europe – History – 18th century.
I. Title II. Series
382.4'282'094'09033-dc22

ISBN-13: 978-1-138-66141-7 (pbk)
ISBN-13: 978-1-8489-3087-2 (hbk)

Typeset by Pickering & Chatto (Publishers) Limited

CONTENTS

ACKNOWLEDGEMENTS

This book would not have been possible without the support and inspiration given by many people. First of all I want to thank Prof. Diogo Ramada Curto, who has provided excellent guidance while I was at the European University Institute in Florence. Prof. Anthony Molho has always been available, and has read many of my incomplete writings, providing useful and honest comments. Niki Koniordos's office was always open, and she always helped me out when needed. I also want to thank Prof. Jan de Vries for his useful comments and his encouragement. I greatly benefited from my participation in the seminars on economic history and Europe in the early modern world during the spring term of 2008 at UC Berkeley. I am grateful to Prof. Larry Neal and Dr Joost Jonker for helping me with the technicalities regarding to bills of exchange, and I equally wish to thank Prof. Francesca Trivellato for her constructive comments on my writings. In the transformation of the thesis into a book, the suggestions given by an anonymous referee have been most helpful. My research would not have been possible without the generous assistance given to me by the people working in the different archives I consulted in Belgium, the Netherlands, the UK, the US, Portugal and Brazil. My enquiries by email were without exception answered with a friendly invitation to come to the archives, where help was waiting. I appreciate very much the correction work done by David McCourt. I am grateful for the technical assistance given to me by Rein Vanneste and Maarten van Tongel. I enjoyed very much the talks on history and the inspiring comments given by Brett Auerbach-Lynn, Knightcarl Raymond and Dr Oscar Gelderblom. This book has benefited from remarks given to me by Karin Hofmeester. I also want to thank Dr Gelderblom and Beate Völker for giving me the opportunity to research diamonds in different archives. A last mention goes to the good care given to me by Trees de Geest and Anastasia Jamin. I am very obliged to Pickering & Chatto and Daire Carr for giving me the chance to write this book. I am greatly indebted to Stephina Clarke for editing this monograph. I also want to thank Eleanor Hooker for taking care of the marketing. All mistakes still in this monograph are my own. I dedicate this book to my mother Trees de Geest and to Anastasia Jamin. I couldn't have written it without them.

LIST OF FIGURES AND TABLES

INTRODUCTION

At a time when globalization is seen as one of the most important characteristics of our present-day world, it is not surprising that the debate on the roots of it takes a very prominent place in historical writing. A growing tendency to see one interconnected world today has created a need to write a history of such a world.

Two big issues dominate this field, and economic development plays a fundamental role in both. The first approach to world history looks for an explanation for global economic divergence. Economical, but also cultural and technological advantages have been incorporated into macro-historical accounts explaining the different speeds of growth of different regions. Rationalization, specific cultural, social or legal underpinnings of societies, religion, political systems and technological development all have been analysed as reasons why some regions of Western Europe were able to experience a unique economic growth.[1] A body of literature confirming European superiority has been questioned by opposing scholars who argue that the gap between the West and the rest of the world was not as wide as is sometimes assumed.[2] An important part of their analysis is that many of the qualities considered present in European societies were not as unique as they are sometimes made out to be. Part of this critique stems from the fact that the analysis of difference has too often been directed by a biased methodological point of view, complemented by a lack of empirical knowledge of non-Western source material.[3] A second problem often attributed to global histories of divergences is that they depart from a too static comparative basis: 'a major difficulty ... has been the tendency to view civilizations as timeless essences whose fate is predetermined at the moment of inception by their constituent elements.'[4] The second big question in world history opposes this comparative framework in which civilizations are looked upon as closed entities. It offers an analysis of the elements that tie the world together, and in this sense, it is dominated by the question of when globalization began. There are about as many definitions of globalization as there are historical narratives of it, and opinions about its relevance in different fields, such as politics, culture or economics, are divided. What does seem clear is that any definition needs to rely on the notion of global interconnectedness caused by human interaction. One of the forms of interaction that has been considered as one of the strongest causal factors for a growing global interconnectedness is international trade and the question about the origins of globalization becomes a matter of analysing when the density of international trade circuits became high enough for them to serve as proof of an integrated world.

Out of a desire to explain the world we are living in today, globalized and regulated by free market exchange, historical discourse on trade has often taken a macro-perspective. It is clear that in the eighteenth century, the world was not the global village that it is often perceived to be today. Analyses of global interconnectedness based on hard economic terms, such as price convergence on international markets or the volume of international trade, has led to doubts about the existence of a pre-modern globalization.[5] In recent years, and inspired by legal scholars, anthropologists and sociologists, economic historians have come to focus more on a micro-perspective of trade. Rather than seeing commerce as the main organizer of our modern world, explanation is sought in analyses of the organizational forms that make trade possible. This shift in perspective also means a change in methodology: a Weberian, structure-based approach is challenged by a Durkheimian type of economic analysis offering a more central place to human agency. One of the benefits of game theory in analysing economic behaviour has been that

> Rather than assuming that individuals follow rules, it provides an analytical framework within which it is possible to study the way in which behavior is endogenously generated – how, through their interactions, individuals gain the information, ability, and motivation to follow particular rules of behavior.[6]

The insertion of the human aspect has in turn led to different schools of thought, relying on fundamentally different notions of what aspects of human behaviour are relevant when discussing commerce. Analyses of commerce that rely on social embeddedness and cultural norms often stand in contrast to narratives on trade that rely on the development of institutions as efficient and problem-solving instruments. While the first category of theories uses concepts such as networks, diasporas and commercial friendship as successful social vehicles to overcome problems of commercial trust, the second by-passes such concepts by considering the importance of self-interest and rational calculation. The central issue concerns cheating: why would a merchant trust another one, who he might have never met? New economic sociology, building on Mark Granovetter's work on social embeddedness, has concentrated on the importance of social ties in this regard. Cheating is avoided because the social price to be paid would be too high, such as excommunication from the community, or because social control is too strong. Others have focused on rational behaviour as the incentive for sustained commercial relationships: cheating is, in the long run, harmful to the self-interest of the cheater.[7] In this sense, the concept of trust has been criticized for being useless in explaining commercial relationships, as it can be considered to be a rationally created device to overcome the concrete problems of trade posed by long-term commitments between merchants living far away from each other. The argument made in this book will rely on a notion of commercial trust that is partially based on rational choice but also on non-rational elements that have origins in a socio-cultural setting that encompasses business alone.

The idea of a social embeddedness of commerce has been influential with regard to economic history and the macro-perspective of international trade. The role of widely dispersed diaspora communities is considered to be fundamental in the development of large-scale connections.[8] Important in these studies is a focus on the human element as a basis for a growing interconnectedness. The ability of a trade diaspora to pass geographical and political boundaries gives it such a prominent place in global history. Diaspora communities are seen as offering a socio-cultural setting in which commerce can flourish and trade networks based on diaspora movements function by using communal control and the adoption of shared norms and values. A strong tendency towards intermarriage fortified such mono-cultural networks.[9] But not all international trade connections resided within mono-cultural, mono-religious or mono-ethnic blocs. At some point, merchants belonging to a diaspora engaged in business with traders belonging to different communities. In this sense, international trade bears a strong cross-cultural mark. Commercial contact between merchants with different backgrounds becomes relevant if such contacts took place on a regular and stable basis. With regard to globalization, it is of vital importance to study the cross-cultural aspect of international trade. It shifts attention from the study of relationships between groups instead of an analysis of what made commerce work within one specific group.[10]

The definition of globalization through commerce can be refined to incorporate not only the density of international trade circuits, but also the degree of cross-cultural interaction. To support the claim for early modern globalization, a study of commercial networks is needed. This book is about a specific cross-cultural trade network of diamond traders who were active in the eighteenth century. It is a study of commerce as it took place between merchants who did not share the same religion, nationality or background, but who were all members of a commercial society, with its own logic, its own organization and its own language. The main question is micro-historical in scope: how was trade organized between merchants of different origins? The answer points to the use of reputational mechanisms. A merchant's reputation was his most important asset. It was built upon past conduct in trade, creditworthiness and the regularity of his commercial correspondence. The relevance of personal reputation in commerce should not be underestimated. History has a large tradition of explaining certain developments in terms of the personality of actors, but such human-based analysis always seems to have held more power when analysing the roles played by rulers or thinkers than when considering the role played by groups such as merchants. By asserting the importance of formalized personality-based criteria in commercial society, a larger agency is given to the human element in the historical development of international trade. Reputation plays a role both in the construction of privileged network relationships and in a merchant's valuation in a larger business community. The international mercantile society was not a formal body of merchants all acting according to well-established rules, but rather an informal set of negotiated norms and commercial customs that were adopted amongst a wide variety of trade relations. Although in essence, self-interest was a crucial motivation for every merchant participating in international trade, merchants were aware that they could only serve their own interests by looking out for the interests of others and the common language developed between traders is often a language stressing mutual benefit. Albert O. Hirschman has stated that 'the by-product of individuals acting predictably in accordance with their economic interests was ... not an uneasy balance, but a strong web of interdependent relationships'.[11] This is crucial in understanding the role played by socio-cultural elements with regard to commercial behaviour. Self-interest is by no means absent, but became a recognized principle within commercial society in the sense that self-interest in others was also accepted. According to Amalia Kessler, 'anti-commercial norms of selflessness served to promote commercial self-interest'.[12] I. Ben-Amos considers that the evolution towards modernity 'has typically centered on the supposed decline of personal obligations and the emergence of more calculating, selfish norms'.[13] Rather than seeing a substitution of a system based on social and personal relationships with a system based on rationality, early modern commercial society managed to construct commercial relationships by incorporating social customs. Eighteenth-century commercial society developed in a way that anti-commercial norms of selflessness were used as a common language on which long-lasting and regular trade relationships could develop that served mutual interests.

This idea makes traders more than individuals in a market society. Human agency with regard to worldwide integration is not given to the individual, nor is globalization explained by structural economical conditions. Attention to networks rather than individual entrepreneurs is one of the most important developments in business history in recent years. In establishing the historical agency exerted by networks of trade, finance and information, the role of the individual entrepreneur is taken out if its cadre of rationality and self-interest to be inserted into a theory in which cooperation and interaction are the crucial forms of agency.[14]

The merchants whose activities serve as the empirical basis for this book were all active in the diamond trade. There are two important reasons why the diamond trade is an excellent case to test the hypothesis that social relationships are crucial to successful commerce. A first argument is that the international diamond trade was a branch of business that built upon a relatively high degree of cross-cultural cooperation. Commerce in precious stones is generally considered to be a closed world of orthodox Jewish merchants. This stems from the historical assumption that the trade in precious stones has been dominated for centuries by Jewish traders. Relying on the idea that diamond trade was exercised within a relatively closed and homogeneous group, social and cultural explanations for the self-regulating and extralegal nature of the business are popular.[15] Historical evidence, however, suggests that diamond trade was not as closed as presumed. Intercultural partnerships are found commonly in lists of merchants active in the Indian diamond trade and existing commercial correspondence suggests the importance of non-Jewish diamond merchants.[16] Francesca Trivellato has studied a cross-cultural diamond network spreading from Lisbon to London and India, demonstrating that other ethnic groups played an equally crucial role in the trade.[17] Owing to a lack of source material, the flow of diamonds to the Mogul court, China or Arab and Persian regions cannot be analysed in a structural manner and in general the historical role of Indian trade networks in serving Asian markets remains undervalued. Another element challenging the idea of diamond trade as dominated by one ethnic group is that the homogeneous nature of Jewish merchants as one group is, from a historical point of view, highly questionable. Sephardic Jews coming from the Iberian Peninsula were clearly distinguishable, economically but also socially, linguistically and culturally, from the Ashkenazim that came from Eastern Europe in the seventeenth and eighteenth centuries. A second reason is that a great deal of the trade in diamonds was secretive. From the 1750s onwards, Brazilian diamond imports to Europe were limited by a royal monopoly. At various times, the trade in Indian diamonds has been regulated by the different European East India Companies. Import duties had to be paid, and at times private trade in precious stones was forbidden. The large amount of illegal commerce and smuggling made the diamond business dependant on personal relationships, which enhanced the importance of commercial trust.

This book is about one of many different networks active in the diamond trade in the first half of the eighteenth century. James Dormer was a Catholic Englishman living in Antwerp and as a merchant he had not specialized in a specific commodity. As many merchants of his time, he traded in everything that could yield a reasonable profit. In this sense, he was no different from other eighteenth-century merchants.[18] As a result of this lack of specialization, Dormer developed an extensive correspondence with different traders. Between 1735 and 1765, he and his son, who took over the firm after Dormer died in 1758, wrote an average of 509 letters per year. The fact that this number is not extraordinarily high for a merchant at the time shows perhaps that Dormer was not one of the bigger firms, but it nevertheless indicates that traders spent a lot of time writing letters to business contacts. With only a few of those business contacts did Dormer develop a close relationship and the duration of most of his correspondences was short: more than 75 per cent of them stopped within five years. Only 13 per cent of the merchants with whom Dormer corresponded remained in regular contact with him for longer than ten years.[19] An important part of his activities were embedded within the international immigration of English Catholics. Although Dormer tried, and succeeded by marriage, to gain entry into the world of local lower nobility, he also considered himself to be a part of the international English Catholic diaspora. 48 per cent of the traders with whom Dormer corresponded for longer than ten years were English, Irish and Scottish, and a lot of them were Catholic. He offered credit to English travellers and one time he personally rescued an English alcoholic army captain from prison.[20] It is not surprising that a merchant relied heavily on other merchants sharing a similar background. The familiarity created by a shared religion, nationality or language might serve to deter merchants from cheating on a business partner and it seems logical that many merchants were naturally attracted to trading partners living far away who shared origins in the same community.

International commerce, however, was not exclusively based on such monocultural networks of trade. Although Dormer had not specialized, over time he did develop specific interests. The insurance company he founded in 1754 was important for him, as well as his banking activities. In commodity trade, he developed a focus on diamonds and textiles. It is in the diamond trade that Dormer associated himself with traders who did not share a common religion, kinship ties or nationality. His first transactions in the diamond trade were conducted with the Sephardic Jewish firm of Francis and Joseph Salvador. These merchants were, more than Dormer, active on an international scale and in other branches of trade and finance. Around their commercial association, a trade network developed itself that remained operational until Dormer's death in 1758. The network spanned four cities: Amsterdam, London, Antwerp and Lisbon, and different religions, ranging from Sephardic Jews, English Catholics and Protestants, as well as French Huguenots. It remained active on a regular basis for a period of fifteen years and with all the network members living abroad, Dormer had established a regular correspondence for that period, making the network merchants exceptionally intimate trade contacts with Dormer. Although the network focused on diamond exchange, its members interacted with each other in different trade operations such as textile trade, insurance and financial operations. For the sake of simplicity, this network will be referred to throughout this book as the cross-cultural diamond trade network. The interest of Dormer in diamonds is somewhat remarkable. In the first half of the eighteenth century, Antwerp suffered an economic crisis and commercial activities were in decline. This was also noticeable in the diamond trade and only twelve diamond merchants were known to be active in Antwerp in that period.[21] Amsterdam and London had overcome Antwerp as Europe's most important centres in the trade of precious stones. For the merchants active in the cross-cultural network that emerges from the correspondence sent to Dormer, Antwerp remained an important market to sell polished diamonds. Taste differed locally, and although London and Amsterdam were by far more important as diamond import centres, Antwerp could still rely on a diamond cutting industry and on a local consumer market.

The main commercial instrument used by merchants working together was business correspondence. The regular writing of letters to one another allowed for international business to take place, as it turned discussions on commercial opportunities into concrete commodity transactions. But letters sent were much more than tools used in commerce; they also allowed for the construction of intimate commercial ties that made the relationships between the merchants of the cross-cultural diamond trade network privileged. Apart from a direct function related to commerce, the letters merchants wrote to one another served a number of other purposes. In their cohesive function, through reciprocity and mutual interest, business correspondence assured that the network was profitable for all merchants involved. It is the main reason why such a business organization remained operational. In their social function, these trade letters created a sense of intimacy and friendship between merchants and hence worked to create a familiar world within which it became easier for them to trust one another. It adds to the idea that a network is an organization and not just of businessmen sharing an interest in the diamond trade, but also of a group of privileged merchants who had developed a routine exchange of letters between them, in contrast to a world of outsiders and competitors. In this sense, it is correct to use the term commercial friendship. According to Luuc Kooijmans, friendship in the seventeenth and eighteenth centuries should not be mistaken with our modern notion of friendship as being free from self-interest. In a time when protection and support from the government was minimal, individuals became engaged in relationships with people who would be willing to help in case of need. Relationships had to be maintained by regular contact and the assumed promise of reciprocity.[22] These conditions were present in the privileged relationship between Dormer, Francis and Joseph Salvador, Berthon and Garnault and others. Such friendship was not exclusive, however, and none of the merchants who were active within the network devoted all their commercial activities to that network. All merchants had other trades, other interests and other correspondents. A few examples given above suggest already the willingness to use these other contacts on behalf of network trade, but it seems clear that the relationship between network insiders and outsiders was more complex than that, especially because a differential in commercial activities meant that different webs of correspondents not always meant that they were competitive webs potentially harmful to network trade activities. The attachment of merchants to different international circuits of commercial correspondents shows that the cross-cultural network did not operate in a vacuum; it was but one of many different possible organizations of long-lasting business relationships. What these relationships had in common was that they had become more and more international and diverse, and that they increasingly relied on a set of informal norms regulating commercial behaviour. More privileged relationships of commerce were embedded in the larger world of commercial society and a third additional purpose of commercial correspondence was the maintenance of ties with this outside commercial community, by providing information on the reputation and creditworthiness of other merchants. The divulgation of reliable information not only added to the reputations of merchants within a web of privileged relationships, it also opened up new opportunities – something that always interested a trader.

A last purpose of trade letters was the arrangement of credit operations. The amount of letters sent by merchants that discuss concrete commodity transactions is far lower than the amount of letters discussing financial operations, especially credit. In international commerce, most payments for goods contained an element of future payment. The dependence on credit tied the mercantile community together, and payment instruments such as the bill of exchange were the physical expression of these ties. The bill of exchange was a technical invention making international payments possible. In the eighteenth century, the bill of exchange was no longer exclusively attached to commodity trade. The invention of the endorsement had made it a negotiable commodity and bills could contain a whole list of signatures on the back. The valuation of these strings of credit was based on trust, meaning the punctuality of the payer, but also indicating the belief that he would indeed pay. The lack of specialization of most eighteenth-century merchants was also visible in the giving and providing of credit. According to Stanley Chapman, 'the loan business was quite conveniently run in harness with that of the merchant'.[23] Merchants developed skills in both commodity trade and finance and both were strongly interwoven.

Apart from the large attention to credit, correspondence contained a lot of information regarding possible transactions. In writing about many events, market possibilities and possible engagements in future trade relations, James Dormer and his correspondents have provided us with the material required to reconstruct their image of the world. The number of transactions that traders looked into is far greater than the number of transactions that became concrete. If analysis were to be restricted to the actual commercial operations of traders, it would provide a limited image of the world as it was perceived by merchants. David Hancock has described two ways of analysing transatlantic trade: statistical and biographical.

His main problem with a statistical approach is that it 'reveals patterns in their entirety of which the participants could not directly have been aware'.[24] International merchants considered the world as a place of possibility.

This is best shown by the experience of Francis and Joseph Salvador who were active as international merchants, engaged in different enterprises that were often international in scale. Their firm had representatives in India and they were involved in the trade monopoly in Brazilian diamonds. Joseph Salvador bought land in South Carolina, where he lived the final two years of his life and his son-in-law died fighting for American independence. Their international connections influenced their mindset; the world was an open place to them, a place in which they were constantly looking for new opportunities by contacting traders who lived far away.

The opportunistic mindset of a merchant was complemented by a curiosity in the world. Joseph Salvador was interested in geology and astronomy, and within the network he was not the only trader with a passion for science. These interests enhanced the merchant's view of the world, and they had a notion of it that was more than theoretical. In this way, awareness grew as did the perception of these merchants as cosmopolites. The experience of the Salvadors as merchants, and their financial success, had given them a certain status. Both Francis and Joseph Salvador were on different occasions consulted by the Portuguese and British governments. They had an influence on adopted international policies, because they were seen as people with an international outlook. It is often this label of cosmopolitanism that has created the perception of merchants as the main actors in the development of globalization. It is difficult to reconcile an idea of geographical integration through human interaction if the people involved were not attached to their surrounding societies. In her analysis of cosmopolitanism, Margaret Jacob has justly pointed to the need to consider physical places where strangers could meet.[25] It was often centres of international trade, such as port cities, that were considered as cosmopolitan places because of the different ethnic groups established there and their occupation in commerce.[26] However, early modern globalization seems hard to sustain if its existence is based on the actions of a minority group of international traders living in a number of port cities. Chapter 5 will show that members of diaspora movements were embedded in the social environment in their host society, in a more profound and nuanced manner than is usually assumed. Placing the actions of diaspora traders in a paradigm that is based on the search for acceptance by the host society is reductive and underestimates the manner in which different diaspora merchants had adopted a national feeling about their host society without abandoning their loyalty to their religion. It reduces diaspora members to 'outsiders to polity with only commercial profit in mind ... their link to their host society [is not] assumed to be anything more than the payments made for a right to conduct commerce as cross-cultural brokers'.[27] According to Francesca Trivellato, 'Sephardic merchants asserted their self-perception as full members of an increasingly tolerant commercial society, but also struggled to diminish the impact of less than sympathetic views that were meant to keep them on the margins of that very same commercial society'.[28]

The combined presence of cosmopolitan outlook and membership of international networks with a successful positioning in a new society offers a solution to the paradox that the same merchants who managed to integrate in remote regions were not really embedded in those regions. The quote from Francesca Trivellato shows that, in the eighteenth century, full membership of foreigners in society was not generally accepted but remained open to fierce debate. It shows that the world was changing due to a larger circulation of people, goods and information. International and cross-cultural commercial networks did not create a global village. But they had started to change mentality and had opened questions about the organization of societies. These developments in turn led to a larger worldwide interconnectedness.

This book is divided into three parts, each containing two chapters. The first part is contextual. Chapter 1 offers a methodological overview of the analysis of commerce. It aims to show that there is a problem with the reliance on individual rational behaviour as the main explanatory factor for economic interaction. The rise of a commercial society is often considered to be one of the main expressions of modernity and historically, as well as economically, the development of free market exchange has become a central element in explaining the world of today. The connection between free trade and democracy has even led to the belief that history had reached an endpoint. Although Francis Fukuyama does not see man as a purely economic animal, the central idea of his *End of History* can be situated closely to positivist and evolutionary narratives with regard to commerce.[29] This belief stems from the way commerce in particular and economic activity in general has been studied in classic economic theory. Economic man is reduced to a self-interested and rational individual, and social and cultural underpinnings to economic activities such as commerce are seen as either irrelevant or archaic. Fukuyama's point of view belonged to a specific time, and in our current worldview, Western-based global history that considers the global spread of free market exchange as an endpoint is very much questioned.[30] In Chapter 1, this classic notion will be challenged by addressing criticisms launched at classic economic theory from different angles. Anthropological and sociological discourse will be used to support economic theory that includes not only self-interest and rationality, but also cultural particularity and social embeddedness. In making economic man a social participator in networks and a culturally diverse individual, cross-cultural trade networks can be said to have contributed to an early modern globalization.

The merchants studied in this book were all active in the diamond trade, and Chapter 2 focuses on the commercial world in which these traders operated. It gives an overview of the history of the diamond trade, with specific attention to the eighteenth century. Diamonds were a valuable luxury commodity in Europe, but also in Arab and Asian countries and in pre-industrial times diamonds were only found in India, Brazil and on the Indonesian island of Borneo. In this chapter, trade networks bringing diamonds from the mines into consumer markets will be investigated. This chapter initially focuses on diamond trade in Asia, moving on to the discovery of Brazilian diamonds and their subsequent entry into international commerce. The finding of precious stones in Minas Gerais greatly altered the international diamond trade and posed a threat to established networks active in trade with India. Another aspect affecting mercantile activities was taste. The last section of this chapter focuses on the consumption of diamonds in Europe, and how international trade networks were spread in Europe to allow diamonds to reach the classic consumption markets for jewellery, such as Paris. One of the most important aspects of these trade networks was that diamond trade was not a typical luxury commerce. Rough diamonds were imported into Europe to be transformed into jewellery but polished stones were also sent to India to be sold there. In this sense, no one-dimensional commodity chain can be traced from diamond mines in Asia and Brazil to European markets.

The second part of this book aims at an empirical analysis of the underlying mechanisms that helped to establish a cross-cultural diamond trade network. Chapter 3 deals with the network itself: its concrete activities and its internal cohesion through commercial correspondence. The first part of the chapter analyses the practical operations taking place within the network. It shows who was involved, what the respective roles were of the network members, and in what way they were active in the diamond business. The second part of the chapter analyses the foundation of this network, and addresses the question of how cross-cultural trade can take place. It is argued that business correspondence plays a crucial role in the establishment of regular commercial ties, and that it served, separate from its role in concrete trade transactions, four other functions that helped to maintain intra-network relationships as well as the connections with commercial society within which the network resided. These functions were the securing of mutual interest, the construction of a form of commercial friendship, the divulgation of information on others and the provision of credit.

These functions were not exclusive to a privileged set of traders and Chapter 4 deals with the relationship of one of the network's members with merchants belonging to another trade circuit. It will show the limits of loyalty but also how merchants used competition as a way to reinforce their own privileged relationships. Dormer maintained an extensive correspondence with a number of firms that were involved in a kinship-based network of Ashkenazi diamond traders. These merchants were considered as commercial competitors by some of Dormer's closest acquaintances and his involvement with them shows that self-interest was a strong motive for commercial action and that group loyalty had boundaries. Similarly to the Sephardim, Ashkenazi merchants were part of a religiously-inspired diaspora, and this element was an important part of their identity. The Ashkenazi diaspora has received far less attention than its Sephardic counterpart, partially because it is commonly accepted that the Ashkenazim were more land-oriented while the Sephardim have been seen as more international and connected to overseas trade. Merchants of the Ashkenazi firms studied in this chapter travelled to other cities or fairs in person, something Joseph Salvador rarely did. One of the aims of this chapter is to show that this difference in mentality cannot be reduced to a paradigm of old-style kinship-based business organization versus a more globalized cross-cultural model.

The final part of this book concentrates on the role played by commercial networks in the development of an early modern globalization. Chapter 5 argues that circuits consisting of internationally-active merchants can only contribute to growing interconnectedness if these merchants were at the same time oriented towards international trade but also attached to the local society in which they lived. Using the example of the Sephardic and Huguenot diasporas, this chapter shows how the dialogue maintained between society and foreign traders went beyond a simple demand for assimilation. Although international commerce and unfamiliar merchants have a long history of being considered as corrosive to the social order in society, the eighteenth century saw the emergence of thinkers who thought of trade as an asset. A growing presence of foreigners in the public space and in different segments of society contributed to mutual change that forced society to reconsider issues of belonging and social and cultural order. Growing cross-cultural interactions taking place on a local scale is a crucial condition to maintain the idea of a form of globalization.

The final chapter focuses on the exact contribution made by merchants who were at the same time outward-looking cosmopolites and inward-looking locals. Different business activities of several merchants active in the cross-cultural diamond trade network will be investigated, as well as the attachment of merchants to far-away regions. It was through the opportunistic participation of merchants in different commercial ventures with diverse traders that a new world of commerce came to take shape in the perception of these merchants with regard to the world. The combination of a changing mentality and awareness of the world with a growing attachment to specific communities and a normalization of commercial relationships with strangers is what justifies use of the term globalization in pre-industrial times. In this sense, the importance of traders as agents of worldwide interconnectedness goes beyond their professional activities. After all, the historical relevance of groups of people such as traders cannot remain limited to their employment alone.

1 MODELS FOR TRADE AND GLOBALIZATION

Social relationships are crucial to successful commerce. They are able to overcome the two factors that most contribute to the success of trade: good information and the prevention of cheating. These two criteria, together with the possibility of profit, determine if repeated transactions occur. Social embeddedness theories of trade answer why a merchant would trust another merchant whose actions might be beyond direct control or punishment. In the early modern period, the world did not have an integrated market and information travelled slowly. Trade did not yet shape the world, but was embedded in a society arranged on personal ties such as kinship or religious affiliation. Social ties and cultural norms and values were shared. In such a familiar world, a trader could reasonably predict commercial behaviour of another merchant. The fact that modern commerce was based on impersonal market exchange seems to suggest that the social embeddedness thesis is only valid for pre-industrial times. Historians have come up with institutions that were invented to replace social relationships in commerce, relying on the pursuit of self-interest by the rational individual.

Different scholars argue, however, that social relationships remain crucial in answering the question of repeated transactions. Trade is a form of human interaction, and a theory explaining its organization based solemnly on self-interest seems hard to sustain. Game theory, new economic sociology, institutional economics and network analysis all have in common that they analyse solutions for the problems of monitoring behaviour through information and the punishment of cheaters. In order to assess the validity of the claim that social relationships are important, commerce has to be analysed taking their conclusions into account. This can only be done by an analysis of the solutions applied by merchants to overcome problems of regular and long-distance cooperation. The social foundation of trade becomes especially relevant when considering the rising cross-culture nature of trade and its international expansion after new sea routes opened up to Asia and the New World. If social ties are so crucial, what sort of relationships were formed between people who entered into commercial transactions together who did not share kinship ties, a common religion or a similar background? This question becomes all the more poignant because it is often the rise of international trade that became central in explaining our modern economic system. In this first chapter, a theoretical framework will be discussed that will allow for a socio-cultural analysis of cross-cultural trade networks. This framework will be connected to a soft definition of early modern globalization that relies on the ability of international and cross-cultural commerce to change merchants and the societies to which they belonged in a profound and reciprocal manner.

Commerce as an Economic Activity

Classical Economic Theory, Economic Man and History

Following Adam Smith's *Wealth of Nations*, economic theory has firmly become rooted on the idea of the rational, calculative individual that is looking out for his best interest. Impersonal market exchange between utility-seeking individuals has become the main explanatory element in classical and neoclassical economics. According to Geoffrey Ingham, 'the model of the rational calculating subject is the foundation stone of all economics' and '*all* explanations in economics are based on typifications of individual economizing'.[1] Analysis of behaviour that is based on selfish incentives of so-called *homo economicus* led to classical economics, but it also created fierce methodological debates. Alfred Marshall published his *Principles of Economics* in 1892, and its first chapters showed the 'ubiquity of the calculating, maximizing spirit in economic life'.[2] The idea that it was possible to derive universal economic laws which were able to describe economic events disregarding where or when they occurred came up against strong opposition, not in the least from economic historians. The universality suggested in the theory of economic man is difficult to reconcile with a discipline such as history, wherein the particulars of time and place are essential to analysis. It is also very hard to re-interpret the past in the light of modern theories on man, as there is no absolute truth in the idea that man and his motives have always been the same throughout the ages with regard to economic activity.[3]

If it is accepted that the self-interested search for utility is a fundamental and universal inclination of man, it becomes impossible not to see societies that have made different arrangements with regard to economic activity as less-evolved. Societal economic practices that are not based on free market exchange between individuals become in this manner old-fashioned structures that stand in the way of modern economic development. In this sense, it becomes hard to argue that this type of economic analysis does not contain a fundamental notion of superiority of the free market.[4] A substantial amount of mainly Western historiography has been written with a desire to instruct others on the true nature of things, so that they can better their condition. This is a Western-focused agenda.[5] The idea of superiority is further enhanced by the revolutionary heritage that linked free trade and individualism with freedom and liberalism in general. It is this connection between the organization of the economy and of society based on individual self-interest that goes back to Adam Smith and was elaborated in the nineteenth century. An individual acting freely on the market would take up similar ideas about his freedom in general. A thinker such as Benjamin Constant 'adopted the more standard Smithian view that commercial life universalizes the ideal of the masterless man ... it habituates people to providing for their own needs without the intervention of political officials'.[6] More than an economic axiom, the idea of *homo economicus* became a modern ideal. Each individual, free from oppression, would be able to enter the market in order to transact with other individuals, leading to a mutual optimal fulfilment of self-interest. It has been a common consideration to see modern market exchange, or the capitalist system, as the crown in historical progress. The idea of a society arranged on self-interest as modern is an evolutionary idea that had already found its origins before Adam Smith.[7]

The interdependency between the development of classical economics based on the *homo economicus* paradigm and economic progress is remarkable, and has led to a mainly Western vision of economic activity and its contribution to progress of society. This vision suggests that scientific progress is economic progress, and economic differences are often explained in terms of knowledge differentials, which still does not explain where that gap in knowledge comes from.[8] Two different types of society can be distinguished: one in which rational individuals know what they are, and another in which they do not. Rationality means that once a society is aware of the fundamental human nature of its subjects, it can take fate into its own hands. In the modernity discourse, this is what happened in the West. Other societies have not experienced similar success because economic science has not advanced sufficiently to make them aware of the existence of fundamental laws based on economic human behaviour. Once they had advanced sufficiently and had become self-aware, there would be no rational reason why individuals living in such societies would not respond accordingly. It is not a coincidence that many eighteenth-century thinkers wrote about universal economic principles with an explicit agenda of making the government aware of these principles, so that they could act accordingly. The fact that a theory leads to a hierarchical world view does not in itself mean that such a theory is wrong. Universality of economic theories has also been attacked on the grounds of providing an analysis of ideal situations. Albert Hirschman considered idealized markets that consisted of 'large numbers of price-taking anonymous buyers and sellers supplied with perfect information'.[9] Classical economics might not always explain how things worked, but how they should work under specific and ideal circumstances, making abstraction of socio-cultural and historical elements that influenced economic behaviour. This is acknowledged by the development of institutional economics, a discipline that deals exactly with the imperfect nature of market relationships, and human-built institutions to overcome such imperfections.[10]

In economic theory based on *homo economicus*, there was no need to study culture, or to include human interactions that took place outside the anonymous market. Such matters came to belong to sociology or to anthropology, and this division led to a separation of research objects and created a lesser interest in cross-disciplinary approaches.[11] Eric Jones has written that 'economists agree about many things ... but the majority agree about culture only in the sense that they no longer give it much thought'.[12] The determinism that society is based on economically-driven actions of man separated the field of economics from the human sciences that dealt with society. This methodological separation is all the more remarkable since economics as a science had developed itself out of an analysis of society. When economics accepted the self-interested motive of man as the basis for his economic behaviour, man was made economic man, and other aspects of his character had lost their place in economics as a science. This also rang true for economic history. According to Emma Rothschild,

> historians have chosen, mostly, to describe the exterior events of life. The history of economic relationships has come to be seen, in particular, as a matter of quantities and commodities, of canals and paper money and the bullion committee. Economic thoughts (the thoughts of economic theorists, and of public officials, and of individuals in their economic lives) have come to be seen as something less than events.[13]

The idea that the thoughts of individuals in their economic lives no longer matter is especially relevant for this discourse. The acceptance of rationality and self-interest as the only human characteristics that matter when it comes to economic behaviour has made man a slave of his own nature. He seems not to have had much choice but to act in an economically rational manner, and the search for other motives regulating his behaviour was stopped on the grounds of irrelevance, at least in economic theory.

The separation between economics and human sciences goes back to an older division between ethics and economics. Historically, there has been a strong tendency to consider trade in a moral perspective.[14] According to Amartya Sen, economic theory has taken moral consideration out of its analysis.[15] The centrality of the rational and self-interested individual as an explanatory element in economic theory might have driven ethics out of classical economics. Ethics can be considered a field that analyses inner man. In its acceptance of self-interested man as the basis and its separation from ethics, classical economics has lost interest in culture or social group interaction precisely because it did not matter. The paradigm of *homo economicus* has driven questions on other motivations of man to other scientific disciplines. In universalizing human motives and by explaining the world in terms of economic performance, individual agency has become institutionalized. Economic science has embraced the *homo economicus*, but in doing so, it has also marginalized human agency or the importance of historical change. If human nature is fundamentally the same everywhere and at any time, it ceases to be an explanatory element. It is no coincidence that some of the strongest adversaries of classic economic history were sociologists and anthropologists. Scholars working in these disciplines are not so much concerned with the individual, but with interaction between individuals and groups in societies.[16] They argued for a more nuanced view of economic man by showing that other types of commercial exchange and relationships existed, historically as well as contemporaneously.[17]

The Rational and Self-Interested Mindset as a Cultural Construction

The challenge made by anthropology to the economic model based on rationality and self-interest is concentrated on its alleged universality and consequent superiority over other models. Anthropologists are well placed to confront the classic economic model, as they often examine societies wherein economic activity is based on other motives than individualism and profit maximization. It is not an anthropological prerogative to question the universality of individual character. The vision that human nature was fundamentally the same has never been without criticism. In his posthumously published *History of Economic Analysis*, Joseph Schumpeter criticized Adam Smith for the 'equalitarian tendency of his economic sociology'.[18] According to Schumpeter, Smith saw humans as fundamentally alike, attributing differences to different training or environment. For Schumpeter, economic progress lay in the action of the entrepreneur, who caused economic growth by coming up with an innovation.[19] The Schumpeterian entrepreneur broke out of a rhythm of daily life based on routine, something that required leadership skills, and a particular and rare mental state.[20] The Schumpeterian entrepreneur was rational and self-interested. He was an innovator who changed the economy in a dynamic manner. In his discourse on the importance of the entrepreneur with regard to economic progress, Schumpeter did not fundamentally challenge the idea of *homo economicus*. He made him a rare character, perhaps not to be found in all societies or at all times. He opposed universality, but he maintained the notion of exceptionalism based on the same economic qualities: rationality, individualism and self-interest. His individual possesses the same agency as is given to him by classical economics, but he is not a faceless individual. Schumpeter's theory implies that economic inequality can be explained by differences in human nature. The fundamental link between economic performance and *homo economicus* is not challenged, but the idea that everybody is a *homo economicus* is. It replaces the question of why certain societies had more economic success than others with the question of why certain societies had more entrepreneurial characters in their ranks than others. In this way, global differences are put in terms of human actions and motivations.

Schumpeter's entrepreneur possessed, however, another important character trait: in order to overcome resistance, he had to be self-aware. The idea of resistance was very important in his analysis, and it made the entrepreneur an extraordinary figure. In fighting resistance from people who were interested in preserving traditional circumstances, the entrepreneur had to be aware of his difference from most others.[21] Self-awareness is another way of explaining economic differences, but it allows for a preservation of the idea that humans are universally the same. In fact, self-awareness is a crucial aspect of economic man and plays a vital role in the parallel between scientific and economic progress. It leads to a deterministic idea of inequality. By making Western economic progress the measure of things, it is implied that other societies could arrive at a similar success, if they too became self-aware. This is a judgement of rational man towards another, but such judgement might not be an obvious truth. Jack Goody wrote that it is generally true that people see conformity to norms as a mark of the other, while they themselves are governed by individualistic and rational criteria.[22] Self-awareness can easily be mistaken for a universal truth by which others are measured. The self-awareness certain societies have constructed, also through scientific discourse, becomes a shortcoming for others. If human nature is unequal, that discourse becomes harder to maintain. Superiority is challenged, and one notion of awareness might not be a universal one. The causal link between self-interested human behaviour and successful economic performance is put into question. At the same time, the one-way association that man made society, and particularly that self-interested man made commercial society, was also challenged.

This allowed for a return to cultural and social explanations in economic theory and consequently in economic history also. A number of scholars have argued for the contextualization of rational and self-interested man, and for the necessity of placing him in a specific time and society. Self-interest was to become one of many different possible motivations of man and overly selfish behaviour no longer had to be seen as leading to market society, but was also considered to be a product of it. The relationship between certain characteristics of certain people and the society they live in becomes reciprocal:

> It has been suggested that homo economicus produced capitalism, meaning roughly that human nature being what it is, the evolution of the capitalist rules of the game is both likely and desirable. But this may be just backwards, or at least one-sided; one could equally argue that capitalism produced homo economicus.[23]

This approach made economic man and the society he lived in a possible object for anthropological or sociological study, but undermined the notion of classical economics. According to Robert Solow, 'the attempt to construct economics as an axiomatically based hard science is doomed to fail'.[24] He attributed this failure mostly to the impossibility of using hard scientific methods such as the testing of hypotheses by experiment, but also to the problematic nature of economic man. The anthropologist Marshall Sahlins wrote that 'the notion of a competitive self-interested human nature as the mainspring of history is itself a particular cultural self-consciousness'.[25] Others have also claimed that capitalism is a product of a specific society, a specific culture and a specific mindset.[26] Thorstein Veblen was very aware of this problem when he wrote that 'as is true of any other point of view that may be characteristic of any other period in history, so also the modern point of view is *a matter of habit* ... this modern point of view, therefore, is limited both in time and space'.[27] Georg Simmel considered modern life rational, something he connected with the money economy and distinguishable from pre-modern times, with a 'more impulsive, emotionally determined character'.[28] For Simmel, psychological character traits were connected to scientific attitude. It should be taken into account that the perception of the present as a time of modernity, rationality and progress influenced scientific methodology. This rings especially true for economics as economic progress and economic thought have been strongly connected historically. Simmel not only saw a historical change in mentality between modern times and the pre-modern era, but also connected it to a certain vision of the world that has to do with the mentality of the ones envisioning it:

> This measuring, weighing and calculating exactness of modern times is the purest reflection of its intellectualism which, however, on the basis of abstract equality, also favours the egoistical impulses of the elements. Language, with fine instinctive subtle insight, interprets a 'calculating' person simply as one who 'calculates' in an egoistic sense. Just as in the use of 'reasonable' or 'rational', so here too apparently non-partisan formalism of the concept is basically a disposition to cover over a specific biased content.[29]

Not only should rational, self-interested man be seen as living in a particular society, in helping to create it and being a product of it, but scientific analysis that aims at global comparison and universal explanatory power should be re-evaluated as well. The idea, as expressed for instance by Joel Mokyr, that 'the Enlightenment in the West is the only intellectual movement in human history that owed its irreversibility to the ability to transform itself into economic growth' needs to be nuanced somehow.[30] Seeing *homo economicus* as belonging to a particular time and place, and a specific society, allows the return of history in economic discourse, and confirms the old adagio that any object of study is determined by who is looking at it.

If rational *homo economicus* is a cultural construction, it becomes necessary to bring culture back into economic explanation. It is one of the main goals of this book to discuss commerce, as an economic activity, in a social and cultural framework. This will not mean a total abandoning of the observation that economic agents, such as merchants, do act in a substantial way in their own interest, and on a rational basis. But this book aims to show that forms of human interaction, especially cross-cultural trade, cannot be analysed as being based exclusively on a *homo economicus* model and that they need cultural context. Turgot has written that

> Merchants, through the huge amount of the capital that they have at their command, and the extent of their connections with other merchants, by the promptitude and exactness of the advice they receive, by the economy that they understand how to place in their operations, by their practical experience in all matters of commerce, have the means and resources lacking to the most far-sighted, clear thinking and most energetic administrators.[31]

This is an interesting comment, not only referring to an imperfect market reality for traders, but also to the importance of connections. This book will analyse in detail how mercantile relationships are a fundamental underpinning of commerce, in the sense that the development of these relationships in a structural, formal and stable manner is the central driving force behind commercial development in the eighteenth century. It is not just a matter of capital, of information or of understanding belonging to individual traders. Turgot was very right to mention connections with others as well.

Interaction with the other not only implies a socio-cultural analysis, it is also followed by a need to bring ethics back into economics.[32] Merchants had to rely on certain business ethics in order to make their relationships stable and successful. In an international context, such business ethics became more important, as they had to replace at least partially face-to-face contact, but also because a diverse international theatre of trade also meant different opinions of and approaches to what was considered ethical in commerce.[33] Ethics is needed because of the social nature of commercial interaction. As Turgot wrote, their extensive connections with others made merchants resourceful and intelligent. Beyond the need for cultural and ethical explanation about how such connections could last and expand, their existence shows a further need to socialize economic analysis.

Institutionalism and Embeddedness

The publication of Mark Granovetter's seminal article in 1985 was the starting point of new economic sociology, which saw economic activity as embedded in social relationships. The term 'embeddedness' was borrowed from Karl Polanyi and referred to the basic idea that people are social creatures conditioned by their participation in networks of social relationships.[34] This is also valid for the economic activities of individuals or groups of people. Economic interaction is considered to be embedded in society, in different networks that were not all purely economic in kind. New economic sociology is an important current in economic theory that often enters in dialogue with institutional economics and can be situated close to it. Institutional economics proposes an economic analysis by investigating man-made solutions to market problems. Different sub-schools exist, focusing on different problems. Transaction cost economics argues that commercial and other institutions, both formal and informal, came into existence to lower the transaction costs of different interactions.[35] New institutional economics has argued for forms of bounded rationality, caused by limited information.[36] This variety of approaches means that no single definition of an institution exists. According to Douglass North, institutions are the 'rules of the game a society adopts'.[37]

Avner Greif has summarized different existing definitions, and pointed out that they shared some common features, not in the least an emphasis on the human origin of institutions.[38] Greif distinguished a Weberian and a Durkheimian current in economic analysis, the former grounding its analysis on structures, the latter on human agency. According to Greif, institutional economics provides the possibility of reconciling both approaches. He defined institutions as 'a system of such social factors that conjointly generate a regularity of behaviour'.[39] This is a very useful definition, and it also allows for the incorporation of human organizational structures based on social and cultural elements. Institutions could be for instance commercial networks or kinship relations, but also legal rules about contract enforcement or property rights. The main problem with institutional economics might be that it still sees anonymous market exchange based on the self-interested individual as the model to be explained, and combines this adherence with a sense of functionalism, meaning that institutions were too often explained in terms of their results. New economic sociology has addressed the functionalism present in institutional economics. History is of vital importance in this debate, as an existing argument is that an economy, and commerce, based on social relationships has been replaced with more efficient institutions that rely on profit maximization.[40] This is a rephrasing of the superiority debate that has been addressed above.[41] An economic analysis based on social relationships could be useful to study backward societies in pre-modern times, while the different institutionalist schools could focus on efficient market change brought about by the birth of the capitalist system.

There is, however, an important binding aspect between new economic sociology and institutional economics. A common agenda of both lines of thought is the focus on human agency, although opinions differ on whether or not both disciplines do successfully incorporate human agency in their methodology. Individuals or groups shape institutions; they connect with each other and set rules. In turn, institutions do not only provide practical solutions for economic problems and inefficiencies, they also set boundaries. One example of a boundary is the corrosive force attributed to commerce by conservative thinkers. They saw commerce as a threat to an existing, different set of man-made rules – those of a traditional society.[42] This does not mean that both institutional economics and new economic sociology share the belief that economic activity cannot be analysed as separated from society and societal structures. The threat felt by conservatives such as Edmund Burke with regard to commerce already demonstrates the connection between trade and society.

In a way, both disciplines want to retain the importance of human behaviour that was hailed in classical theories, but both attempt to expand it also. An attempt was made to solve the problem of facelessness. In economic theory, individuals have no real character, since they are all anonymous actors whose behaviour is predictable. This is essentially an accusation of the ahistorical character of economic thought.[43] The individual in institutional economics and new economic sociology is not necessarily attributed with a character and a face, but he receives a higher agency in being an active participator in institutions and social networks, shaping them but also being a member of them. Granovetter and other sociologists have challenged the vision of the faceless individual, for the most part by emphasizing the group or networks as important. A network is more than a sum of its parts. It has a characteristic of its own, and it also possesses explanatory force on its own. In this sense, the idea that behind every institution, individual self-interest can be traced is challenged.

A network is more than just an informal type of organization of individuals to solve functional problems of information. In still maintaining the individualist notion at the core of network formation, new institutional economics undersocializes man.[44] It means that the idea of social man was important for different reasons, in that social network participation helps to explain economic activity, since the two are connected, and in the idea that social participation 'can give rise to alternative sources of motivation that can dissuade them from opportunistically pursuing their self-interest'.[45] In other words, economic analysis becomes different owing to the entrance of another explanatory field, that of social action, changing both the economic activity in itself as well as the notion of *homo economicus*.

The use of the term 'economic sociology' goes back to Max Weber, and his ideas about economics and society, mainly through societal features such as religion, law and politics, are excellently addressed by Richard Swedberg. According to Swedberg, one of the two great insights of Max Weber on the relationship between religion and commerce was that they were linked to each other through the moral evaluation of economic activities.[46] It was perhaps partially in response to this evaluation that certain eighteenth-century writers had constructed different economic theories, and their body of work certainly stands in contrast with the traditional religious account. Weber's other basic insight was the link between ascetic Protestantism and rational capitalism, and it is in this aspect that he differs from, for instance, Mandeville, since luxury was considered a morally wrong motive for pursuing wealth. One should work hard and constantly as an end in itself, and should wealth occur, it was important not to just use it for personal pleasure.[47] It was this idea that worked well with capitalism, of which one of the main characteristics in Weber's discourse was the tendency to view work (including commerce) as an end in itself.

Sombart's work on Jews was partially a response to Weber, and it has been pointed out that his argument was very Weberian. It explained a phenomenon (the rise of capitalism) by the ethics and morals of a single religious group.[48] Weber has received criticism that his work was not sufficiently rooted in empirical evidence. Gordon Marshall argued that, at best, Weber's thesis was 'not proven'.[49] Marshall pointed out that several of Weber's claims were to remain unproven simply because the data does not exist, but he uses a case study by using the business records of a seventeenth-century Scottish firm that largely confirms Weber's findings. However, he still argues that the evidence of the causal relation between the Protestant spirit and the rise of capitalism is not waterproof.[50] This indicates a difficulty with regard to the sociological approach. Weber's work was historical, but he also aimed at universalism. He had given a course in Munich entitled 'Outline of Universal Social and Economic History'.[51] It is difficult to prove a change in mentality empirically, and to combine a universalist agenda with historical particularities. For Weber, the capitalist process was long, and the Protestant ethic had helped to bring about a change in economic mentality, while economic organization remained unaltered.[52] His economic sociology was very close to the study of mentality and culture; the main social aspect of his work was concerned with how they were influenced by society and how they compared between different societies. This shows that the distinction between a social and a cultural critique of classical economic theory is not always easy to make.

The new economic sociologists were very much concerned with organization, and were not always exclusively attached to evolutionary processes taking place in the long run. The evolutionary approach to institutional change was one of the most criticized elements in new institutional economics. Economic institutions do not always arise out of a functional need, nor are they always efficient. Historical contingency should be taken more into account, something that can be achieved by studying the relationship between social networks of people and economic circumstances.[53] What is important is that these networks were often informal, loose organizations of people. The idea of network departs from the inclusion of horizontal relationships. Granovetter criticized Williamson's model for new institutional economics as 'a rediscovery of Hobbesian analysis, an over-emphasizing of hierarchical power'.[54] Markets and hierarchies were two ideal types of economic organization dealing with the problems of bounded rationality and imperfect information. As was the case with Weber, such a general and idealized approach might be difficult to rhyme with historical reality. In an article on business organization, Naomi Lamoreaux, Daniel Raff and Peter Temin argued that Williamson's core idea that institutions served to solve problems of information and transactions should be maintained. They also argued that economic actors resolved these problems in a wide variety of ways, and that three general types can be distinguished, the one-shot market exchange, a hierarchical organization and in the middle, the voluntary continued relationship.[55]

It is perhaps this intermediate type of relationship that demonstrates best the need for social embeddedness. This is not to say that single market exchanges or the organization of hierarchical firms can be researched exclusively on economic terms, but the search to reduce risk was important for merchants. They often sought to establish longer-lasting relationships, on a voluntary basis, and it is in this area that the need for social embeddedness becomes clearest. An informal association brought about by human choice implies the idea that choices could have been made differently, and it also raises the immediate question on what criteria choice was based. It is in this manner that social networks gain entry not only in economic mentality, as was for instance one of Weber's research fields, but also in economic organization. Empirical evidence shows that the choice for merchants was not restricted to that between working in a hierarchy or by means of anonymous, multiple market exchanges.

Networks came into existence in commerce, as loose organizations that had strong social components, as is the case of diaspora circuits. Merchants preferred to establish long-lasting relationships, since it reduced risk and could create a reasonable expectation about future behaviour. If man is social, it seems a natural inclination to want to associate with others. These associations were not merely economical and functional. It will be argued that trade networks show that Granovetter's claims about the need for embeddedness are confirmed by a concrete network analysis. At the centre will be the interplay between cultural, social and economic aspects arranging the stability of a commercial network, and making it work.

Historical Network Analysis

Network Analysis as Economic History

So far, a different vision of man as an economic agent has been contended. Instead of the picture of economic man as an individual, trying efficiently to maximize his profit on the market, man is considered to be a social animal, carrying culture with him. Surely he or she tries to be rational, but the assumption of full rationality might be making him too conscious of himself as an economic actor.[56] Certainly, man seeks gain, but other considerations also cross his mind. In engaging in economic relationships with others, family or not, belonging to the same society or not, a whole set of factors engage in interplay. This interplay determines his economic engagement, and this engagement is not universal, exactly because it depends on different varying circumstances that are both internal to human nature as well as external to it, determined by time and place. So far, different economic theories have been analysed to provide a nuanced picture of economic man. Network analysis is a type of economic history that wants to assert the role played by social interaction and cultural background when it comes to trade. It builds its discourse not on a macro-historical perspective, but departs from a micro-historical point of view, by trying to find an answer to the question as to what made durable and long-distance trade work. Human agency is a key element in this discourse.

In his *Civilisation matérielle*, Fernand Braudel analysed trade in all its aspects between the fifteenth and the eighteenth century. His analysis shows a serious appreciation for trade as a human activity, and he tried to do justice to the dynamism that these people, merchants of all kinds, developed over time, adapting themselves to changing circumstances, circulating around the globe.[57] This large-scale approach has its shortcomings. A macro-analytical study of any human activity tends to overlook certain mechanisms taking place in a smaller environment, more defined in time and place. The same type of criticism can be found in Claude Markovits's assessment of South Asian diaspora studies. He stated that these tend to assume the existence of a single South Asian diaspora, studying the role of this movement in the world economy. A loss of focus demonstrating smaller-scale differences is often the consequence of a macro-historical approach and Markovits has stated his intention to deconstruct. He does not believe in a single, unitary South Asian diaspora. Instead, he chose to focus on two merchant networks, originating from two different towns in the same region. In doing so, his base of attention shifts from the points of arrival to the point of departure, the Sind area.[58] His deconstruction opens space for the analysis of particularities that would have been lost in a more general approach.

In recent years, a growing amount of scholars have adopted a similar micro-analytical approach, moving away from Braudel's *histoire totale*. They take a position that seems to be inspired by a modern world view that can be situated between a sense of fragmentation of our current world and a feeling of globalization. Their methodology challenges a vertical approach towards trade mechanisms, using the concept of trade network. Authors such as Philip D. Curtin, Avner Greif, David Hancock, Bernard Bailyn, Claude Markovits, Gunnar Dahl and Francesca Trivellato have all been concerned with trade networks.[59] These scholars are concerned with the fundamental question on the organization of long-distance trade. Different types of associations existed within which commerce could take place: joint-stock companies, partnerships, diaspora circuits, kinship networks, partnership relations or state-given monopolies.[60] One could argue that network analysis is a sort of particular institutional economic history, in analysing networks as institutions created by merchants in order to overcome a number of problems that they encountered. In international commerce, it was often hard to meet in person, and one would have to be able to trust a partner who lived overseas. In times when information travelled slowly, it was also important to gain access to reliable information on market opportunities or the behaviour of fellow traders. A prevention of cheating, combined with monitoring behaviour, and the access to good information are perhaps the two most important measures a merchant has to have in place. As is argued by new economic sociology, the embeddedness of commercial relationships in social tissue offers a solution to these problems. It is a tempting and almost obvious idea to think that in a socially or culturally familiar world, stable trade based on repeated and routine-like transactions occurred more often. Apart from some sort of natural trust that follows familiarity, it would also be easier to punish cheaters in trade, as they could be thrown out of this familiar world.[61]

Different historical studies have analysed such familiar networks, which were indeed embedded in a social or cultural environment. These were international trade circuits that relied on kinship relations or the sharing of a common religion. Studies of groups that have been seen as classic trade diasporas, such as Armenians, Greeks or Jews have been very important in the development of the idea of trade networks, and these minority groups have historically held a very strong attachment to international commerce.[62] Networks that were arranged on kinship or religious ties, with the two often overlapping, had the advantage that the incentives to cheat were smaller, and that the trustworthiness between network members was larger than would be the case for transactions that took place with non-network members. Certain cultural rules were shared by diaspora merchants, and their belonging to a specific community made it more difficult to betray other members of the social environment, especially since many of these diaspora communities were closely knit together by marriage, which was used as a conscious strategy to keep interest close at heart. Also, in a number of important cities diaspora communities were tolerated and they were allowed to have their own officials that had a certain jurisdiction over community members. This way, merchants that had cheated on others could be punished by officials, who were sometimes traders themselves.[63] At the same time, the importance of social and cultural environment for commerce should not be overstated. The fact that merchants belonged to the same religion did by no means exclude cheating behaviour and trust is not synonymous with kinship. Furthermore, to a certain extent, international trade is essentially a form of interaction between different religious and ethnic groups. These groups had always been engaged in commercial relationships with one another, but the social embeddedness of trade was more and more undermined by the international expansion of commerce after sea routes opened up to both Asia across the Cape of Good Hope and to the New World.

The publication of Philip Curtin's groundbreaking work on cross-cultural trade inspired scholars to shift attention from trade networks based on kinship or religious ties to commercial relationships between merchants or groups of traders that did not share such origins. Network analysis, and in this it distinguishes itself from diaspora studies, analyses such relationships, if they occurred in a regular and long-lasting way. A good definition of cross-cultural trade as object of study is given by Francesca Trivellato, who sees it as a collection of 'relations d'affaires dans le commerce à longue distance, à savoir la création d'échanges commerciaux durables et volontaires entre les communautés marchandes qui ne partageaient pas les mêmes valeurs culturels ni les mêmes normes'.[64] Apart from referring to the cross-cultural nature of such relationships, and the following difference in cultural values and norms, she also pointed to two other important characteristics: the fact that such relationships were voluntary and durable. Although commercial relations based on singular transactions were also important, and resided in a similar atmosphere as more durable relationships, the question regarding the organization of trade becomes particularly interesting when researching exactly cross-cultural associations between merchants that existed over a certain period of time and were constructed out of the free will of the participating traders of such associations. It suggests that the relationship became privileged, that it was distinguishable from other relationships. This is what characterizes a network the most: it is an association between more than two merchants who become engaged in a business relationship that considers insiders and outsiders. A certain number of traders belonged to the network, and others did not. It depends on definition whether a network is considered a formal or an informal structure. Although some relationships within a network could be formalized by written contracts, a mercantile network did not generally operate on a written agreement. Philip Curtin used a definition of network that includes formal commercial structures as well:

> These networks were organized in many different ways, some so informally that the individual settlements were linked by little more than the solidarity of a common culture. Others, like the great European trading firms of the seventeenth and eighteenth centuries, were formally organised, chartered by European states, granted certain monopoly rights, empowered to govern as well as trade, and to use their own military and naval forces.[65]

Curtin refers both to mono-cultural networks as well as to formal structures, and in order to make a clear distinction between informal networks of merchants and formal circuits based on monopoly contracts or international trading companies, this book will not call the latter networks, but rather institutions that competed, interacted and also overlapped with trade networks. This is a central issue in network analysis: it studies a particular form of business organization, within which social ties and cultural underpinnings play an important role. In claiming the coexistence of different forms of business associations, both formal and informal, network analysis offers an alternative towards the evolutionary approach towards business history as is advocated by new institutional economics. Social embeddedness of trade did not give way to more efficient forms of business organization, they instead coexisted.[66]

In this book, a definition of a network will be used that is close to Francesca Trivellato's description of criteria.[67] It is considered to be a free and informal association of merchants, who engaged in business in a stable, long-lasting and mutually beneficial manner. It is also considered to be a privileged association. There are insiders and outsiders, network members and competitors. Throughout this book, it will be maintained that, although network members did not deal exclusively in business taking place within the network, an idea of belonging to a privileged group did exist, and this was particularly visible through their dealings with competing trade circuits.[68] Mono-cultural circuits of trade fall within this definition, and in that case, it is simpler to distinguish membership as it can be based on common features that extend beyond the commercial sphere. In studying networks from Sind, Markovits stated that one criterion on which the networks he studied were based was a common regional origin. Although networks could be composed of merchants from a shared background, one of the main reasons for elaborating the concept of network analysis is exactly that this commonality was not always the case.[69] The trade circuit that will be analysed in this book was an international and cross-cultural network, and one of the main shared features was commercial: a desire for profit.

Trust and Reputation

Network analysis poses a double question: why would a privileged relationship be established between merchants of different origins and, with the lack of a cultural and social bond, how were these relationships maintained? The concept that is most used to address these questions is trust. It is a disputed concept, as a number of economic historians maintain that trust is not needed to explain long-term business associations.[70] Nonetheless, a rationally acting individual needs to trust his business associate to do the same and it is debateable whether this presumption follows from rationality, or not. Even if a rational merchant makes the assumption that the person he is trading with is similarly self-interested and thus does not cheat, the assumption of rational behaviour from others is a form of trust.[71] It is a form of rational trust to assume that a merchant would act in a way that would be eventually the most beneficial to him. Cheating on trading partners could mean good short-term profits, but in the long run a corrupt merchant would find himself without options, without anybody to trade with. This rationality does not, however, exclude the possibility of cheating. Not every merchant is necessarily interested in the long run and a certain number of transactions were meant not to be repeated. It can be said that the social embeddedness of trade provides an additional instrument to prevent such cheating, by offering social punishment as a means to avoid breaking rational trust. It has often been argued that social punishment in response to commercial unjust behaviour corresponds with an archaic form of trade, and that modern commerce has replaced social punishment by formal institutions that could enforce just behaviour.[72] A number of such institutions did indeed exist, such as commercial courts or legal rules concerning bankruptcies, but these did not provide a legal international framework. Furthermore, litigation could be costly and long, and merchants preferred to settle disputes within their own professional sphere.

Avner Greif tackled the problem of trust in long-distance relationships by using game theory. It departs from the observation that in international commerce, many merchants used intermediaries. By paying an agent a wage that is high enough during the periods in which that agent is known to be honest, a merchant can ensure that that agent's value and utility is greater than his potential profit gained by cheating. Hence, the best thing for the agent to do would be to act honestly. This means that rationally, the merchant can trust him.[73] This example is not exemplary for all trade associations. It is based on a hierarchical relationship, and indicates that more control mechanisms are needed than simply a reliance on rationality of the other. In Greif's example, the problem is a problem of asymmetric information. The profits the agent made for his employer could not directly be controlled by the latter. It would thus be easy for the agent to increase his own profits by misreporting to his employer, and producing falsified numbers. The merchant would need more to be able to trust his agent or find a way to obtain information on his actions. The rational trust problem becomes a problem of information. Access to information about the dealings of other merchants meant that the choice whether to become engaged in business with somebody or not can indeed be made on a rational basis. This is indeed the focus of a substantial body of institutional economics.[74] Their focus on information does not make trust unnecessary, exactly because good information was not always readily available, and merchants sometimes, in the search for business opportunities, had to make quick choices. Secondly, information channels had to be trusted, as information often came from others.

So, rational behaviour and trust are not mutually exclusive. Instead, a form of commercial trust is based on rationality. In the first part of this chapter, an attempt has been made to address the problematic assumption that economic man was a rational and self-interested individual. By accepting the relevance of social embeddedness and culture for economic activities such as trade, one also has to accept the necessity of social trust. The importance of social and cultural elements means that, in cross-cultural trade, the concept of the 'stranger' cannot be avoided. Self-awareness in a cultural way means that the reflexive person is also able to distinguish himself from others, coming from different cultures and social backgrounds. This makes a reliance on rational trust less secure, because if one does not know which normative systems contribute to determine a stranger's activities, he cannot rely on that stranger to make the same kind of rational choices as himself. A substantial body of literature has studied social trust, in the sense that it is a type of judgement to which normative and formative functions are attached regarding social order. Trust is something inherent to social relationships, ranging from friendship to order within societies. It has to do with expected behaviour, as defined within values and norms of a given society. It contains a strong element of time: trust placed in somebody might be derived from the past, but it is applicable in the present as well as in the future, at least until such judgement is proven wrong. Essential in this notion of social trust is that it, by definition, incorporates the possibility of erroneous judgement. Trust cannot be an absolute truth; it is a human form of predictability passed on others.[75]

In this book, a definition of trust will be advocated that combines the two definitions from above: commercial trust has a rational and a social component. It will allow for a vision of mercantile relationships as being organized on individual self-interest, social embeddedness and cultural norms. Commercial trust is defined as the personal valuation of the reputation of another merchant with regard to future behaviour. The reputation of a merchant is based on his past behaviour and on the degree of intimacy that he shares with the trustee. Past behaviour can be monitored either by personal experience or by information obtained by other merchants who are already known to be trustworthy. The degree of intimacy depends on the social connection maintained between merchants, but also on the sharing of a certain number of cultural elements, such as religion. Commercial trust as it is defined here possesses two crucial characteristics that give it a central place in the study of cross-cultural and international commercial relationships. First, such trust is reciprocal. Merchants were aware of the fact that they needed others in order to trade, and a trustworthy relationship meant that all the parties involved could benefit from it. This means that relationships were established in a two-directional way. Secondly, reputation was a very important form of commercial capital. Trust based on reputation was not only valid in a personal trade relationship, used to make the choice whether to engage in business with someone or not. Reputation developed over years, and circulated internationally. Trust played a general role in organizing an internationally developing commercial community.[76]

Historically, merchants involved in international trade did not meet face-to-face regularly, and some never did. They had another instrument at their disposal that replaced physical meetings and that served not only as a vehicle used to conduct concrete commodity transactions, but also as a carrier of trust and reputation. This instrument was business correspondence. Merchants wrote a lot of letters to each other, and network analysis relies to a great extent on an empirical analysis of business correspondence. What makes this source interesting beyond the richness of information on trade is that correspondence itself was a type of institution. Francesca Trivellato has pointed out that trade letters historically became increasingly standardized, and letters had a certain legal meaning in commercial litigation.[77] It is in this sense not surprising that most early modern correspondence that still exists has survived in legal archives.[78] Correspondence was what was used to keep a network together, and at the same time it served as a connection to the outside world.

Reputation and trust had to circulate in a public sphere. Connections were not only important when they existed, but also in the idea that existing connections could be expanded to include new contacts. The vital importance of reputation and trust within trade circuits and the idea that merchant networks were an important constructive part of the world of commerce suggest the existence of a mercantile society. This community had its own customs, its own language and its own mechanisms of negotiating relationships.[79] It lends nuance to the Smithian idea that one important characteristic of the rise of a commercial society was the separation of friendship and functional relationships. In Smith's evolutionary theory, pre-commercial society was characterized as a world where the space between friend and enemy was filled with uncertain and menacing possibilities.[80] That intermediate field was, in commercial society, replaced by a field of strangers where everyone in society was as independent of every other, as a stranger.[81] This idea of independence is challenged by the insight that friendship existed in business, and that business correspondence and credit connections aimed at tying the commercial world together, friends as well as strangers.

Network analysis aims at gaining an insight into the mechanisms of merchant relations within commercial networks and the wider trading community. Moral values derived from a social and cultural environment have been called upon to tame the negatively-labelled pursuit for commercial gain. Similar control mechanisms that served in personal commercial relationships contributed to the development of a concretely applicable set of merchant customs. Often, values applied within a mercantile sphere were not always that different from general social values and customs. Reliability, trust, different degrees of friendship and reputation were all social human assets and part of human interaction in general.[82]

This does not mean that merchants were merely using values that they possessed as humans in order to trade, without any special attributes for these values with regard to commerce. Mercantile society was fundamentally different than society in general, since it was based on the forging of social ties within a community that was physically dispersed and diverse in nature. Where traditional society formed over time in defined space, and ultimately with a government that had defined jurisdiction, merchant society did not possess such cohesive factors, which explains for the development of other factors, such as trust and reputation. It is difficult to assert what defines society. Internal cohesion, the adherence to a shared set of identities, belonging and values seem all to be fundamental. As such, a society can perhaps be described as necessarily monolithic (to a certain extent of course) in two different aspects: the material and the spiritual, both connected to each other since the material is partially defined by the spiritual, containing values, belief systems and identity.

In defining society, the concept of culture is very useful, and could be used to incorporate both spheres, the material as well as the spiritual. Often, culture has been narrowed to 'high culture', which made it restrictive. Jack Goody has defined culture differently, as an inclusive concept, following a definition by E. B. Taylor in 1871. In his definition of culture, which can be said to be anthropological, he included material culture as well as ideologies, beliefs, systems of meaning and family culture. This definition has the advantage that it incorporates a social element and that the concept of culture can also be applied to relationships between people. In this manner, culture is not simply a separate category of human behaviour besides the social and other categories.[83] Using this definition, the idea of merchant culture becomes very plausible. It not only points to the existence of merchant community, operating on certain terms in a social, concrete and material way, but also includes the idea of values, and their concrete use in daily practice. It means also that the trust generated by personal ties did depend on culture,

> Without adding a cultural dimension to structural accounts of embeddedness, it is difficult to understand the negotiated, emergent quality of trust in many concrete settings, and the ability of entrepreneurs to construct networks out of diverse regions of their social worlds.[84]

Network analysis as applied to concrete case studies of trade circuits appreciates the foundation of commercial relationships in a set of adopted values and manners, and tries empirically to determine what these manners were and how they regulated trade. This not only allows for a thorough study of the underpinnings of commerce from a historical perspective, it also offers the possibility of making a connection to macro-historical developments such as globalization. The development of international and cross-cultural connections in trade has been seen as one of the main catalysts for modernity, and our present-day world is often considered to be a world dominated by the culture of commerce. The discourse of the development of a commercial community that was to an important extent regulated by specific and informally accepted types of behaviour makes network analysis a good candidate to address questions of historical global integration.

An Early Modern Globalization through Trade

Large-Scale History, Human Agency and Networks

It stands beyond doubt that the development of international trade routes during the early modern period has contributed to growing connections between regions on a worldwide scale. Whether this development can be labelled as a form of globalization or not is open for debate. In a very interesting article, Jan de Vries distinguishes two definitions of globalization. A hard definition is based on a convergence of commodity prices in markets in Asia and Europe. The absence of such convergence leads to the conclusion that there was no early modern globalization, and that this was to a large extent caused by the monopolies established by the European East India Companies.[85] Similarly, Acemoglu, Johnson and Robinson have cited the lack of evidence for a quantitative contribution of trade as one of the main problems of identifying intercontinental trade as a step along the road towards modern and global economic development. According to them, the volume of international trade and the profits made from it were not sufficiently high to justify the idea of globalization in pre-industrial times. The belief remained, however, that trade was highly influential in tying the world together and in the same article the importance of the combination of Atlantic trade and institutions securing property rights in Holland and England was considered vital for modern development.[86] Their theory suggests the importance of elements that were not directly quantifiable. Other scholars have also hinted at a qualitative influence of international commerce that could justify the term globalization for the early modern period. Larry Neal has written about the development of capital markets and international networks of information, while Austen and Smith argued that international trade changed the demand pattern in Europe and thereby the material and consumption culture.[87] While claims on the contribution of international trade often focus more on modern Western economic development than on global interconnectedness, they indicate that early modern trade can still be considered a globalizing factor.

One of the difficulties in asserting the historical role that commerce has played on a worldwide scale is that, from our present-day point of view, it seems to be intuitively true that the history of globalization has known a straightforward evolutionary path to arrive at the present, and that large-scale factors are responsible for this. This causes a positive correlation between commerce and globalization, without necessarily showing how exactly trade was able to contribute to interconnectedness. The fact that it was expanding over time seems often sufficient and the ethical connection that has been made between commerce and peaceful coexistence makes the idea that trade shaped the world almost self-explanatory. Evolution might be captured by positivists in the fact that commerce has freed itself over time from state regulation or historical abuses done by the trading companies, or by negativists by pointing to growing anonymity and similarity in the modern world, but the connection of trade and globalization in itself is not fundamentally questioned. In a way, trade is abstracted: it becomes instrumental and ideological. Popular publications in the field of world history also tend to satisfy an exotic curiosity about commerce with remote lands inhabited by people of a different culture. Trade itself is the main explanatory factor, not the behaviour of the persons participating in it.[88] As a global force, commerce has too often been considered as an organizational principle for the modern world. Much historiography related to the international integrative capacities of commerce has remained structural in essence in the sense that commerce in itself is considered the driving motor behind integration, and not the human element that underpins commerce. This explains the negative evaluation of early modern globalization based on a hard definition.

A second problem with the idea of worldwide integration through trade is that, when human agency is taken into account, it is often derived from a hierarchical system. Global influence is often preserved for the large national trading companies or groups of imperial agents, entrepreneurs, bureaucrats and politicians, paving the way for the era of global commerce.[89] World history as seen through the lens of empires, trading companies and elites does not deny the historical involvement of other groups in economic progress. It is rather the reduction of their role to that of a socially subservient group within a hierarchical division that is most problematic. For example, the argument is made that the Atlantic crossing of slaves from Africa matters in the historical process of worldwide integration, but at the same time their role is reduced to that of a group that was put in ships and sent to the Americas to work by their masters, while the merchants who invested in the slave trade were considered to be the main global actors.[90] This hierarchical division contributed to Eurocentrism, in emphasizing European states and companies as the driving forces behind change. It is the rational-economic idea that their search for profit transformed the world into a global market. In writing about Indonesia, J. C. van Leur stressed the point that identifying Indonesian history with the history of the Dutch East India Company's presence was a very Eurocentric one. In concentrating on Western evolution, a lower value is attributed to other regions in the world.[91] Since the elite standing high in the hierarchy with regard to international trade were generally European, a hierarchical framework of commerce has also contributed to a hierarchical framework of regions and continents, further enhanced by national economic histories, stressing the uniqueness of a particular region.[92]

It seems that another definition of globalization might help to solve some of these problems. It is clear that such a definition has to rely on human interaction. For Dennis Flynn and Arturo Giraldez, a permanently established global trade had to exist 'on a scale that generated deep and lasting impact on all trading partners'.[93] Jan de Vries also refers to the importance of direct physical contact and consequential interaction between people of different background and cultures, in a way that affected all parties involved.[94] In recent years, several fields of large-scale histories have focused on human agency in tying historical spaces together. Such histories share the characteristic that they do not limit themselves to human circulation within areas defined by political boundaries alone.

The development of commercial routes meant that regions that were remote became increasingly interconnected owing to streams of personnel, goods, money or information. Their connection also depended on shared characteristics that allowed for the distinction of an international space that was internally interconnected. An empire is a transnational historical space whose existence can be derived from the fact that the whole area, or collection of areas, resided under one rule. Apart from unity deriving from an overlaying political structure, large-scale histories have come to focus on internal cohesion of areas through human activity. Transnational regions became relevant objects of study themselves and different circuits of human exchange have led to different disciplines studying particular areas, such the Mediterranean, the Atlantic and the Pacific.[95] Atlantic history, for instance, fully acknowledges human interaction in the construction of historical spaces. One of the main focuses when studying interactions in a certain geographical area has been commerce. It is precisely through human agency connected with different forms of interaction that historical spaces have been defined. And in that sense, they can overlap.[96] A country such as Portugal can be a nation, but also the origin of an empire, connecting it with territories in the Indies and in Brazil. At the same time, some of its territories can be integrated in another system based on interdependencies and human flows, such as the Atlantic.

In explicitly making human interaction a fundamental criterion in the definition of what makes a historical space, different large-scale histories have put the question of agency central in their analysis. In defining Atlantic history, Bernard Bailyn has written of the need for 'emphasis on the human, individual, entrepreneurial aspects of commerce'.[97] In an introduction to a set of essays about oceans as connective spaces in history, Kären Wigen has argued that 'the Mediterranean was the first to be colonized by networks of routine, round-trip exchange'.[98] It suggests a strong sense of agency that networks of trade can play in connecting different regions, once these networks become based on a certain routine.[99] An important aspect of Atlantic history writing has been the emphasis on the idea of the Atlantic as a definable historical space, meaning it possesses characteristics that allow for its distinction as a singular area, interconnected within itself and distinguishable from an outside world. These characteristics have to do with the people living there. Fernand Braudel wrote that 'ce n'est pas l'eau qui lie les régions de la Méditerranée, mais les peoples de la mer'.[100] Perhaps the most important characteristic that is attributed to the Atlantic is its quality as a commercial system. One of the concepts used to assess the human constituent of commerce is trade networks. Bernard Bailyn wrote that 'Earlier historians – Chaunu, Mauro, Godinho, Haring, Hamilton, Vicens Vives – had produced the elements for the construction of an Atlantic economic system bound together by a multitude of trading networks, monetary and capital flows, intercontinental labour markets, and pan-oceanic distribution patterns.'[101] These authors, also working in the time they lived in, were limited in their analysis by relying too heavily on national boundaries. Younger post-war historians, on the contrary, pushed these borders and began to unravel a more complex world leading to large-scale historical writing that was far from a collection of national histories.

Newly emerging disciplines that study a particular historical space have the great advantage that they encompass national histories without falling into the trap of universalism. A field such as Pacific history allows for an analysis of similarities, differences and interactions between different localities in a wider sphere. This analysis can be cultural, social, political or economical, and it avoids fundamental problems such as a cultural analysis restrained within a politically defined territory.[102] Large-scale histories based on human interaction have the additional advantage that they allow for an expansion of human agency. More power is given to slaves, sailors, peddlers, fortune-seekers and merchants of all kinds, who, rather than being instrumental in the hands of an elite group, shaped different historical spaces. This tendency is not only visible in the relative recent fields of oceanic histories, but has also had influence on older large-scale disciplines such as imperial history, adding a sense of dynamism.[103] In a similar sense as the above-mentioned spatial histories, world history can be defined as the study of an international space, the world, by seeing it as an interconnected area. In this manner, world history becomes the history of the development of such interconnectedness, or, in other words, the history of globalization. Its task becomes the analysis of worldwide integration within the global historical space by analysing human interaction that took place within this space. A soft definition of globalization fits perfectly within this framework, in its emphasis on human change brought about by permanent global international relationships. These relationships can be commercial, while human change can be social, cultural, commercial or political. This definition of world history is perfectly compatible with historical network analysis.

Combining Two Notions of Networks

If trade is to be seen as a worldwide integrative force, it should first be analysed from within. Fundamental to the idea of international commerce as one of the main carriers of globalization and economic growth is the observation that at some point in the exchange line, it became cross-cultural, meaning merchants who belonged to a different culture, religion, nation or background were doing business together. In a very interesting article, Jerry Bentley has put forward the idea that different degrees of cross-cultural interaction allow for a periodization of world history based on the level of worldwide integration.[104] A changing perception of the world we live in today has caused historical explanation from a transnational point of view to a cross-cultural one. Jonathan Israel attributed to Sephardic trading networks an important role in European maritime expansion from 1492 to the end of the eighteenth century, and in doing so he claimed that this vital role was not caused by '"idiosyncratic" Jewishness but by very specific, novel and complex sets of international circumstances forging a new, world-political context interacting on characteristic Jewish forms of community and social organization'.[105] This suggests that cross-cultural relationships in commerce went beyond the establishment of a mutual understanding in trade, and that it also affected society in a more general manner.

Secondly, in theorizing about market exchange, economics has at times oversimplified the process of exchange. It was rarely a matter of a bi-atomic transaction between a buyer and a seller. Others were involved: agents sending packets on ships, brokers negotiating prices or correspondents taking care of a sale for a remote partner. The double observation that all international trade was at some point cross-cultural, meaning it involved contact between people of different backgrounds, and that many commercial exchanges in fact consisted of a string of transactions, lead to the conclusion that the question on the organization of trade is very important in order to understand its potential contribution to early modern globalization.

So far, two different notions of networks have been used. First, a network has been considered as a form of informal business association between merchants. Network analysis sees such associations as valid research objects in order to develop a thesis regarding the internal organization of commerce. Such organization is man-made and serves to develop problems that occur in long-distance trade: the need for trust and the lack of information. Secondly, networks have been considered as human associations that are able to interconnect historical spaces. These two uses of the term 'network' refer to one historical reality: actual commercial networks that have existed in the past.[106]

Granovetter's claim about the importance of social networks for the study of economic activity is not the same as the use of networks in large-scale histories.

The sociologist's claim was that economic behaviour needed to be embedded in society, and thus was concerned with an incorrect economic analysis due to an incomplete consideration of the elements that were important. It is not a call for human agency, but for expanded human agency. It shifts the idea of man as an economic actor above all to that of man as a social actor. The idea of trade networks in large-scale histories is an agenda to put human agency back into the centre. Although both lines of thought agree on the need to analyse human networks, there is a problematic issue between the two that needs to be addressed. Granovetter has made it clear that economic activities should be embedded in society. The idea of society is harder to maintain within a discipline that connects different societies, or wishes to explain how they were shaped by outside contacts but that does not put trade networks in one particular society, for it would be hard to argue that the specific historical space formed by different human circuits, such as the Atlantic, coincided with a particular 'Atlantic society'.[107] Further, even if one could argue for such a society, large-scale history has made networks an integrative force, meaning that the historical spaces they studied existed because of the establishment of human circuits. Social embeddedness relied on the inverse idea that economic activity such as trade is not integrative, but needs to be integrated.

This discrepancy between the two different applications of networks can be solved. People belonged to different social circuits that were not all based on the same inner logic. It would be wrong to see merchants as just merchants. They also lived in a certain society, considered themselves as belonging to a certain nation, practised a certain religion and had a certain financial status or not. Network analysis cannot content itself with an analysis of trade mechanisms taking place in a space that was separated from society, the network, or the collection of networks constructing a merchant community. First of all, matters such as trust and reputation were not exclusively commercial. These were values and assets that had multiple meanings beyond the economic sphere. Traders were also more than that; they had acquaintances who were not merchants, they sought acceptance in circles outside the trading communities in which they operated, and many of them had other interests as well.

In writing of the utility of the concept of culture, Jack Goody stressed that it should not become a category in which the non-economic is placed.[108] The economic and the cultural are not two separable things. As such, it is critical towards approaches that study the influence on one area on the other. In sociological or anthropological analysis, the economy is part of the social system and part of culture. It is with this inclusive definition in mind that network analysis can be significant, in studying cultural and social factors, such as human interaction as a type of economic history. However, one should be careful not to reduce cultural or social factors such as trust, reputation or behaviour to their economic meaning in this way. Merchants were not rational in the sense that all their actions were consciously constructed to make their business more efficient; they also relied on values because they were already used to mercantile custom, meaning that they were not always re-negotiated in each individual mind against the preoccupation of profit and self-interest, and also because such values were values of them as humans, as participators in society that was more complex and diverse than based on a one-dimensional division of class, status or membership. If trade networks did indeed tie the world together, historians need to analyse how network members related to society and to their immediate surroundings.[109] This means that the underpinnings of commerce cannot always be described in abstract economic laws. This attention to the particular is shared with micro-historians. Their work has tried to escape universalism by focusing on the particularity of their research objects. This school aimed directly at focusing on the individual experience, and on 'relationships, decisions, restraints, and freedoms faced by real people in actual situations'.[110] Macro-history can all too easily lead to a type of historical analysis in which abstraction was made of human action. Human agency can still be formally at the centre of historical explanation, but the particularity and contingency of historical human behaviour is sometimes lost in large-scale narratives. Micro-historians, to the contrary, were trying to avoid the risk of 'losing the complexity of the relationships that connect any individual to a particular society'.[111] The interaction between merchants, commerce and society was fundamental, not in the least because of the importance of social ties and cultural norms. The connection between network analysis and global histories has to be made by placing merchants belonging to particular trade networks in the society they lived in. In this manner, trade remains a catalyst for global integration, but not in an abstract manner. In analysing its internal functioning and its social embeddedness, the historian is better equipped to analyse why commerce served as a carrier for globalization, through an explanation of what made cross-cultural interaction work. This discourse relies on an economic, social and cultural analysis and reflects the methodological discourse for commerce as determined, next to self-interested considerations, by social and cultural fundamentals.

2 A SHORT HISTORY OF THE DIAMOND TRADE

Diamonds have been a source of fascination for mankind ever since they were first discovered. Before the eighteenth century, diamonds came from a number of regions on the Indian subcontinent and were also found on the island of Borneo. Suggestions that references to diamonds can be found in the Bible or in Egyptian texts cannot be supported by historical evidence and have only added to their mysterious status.[1] Originally, diamond was valued because of its magical powers that derived from its status as the hardest natural material on earth. In certain cultures, bearers of diamond amulets were considered invincible. It was only after the discovery of cutting techniques in the fifteenth century that diamonds were appreciated for their beauty and their capability to reflect light.

Trade routes connected the Indian diamond mines with China, Europe, Persia and Arab countries, where local rulers and rich inhabitants wore jewellery that included precious stones such as rubies, sapphires and also diamonds. The Portuguese exploration of the African coast and the discovery of a new sea route to Asia brought more European traders to India. Initially they engaged in private trade with local merchants, but soon enough different East India Companies were established that tried to regulate diamond trade. Around the middle of the seventeenth century, the English East India Company managed to reduce Portuguese and Dutch diamond exports to Europe. Although several English traders, alongside other Europeans, were also active in the intra-Asian trade, the role of Hindu and Muslim merchants in serving Asian markets is very important. Some Indian merchant princes became very wealthy thanks to diamond trade, which became an exchange trade, with the export of rough diamonds to Europe against the import of silver, polished stones, jewellery and coral.

In the 1720s, this system came under heavy pressure with the discovery of diamond fields in Brazil. The European market saw its prices for diamonds drop drastically; traders tried to establish new connections in Lisbon, and the Portuguese government adopted mining and trading monopolies in an effort to control Brazilian diamond imports.

Yet the profits made by diamond merchants did not only depend on supplies. Taste shifted and followed technical innovations and the European and Asian consumer markets for diamonds were locally different. In trying to obtain the best price for their commodities, diamond merchants were used to sending parcels of precious stones back and forth between cities trying to conclude the best deal.

The Era of Indian Diamonds

The Diamond Trade until the Seventeenth Century

Godehard Lenzen has concluded that the earliest reference to diamonds can be found in a Sanskrit text on Indian economy and law entitled the *Arthasatra*, dating from the fourth century BC. The oldest reference found in Western antiquity is generally considered to be Pliny's *Naturalis Historia*. Until the eighteenth century, India and the island of Borneo were the only known regions that contained diamond mines. From there, diamonds found their way to the West using the overland trade routes passing through the Middle East. Diamonds also reached China via commercial connections between the Romans and the Han dynasty.[2]

Although a changing cultural appreciation due to the growing influence of Christianity and a lack of gold to pay for diamonds caused a temporary decline in diamond trade to Europe, the commercial routes that existed in antiquity continued to transport diamonds during the early Middle Ages.[3] Precious stones reached Europe through the Red Sea, by way of Aden and Alexandria, or through the Persian Gulf, Ormus, Aleppo and Constantinople. A number of diamond traders lived in Cairo at least since the eleventh century.[4] Trade to Arabia, Persia and China continued or even expanded. From the eighth century onwards, Venice had become an important gateway in the Oriental luxury trade, including pearls and gems, but diamonds are only mentioned a few centuries later.[5] The volume of diamond trade started to grow significantly after the invention of cutting techniques, leading to a new appreciation for diamonds based on beauty rather than magical powers. It seems that the 'table cut' for diamonds came from Venice, where it had possibly arrived from India. The technique of diamond cutting is mentioned in Antwerp in 1482 and in Augsburg in 1538.[6] In Amsterdam, a wedding act from 1586 mentions diamond cutting as a profession.[7] Four years earlier, the *Robyn- en Diamentsnydersnatie* ('nation of ruby and diamond cutters') had become an official guild in Antwerp.[8] By that time, cutting techniques had already further developed by several technical inventions such as the polishing of facets by using a polishing wheel and diamond dust.[9] At that time, European diamond trade was centred on the axis Bruges–Venice.[10] The importance of Venice as a trading centre diminished after 1498, when a direct sea route to India across the Cape of Good Hope was discovered, but it still remained an important centre for cutting diamonds and other precious stones. In 1636, there were still 186 diamond cutters working in Venice, while Antwerp in 1613 counted only 164.[11] Trade routes shifted to an axis that connected Goa, the Portuguese capital in India, with Lisbon and Antwerp, where the Portuguese trading factory had moved from Bruges in 1499. Several Italian merchants active in diamond trade settled in Antwerp, such as the Affaytadi firm, who were also important spice traders.[12] Two indexes on lost business books from 1548 and 1560 indicate that they bought rough diamonds in Lisbon: 'diamanti di contto de mi di Lixbona'.[13] Lisbon was now the most important distribution centre for uncut diamonds in Europe and Portuguese traders started to travel to the diamond mines. They sold precious stones in China and the Philippines, from where they were even shipped to New Spain.[14] Other Europeans followed, often on board Portuguese *Carreira da India* ships. Already early in the sixteenth century, Flemish merchants were trading in diamonds, jewels and precious stones. In 1528, Guylherme de Bruges sent jewels with sapphires and rubies to a merchant in Cochin, in order to ship them to Lisbon. In the 1530s merchants from Antwerp and Nuremberg were trading in Vijayanagar, a region containing diamond mines, and in 1545, a certain Pero de Bruges was active as a dealer in precious stones. Linschoten mentioned the story of Frans Coningh, a diamond cutter who was eventually murdered in Goa in 1588 by his wife.[15] The diary of Jacques de Coutre, a diamond merchant from Bruges who travelled in India between 1591 and 1627 mentions the arrival of Portuguese vessels in Goa carrying jewels, rubies, emeralds, pearls from New Spain and also coral.[16] This exchange trade was to become a typical element of the diamond trade between India and Europe.[17]

Another important characteristic of European presence in India was that different merchants travelled to the diamond mines in person, where they bought rough diamonds from local traders, who had received the privilege of buying directly from the mine-owner, who was regularly the king or sultan on whose territory the mine was found.[18] Indian merchants were more than intermediaries between mine-owners and Europeans. Some Hindu and Muslim merchants became so successful that they had their own agents at the diamond mines and could rely on extensive commercial networks.[19] Two of the most famous Hindu merchants were Shantidas Zaveri (*c.* 1585–1659) and Virji Vora (*c.* 1590–1670). Zaveri designed and sold jewellery, and sent agents to the diamond mines in the kingdom of Pegu. He had established himself in Ahmedabad, where jewellers lived in a separate settlement. Zaveri had good connections with the Mogul court, to which he sold diamonds and jewels, as well as with European traders. Although he was considered by European travellers as belonging to the Gujarati Banyans, he was in fact a Jain entrepreneur like most Hindu merchants active in diamond trade. Virji Vora was another Jain entrepreneur; a money lender to Europeans and a wholesale trader who bought coral and made huge profits by selling pepper and other spices. His business house relied on a large network and there were branches in Ahmedabad, Agra, the Deccan and Golconda, where some of the best-known diamond mines were found. The English considered him one of the richest persons in the world and were impressed by his power.[20] Virji Vora and Shantidas were not representative of Jain merchants in general, but their commercial success, good connections and commanding position indicate that the relationship between European and Indian merchants was more complex than the latter acting as agents for the former, and several Gujarati merchants established commercial routes with Arab and Persian cities that did not include Europeans.

The zenith of Zaveri and Vora's activities coincided with the establishment of different East India Companies. The Dutch East India Company, the V. O. C., was founded in 1602. They were granted the exclusive right to Indian trade in the Dutch Republic. Pepper and other spices were their most important commodities, but the Company was also interested in diamonds. With the foundation of several national trading companies, the structure of diamond trade between Europe and Asia was to change structurally. Initially, diamond trade was free, but the Dutch East India Company rapidly tried to control the diamond trade of its servants and they forbade private trade in 1631.[21] In spite of several efforts, Dutch activities in the Asian diamond trade were never sufficiently high to outshine the Portuguese.[22] Lisbon never developed a diamond cutting industry and thanks to the good commercial ties between Portugal and the Low Countries, a lot of the Indian rough diamonds that arrived in Portugal were sold in Antwerp and Amsterdam. There is little material available to analyse the intra-European commercial routes in the first half of the seventeenth century. Only the firm of Paolo du Jon, active in Antwerp, has left some business books and letter copy books, dated between 1622 and 1654.[23] These sources show that Portuguese and Italian firms in Lisbon were the most important suppliers. Du Jon traded with Lisbon, where his agents André de Saintes and Francisco Wallis, who was family of du Jon, had direct contacts with an important Portuguese merchant in India named Balthasar da Vega, who had resided in Goa since 1618 and was arrested in 1644 by the Inquisition on the suspicion of being a 'judaiser'. He had escaped earlier arrests owing to good connections with officials, and Goa's viceroy carried a shipment of diamonds of da Vega with him to Lisbon in 1636.[24] One source is not enough to draw definitive conclusions, but it shows that, at a time when the Portuguese factory in Antwerp had already been closed, rough diamonds found their way from Lisbon to the most important cutting centres.

Dutch, Portuguese and Hindu merchants were not the only ones competing over rough diamonds. A Dutch letter written in 1626 complains of competition from traders coming from Atchin, Gujarat and 'different other nations' who bought almost all the diamonds.[25] In 1658, representatives of the V. O. C. stopped buying diamonds because large purchases by Armenian traders had raised the price by 40 per cent.[26] A few decades later, the Armenian trader Rupli set up a business in precious stones together with French traders.[27] In a text dating from 1663 included in Pieter van Dam's history of the V. O. C., a diamond mine in Bengal was said to be visited by French and Portuguese jewellers.[28] All this competition made the search for new diamond deposits interesting, and the Dutch could count themselves lucky with regard to the location of their Asian spearhead, Batavia. Close by, the Indonesian island of Borneo contained an unknown number of diamond deposits. Diamonds were found not far from Succadana, on the western side of the island. Samuel Blommaert, chief factor of the Dutch East India Company on Borneo was instructed in 1609 to reach an agreement with the King of Banjermassin about a trade in diamonds. Blommaert mentioned that Chinese traders were already active in that trade.[29] English sources confirm that in around 1609, Dutch or Flemish merchants were already active in the Borneo diamond trade:

> I have many times certified your worships of the trade the Flemmings follow to Soocadanna which place yieldeth great store of diamonds, and of their manner of dealing for them for gold principally which comes from Baniermassen and blue glass beads which the Chinese make and sell[30]

Another effort was made in 1619, when the Dutch sent 'one of the best diamond connoisseurs' to the diamond deposits. It seems that Dutch merchants never really gained ground in the diamond trade based in Succadana. They suffered from foreign competition and in the 1640s, merchants from the island itself, and from other nations, came by boat to Batavia to sell diamonds.[31]

In the first half of the seventeenth century, diamond trade was not very stable and regular. This irregularity was exacerbated by the fact that the European Companies never managed to make formal agreements with the rulers in whose kingdoms and sultanates the mines were found, which meant that merchants could not always count on a steady flow of diamonds. For example. the King of Visapur decided to close his mines in 1626: 'de diamantmine was voor de cooplieden geslooten, den Coning dede voor sijn particulier daerin graeven'.[32]

Anglo-Indian Commerce in Precious Stones

English merchants were trading in diamonds in the first half of the seventeenth century, and the East India Company had forbidden private trade in diamonds by English subjects in 1609. However, in 1625, servants of the Company were allowed to conduct a private trade in precious stones. English diamond traders quickly started to challenge other Europeans and declining purchases by the Dutch was attributed to English interference: 'Alsoo de Engelse libertijten schijnen meer particuliere capitalen bij te brengen als de onse'.[33] Dutch diamond exports declined from 1660 onwards and fell into insignifance after 1668.[34] Around 1635, Portuguese diamond exports through Goa had strongly diminished as well. These used to amount to 2 million *cruzados*, but at the middle of the seventeenth century exports only valued 3,000 *cruzados*.[35] During the 1650s and the 1660s, the East India Company also allowed ship owners and ships' officers to import diamonds, pearls and other precious stones from Asia.[36] In 1664 the East India Company decided to open up the trade completely, providing the payment of duties to the Company. Exporters of precious stones and importers of rough diamonds paid 2 per cent, provided they were Company stockholders. Otherwise, the import duty was 4 per cent and foreigners paid an additional duty.[37] This policy proved to be a decisive step towards the establishment of an Anglo-Indian trade circuit between Surat, later replaced by Fort St George (Madras) and London as the most important route for the import of diamonds in Europe.

The regulation of the Anglo-Indian diamond trade as an open business coincided with the arrival of Portuguese Jews, the Marranos or New Christians, in London. It was at that moment, according to Gedalia Yogev, that the diamond trade between Europe and India transformed from a business based largely on chance transactions into a regular trade.[38] Although it is true that there was a relatively high participation of Jewish merchants in the Anglo-Indian diamond trade, it would be wrong to assume that Jews controlled all trade in precious stones, as it would be equally unjust to presume that their arrival in England formed the start of their activities in the diamond business. New Christian involvement in the Indian diamond trade already dated from the time when the Portuguese were dominating the trade with Europe in precious stones.[39] Because of a shift in European power in India, many diamond merchants had started to use English vessels to ship their diamonds to Europe and in the second half of the seventeenth century, there was a move of New Christian wealth and business branches from Seville, Lisbon and Madrid to London, Hamburg, Amsterdam and Paris.[40] Many of the Portuguese Jews arriving in London at that time had come from Amsterdam, where they kept good commercial relationships with remaining family members.

Jewish merchants often imported Indian diamonds under the cover of English merchants to avoid the higher duties they had to pay.[41] In 1687, the East India Company abolished the difference between foreigners and Englishmen in the payment of duties, and they re-installed the difference between stockholders and others. With the appearance of the international stock exchange, Jews could also possess East India Company stock and they did not need to use English cover anymore.[42] This did not diminish the regular partnerships between Jewish and non-Jewish merchants, and rather than considering the Anglo-Indian diamond trade as Jewish, it should be seen as a branch of business with a high degree of cross-cultural cooperation. A written agreement dating from 1721 demonstrates such a partnership. It was made between Robert Nightingale of

London acting for George Drake and Anthony da Costa of the same city and acting on behalf of Joseph Osorio from Amsterdam. Osorio and da Costa were Sephardic Jews, and an agreement was made to begin a partnership in the trade of diamonds. Nightingale and da Costa were to settle in Fort St George, to sell goods and to make returns in diamonds and bills of exchange.[43]

The introduction of less discriminatory duties was one element that contributed to an expansion of diamond trade in London. In the 1670s, trade in coral became increasingly controlled by diamond merchants thanks to East India Company regulations. Coral was a popular commodity that was sent to Asia for the purchase of rough diamonds. It came from regions in the Mediterranean such as Marseilles, Leghorn, Genoa and Naples. Coral was not only sent to India, where it was popular for use in jewellery, but also to China by English diamond traders.[44] However, the new policy that was adopted in the 1680s did not halt the instability in regulating the trade. Towards the end of the seventeenth century, the exchange trade came under pressure due to restrictions in the export of silver. Imports dropped drastically, and while in 1698, £92,000 worth of rough diamonds arrived in London, the yearly value of such shipments in the first decades of the eighteenth century was never higher than £12,000. In compensation for prohibitions on silver exports, the coral trade was opened by the Company in 1709.

A decade later, private diamond trade was finally stabilized and the organizational framework established by the East India Company remained the cadre within which private trade was conducted until the beginning of the nineteenth century.[45] A London class of diamond merchants with good contacts in Amsterdam developed, and they were mainly concerned with the import of rough diamonds and the export of silver, coral and finished jewels. Most of these commodities arrived at Fort St George, the most important Indian diamond centre for most of the eighteenth century, although some were destined for Surat, Fort St David and Calcutta. Next to a considerable Sephardic presence amongst these merchants, East India Company officials also played an important role. Gedalia Yogev suggests that the election of Josiah Child as chairman of the Court of Directors of the East India Company in 1681 might have been decisive in putting a halt of new efforts by the East India Company to forbid private diamond trade. Child maintained good relationships with Jewish merchants and even instructed the governor of Fort St George to persuade Jewish diamond traders to move to that city. He also participated in negotiations with Armenian merchants who wanted to establish commercial privileges there.[46]

Another important East India Company official with a personal interest in the diamond trade was Thomas Pitt. Born in 1653, he went to India for the first time in 1674. After disputes with the Company due to private commercial ventures, he was named governor of Fort St George in 1697. As a diamond trader, he was advised by his good friend Alvaro da Fonseca, an important

Sephardic merchant. The famous Pitt diamond was named after him.[47] Pitt had good connections with a number of important diamond traders, both in London and in India, including Jean and Daniel Chardin who were active at the end of the seventeenth century. They were French Protestant merchants settling in London in the 1680s out of fear of religious prosecution. In the 1660s and 1670s, Jean Chardin had travelled much in Asia, where he was active as a jewellery trader who sold to the rich and powerful, such as the Persian Shah.[48] In London, the Chardin brothers established good commercial relationships within as well as outside the East India Company. Jean Chardin was a good acquaintance of Josiah Child, and the Chardins made a partnership with two Jewish brothers in India in 1682, Salvador Rodrigues and Francisco Salvador.[49] Jean remained in London, where he was now a sort of celebrity thanks to his travels, which had gotten him the attention of the Royal Society and the likes of those such as John Evelyn.[50] Daniel went to settle in Fort St George, from where he was to conduct a regular and equally advantageous diamond trade with the Jewish partners.[51]

This partnership is another example of cross-cultural cooperation and shows how, in the diamond trade, at the level of international imports and exports, merchants of different religions and Company officials were interconnected at a personal and a commercial level, both in London as well as in India.[52] It was this mixture of people who would remain the most visible in the Indian diamond trade in the eighteenth century, although these established networks came under growing pressure from outside factors. Only a few years after stability was finally found in the Anglo-Indian diamond trade, diamonds were discovered in Brazil. Prices for rough diamonds fell rapidly in Europe, which caused great fear amongst the London merchants. David Jeffries, an English jeweller who published a treatise on diamonds and pearls in 1751 remarked that

> [the discovery of Brazilian diamonds] occasioned many, even of the most capital traders in London, to believe, that Diamonds were likely to become as plenty as transparent pebbles; and they were so far influenced by this opinion, that most of them refused to buy Diamonds on any terms.[53]

It is exemplary for the rapidly changing circumstances in early modern commerce that, at almost the exact same time when the internal organization of Anglo-Indian diamond trade was finally set on a firm and stable basis, a new and this time outside threat almost immediately presented itself. This did not prevent the first half of the eighteenth century from being a very successful period for the Indian diamond trade. The networks that had established themselves between London and India extended to other regions within Asia but also to Amsterdam. A lot of Jewish merchants had kinship ties in the Dutch capital, and London's cutting industry never competed with the one in Amsterdam. According to Jonathan

Israel, 'there were many more Jewish brokers, a much larger Jewish diamond- cutting and polishing industry ... [in Amsterdam] than in London'.[54] David Jeffries attributed the different magnitude in the cutting industry to the fact that the wages of English workmen were too high in comparison with Amsterdam.[55] Yogev has provided us with a better explanation, namely that a possible transfer of diamond industry to London would have been accompanied by a transfer of skilled diamond cutters and that such an emigration did not take place.[56] The cutting of the Pitt diamond by Joseph Cope in 1702 indicates that, notwithstanding Dutch predominance, a diamond industry had developed itself in London.[57]

These international circuits of trade were diversified after the discovery of Brazilian diamonds. Several merchants tried to switch to trading in Brazilian stones and the commercial monopoly in Brazilian diamonds established in the 1750s caused a greater Dutch participation, as well as a bigger involvement of non-Jewish merchants.[58] This diversification was also brought about by the growing number of Ashkenazi diamond traders. More and more of them sent agents to India in the early eighteenth century. In Europe, the lack of connections with the Mediterranean and Leghorn made the Ashkenazim more active in bullion rather than coral trade. The export of English silver was still restricted, so often Spanish pieces of eight and other foreign coins were bought up for shipment to Asia. The Ashkenazim were able to sell diamonds and buy bullion on markets in Germany, and in doing so they challenged existing trade networks.[59] In 1765, a large smuggling affair was revealed, involving nineteen firms, eight of which were Jewish, all Ashkenazim.[60] Their rise in commerce can be demonstrated through their rising financial status. Around 1750, no Ashkenazi merchant possessed the same wealth and influence as the foremost Sephardic traders, but by the end of the century, members of the Goldsmid family had become the most important businessmen in the city.[61] Contemporaneous to this growing Ashkenazi trade in London, Amsterdam saw a gradual replacement of Portuguese with Ashkenazi jewellers and workers.[62]

More than competition, the discovery of diamonds in Brazil allowed for the incorporation of a larger number of diamond traders in the business, and an equilibrium was reached, with many merchants in London, Amsterdam and Antwerp trading both in Indian as well as in Brazilian diamonds, although the latter were sometimes said to be of a lesser quality. This period came to an end in around 1765, when Anglo-Indian merchants faced a severe crisis due to problems with remittances from India. Englishmen gained increasing wealth from trade in India, and they tried to send their fortunes back home in a number of different ways. Often, bills of exchange were used, but the East India Company made some restrictions for fear of a lack of funds. Diamonds became increasingly used in order to make remittances, which caused import numbers in England to boom. Further, a typical sellers' market was created in India, causing prices to rise, while in Europe, too many stones were in the hands of outsiders, of people who did not have an interest in the international diamond trade.[63] At the end of the eighteenth century, productivity of the mines had started to decline – something that also occurred, not much later, in Brazil. The golden era of Brazil and India as the world's diamond producers was to come to an end, and in the course of the nineteenth century, diamond trade was to take a different outlook.

The Brazilian Monopoly

The Discovery of Diamonds in Brazil and the 1753 Crisis

The exact circumstances surrounding the discovery of diamond deposits in Brazil are still surrounded by myth. According to most accounts, they were first found towards the end of the 1720s. Minas Gerais, the captaincy where the discovery was made, had already been known as a region rich in gold, which had been found at the end of the seventeenth century, creating a true gold rush to the region around Ouro Preto.[64] Often, the discovery of diamonds is attributed to a certain Bernardo Fonseca Lobo.[65] According to several stories, a priest who had been in Golconda or Goa was the first to recognize Lobo's stones as diamonds.[66] The veracity of these stories cannot be assured, but Bernardo Lobo was a real person. One of his slaves is mentioned as a runaway in a registry of slaves, licenses and shops in Tejuco, the city that was to be the centre of the diamond region.[67] Portuguese officials were aware of the existence of diamonds in 1729 at the latest. In December of that year, the governor of Minas Gerais sent a dispatch to Lisbon mentioning the discovery of diamonds.[68] A few months earlier, a letter sent to the Lisbon merchant Francisco Pinheiro mentions new discoveries of diamonds in Serro do Frio. Its author asked Pinheiro to determine the value of diamonds that he would send to him, and to have them polished.[69] This letter shows that diamonds quickly found their way to Europe. Diamond mining in Brazil was to develop at a rapid speed.

At first, the mining of diamonds was permitted for anyone willing to pay a head tax for each slave that they employed. This permissive policy caused a rise of diamond supplies in Europe. Lord Tyrawly, English consul in Lisbon, remarked to the Duke of Newcastle in 1732 that

> The discovery of the Diamonds in the mines of the Brasils, has put a stop for the present to that Trade from East India, thô not to the London market, on accompt of the advantage which England has over its neighbours in the Trade with Lisbon...so that the much greater part of the Diamonds that come from the Brasils have hitherto gone to London, from whence they are distributed to the rest of Europe.[70]

Prices for rough diamonds fell drastically, and important merchants in Amsterdam such as Andries Pels & Sons complained that Brazilian diamonds harmed the exclusive nature of their trade. The firm of Meulenaer in Antwerp lamented that he almost found no more buyers and it was said that in 1732, the amount of imported Brazilian diamonds was four times higher than Indian import figures.[71] The first reaction of the Portuguese Crown was to control production, and in 1734 the governor of Minas Gerais ordered the diamond mines to be shut down.[72] This was a very severe measure, especially since other solutions were suggested. In 1733, the viceroy of Brazil had written to D. João V indicating that selling a monopoly to a mining company was an ideal solution against the problems of declining prices and contraband.[73] One year later, several merchants sent proposals to the Crown in order to obtain a combined mining and trade monopoly. In February 1734, six European merchants living in Lisbon, of French, Dutch and English origin but also counting three Portuguese traders, made a united effort to obtain a diamond monopoly, but they did not succeed, as a full closure of the diamond mines was issued shortly thereafter.[74]

In January 1739, after five years of prohibition, the colonial authorities advertised that they were searching for a company interested in obtaining a monopoly in diamond mining.[75] Several meetings took place between inhabitants of the diamond region and the governor of Minas Gerais. The offer of a Portuguese merchant, João Fernandes de Oliveira, was accepted. As was the case for many immigrants who settled in Minas Gerais, he came from the north of Portugal, from a region called Minho. João Fernandes was a member of a large family of traders, most of them living in Brazil.[76] He had left for Rio de Janeiro at the beginning of the eighteenth century, but drawn by the prospect of gold, he quickly decided to go to Vila Rica de Ouro Preto, the capital of Minas Gerais. He did not stay there long but moved to Vila do Ribeirão do Carmo, present-day Mariana, where he founded a company with some others and managed to get the contract to collect the royal tenths in the region. In 1727 his wife, the daughter of a Rio de Janeiro-based merchant, gave birth to a son who later followed in his father's footsteps and obtained the diamond contract in the 1760s.[77]

The mining contract was granted to João Fernandes on 20th of June 1739 and was to last for a period of four years.[78] He was to pay a yearly taxation of 230$000 *reis* per slave that would work in the diamond mines, with a total of 600 slaves to be employed. Illegal mining and contraband trade were severely punished. Dragoons patrolled in the diamond region and all inhabitants were subject to severe requirements. Whoever did not exercise an official employment was ordered to leave, and traders were banned. People who were caught in the district without a valid reason for being there had to leave within two months.

Another regulation was concerned with the transport of diamonds. Discovered stones were to be kept in the office of the *intendente*, a specially-appointed government official, and at specified times the stones were sent to Rio de Janeiro, where they were loaded onto Portuguese *naus de Guerra* headed for Lisbon. The mining company's representatives in Lisbon then sold the stones to different merchants.[79] These representatives were named *caixas*. There were two of them and, although chosen by the contract holders, they had to answer to the Portuguese State.[80] Officials of the King had the first choice of purchase, and they were to pay within four months. After that, the *caixas* were free to sell, in the presence of a Portuguese minister and after an official agreement by the King.[81] The first contract ended on 31st of December 1743, but was prolonged for another four years. João Fernandes maintained a good relationship with the governor of the captaincy, and he employed many more slaves than was officially allowed.[82] The *História Chronológica* mentioned the use of 3 to 4,000 slaves.[83] Financial problems made João Fernandes decide not to apply for a third contract, which was given to Felisberto Caldeira Brant and his brothers. Brant was born in Brazil, a *Paulista*, and already had mining experience. He had been in Goías in 1735 when precious stones were discovered in riverbeds there.[84]

Although diamond mining had become restricted in 1739, the commerce in Brazilian diamonds had remained free. The diamonds that arrived on the Rio fleet were bought in Lisbon by merchants who had good connections and who were often foreign. In Brazil, Felisberto Caldeira Brant, whose contract was to end in 1752, had maintained a good relationship with the steward that was to overview diamond mining on behalf of the Portuguese Crown. He was also a personal friend of the governor of Minas Gerais.[85] Things went well until 1751, when the steward was replaced and the governor left for Rio de Janeiro. Those newly made responsible quickly accused Brant of illegal activities. He was accused of working with 5,000 slaves instead of the permitted 600, the bills of exchange he had issued to cover his expenses were no longer deemed trustworthy and he was also accused of selling large diamonds to private merchants rather than handing them over to the government for shipment to Europe. In January 1752, a letter was sent to Lisbon demanding his arrest and sequestration of his goods.[86] In response, Brant accused the steward of the theft of 386 carats of rough diamonds.[87] At the same time, João Fernandes was in Lisbon to negotiate terms for the next mining contract. He had to deal with a new king, D. José, since D. João V had died in 1750, and a new man who was to become Portugal's most important figure in the years to come, Sebastião José de Carvalho e Melo, the future Marquis of Pombal, who was at the time secretary of war and foreign commerce. De Oliveira was granted an audience with the King in March 1752 after which the King granted the mining monopoly for four years to him and his two partners, Antonio and Manoel Barbosa Torres.[88]

On 16 January 1753, shortly after the contract had been signed, the Rio fleet entered Lisbon with money, diamonds and promissory notes payable to merchants that had made investments in the diamond mines. The investment money was used to pay the slaveholders and to pay for technical equipment and the bills were to be paid out in Lisbon by the local representatives of the contract holders, the so-called *caixas*, with the proceeds of diamond sales.[89] The foreign firm of Sebastian & Manuel Vanderton was one of Brant's important business contacts.

According to Dormer's Lisbon agents, they were a 'chief limb of the Brazeel contracters', and Vanderton bought 'all that comes to his hands'.[90] When there was talk in town about the involved parties of the new diamond contract in 1752, they wrote to Dormer that rumour had it that the Vandertons were involved, a rumour that they did not believe.[91] It seems that the Vanderton firm was the major buyer of rough diamonds shipped on the fleet that had arrived in January 1753.[92]

The bills that had arrived on the same ships were issued by Brant. When presented for acceptance, the Lisbon *caixas* made an official protest and refused to pay.[93] To make things worse, Sebastian Vanderton, who had purchased diamonds on credit, had pawned many of the stones he had bought to different firms in Lisbon. The *caixas* had done the same thing with several parcels of diamonds and they were indebted with private merchants but also with the Portuguese government. The consequence of the protested bills was that the diamonds belonging to Brant's contract could not be sold. This caused the diamond trade to come to a standstill and the lack of circulation of money paralysed the whole trading community of Lisbon. A court decision put the pawned diamonds up for public sale, but they were sold for very low prices and a new diamond crisis occurred.[94] The authorities decided first to deal with Brant. In February 1753, the King sent a letter to the judge in Tejuco, wherein he stated that Felisberto had abused the terms of the monopoly contract by selling diamonds illegally.[95] One month later, a large parcel of contraband diamonds was discovered in the port of Lisbon. The authorities concluded that such an operation could not have taken place without the complicity of the contract holders and Brant was imprisoned.[96] In April, Berthon & Garnault informed Dormer about the 'recherche tres rigoureuze' that was taking place. According to them, the whole affair would 'occazioner des terrible embarras surement au Brezil' and perhaps create more problems in Lisbon.[97] Three weeks later, people were still being interrogated and people were hoping that the Rio fleet would sail quickly again, so that also the circulation of news and the Crown's decisions would be known on both sides of the ocean.[98] The firm of Sebastian & Manoel Vanderton, which was partially responsible for the crisis, remained in difficulties. According to rumour, they had stopped all their payments, but they tried to maintain their reputation:

> they feed their creditors with the hopes that when the Rio fleet will come the King will put em in a condition to pay what they owe and at same time, take in of courze the pawns that many of them have had laying in their hands for years.[99]

The Brazilian Diamond Trade Monopoly

The events of 1753 led to a total re-structuration of the Brazilian diamond trade, and its architect was the Marquis de Pombal. When the King left Lisbon for eight days, Pombal declared that 'I could be locked up in my cabinet, without being interrupted'.[100] Pombal had been frustrated that a lot of that trade was in foreign hands, and he wanted to preserve a bigger role for a Portuguese commercial bourgeoisie.[101] He remarked in his manuscript that 'their position [of Portuguese merchants] was substituted by many foreign merchants to sell their merchandize for themselves with an insupportable arrogance'.[102] At the same time, he realized that English and Dutch merchants had more expertise and financial means with regard to diamond trading, and he was also afraid that the trustworthiness of Portuguese merchants was affected following the refused payment of the bills by the Portuguese *caixas*.[103]

He decided to grant, next to the existing mining privileges, a commercial monopoly in Brazilian diamonds. It was sold to foreign merchants, but a diamond administration was established in Lisbon that was dominated by Portuguese merchants employed by the state. A new and rigid law was issued in August 1753 attempting to prevent illegal mining and contraband trade in the diamond district in Minas Gerais.[104] It was after the issuing of the separate monopoly that the European trade in Brazilian diamonds became firmly in the hands of English and Dutch merchants. The first monopoly was given to John Bristow and Hermann Joseph Braamcamp. Braamcamp was a Dutch Catholic merchant who had settled in Lisbon and had been the representative for the Prussian government at the Portuguese court during the early 1750s.[105] His brother, known as a wine dealer, possessed a magnificent collection of art.[106] John Bristow was a partner in a firm called Bristow, Ward & Co., one of the biggest English firms operating in Porto and Lisbon that possessed considerable credit, as he subscribed £150,000 in an English government loan in 1744.[107] Pombal knew Bristow personally, as he had interfered on his behalf when the Englishman got into trouble with Portuguese authorities who suspected him of smuggling bullion out of Lisbon on an English ship in 1752.[108]

On 10 August, the first monopoly contract was signed between the Portuguese Crown, John Bristow and Gerard Braamcamp, who agreed to buy 35,000 carats of diamonds per year between 1754 and 1759. Two Portuguese merchants, Domingos de Bastos Viana and Antonio dos Santos Pinto, were named as *caixas*.[109] The partners of the first monopoly contract did not have the luck of seeing the four year term through. In 1757, Berthon wrote to Dormer that the contract was taken from Bristow and his partners, and that it was given to 'Vaneck, Gore & some others'.[110] The rumour had spread that Bristow and Braamcamp were associated with a secret Jewish partner, the Salvador firm in London, much to Pombal's anger, and an envoy was sent to London with 'orders to keep an eye at all the wealthy merchants at the Bourse of London, to choose three or four, who possess the greatest capital and best established reputation'.[111] The Lisbon earthquake of 1755, an event that catapulted Pombal to an almost absolute power, was the final blow for John Bristow. He lost a considerable sum of money because many of his debtors could not repay him.[112] Enquiries in London had led to talks with two merchants willing to take over the contract, Joshua van Neck, a merchant-financer from Dutch origin living in London, and John Gore, an English merchant.

Their contacts in Lisbon, Gerardo Devisme and David Purry, signed the second monopoly contract in December 1756.[113] For the duration of the contract, three years between 1757 and 1759, Gore and van Neck engaged themselves to buy 50,000 carats of rough diamonds each year, for 9$200 *reis* per carat. The contract could be renewed every three years, with a rise of 200 *reis* of the price per carat.[114] For a second time, the contract would not be fulfilled, as the partners tried to get out of it in 1758. Pombal, who had labelled Gore as a man of 'great and known talents', saw Jewish pressure as the reason why Gore and van Neck tried to terminate the contract. He wrote that the 'nation of Jews' tried to break the Brazilian diamond trade, and had attempted to destroy creditworthiness of the Portuguese merchants.[115] The commercial interest important diamond traders maintained with India caused problems and it should not be excluded that merchants who had been active in the Indian trade considered the Brazilian diamonds as a serious threat, and tried to discourage London merchants to become engaged in that trade. After all, control over imports of Brazilian diamonds came into the hands of only one partnership, while the import of Indian diamonds had remained a competitive business that was virtually open to anyone interested. It seems only logical that this situation created unhappiness in the circles of Indian diamond merchants, as they could not gain entry into the Brazilian diamond imports and from that side, they would have to content themselves with buying from the contract holder and selling to other markets. Earlier, in the first years after the discovery of Brazilian diamonds, a number of worries were expressed by well-established diamond merchants, and their exclusion from the monopoly must not have silenced these voices.[116] Whether it was directly owing to difficulties in London or not remains unclear, but Pombal decided to bypass London and searched for a new privileged partner in Amsterdam.

The failures of the two first contracts made Pombal seek for a more durable solution, something he found in the person of Daniël Gildemeester. This Dutch merchant, considered to be the 'merchant in Lisbon who, by common opinion, had accumulated the greatest financial capital', was already experienced in the diamond trade and the name of his brother Jan figured on a list of buyers of diamonds of Sebastian Vanderton in 1753.[117] Jan Gildemeester was also correspondent for the V. O. C. in Lisbon, and his son, born in 1744, was consul for Portugal in Amsterdam and a famous art collector in his time. In 1761 the third monopoly contract in Brazilian diamonds was signed by Daniël Gildemeester. For a period of three years, he promised to buy 40,000 carats per year, at 8$600 *reis* per carat. It was the first contract without the involvement of London merchants and it was considered to be so successful that it would be prolonged in

1764, 1767 and 1776.[118] The whole structure of Brazilian diamond mining and trading had found equilibrium. João Fernandes de Oliveira and his son still possessed the contract of mining in Tejuco, Gildemeester now held the trading monopoly, and the Portuguese merchants active on the diamond board came from a selective group of families, da Cruz Sobral, Bandeira and Quintela, who all played a large part in Pombal's project to enlarge the body of Portuguese merchants in colonial trade. This had included the foundation of a trade council, and two trading companies for Brazil, the *Grão Pará e Maranhão Companhia* and the *Companhia de Pernambuco*. José Rodrigues Bandeira and José Francisco da Cruz were among the first directors of these companies. Da Cruz also would become the first treasurer of the Royal Treasury (Real Erário) in 1761. Members of all three families would be active in other organs of national manufactories and international trade, and a Quintela was named as special judge to deal with conflicts including English merchants in Lisbon. They were the visible expression of Pombal's nationalistic policy.[119] Bandeira and da Cruz were appointed *caixas* in the diamond trade monopoly. Members of these families held these posts until the end of the Gildemeester period in 1787. It is very interesting to note that these Portuguese mercantile families became connected with the contract holders through marriage and social acquaintance. The da Cruz Sobral family became intermarried with the Braamcamps. Gerard Braamcamp, Hermann's brother, had possessed the tobacco trade monopoly in the same period, the 1750s, together with da Cruz.[120] In 1778 the French ambassador visited the house of the Gildemeesters, where Daniël and Quintela were discussing the marriage of Daniël's son with the daughter of a Portuguese merchant.[121] The presence of Portuguese families in the diamond trade administration is also acknowledged in a list from 1770 that contains the names of merchants waiting on returns of investments made in the diamond mines. 29 per cent of the financial value of the investments came from people with ties to the Bandeira, Quintela and da Cruz Sobral families.[122]

For several years, Gildemeester bought more diamonds than was officially demanded. This changed in 1770, when he only purchased 55,414 carats of rough Brazilian diamonds. The year before, he had still bought 76,689 carats. A year later, João Fernandes de Oliveira the younger's contract had ended. His leniency towards smuggling led again to a change in Portugal's approach to diamond mining: in 1771, the mining monopoly was abolished. Mining was put under the direct control of colonial authorities, the *Real Extracção*. In August 1771, the new stipulations were made public in a law containing fifty-four articles that dealt with illegal mining, smuggling, the use of slaves and the settlement of people. Besides introducing a colonial system controlling the mining, most stipulations were re-iterations on the rules of 1753.[123] At the same time, similar problems as in 1753 occurred, showing a weakness in the system of investments. Bills of exchange were to be paid out in Lisbon by the *caixas*, and this relied very much on Gildemeester's purchases and sales. In the early 1770s, he had started to buy less and less, and again, the system of credit was at risk by a growing possibility that bills could no longer be paid out. Rumours were spreading that Gildemeester would be replaced, perhaps even by a Portuguese firm. The possibility of constructing a diamond polishing industry in Lisbon was also considered. A lapidary existed in the early nineteenth century, in the Campo Pequeno neighbourhood in Lisbon, but it did not survive for long.[124]

Gildemeester had become very rich and lived outside Lisbon, in the Palácio dos Seteais that he built in Sintra. He wanted to keep the contract, which the government allowed in exchange for a higher level of control. It was now the Portuguese State that would stand as guarantee for the payment of future bills of exchange. The *caixas*, still members of the Bandeira and da Cruz families, were given a larger influence in the selling of Brazilian diamonds.[125] These measures could not stop the decline in production.[126] In the 1780s, Gildemeester's purchases were fewer than ever before: of the 62,038 carats of rough diamonds arriving in Lisbon in 1784, Gildemeester had only bought 37,500. In 1786, the authorities let him decide personally, accompanied by two Portuguese cutters, what diamonds he chose to buy, but this did not stop the Dutch merchant giving up the contract in 1787. In the same year, the famous Englishman William Beckford described Gildemeester as 'the old diamond dealer'.[127]

It is not clear who gained the commercial monopoly thereafter. Between 1790 and 1800, Joaquim Pedro Quintela bought 158,168 carats of Brazilian diamonds, although it remains unclear whether his purchases were made within a monopoly or not.[128] By that time, Portugal was threatened by a French invasion and was in financial difficulties. Brazilian rough diamonds were used to repay loans the government had made in London, with Baring Brothers & Company, and Amsterdam, with Hope & Company.[129] The Hope firm was a very considerable merchant-banking house and they had previous experience in diamond trade. At various times they attempted to obtain the Brazilian diamond contract. In 1765 they tried a last time, invoking the help of the Danish court. Their envoy in Lisbon tried to plea in their favour, but the contract was given to Daniël Gildemeester.[130] They were correspondents of Dormer, with whom they were engaged in a few diamond sales. They had good contacts on consumer markets in Turkey and Russia, and balance books for the 1760s show that they made regular sales in Constantinople.[131]

Diamond Consumption in the Eighteenth Century

James Dormer, a Small Merchant Banker?

In 1716, London's *Saturday's Post* contained a small article on the already famous Pitt diamond:

> There is news about the Pitt diamond, that it's carried to France, and is of so great a Price, that it cost 100000 Livers to cut it and that the Chips that they cut off from it, are worth 150000 livers; as for the diamond it self, 'tis said to be the greatest that ever was seen in the worlds, and not only so, but of the most perfect beauty. The French jewellers say 'tis worth 20 Millions of Livres, and that as there was nobody found rich enough in England to buy it, so 'tis thought they have carry'd it to a wrong market in France; or at least at a wrong Time, the Regent being too good a Husband to part with so much money.[132]

This text contains all the elements that have made the diamond the successful luxury item it still is today. It has always been an international commodity, found in exotic places and remote mines and sold on exotic markets in Persia, Constantinople and Russia. Only after human intervention could the diamond, the hardest gem stone on earth, be transformed into a thing of beauty.[133] Legendary diamonds were often named after people who consequently shared in the myth, and they were seen as adornments for the extremely rich. Stories like this one fed the desire of consumers and contributed to the role diamonds played in the eyes of purchasers of jewels and other luxury products. This article was read by merchants, but also by consumers, and in buying jewellery set with diamonds they could gain access to this international world of luxury, even if it was a ring set with a small diamond.

The merchants that play a part in this book hardly came into contact with consumers dreaming of precious and exotic stones. Their networks were circuits involving fellow traders and jewellers. Yet, they could not operate without knowing what customers wanted. In Asia, merchants such as Jean Chardin and Jean-Baptiste Tavernier travelled to different courts selling jewels that were largely manufactured in Europe. They needed to know, or at least reasonably guess, local taste, so they could decide which jewels to purchase for their trips. Constantinople, Milan, Paris and other European cities were vital markets for the sale of cut diamonds and other forms of jewellery. Where they were sent, and in what manner they were constructed, depended on taste. So far, the international diamond trade between India, Brazil and Europe has been analysed. It has been pointed out several times that the geographical spread of commercial circuits not only depended on the establishment of networks of merchants or the place of the diamond mines, but also on the establishment of diamond cutting industries and of consumer markets. More than a matter of consumer taste, fashion in the diamond industry was greatly dependent on technical progress as well. Diamonds only developed as a luxury product after the discovery of cutting techniques enabled consumers to value diamonds for their beauty and light effects. This puts diamonds, and other precious stones, in a particular position, as they are natural materials that are transformed by people to become a part of culture.[134] This means that the use, and value, of precious stones is determined by the cultural appreciation for it, but also that the role played in culture by such commodities depends on what can be done with them. Godehard Lenzen has shown that it was a combination of cultural change, economic possibilities and technical advance that eventually replaced the mythical meaning of the diamond as the hardest material with a meaning of beauty and luxury.[135]

This book is concerned with the activities of international diamond traders and how these contributed to a movement of globalization, and is therefore not concerned directly with the consumer market for diamonds and other precious stones. A history thereof would lead too far away from the main subject, and a lack of studies connecting diamond trade with consumption patterns makes it a difficult task to summarize a century-old history of the use of the diamond as a jewel. Notwithstanding, consumer's choice is of vital importance to the international diamond trade, and even to the traders who were not themselves delivering products to final customers. They still had to know what was in fashion, not only in order to buy the right type of product, but also to make a choice in cutting. The cutting and polishing of rough diamonds was a delicate business, as a cutter could greatly enhance the value of a stone. Next to fashion, the shape of a particular diamond determined how it would be cut, together with the technical skill of the cutter. Different merchants active in Europe bought rough diamonds and ordered them to be cut before they were sold to jewellers or other diamond merchants. No trader could permit himself to remain ignorant regarding the general aspects of diamond cutting or the fashion of certain types of diamonds. Because of the relevance of information regarding these elements of the diamond business to the decision making process of merchants, their point of view with regard to the consumer's market will be analysed, rather than presenting a general overview of the history of diamond consumption.

One of these merchants was James Dormer. He was involved in an international and cross-cultural diamond trade network and his surviving correspondence shows the state of Europe's diamond consumption in the first half of the eighteenth century. Dormer was one of eleven sons of Charles, fifth baron Dormer. James was born in 1708 and died in 1758 on a secret mission for the Habsburg emperor. He was a friend of Alexander Hume, governor-general of the colonies that the southern Netherlands possessed in Bengal and became a merchant working for the *Company of Ostend*.[136] Between 1728 and 1732, Dormer was accepted as an apprentice in a small English trade firm located in Bruges. Thanks to his brother's good relations with Hume and with the directors of the company, James got the opportunity in 1732 to go on an expedition to Canton, which lasted a year. When he returned, he completed his training as a merchant and decided to settle in Antwerp. He married in 1735 with Maria Magdalena Emtinck, who belonged to a rich family. She died when giving birth to a son two years later, and soon enough it was discovered that much of her capital had vanished. He remarried in 1738, with Joanna Theresia Goubau, who also brought a considerable capital with her. He invested this capital not only in trade, but also in a luxurious lifestyle.[137] Dormer's aspiration to marry into nobility was representative of the 'aristocratization' of a number of merchant families in seventeenth- and eighteenth-century Antwerp. For some of these families, the desire for luxury goods and the purchase of country houses and castles led to financial difficulties. Dormer's spending eventually contributed to his firm's bankruptcy after his death.[138] He traded in a variety of goods, such as textiles, rice, oil, indigo, skins, French wine, tapestries and grain, but diamonds were his most important commodity, in absolute and relative terms of profit.[139] He had not specialized in a specific trade, and in that regard he was no different from most eighteenth-century merchants.[140] He managed to make a good profit acting as a paymaster for the English army during the Austrian Succession War.[141] Other income was derived from his activities in ship-leasing, insurance and banking.[142] These activities remained relatively small, and the total amount of interest that Dormer received during his banking career was more or less the same as the interest that Charles Proli made in one year.[143] Erika Meel concluded that Dormer's firm can be seen as an example of a medium-sized firm with an international character in the first half of the eighteenth century. As a merchant, she characterized Dormer as flexible, opportunistic and prepared to take initiative. However, she also stated that he was rather traditional, and preferred trade activities that had already proven their profitability.[144] Through his connection to local lower nobility, Dormer's close relatives, such as his wife and children, became consumers of the products related to diamonds that Dormer sold, and on some occasions the English merchant noted in his diamond books that some stones he possessed were taken out of circulation: 'the two yellow drops were taken & sett for my wifes Earings'.[145]

The origins of his interests in the diamond business will probably never be known, but Dormer had started to make inquiries about the trade in 1737. He had established a correspondence with the Salvador firm, important merchants active in the Anglo-Indian diamond trade by buying twelve pictures for Francis Salvador. Francis's sons Joseph and Jacob were partners in the firm, but Jacob died in 1749. Joseph Salvador (1716–86) built himself a reputation that would bypass his father's name and he became one of London's most prominent Jewish figures.[146] Apparently, Dormer was introduced to Francis Salvador through Alexander Hume and he quickly enquired about a possible cooperation in diamond trade.[147] In a letter Salvador wrote to Dormer in September 1737, he mentioned that nothing could be done in the diamond trade: 'they are so excessive dear in this place and we have not any from India nor Brasil when there is shall send you some for a tryall'.[148]

A regular trade was not established until a few years later, and a cross-cultural and international trade network developed itself involving both Dormer and the Salvador firm. They bought and sold diamonds on a co-partnership basis, but also acted at times as agents for each other. Other important merchants involved were the Nunes firm in Amsterdam, who were cousins of the Salvadors, and the Huguenot partnership of Berthon & Garnault, who had established themselves in Lisbon and sold diamonds on behalf of Dormer and Salvador. Joan Osy & Son was a French firm who often acted as transportation intermediaries in Rotterdam, and Bernardus Edmundus van Merlen and Isabella de Coninck, husband and wife, were partners in purchase and sales of Dormer but acted as itinerant intermediaries who often went to Amsterdam. They were also responsible for sending rough diamonds to the diamond cutters. Also involved were the three biggest banking houses in eighteenth-century Amsterdam: Hope & Company, Andries Pels & Sons and George Clifford & Sons. Dormer maintained an extensive correspondence with all three of them, and apart from sharing interests in the diamond trade, a lot of financial activities took place between them.[149] The network counted four nationalities (Dutch, English, French and Brabant) and three religions (Judaism, Catholicism and Protestantism) active in Lisbon, Amsterdam, London and Antwerp, Europe's foremost centres in the diamond trade.

The exact nature of the relationships established between these merchants of diverse origin will be the attention of the following chapter. At this point, it is important to note that the information drawn from the extensive correspondence they maintained with each other allows for an insight into the way the European market for diamonds worked at a time when it was dominated by both Brazilian and Indian precious stones.

Complementary Markets

London has often been seen as the most important diamond centre in the eighteenth century, with Amsterdam in second place. This is based on London's crucial role with regard to diamond imports into Europe and Amsterdam's leading cutting industry. Nevertheless, London possessed a diamond industry that even served Indian customers as is shown by the following message that appeared in the *Middlesex Journal or Chronicle of Liberty* in January 1771:

> On Friday Policies of Insurance were opened at Lloyd's coffee-house at 10, 20, 30 and some at 40 per cent, on one of out homewardbound Indiamen, which has on board a rough diamond single stone, valued at 100000l. sterling. It is sent in its primitive state in order to be manufactured here by our ingenious countrymen, for the use of an Indian Nabob.[150]

At the same time, Amsterdam was a major import centre for Brazilian diamonds thanks to the Dutch merchants controlling the Brazilian diamond monopoly.[151] Roughly, both cities offered the same opportunities in diamond trade, although not to the same extent. Philip Curtin has described a hierarchy between cities in urban networks, based on a functional dependency between them.[152] For diamond trade, the functions are: international import, wholesale, jewellery sale to consumers and the cutting industry. No city played a leading role in all four of these functions and the distinction that should be made is not between cities, but between competing networks, relying on their own suppliers, their own contacts with cutters and their own clientele amongst the jewellers. These networks were always international and competition should be seen as an element between merchant circuits rather than between cities. In this manner, cities become locations, offering different possibilities to trading networks that operated between different cities.

As other branches of commerce, the diamond business depended to a great extent on supply and demand. Dormer received rough diamonds from Brazil and India, through London and Amsterdam. He also developed a trade in jewellery and polished precious stones. Both sorts of diamonds came from different channels. Amsterdam had the most important cutting industry, and the Dutch capital provided regularly polished and cleaved diamonds. Owing to the good connections London merchants had with Brazil and India, large supplies of uncut diamonds came from England, but occasionally also from Lisbon. For Dormer, Amsterdam and London were two complementary suppliers. This complementary nature can be extended to other cities that played a nodal role within the cross-cultural network, not only on the supply side but also on the demand side. In Dormer's time, supply channels did not change over a considerable period, although the frequency of individual imports might differ greatly over time. An important factor influencing supplies was the political and economical situation at the diamond mines. Productivity of the mines was also important, although this never became an issue in Dormer's time. Transportation was a second element influencing the supply side. Merchants had to await the arrival of the fleet from Rio de Janeiro and of the India ships. Their arrival was often surrounded with uncertainty, and the exact volume of diamonds arriving often remained unknown.[153] Since the trade with India depended greatly on the shipment of silver and coral, diamond supplies also depended on the trades in those commodities. Salvador mentioned the exchange trade in coral and diamonds:

> it is possible we may have but one ship more with diamonds this season and as the coral ships are not arriv'd this year att India the returns of diamonds will fall short this season, there are likewise 3 more of our ships arriv'd or on the coast as likewise 7 Dutch Indiamen perhaps they are now in the Dutch ports[154]

This uncertainty, caused by the international nature of the trade and the slow travelling of information, was a basic characteristic of the imports of diamonds. Dormer received similar information on the arrival of fleets at Lisbon: 'our Rio fleet will be here in about two months and then we hope that things will mend'.[155] English Indiamen regularly made stops in Lisbon before heading home and occasionally this gave an opportunity for buyers in Lisbon to get some diamonds from the Indian mines: 'there is an India ship expected now very soon, and we hear of severall that expect parcells of Diamonds by her'.[156] When a monopoly in Brazilian diamonds was issued by the Portuguese Crown, clandestine trade grew and Berthon & Garnault informed Dormer of the possibility of purchasing diamonds out of the official circuit: 'the publick has not been informed what rough diamonds the last Rio fleet has brought tis thought it has been a reasonable quantity very few out of contract have appeared and they have been sold very dear'.[157] News about contraband diamonds also arrived in Amsterdam, where the Nunes brother wrote in 1741 that 'l'on dit que avec les flottes arrive a Lisbonne viennent 1208 octaves diamants s'il ne vient plus hors du registre ce n'est pas grand chose'.[158]

Most of the rough diamonds that Dormer received from different channels were sent to be cut and polished, which was done mostly in Amsterdam. After this process, diamonds were sold in Antwerp, Amsterdam, London and Lisbon. Only on a rare occasion sales were made outside these places, but only on a personal agreement with a local buyer. Most of Dormer's buyers came from Amsterdam, but they bought smaller amounts than his customers in Antwerp. This suggests that he traded more with wholesalers in Antwerp, while he sold more to jewellers in the Dutch capital. The fact that Antwerp was the most important sales market for Dormer is not very surprising, as one of his main tasks within the network was his function as a sales agent for other merchants.[159] The fact that important merchants such as the Salvadors, who maintained good kinship ties in Amsterdam, considered Antwerp to be a valuable sales market is more surprising, especially when considering its vicinity to Amsterdam, where both imports and cutting industries flourished in the eighteenth century, and Paris, one of Europe's most important jewellery centres.[160]

Dormer's sales in various cities were not only determined by his supplies; the demand side was equally important, and local differences in demand might help explain why Antwerp was still considered to be an important market for diamonds. As was the case for supply, demand depended to a certain extent on the rhythm of ships arriving from India or Brazil in European ports. Anticipated arrivals of diamonds not only helped to set prices, it also contributed to the flow of trade in general, as the arrival of India and Brazil fleets caused cash circulation, and acted as an accelerant for trade: 'the jewellers shopkeepers being now most out of money they wait the arrival of the Rio fleet about latter and of August to rule themselves'.[161] The availability of cash and credit influenced the demand for luxury products and this information was crucial to diamond merchants, who were very conscious of these fluctuations:

> if an opportunity should offer for sale, it's the mizery of the people on one hand which has been cauze of the few sales there has been ... add to this the dearness of all eatables makes that many that formerly lived comorftably are now nigh starving the dearness of corn in particular ... so that ordinary Jewellry has but little vend, and the better not much neither, but still some ordinary goods go off.[162]

Demand for luxury goods was not purely influenced by economic and financial factors. Polished diamonds were mostly used in jewellery and their demand depended on taste and fashion. Diamonds were cut in different ways. The table cut was the oldest, but after technical innovation first roses and later brilliants became the most popular cuts, as they enhanced light effects within the diamond and magnified their beauty. An extract from a letter sent from Lisbon indicates that wealthier buyers preferred the brilliant, as it was technically superior to the rose, but also more expensive: 'mais de telles Rozes ne sont point en mode Icy; ceux quy peuvent depencer une somme; le veullent faire en gouet cest a dire dans un bon Brillant'.[163] The appreciation for different types of diamonds also depended on time and place. In his treatise on precious stones, the English jeweller David Jeffries wrote about different ways to polish diamonds, and remarked

> that nothing can more perpetuate rose diamonds on the esteem they have hitherto had in the world, than maintaining the truth of their manufacture. Nor was it ever more fit to be recommended than at present, on account of the corrupt taste that has of late prevailed, in converting rose diamonds into brilliants, under pretence of rendering them, by that means, a more beautiful, and excellent jewel.[164]

This practice of cutting polished diamonds again, but in another form, indicates a shifting taste. This difference did not only occur over time, but also over space. In Lisbon, consumers preferred other diamonds than in Paris and merchants kept each other informed on local differences in taste. As a consequence, many parcels of diamonds were sent back and forth between London, Lisbon, Antwerp and Amsterdam in order to obtain the best possible price. On various occasions, a merchant procured a specific kind of diamond with a specific market in mind. In 1738, Dormer tried to get specific stones from Salvador for the Antwerp market, but Francis Salvador answered that he could not obtain the diamonds that were popular in Antwerp.[165] In 1743, the English merchant asked Francis Salvador about the possibility of buying rose diamonds in London, but the latter responded that it was not possible: 'the roses are not to be bought here since all comes from your place'.[166] Later, Salvador frequently mentioned to Dormer that he had received good parcels that were fit for the Antwerp market.[167] When

George Clifford & Sons wrote to Dormer to show their interest in the diamond trade, they made specific requests, and they asked Dormer if he could obtain stones that would among the five most wanted sorts in Amsterdam. They were quite clear about what they wanted: 'rozes that are well spread x pretty clear, but not quite of the first water'.[168] When the Nunes firm of Amsterdam heard that a certain sort of diamond was in specific demand in Antwerp, they wrote that they would address Francis Salvador, to see if he could buy the specific kind.[169] Dormer made several specific requests to different network members about the diamonds he wanted because of their demand in Antwerp. Sometimes, his requests could not be fulfilled, as was the case for his order to Thomas and Adrian Hope in 1750 for 'diamants fins de 2 a 10 au Kt'.[170] The prices mentioned by Dormer were too low for them, at such selling price they could not make a good deal, but they asked Dormer to continue trying to get better prices.

Dormer's correspondents in Lisbon also kept their eye open for what was fashionable. On one occasion, Dormer had sent Berthon & Garnault yellow diamonds, while the Portuguese wanted white stones: 'on veut du blanc tant en rozes quen brilliants & en surplus en ces derniers on les recherche parfaits bien taillés et surtout bien estendus'.[171] Mostly, Berthon & Garnault used brokers to look for customers, but sometimes they met themselves with prospective buyers and one letter from them contained a fragment in which they described such a meeting:

> we immediately cal'd a buyer, the best man here he lookt' em over and told us that as to the 2 papers of brilliants ... they were insaleable amongst the Portugueze, that what was in demand amongst em was only very small brilliants perfect in coullour & cleanness and from 20 to 30 to ye. Kt.[172]

After this negative advice, they consulted a broker, who concluded the same and the diamonds were sent back to Antwerp. The frequency with which diamonds were sent back and forth between markets, the often specific demands merchants made to each other to obtain specific types of diamonds and the constant inquiries about prices lead to the idea of complementary markets, on which merchants tried to make the best profits and looked out for every opportunity. Dormer and his correspondents tried to play the markets, send types of diamonds to the city where they were the most wanted and where they could obtain the best price. It seems probable that, if Dormer had not operated within a network, he would have had to choose between the commerce in polished or in uncut diamonds. Commodity circulation would have been more difficult outside the network, and the ease with which diamonds were sent to one of the four markets in which Dormer was active is a vital mechanism from which the network derived its flexibility.

Although these fragments of letters sent between traders demonstrate that merchants considered markets to be complementary, the fact that the occupation of most of Dormer's purchasers remains unknown prevents a more detailed analysis of how taste and other demand mechanisms shaped the consumer's market for diamonds in the eighteenth century. Another difficulty is that Dormer's correspondence is not covering the entire scope of activities of the cross-cultural diamond network. Unfortunately, no separate correspondences or business books of other merchants involved have been preserved, with a few exceptions such as material relating to the firm of Hope & Company. This problem poses itself most at the boundaries of the network, where diamonds were sold to consumers. A few fragments in the trade correspondence indicate that the circulation of precious stones did not stay limited to network members, as is to be expected. Sometimes, diamonds were sent to jewellers in Paris and there are signs that network members sold diamonds at more distant markets. Thomas and Adrian Hope wrote to James Dormer in 1747 that a correspondent of theirs in Russia desired thirty carats of brilliants, cut in a special way. They asked Dormer to provide them with a sample that they could send to Russia.[173] In 1749 Berthon & Garnault wished they had some rose diamonds, fifty to 100 stones per carat, and they claimed that they could ship them on the fleet to Brazil, because there was a great demand for such roses in Rio de Janeiro.[174] In June 1758, the firm of Aaron & David Fernandes Nunes, based in Amsterdam, returned a letter of James Dormer in which he had sent them diamond prices in Antwerp. They were high, a fact that the Amsterdam merchants did not understand, 'attendu que presentement il n'y a la moindre sortie pour la Turquie, comme vous le saurez sans doute'.[175] It seems that fashion in other consumer's markets determined the circulation of goods in London, Amsterdam and Antwerp. When Dormer wished to sell some polished diamonds, Francis and Joseph Salvador replied that there was 'no Demand at present for small Roses on Account of the Turkey Trade being at present Stopped'.[176] At least on one occasion did one of the members of the cross-cultural trade network travel to Turkey. In 1746, James Dormer asked him to go to a public sale in Amsterdam, but van Merlen let him know he was unavailable because he had just returned from the Turks and had plans to undertake another voyage.[177]

3 A CROSS-CULTURAL DIAMOND TRADE NETWORK

James Dormer was an all-round merchant living in the first half of the eighteenth century. His main occupation was the trade in diamonds, and he managed to become involved in a circuit of traders that had different backgrounds. He worked on a reciprocal and regular basis with Jewish businessmen in London and Amsterdam, Brabant traders in Antwerp, French Huguenots in Lisbon and Protestants and Catholics in Holland. In analysing their daily operations as well as the underlying structures that made a regular and stable trade possible, the example of Dormer and his partners shows the relevance for a socio-cultural economic analysis. This network was constructed out of a search for profit, and as was the case for all trade, the self-interest of individual network members played a role. This did not mean that egoistic behaviour was sufficient to ensure a smooth series of transactions that were mutually satisfying. Traders relied on a series of mechanisms applied in their mutual correspondence to build trust between each other. It relied on personal reputation, and information regarding this commercial characteristic was divulged in trade letters. This led to a form of cohesion within the informal trade circuit of which Dormer was a part, but also connected merchants to a larger commercial society. Reputation was a negotiable commodity that circulated within this informal society and it was based on past conduct, judgement from others and creditworthiness.

The study of internal mechanisms that bound these merchants together answers the question of how cross-cultural trade was possible. In an article analysing Turgot's writings on a famous court-case in Angoulême in 1769, Rothschild found 'a story of intense emotion ... not what one expects to find in economic history'.[1] The fundamental importance of reputation, a creation of familiarity and the reliance on the judgement of others, suggests that a form of emotional behaviour can be expected in business relationships. One should just be careful not to see this emotion as proof of fundamentally non-rational origins in the mechanisms of business, nor as a utilitaristic tool to create trust. Merchant society was not consciously constructed by its members. It grew with time and within it, habits, traditions, novelties and customs were developed. These can all be traced in the large amount of letters that Dormer wrote and received.

Commercial Operations

The Establishment of a Cross-Cultural Cooperation

Besides the great deal of correspondence of James Dormer that has been preserved in the city archive of Antwerp, Dormer's commercial books, in which he registered all his transactions in diamonds, have also been conserved. From these four books a number of people return who can be considered close associates of Dormer in the diamond trade. Between 1744 and 1758 (the year in which Dormer died unexpectedly), a regular and routine-like trade developed between these people, and their cooperation can be labelled a cross-cultural network. Its members and the functions they performed are summarized in Table 3.1.

Table 3.1: The diamond network.[2]

Merchant firm	City	Activities in the network	Period of correspondence	Number of letters sent to Dormer
James Dormer	Antwerp	Partner, agent	-	-
Francis & Joseph Salvador	London	Partner, supplier for Dormer	1737–58	672 + 4
Bernardus Edmundus van Merlen	Amsterdam	Travelling agent, broker, partner, responsible for cutting and cleaving of diamonds	1746	3
Isabella de Coninck	Antwerp/ Amsterdam	Travelling agent, broker, partner, responsible for cutting and cleaving of diamonds	1750–8	9
Paul Berthon & Peter Garnault	Lisbon	Sales agent	1747–56	149
Paul Berthon	Lisbon	Sales agent	1756–8	26
Aaron & David Fernandes Nunes	Amsterdam	Agent, representative for Salvador in Amsterdam	1740–58	163
George Clifford & Sons	Amsterdam	Transport agent, financer	1746–58	680
Joan Osy & Fils	Rotterdam	Transport agent	1742–58	489
Francis Mannock	London	Agent, Representative for Dormer in London	1728–58	850 + 2
Joseph de Marcour	Antwerp	Broker	-	-

The number of letters refers to the total amount of letters written by that correspondent, not only the letters relating to diamonds. Many of the letters contain information about credit, general commercial opportunities, other merchants and political events. For the network members, the main topic was the diamond trade. For Joseph de Marcour, no correspondence exists, which must be attributed to the fact that Dormer and Marcour lived in the same city. The correspondences with van Merlen and de Coninck are incomplete, which is proven by references to other letters that have not been preserved. It has been seen in the previous chapter that the establishment of a correspondence with the diamond traders Francis and Joseph Salvador of London was the first sign of Dormer's interest in the commerce of precious stones. Joseph was one of two sons of Francis active in the same firm, but Jacob died an early death in 1749. They were Sephardic Jews who managed to become part of London's upper class. Some of their relatives lived in Amsterdam, such as Aaron and David Fernandes Nunes who were cousins of the Salvadors and acted as their agents in Amsterdam. Joseph Salvador's aunt had married a Fernandes Nunes.[3] The ties between them form the only kinship relationship existing within the network.[4] The first transaction in diamonds with Salvador that can be found in the diamond books dates from the end of 1745, when Salvador supplied Dormer with two parcels of polished diamonds and fine diamond dust, with a total weight of 496 carats. Diamonds that were purchased were often mingled with other parcels or divided into smaller parcels. Salvador's supplies of 496 carats were divided into four parcels. Two of those, weighing respectively 138.25 and 59.5 carats, were sold in Antwerp by Isabella de Coninck. Two other parcels were given to Bernardus Edmundus van Merlen who had them further polished before selling them.[5]

Although this transaction with Salvador at the end of 1745 was not Dormer's first venture in the diamond trade, it did mean the beginning of a trade pattern involving often the same traders that was to continue until Dormer's death. The different actions relating to the diamond deal in 1745 became very routine-like in later years. A lot of the diamonds that were bought by Dormer, on his own behalf or in partnership with van Merlen, came from the Salvador firm in London. Either they bought diamonds there on Dormer's behalf, or they sold him imports from India that belonged to them. Often, the stones the Jewish firm sent were uncut, in which case they often passed to the hands of van Merlen, who was responsible for the contacts with the diamond cutters. Next to supplying network members with rough and polished diamonds, the Salvador firm was also concerned as a partner of James Dormer in the selling of precious stones in Amsterdam or Antwerp. Dormer acted as Salvador's agent, selling stones on the latter's behalf, for which he received a commission fee. Although less frequent, the opposite also occurred, and Francis and Joseph Salvador made a few sales on behalf of James Dormer and Bernardus van Merlen in London, especially in 1747.

Bernardus van Merlen was a diamond merchant who divided his time between Antwerp and Amsterdam. Nothing is known about his background, but it seems very likely that he came from Brabant. He was married to Isabella de Coninck, who fulfilled different functions for the network in Antwerp.[6] In Amsterdam, van Merlen was acquainted with the local diamond traders, including several Ashkenazi firms, and when he returned from a trip to Holland in April 1746, he did so in the company of Jacob Elias Levy, an important diamond merchant who often came to do business in Antwerp.[7] A lot of these travels related to van Merlen's activities an agent, buying and selling diamonds for network merchants. While van Merlen was responsible for almost all of the network's operations in Amsterdam, de Coninck worked mainly as an intermediary in Antwerp.[8] She started to travel regularly to Amsterdam only after van Merlen died in 1753. As agents, they were also responsible for arranging the cutting and cleaving of rough diamonds.[9] Besides their activities as intermediaries, van Merlen and de Coninck also operated as merchants. Most of the diamond sales recorded in the diamond books were done on behalf of a partnership between van Merlen and Dormer. At times, the former also purchased diamonds from Dormer for his own account – something that was done more frequently by de Coninck after 1753.

Several parcels of diamonds owned by van Merlen, de Coninck, Dormer and Salvador were sold in Lisbon by the firm of Paul Berthon and Peter Garnault. They were French Huguenots who had established themselves in Portugal after a passage in England. Because of their religion and their good contacts with England, they acted as part of the body of English merchants in Lisbon.[10] Their activities as sales agents meant that they contacted brokers and buyers. They concluded sales and arranged payments. If these were late, they often became involved personally in following debtors until their promise was fulfilled.[11] Sometimes they bought rough diamonds on Dormer's behalf and they were a very important source of information with regard to the Brazilian diamond trade. Diamonds that were to be sold in Lisbon were shipped through Holland, by means of the firm of George Clifford & Sons in Amsterdam that acted as transport agent. George Clifford was a merchant-banker, already of the third generation. The Cliffords belonged to the English peerage and they were Protestants who came originally from Cumberland. Part of the family emigrated at the end of the seventeenth century to the Low Countries, where they became successful in commerce and politics. Together with the firms of Hope & Company and Andries Pels & Son, they were considered to be the biggest bankers in Amsterdam during the first half of the eighteenth century.[12] A number of family members became active in the City Council of Amsterdam and one even became mayor of the town. In the nineteenth century, most family members that lived in the Netherlands moved to The Hague.[13] The Cliffords had an interest in diamond trade, and they were allegedly involved for a while in the Brazilian diamond trade together with Francis and Joseph Salvador. However, with regard to Dormer and van Merlen, they only acted as transport agents for diamonds with regard to Lisbon.[14] As bankers, they played a more important role, as their firm was often chosen by network members for the payment and remittance of profits related to diamond transactions.[15]

Another wealthy firm that acted as transport agents, this time between Antwerp, Amsterdam and London, was the firm of Joan Osy & Son, a Catholic Frenchman who had settled in Rotterdam, where the Osys became an important merchant-banking family. They were also active in Antwerp and were tied by marriage to the well-known Antwerp merchant-banker Charles Proli.[16] In 1742, Joan Osy's widow had a yearly income of around 13,000 guilders and she was considered to be one of the ten wealthiest people living in Rotterdam. Joan Osy & Son was active in trade with Cadiz, Bayonne and the Caribbean. One of their most important activities was the wine trade.[17] For Dormer, they acted as agents arranging diamond shipments to and from London, and for a while they also shipped bullion on Dormer's behalf.[18]

Besides the Salvadors, Dormer had another good contact in London relating to diamond trade. Francis Mannock was an old acquaintance of Dormer, with whom he had already started a correspondence in 1728. He was a Catholic who had enjoyed his merchant training in Cadiz, where he lived between 1739 and 1741 before returning to London. While he lived in Spain, Mannock had been working together with Dormer in the grain trade. In the network, he was of lesser importance, and acted as an agent for Dormer and van Merlen in London, buying and selling diamonds on various occasions. He was also involved in financial connections between Clifford, Salvador, Dormer and Berthon & Garnault intended for the remittances of profits to the right persons. A last network member also operated in Antwerp and was a diamond broker, Joseph de Marcour. Not much is known about him, but he worked many times for Dormer as a seller of his diamonds, an activity that in 1753 caused them problems with the diamond cutters guild in Antwerp.[19] On a few occasions and on behalf of himself, Salvador and van Merlen, Dormer sold parcels of diamonds to de Marcour, but this occurred only six times between 1751 and 1757.

All these different merchants engaged in a web of correspondence that was meant to sustain a regular and profitable trade in rough and polished diamonds. Mercantile connections connected Antwerp, London, Amsterdam and Lisbon. Because of the different origins of the merchants residing in these cities, this network can be labelled as a cross-cultural one. Dormer was an English Catholic, the Nunes and Salvador families were Sephardic Jews, Berthon and Garnault were Huguenots, the Cliffords were Protestants, while Mannock, Osy and probably also de Marcour, van Merlen and de Coninck were Catholics. The only characteristic that was shared by all traders was their profession. It remains unclear how the English merchant got involved with exactly those traders, and not with others. The correspondence available does not reveal the origins of the network but it must be assumed, as had been the case for the relationship between Dormer and Salvador, that these merchants had found each other through mutual acquaintances. For almost fifteen years, between 1744 and 1758, this group of merchants collaborated in the commerce of precious stones on an informal basis. No written contracts were made up between them, and although all merchants had commercial relationships that extended beyond the network, it can be considered a homogeneous group of merchants sharing a similar interest and positioning themselves against outside competition. A few times, attempts were made to make the cooperation that existed between the merchants mentioned in Table 3.1 more formal, but these attempts were to fail and even led to a decline in network activities.

Brazilian Ambitions and Decline of the Network

1746 was the first year in which Dormer and Salvador sold diamonds in a partnership.[20] In the same year, sales multiplied and Dormer soon started attempts to make his commerce in diamonds more structured and regular. A first opportunity he considered followed the French siege of Fort St George in 1746. The city was plundered and the captain of the French fleet, Bertrand-François Mahé de La Bourdonnais, was rumoured to have laid his hands on a large parcel of diamonds.[21] When news about La Bourdonnais reached them, Dormer and Francis Salvador decided to form a partnership in order to negotiate with the Frenchman: 'as for mons.r de La Bourdonnayes affair I am ready to Come into it and Back it with all my Credit & Desire in answer to know the terms between us for this is not an affair of your Single agency'.[22] A lot of letters were sent back and forth and the merchants tried to keep each other informed about the situation. In December 1747, a French Indiaman had arrived in a port in Galicia and Francis Salvador suspected that La Bourdonnais was on board. According to Salvador, La Bourdonnais had fallen out with the French government and Salvador thought Dormer could travel secretly to Spain to meet with La Bourdonnais and conclude a deal.[23] No meeting ever took place between the French captain and Dormer, and La Bourdonnais was eventually imprisoned in the Bastille. He died in 1753, two years after his release from prison.[24]

Dormer and Francis Salvador had, in their eyes, missed a big opportunity to dominate the diamond trade:

> The moutfort from Bengall is also arrived this Ship in June was going in to St Paul on the Coast of Africa but notice was given that La Bourdonnaye was in Port on which she tack'd however La Bourdonnaye Came out x Chased 3 hours 'till it was dark this makes me think that our first Ship from Fort St Davids runs some risk in Case she should be taken by La Bourdonnaye the whole quantity of Diamonds from India will Center there x the Coup in buying 'tho the larger will be the Surer as we shall be intirely masters of that branch for the present untill a fresh supply Comes to Europe which Cannot be 'till next year.[25]

A high degree of confidentiality had to be respected however, because this whole affair could cause great harm to Salvador's reputation in London. He trusted Dormer to be able to respect these lines and enough to let him handle all direct contacts. In the same period Dormer also tried to include George Clifford in a proposal about the diamond trade, which might very well have been the La Bourdonnais affair, as in early 1748, Dormer and Clifford sent each other letters about the whereabouts of the Frenchman.[26] In 1750, he proposed another deal to the Cliffords in which George Clifford & Sons, Dormer and Francis and Joseph Salvador would be the three partners who would each receive one third of the profits. The Cliffords were to sell diamonds in Amsterdam; however, they feared competition from Jewish merchants there and in the end, they did not become partners of Salvador and Dormer.[27]

A year later, the Salvador firm became involved in trading Brazilian diamonds: 'We now have made a Contract by which the Greatest part of the Brazil Diamonds will go through our Hands.'[28] At that time, no official commercial monopoly had been established by the Portuguese Crown and the agreement to which the Salvadors refer must have been made between them and merchants in Lisbon or the mining contractors.[29] In 1753, a severe crisis in the Brazilian diamond trade caused the establishment of a royal monopoly regarding the sales of Brazilian diamonds in Europe.[30] English and Dutch merchants were negotiating with the Portuguese government and the Salvador firm was involved as a secret partner of the English Lisbon trader John Bristow. In July 1753, they asked Dormer for information about

> what Diamonds have been sold in your Place to Polish for these 10 years past as we Shall thereby guess the Better what may be done in future and have a view to do something Considerable There in be as particular as the matter will admit as to the Assortments and Prizes and Distinguish if Possible what Brazil and what India and what Goa.[31]

Different correspondents of Dormer informed him that, when the first contract was signed between the Portuguese Crown, Bristow and Braamcamp, Salvador was a secret partner.[32] The Cliffords also wrote to Dormer about the monopoly, and saw in Salvador's participation a possibility for Dormer and themselves: 'we shall be glad by means of your freinds Messrs Salvador of London you may find means to gett consigned to us what is fitt for this markett'.[33] The Salvadors confirmed their engagement to Dormer one month after the monopoly contract was signed:

> We take the Liberty to Inform you that in Company with one or two more we have Contracted for all the Brazil Diamonds that will be sold in some years in Europe we hope to pass many thro' your Hands & when this Affair is fully Settled Shall write you more fully thereon.[34]

The involvement of the Salvadors in the diamond contract with the Portuguese government was very promising, but before the cooperation between Salvador, Dormer and others could be set on a more regular footing, a series of unconnected events led to a decline of network activity from which the merchants never recovered.

Early in 1753, van Merlen had died.[35] A number of sales were made with van Merlen's widow de Coninck as partner, but no new purchases followed and the partnership ended the year after. Isabella de Coninck also stopped acting as Dormer's agent, but she became one of the main buyers of diamonds sold by Dormer and Salvador. De Marcour and an employee in Dormer's firm, Joseph Xavier Thompson, now acted as the main agents in Antwerp, but Dormer's contacts with Amsterdam became more difficult.

A few months after van Merlen died, Dormer and de Marcour got into a dispute with the guild of diamond cutters in Antwerp. They complained about a public sale of polished diamonds that had been organized by de Marcour. The diamonds belonged to Dormer, but the guild thought they belonged to Jewish and Dutch merchants from Amsterdam, and that the sale of such diamonds would harm Antwerp's cutting industry.[36] After Dormer acknowledged that he was behind the sale, it was allowed to continue, but it is not clear from the diamond books whether such a sale took place. Several large parcels of polished diamonds were sold in May 1753, most of them on commission from Salvador. A lot of names that occur as diamond buyers in Dormer's diamond books signed the petition that was sent in order to prevent the public sale. Because it seems unlikely that none of them had an idea for whom de Marcour was trying to sell diamonds, it seems that Dormer, perhaps due to his ambitions, had fallen out of grace.

Later that year, Salvador's secret involvement in the Brazilian monopoly became increasingly difficult. The firm did not have a good relationship with the Braamcamp firm, the third partner.[37] The origins of their dispute remain unknown, but it is not at all impossible that a conflict of interest with regard to markets in the Low Countries was the source of it. This conflict did not prevent Dormer from pursuing a close association with the Brazilian monopoly.[38] In 1754, Berthon & Garnault assured the Englishman that 'it is cheifly Messrs Bristow & Salvador in London, and some say Braamcamp in A'dam who govern the things wholly, and as they chuze ... so as you are well known of thoze in London very likely a simple lettre from you might procure y° their agentsy', which suggests that the Salvadors won the upper hand in their conflict with the Braamcamps. Eight months later, Dormer sent a proposition to the Salvadors in which he projected a partnership with the Sephardic Jews to buy up 25,000 to 30,000 carats of Brazilian diamonds per year for a period of three years; an amount that was not much less than the yearly amount of Brazilian stones to be sold in Europe.[39] A month earlier, Dormer had sold a parcel of 273 carats of Brazilian diamonds sent to him by the Salvador firm on behalf of the Brazilian contractors.[40] Dormer wanted to grasp the moment, because in the same letter the Salvadors expressed their contentment with the sale, they also replied to a proposition made by Dormer for an insurance company.[41] It is probable that in the conflict Salvador had with Amsterdam, Dormer saw a possibility to become the Low Countries branch of the Brazilian diamond monopoly, perhaps even directly motivated by the Salvadors.

Yet this high ambition would never be fulfilled. In January 1755, Dormer received a letter containing the news that Francis Salvador had died. Joseph, his only remaining son, now gave his name to the company.[42] He was unlucky that year and suffered great financial loss as a consequence of the Lisbon earthquake: 'for my part I shall be a Considerable looser ... I wou'd recommend to you not to be hasty in your sales as 'tis not very Clear that the Diamonds were saved at Lisbon'.[43] Equally harmful was the discovery of the Portuguese authorities of Jewish involvement in the Brazilian diamond contract. They broke off the contract owing to Salvador's participation and started to look for other firms.[44] According to Paul Berthon, George Clifford & Sons in Amsterdam might have been one of the new firms in the contract, although no confirmation has been found for this.[45] Joseph Salvador never fully recovered from the combined blow of the earthquake and the annulment of the Brazilian contract.[46] Dormer had already lost van Merlen as a partner, and the attempt of Dormer and Salvador to enter in the Brazilian diamond monopoly had led to a higher degree of commission sales Dormer made for Salvador and possibly other merchants involved in the Brazilian contract, a practice that had undermined partnership deals between Dormer and Salvador.

In 1756, the partnership between Berthon and Garnault was dissolved out of family considerations: Garnault had a son who could not become partner in the firm, since Berthon already had two sons eligible for partnership. Dormer continued to work with the two new firms that arose out of the breakup, but only Paul Berthon still acted as an agent in the diamond trade.[47] The difficult years between 1753 and 1756 lead to problems for all the firms involved in the cross-cultural diamond trade network. Partnerships had ended, Francis Salvador and Bernardus van Merlen had died and although in early 1753 ambitions were high and these merchants intended to cooperate even more closely, the network did not remain a success for very long, although it continued to exist until 1758. That whole year, most of the letters that Salvador wrote to Dormer were concerned with diamonds, and they even planned to engage in more regular and large-scale business operations again:

> With regard to Brazil Diamonds matters are very green & I cannot say my proposal is fix'd but let me know for what price you would go my halves in 5000 carrats refuge [refugo diamonds] of the same quality as I formerly sent you to be taken annually and likewise for 5000 carrats of fine Goods[48]

Similar intentions can be found throughout the correspondence between network members in 1757 and 1758 but before anything structural materialized, Dormer died. In October 1758 he was sent on a secret mission to England by the

Austrian minister Cobenzl. He was asked to sell 50,000 Austrian lottery tickets, while it was forbidden in England to do so. On arrival in Dover on 21 October, Dormer suffered a stroke. His son Jacob Albert contacted Joseph Salvador who arrived three days later. James died the same day.[49] Jacob Albert Dormer took over his father's business, but he was unable to revive the diamond trade. He was a mediocre merchant, not possessing his father's connections or skills. Only a few letters from a few firms indicated that Jacob still made attempts to remain active in the diamond business, but those attempts did not prove to be successful.

Network Boundaries

Failed attempts of network members to gain a control of the European trade in Brazilian diamonds show that the association between the merchants mentioned in Table 3.1 was only partially and temporarily successful. In addition, the network was not based on a notion of exclusivity. All of the traders working with Dormer were engaged in a variety of commercial activities with other merchants, with whom they also maintained a regular and intensive correspondence. Even in diamond trade, most of these traders did not operate exclusively within the coalition.[50] To further complicate things, a part from Dormer's correspondence, the letters these merchants wrote to each other and to others have been lost. The question poses itself whether it is justified for the cooperation between the merchants mentioned in this chapter to be labelled a 'network'. This depends, of course, on the definition of what a trade network is. A number of suggestions have been given in Chapter 1, and it seems important that it is based on voluntary and durable relationships between members, who do not all live in the same place or provide the same service.[51]

I think the definition of a commercial network should remain sufficiently open to include diverse types of networks, but at the same time allow for a distinction with less regular trade relationships. Perhaps a good definition of a trade network is that it is an association between merchants who share a commercial interest that is essentially based on self-interest but operates practically on the acceptance of mutual interest. Network membership has to imply multiplicity, routine, reciprocity and privilege. Multiplicity means that internal links between network members can not all pass through one person. A commercial collaboration that is essentially one-to-one cannot be labelled a network. In the early modern world of commerce, merchants operated on the basis of their portfolio of correspondents. Even if the amount of letters written between two merchants was high, that does not mean *per se* that they were involved in a network. More persons have to be involved on an equal basis, and they also have to engage in a relationship. Two merchants with a string of intermediaries between them doing business for twenty years together are very good correspondents, not the components of a commercial network. A group of traders that share a correspondent who builds his business by working with all of them in the same branch cannot be labelled a network either. There is a need for multiple contacts between different members of a network in order for it to be more than a trade organization centred on one person. Routine refers to durability and stability: the operations that take place within a network have to become, to a certain extent, standardized. A collaboration between merchants cannot be considered a network if, for every new transaction, modalities have to be negotiated about transport and payment. Reciprocity means that all the people involved have to get something out of it, something of which other merchants are aware and willing to take into account. Privilege indicates that network members offer things to each other that they do not offer to others, and that a boundary exists between insiders and outsiders of a network. It is important to observe that a network association can be formal or informal, based on kinship ties, family relations, religion or something else completely.

With these aspects in mind, the cooperation between Salvador, van Merlen, Dormer, de Coninck and others can be categorized as a network. The lack of source material makes it difficult to assess the level of multiplicity in these network relationships. The fact that research of the specific trade collaboration analysed in this book is to a large extent based on correspondence sent to Dormer might create the false impression that he was the centre of the network, and that others did not know each other. Because of their role as intermediaries, Clifford was in correspondence with Berthon & Garnault, which is also shown by evidence from letters.[52] Clifford and Salvador also wrote to each other, especially about financial transactions, as often drafts on the Amsterdam bankers were used to remit money from Antwerp to London or the other way around. Francis Salvador and George Clifford had important common friends such as the English minister Horace Walpole.[53] The Salvadors were also acquainted with Berthon & Garnault, as they sometimes received letters from Dormer through their contact with Salvador in London: 'Sir By the land post we are favour'd with your esteem'd 24 may with copy of one of the 22d, w.ch you wrote via England, its original we received last night under ccouvert of one from mess.rs Fran.s & Joseph Salvador.'[54] The Osy firm, another transport agent, had a correspondence with the Salvador firm: 'Messrs Joan Osy say we must in future value our Diamonds we Desire your advice thereon'.[55] The connections van Merlen, de Coninck and de Marcour had with others is difficult to know, as almost no letters written by them exist. Especially the first two, because of their high degree of travelling, seems to have spoken more in person with other traders.[56] George Clifford & Sons had meetings with both van Merlen and de Coninck in Amsterdam.[57] In 1753, after van Merlen's death, his widow went to Amsterdam to act as Dormer's agent there, and she contacted George Clifford carrying a letter of recommendation on her behalf from Dormer, something that was common practice, and that was first of all meant to provide Isabella de Coninck with a line of credit with the Cliffords.[58] None of the above-cited fragments were unique, and more evidence can be found that several network members maintained a mutual correspondence, something that undoubtedly was also the case for the

Salvadors and the Nunes firm, who were related. Hence not all contacts within the network went through one person.

The network operated on a basis of routine. The typical types of transactions that occurred have been mentioned above. Diamonds were sold in a certain partnership constellation, or on commission, and depending on the place where they were sold, specific merchants were asked to act as intermediaries. Although letters were written to agree on prices or to ask for specific advice, the way in which transactions were conducted, and who was involved, was never put into question. Such routine gives stability to the commercial interaction that took place for a period of fifteen years. The fact that many sales attempts failed adds to the routine-like nature of the network. Diamonds often circulated between merchants because differences in fashion and price often necessitated such circulation, and in these cases traders knew what to do, who to contact and where to send parcels of stones. Routine is also found in the financial system underlying commercial relationships, and remittances were often made through the same channels.[59] Routine also implies a certain level of constancy in the functions fulfilled by different merchants involved in the network. If diamonds were traded in Amsterdam, it was done by van Merlen or de Coninck. In Antwerp, Dormer, de Marcour and de Coninck negotiated with buyers and sellers. About 40 per cent of the total financial value of purchased diamonds that were further sold by network members came from the Salvador firm in London, either because they bought stones in London from others, or because they had consignments of diamonds coming from India. Diamonds that circulated between London and Antwerp were put on board ships by Joan Osy in Rotterdam or the Nunes firm in Amsterdam. The Cliffords sent diamonds back and forth from Lisbon. As far as tasks go, there was a fair division between members. This is not to say that each network member can be identified with only one function.

Different partnerships occurred for different concrete transactions. This is due to the importance of reciprocity: a network based on the interaction between traders seeks a balance between self-interest and mutual profit.[60] The relationships between the merchants studied in this chapter could not have been built in a way that only one or two would gain a structural profit. The most important partnerships in which the network traders were involved and their respective shares in the sales numbers are summarized in the Figure 3.1. Sales have been calculated based on total price, not of weight or profit. Weight of diamonds would be a bad indication to calculate the relative share of a partnership, as it does not correspond to the value of sales. Profit is more difficult to calculate. Diamonds could remain unsold for years. Parcels were often sent back and forth between cities and some were never sold. Because of the cutting process, the commodity sold was very different from the commodity bought. Parcels were often mingled to better suit the market, making it impossible to link a specific purchase and sale to each other in all cases.

A look at the percentages of sales based on their financial value is the best option to analyse the different types of partnerships underlying sales. Dormer and van Merlen sold for a joint account, and that share was the biggest: 43.8 per cent of the financial value of all diamond sales. The second largest part is taken by a partnership arranged on a fifty-fifty basis between the Salvador firm and Dormer, 22 per cent. Not all Dormer's profits from trade with Salvador came from their partnership, as Dormer also acted as an agent selling Salvador's diamonds on commission, which made Dormer gain 2 per cent of the value of the sale. The relative financial weight of this constellation in sales numbers is 15.5 per cent. Dormer also sold diamonds for his own account. Often, the sales chain included one or several network members, as in only 3.5 per cent of the total sales, Dormer sold precious stones for his own profit without the involvement of a network member, against a relative part of 9.5 per cent for sales including at least one but regularly several others, mainly de Marcour, Berthon & Garnault, de Coninck or van Merlen. Dormer also worked on commission for non-network members, mainly for Ashkenazi traders from Amsterdam.[61] Again, a division can be made between sales including other network members, which took up 5.6 per cent of total trade, and sales without any other network member involved apart from Dormer, that took up 0.1 per cent.

These numbers clearly demonstrate that Dormer's activities in the diamond trade were embedded within an association of merchants who decided to do business with each other regularly. Only 5.7 per cent of the sales that involved Dormer did not include at least one other merchant that was active in the network.

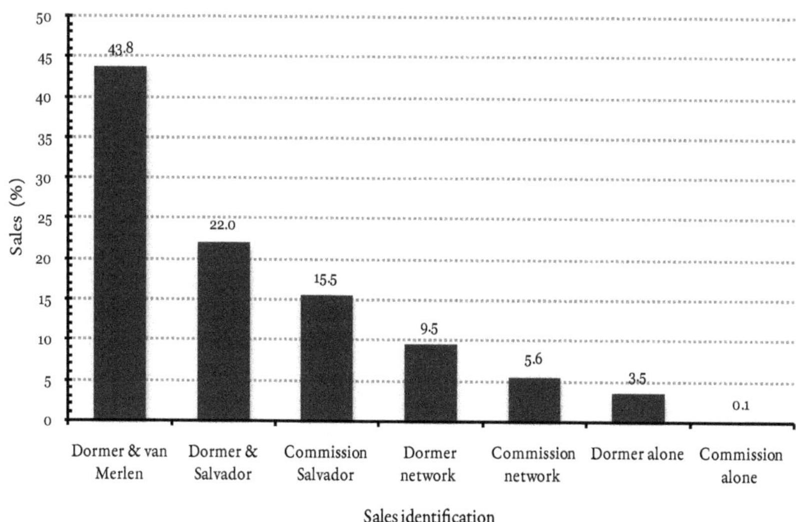

Figure 3.1: Relative share of the financial sales mass of diamond transactions noted in Dormer's diamond books.[62]

For Dormer, diamond trade was his most important business, which is also shown by his ambitions in the Brazilian diamond monopoly, and the correspondents with who he had associated himself in the diamond trade were amongst his closest and most valuable ones. Because of the all-round nature of Dormer's commercial profile, he sought other possibilities, and if he encountered them, he tried to include close acquaintances several times. On 29 November 1754 Dormer was granted the right to establish a Royal and Imperial Chamber of Insurance at Antwerp, which was allowed a monopoly for twenty-five years in Brabant, although individual insurers could still underwrite risks.[63] Dormer wanted to raise a capital of 2 million florins by selling 2,000 shares of 1,000 florins each.[64] He contacted the Salvador firm in London, laying out his plan and hoping that they would be able to draw the interest of Jewish merchants to invest. Salvador bought twenty-five shares and managed to convince some others to buy stock, such as Abraham Prado, a relative of his.[65] Other network members were called upon to act as agents, Berthon & Garnault in Lisbon and Francis Mannock in London. A representative in Hamburg was found thanks to George Clifford.[66]

In 1756 Dormer discussed the idea with Salvador of raising a loan to the Austrian government. Salvador was interested, but reluctant because he thought that 'the raising money will not be allow'd here for any foreign Power att least till the Government is serv'd'.[67] Salvador consulted his government contacts, and turned Dormer down. A year earlier a similar discussion had taken place between the two merchants about the organization of a state lottery in favour of the Austrian government. Salvador agreed to make an attempt to get others involved: 'With regard to your Project on the Lottery it seems well Grounded Mr. Gideon is in the Country I shall send it him but Expect a Success.'[68] The failure of Dormer to get permission made the project collapse.[69] Salvador's service was not only the willingness to become financially involved, thereby helping Dormer in assisting Austrian government, but also to use his own contacts on behalf of Dormer. This shows that for different affairs that Dormer considered important, he relied upon well-established ties within a group of privileged traders who had already proven their worth.[70]

It should, however, be kept in mind that no absolute loyalty existed to one group of merchants. The network was an informal association between merchants who all had other contacts, within and outside the diamond trade. The strong tendency to work only within a limited group in a certain business is what makes this group a distinguishable entity in a wider international commercial community. In the world of early modern trade, correspondence was the most important working instrument for merchants and every trader had many different contacts with correspondents. With them, merchants were involved in a variety of businesses. Some were short-lived and focused on one branch of business only, while other correspondence continued for several decades. The web of correspondence surrounding Dormer was immense and varied. He even maintained a business relationship with a number of intermarried Ashkenazi families who were also active in the diamond trade, and formed a competitive network with regard to the cross-cultural diamond trade network.[71] The fuzzy nature of network boundaries does not make it nonexistent. It makes it embedded in a larger commercial society. The analysis of the denser relationships within a group of merchants who were at the same time very much tied to other circuits, partnerships and associations is a subtle matter. For its internal cohesion, a network depended on the correspondence that existed between traders within such a circuit. It reflects on social and cultural underpinnings of commercial cooperation. But correspondence was also related to an extended world of contacts, and the willingness to introduce new friends to a correspondent was considered an important service. The same mechanisms that made the network work, made commercial society at large work, and were inspired by commercial custom, formal and informal agreements, cultural interaction and social relationships. In order to better understand how a network, especially a cross-cultural one, worked, it is of crucial importance to analyse the letters that merchants sent to one another. It will clarify how merchants saw their relationship with each other and with outsiders, and the positioning of a group of merchants against outsiders who were seen as competition is a very strong argument to attribute a privileged status to such a group.

The Use of Business Correspondence

Mutual Interest and Reciprocal Services: The Cohesive Function

Diamond trade was an international business, and it is obvious from the analysis of the *modus operandi* of the merchants that personal physical contact was rare. Their transactions were negotiated and concluded in extensive business correspondence, often accompanied with copies of sale receipts or bills of lading. A part from their content, the frequency of writing is also an indicative factor for the state of business. In this sense, it is correct to state that the letters traders wrote to one another were the lifeblood of commerce.[72] Correspondence is not only a vital tool for the historian, it was also considered instrumental by the merchants who wrote and received them. A remark such as 'hoping trade may flourish better than these may be ocazions of employing our correspondence' was quite frequent.[73] A part from their direct use as a vehicle for commerce, in which concrete transactions and future possibilities were discussed, trade correspondence served a number of other uses that all related to social cohesion between merchants and their connection with a larger commercial world.

Essential in trade, and in business correspondence, was the idea of reciprocity. Merchants did business together because they believed it could be profitable on both ends. This is essentially a regard for self-interest, but there was also a strong idea that self-interest was enhanced if, in certain privileged relationships such as a steady correspondence, the idea of mutual interest was kept in mind:

> We think ourselves extreamly happy in the personall acquaintance we had the pleasure of making with you, which we shall endeavour to improve by cultivating all in our power a lasting correspondence to mutuall satisfaction x advantage; we are highly obliged to you for laying the first foundation of it[74]

Without the idea of reciprocity in relationships, structures such as networks would not survive for long. It was a basic cohesive element in long-lasting and stable commercial relationships, and this was very clear to the merchants involved in those relations. A business correspondence had no meaning if only one party was to derive a structural profit from it. This meant that merchants assumed different roles in order to guarantee reciprocal interest. Berthon & Garnault sold diamonds for Dormer in Lisbon, but also asked him to try to sell for them in Antwerp. Dormer acted at times as Salvadors's agent, and at other times at his partner in diamond sales. Van Merlen was a partner of Dormer in some sale transactions, but also a travelling agent responsible for the cutting of diamonds. The assumed roles in specific transactions depended on the circumstances, but also fitted the general idea that merchants sought profits in different businesses, easily adapting themselves to new opportunities mentioned to them in the many letters they received. It confirms that the network analysed in this book is first of all a network of traders, who were all interested in personal profit. But because personal profit is not accomplished on its own, merchants involved in a privileged business structure such as a network did care for the interest of others. This prevented the development of a strict hierarchy in the network, and in this sense it is remarkable that a firm like George Clifford & Sons acted often as an agent, receiving and resending parcels of diamonds in which he had no personal interest. Everybody in the network acted at times as agents for the other, or as banker, or as money-lender, or as intermediary in a port city to ship certain packets on boats and deal with the duty officials.[75]

According to Avner Greif,

> the essence of a formal friendship relationship was that two traders operated in different trade centers, providing each other with trade services in their respective trade centers ... Neither received pecuniary compensation. This exchange of services was not based on emotions ... rather it was purely a business matter.[76]

The willingness to offer services to unknown acquaintances of known correspondents can also be found in other types of services offered. A merchant travelling abroad could count on the aid of his contacts, who often arranged for social company, lodging and a line of credit. This was common practice, and supplying it was considered to be a reciprocal favour. It not only occurred between network members, but also with outside acquaintances, through letters of recommendation. In this case, a copy was sent to the correspondent whose services were asked:

> Sir, the bearer hereof is Mr George Hopkins who has lived severall years with us in the counting house and being desirous to make a little excursion into your parts of ye. world, and to accompany a freind of his who is returning to England we take the liberty to recommend him to you as a young gent: we have an esteem for, and should he require any monney, you'll be so good as to furnish him with itt, as far as a couple of hundred Duccatts, taking his receit for ye same x charging our account therewith. We believe after what we have said above he needs no further recommandation.[77]

This was sent by George Clifford's firm to Dormer, and they vouched for the young gentleman as somebody who has worked with them for several years, and thus can be trusted. The writers of the letter indicate that the good reputation of the visitor can be confirmed by passed conduct, as observed by the Cliffords through personal experience. Sometimes, merchants wrote a letter after a visit to the recommender in order to thank him, and as such acknowledge his effort.[78] Generally, the commercially most interesting feature of letters of recommendation was that they often included a demand for credit on behalf of the letter's carrier:

> I shall give a letter of recommendation to monsr. Francois Leferthat will soon be with you x has a house of the first ranck att Cadiz x you may supply him with what mony he may want x I am sure you will find him a pretty gentleman. I shall be oblidged to you for the civilitys you may shew him.[79]

This type of service was meant to be reciprocal. If Salvador could trust Dormer to render services to acquaintances of Salvador, Dormer could also put his hopes in Salvador to return the service. In 1747, Francis and Jacob Salvador sent a letter to Dormer that included a letter of recommendation. Apparently, Dormer was travelling to Paris and the Salvadors had contacted business relations they had there:'Inclosed you'll find a letter recomending you to my good friends messrs Tourton x Baur of Paris to whome I also write p Post giving you an open Credit which you'll make use of in Case of need'.[80]

It not only shows a trust mechanism based on recommendation, but also indicates a way for Dormer and the Salvadors to maintain trust between them, by rendering favours. In complying to Salvador's wishes, helping the young merchant, maybe offer him credit, good advice and lodging, Dormer could prove his reputation to Salvador, and sustain the faith that the London merchant had put in him. The return of favours is a very important aspect to distinguish between normal trade transactions and transactions taking place within a more privileged business environment such as a network. It also implies that, underneath the suggestion of a form of friendly behaviour directed to looking out at someone else's gain, self-interest remains an important underlying factor of reciprocity. The argument here is not that such a selfish motivation is absent, but rather that focusing on pure self-interest provides an incomplete picture in the analysis of commercial relationships.

The important feature of this particular mercantile mix of self-interest and reciprocal services is not that it occurred, but that it happened frequently. After the Lisbon earthquake of 1755, Dormer's most important buyer of textiles suffered severe financial difficulties.[81] Berthon & Garnault asked Dormer to 'show him a Confid[en]ce'.[82] They asked Dormer for help and although this support was seen as a form of charity, it was not free of self-interest.[83] This type of favour was not considered in a framework of a religious or human duty, and the accentuation of merit by reputation made it clear that charitable responsibility was more with the recipient than with the donor. It is in these types of events that the value of the commodity of character and trustworthiness becomes very concrete.

Commercial Friendship: The Social Function

The social function of correspondence is perhaps the most contested one. The introduction of trust and social ties as important business elements have led to the study of business correspondence not only in terms of the commercial activity they represent, but also in terms of their social value, as an element that ties merchants together in a way that sometimes is described as a form of friendship. It is difficult to confirm or deny the development of friendship between traders who wrote to each other regularly over a period of twenty years. In any case, friendship between network merchants was not comparable to our modern idea of friendship. In his monograph on the friendly ties of different families in the seventeenth and eighteenth century, Luuc Kooijmans has defined friends as the people who can be 'talked to in order to reach certain goals or to solve problems'.[84] This definition allows for a categorization of commercial friendship as being different from our modern friendship but nevertheless more than a simple calculative relation. It was the kind of relationship maintained between different merchants of the cross-cultural diamond trade network, especially between Joseph Salvador and Dormer. Regular correspondence allowed for the creation of an intimate bond between correspondents by using rhetoric and information that was non-commercial. The first condition for this intimacy to develop was regularity, and the high volume of written letters in relation to the actual transactions made in them make it clear that one of the mains assets of correspondence was that it allowed communication channels to remain open. Regular contact created an idea of familiarity and if this regularity came to a temporary halt, apologies were issued:

> Since my Father Receiv'd your favour of the 9th october he has been very ill as has Likewise my Brother which I apprehend may have Caused him not to answer yr. said favour I dare assure you no other motive could ever make him Leave so long unactive a Correspondence he so much Esteems[85]

Francis Mannock wrote many letters to Dormer, and one time he complained that the latter had been silent for too long:

> I have endeavourd to mentain the friendship x Intimacy we formerly enjoyd, by several Letters adressd to you both by po[stcarri]er x ship, which I persuade myselfe must have miscari'd or else cant think you would be so forgetfull of your old friends as not to favour me with an answer[86]

Traditional friendship as opposed to the modern concept needs the cultivation of relationships, people have to demonstrate their reliability. This is partially done in the civility of the regular maintenance of correspondence.[87] This friendship was often expressed in and forged by discussions relating to personal affairs. The letters between Salvador and Dormer reveal a great deal of intimate information, and the same goes for other network members. Many expressions of friendship can be found throughout the different correspondences. Best wishes to each other's family members were a common way to start or finish a letter, and expressions of friendship were multiple. Similar fragments can be found frequently in different letters Dormer received from his correspondents. At special events, such as Christmas or New Year, best wishes were sent. Salvador wrote in 1741 to Dormer 'comme nous sommes a la fin d'anne nous vous souhaitons le prochain tres heureux suivi de plusieurs autres avec toutes forses de prosperités tant corporels comme spirituels aussi bien que a tout votre chere famille'.[88] The term 'friend' was commonly used. Aaron and David Nunes repeatedly referred to Dormer as a good friend, and on occasion called him 'un de nos meilleurs amis'.[89] Shortly after the death of Dormer, the firm of Paul Berthon sent a letter to his widow, stating that a long and sincere friendship had existed between him and her late husband, and he wrote that he was 'aussy sensible que les liens du sang nous unissent'.[90]

In a way, the use of language implying friendship and intimacy is formal, merely a way of being polite and of respecting the norms for business letters that had become more and more standardized.[91] Nevertheless, there are a number of reasons to assume that, although partly functional, a certain intimacy on paper developed, but never in such a way that it made commerce a secondary factor in the relationship. The type of intimacy shared at times was too personal to simply label them as products of purely rational, calculated and self-interested behaviour. Friendship found expression in mutual inquiries about one's health problems, marriages and other family affairs. After the wife of Salvador's son gave birth, he wrote to Dormer that 'she is very well, thank God, as also his son and my son Josephs girl grows every day more entertaining they all particularly thank you for your kind remembrances'.[92] References to illness do occur, something that might not seem commercially interesting: 'my Father has been sometime Indisposd of a Palsy & is now att Bath for the recovery of his health'.[93]

Friendship did not limit itself to expressions on paper. Merchants visited each other from time to time, and enjoyed each other's hospitality.[94] Aaron and David Nunes sent a thank you and the compliments from one of their sisters and one of their cousins, who visited Antwerp a short time and could benefit from Dormer's hospitality.[95] In 1751 Joseph Nunes, a third brother who had become a partner in the Nunes' firm went to visit Antwerp. Aaron and David wrote that they had no doubt that Dormer would be a generous host to Joseph and his wife, in the same way they acted when somebody of Dormer's relations went to Amsterdam.[96] Francis Mannock visited Brussels in 1741, and when Dormer heard this, he offered him lodging in his own house, which was accepted.[97] Francis Salvador went several times to Antwerp; the first time he visited Dormer at home was in 1737. The Jewish merchant did not wait until his arrival home to express his gratitude. From Lille he wrote to his English friend 'to accept of myne x my sons humble thancks for the favours we received During our stay att Antwerp x hope in time to see you in England x that the young gentleman is well x our humble service to your good Brother'.[98]

After Dormer visited London, he sent a letter informing the Salvadors that he had safely returned home. Salvador replied that:

> especially the last [letter] brings me the agreable news of yr safe arrival at home in health and that you found Mrs Dormer & yr little ones well you have my wishes & of all my family for yr wellfare & all that belongs to you, my son Jacob has been blessed with a fine boy as you prognosticated soon after you went away & the child & the mother are both extremely well, my son Joseph at Bath is recovering a pace & thank God almost well, I hope to see him in a month intirely recovered, I am much obliged to you for yr kind enquiry.[99]

This fragment hints at the existence of a personal friendship between the two correspondents: they visited each other, and on such occasions they talked about private affairs. These personal visits enhanced the intimacy that was created in a long-lasting correspondence, and it was the only practical outing of it. It was the expressions of friendship and the inquiries about family, complemented by a rare visit that formed the familiar world in which trust could reside. It helped to shape an environment that adds to the idea of a trade organisation, a network, a coalition as Avner Greif would call it that possesses a notion of a community, with a certain unity being inherent to it. The way in which ties of friendship were 'constructed' and contributed to more durable relationships reminds us of the importance previous scholars have attributed to the role of social control systems and ethics, although these were more studied within groups that had more natural social ties, such as clans and tribes.[100]

Trust has to be achieved within a familiar world.[101] In studying cross-cultural relationships and inter-group relations, a certain familiarity disappears that is present amongst groups with a similar ethnic, religious or cultural background. In such an environment, trust and reliability does not limit itself to commerce and trade. It stretches itself over different aspects of the community, and both are important elements to keep the community together. Blood ties and religion, especially in the case of a diaspora, are important elements to preserve a society. Social cohesion is represented by symbols and symbolic events, be it family gathering, the organization of masses or specific festivities. Such events contribute to a certain unity in which it is easier for its members to operate, also in trade activities.[102] Cross-cultural trade networks lack the same cohesion, and other symbolic events have to be constructed to replace it.[103]

Several scholars inspired by Max Weber have stressed the role of ethics in overcoming problems of trust in trade transactions.[104] Ethics is connected with the idea of social control systems: it would be more difficult to betray family or friends. Once Dormer got to the point that he would visit Francis Salvador at home, and made guesses about the sex of his future grandchild, it became more difficult, and certainly more unethical to cheat on his friend. It seems that traders at least partially based their loyalty, and expressed it, in a semantic field, by the language they adopted in their letters. This use of semantics can be seen as parallel to the use of symbols to create a familiar world in which trust can reside.

Instead of using the term commercial friendship, it might be more accurate to label what pertains to the personal sphere in a business correspondence as belonging to intimacy. The fact that this sometimes meant an unusual glimpse in the private life of others is shown by a particular favour asked by Joseph Salvador to Dormer. In May 1758, Salvador sent a letter to Dormer in which he expressed his desire to buy a painting for a large room in a house he had bought the year before. He gave Dormer a certain amount of freedom to choose an appropriate picture, but also mentioned that 'I am likewise deprived the use of the History of the New Testament & d° by the forms of my Religion.'[105] This request let the Catholic Englishman in on the personal religious experience of Salvador, at a time in which his belief was not a generally accepted one. Salvador had made such a request for the first time in 1738 and in 1757 he had asked for information regarding a number of painters from the Low Countries and the esteem they were held in.[106]

The most convincing evidence found that some merchants developed a form of friendship that was born out of a commercial relationship but came to surpass it can be found in the letter sent to an employee in Dormer's firm by Joseph Salvador, wherein the Jewish merchant informs him of Dormer's death:

> Je ne scauray exprimer la douleur que ma Cause le malheur inopine et funeste arrive a votre sieur Dormer je ne viens d'apprendre son arrivée quand jentends quil est attaque dune maladie violente Je vais lembrasser a peine je luy trouve les sens tout etourdi il ne m a dit que des Paroles errans dont Je n'ay pas pu comprendre la signification Je n'ay rien compris autre que des preuves continuelles de son amitie[107]

A last important thing to say regarding intimacy is that it was linked to the identification of insiders and outsiders of the network. In creating a familiar world, intimacy also established an outside world, in which Salvador would not ask Dormer to buy a painting in accordance with the Jewish religion, and in which not everybody would know when his father had fallen ill or when his wife was pregnant. This division goes hand in hand with the secrecy that was observed regarding some commercial information.[108]

Information on Others: The Institutional Function

The first three functions of commercial correspondence can all be related to a smooth functioning of the network. But this network was not exclusive, and all merchants had other correspondents as well. The merchants that dealt in diamonds in the cross-cultural trade network were operating within an international mercantile community. Of course, this was not a community that existed in an all-encompassing sense of the word, but there was a growing sense amongst merchants of belonging to a commercial world, within which they worked, travelled and established contacts. The same things that held the network together also regulated the inner life of commercial society that became increasingly based on mercantile custom, which also found expression in the standardization of business correspondence.[109] One of the important aspects of institutional economics is that it considers an institution as a human-built structure to overcome efficiently the information problem.[110] For trade to run smoothly, it is of vital importance that its participants possess the best possible information in order to make their decisions.

One of the main problems of the circulation of information in pre-industrial times is that it travelled slowly.[111] A second issue is that it could come from different channels. A number of these were public, such as newspapers; others allowed for the sharing of information in a public space, such as the bourse or the *salons*. People who shared interests in the same type of commerce could meet and exchange all types of relevant information. Business correspondence can be considered as an institution by which a lot of information found its way to others. In order to do business, it is not only important to know market opportunities, it is also crucial to know the possibilities with regard to trade partners. Personal reputation was the asset by which a trader was judged, and this relied on past conduct. If merchants had dealt before with each other, it is perhaps fairly easy to establish a one-to-one reputation, as it goes without saying that a successful string of transactions between two merchants can be incentive enough to try to continue business. But merchants had many contacts and they were always looking for new opportunities and new correspondents. For this, merchants often wrote to already established contacts for information:

> the Houze you enquire after DeW[?] R[?] & C[°] is no houze at all, we had not so much before your mentioning heard of such peoples existing; of we beleive fifty people we spoke to of different houzes, not one could give us the least tydings, till at last we mett with a person, who told us he knew thoze we were inquiring about; that the first was a Rogue, and the second not much better: and that they had put their names together to represent abroad the appear[an]ce of a houze of buziness[112]

This fragment indicates that Berthon & Garnault did not know the firm Dormer had enquired about personally, but that they had taken the effort to consult contacts of theirs. Strings of contacts become exposed, by which information eventually found its way to Dormer in Antwerp. This use of correspondence was very important, and a number of firms devoted a lot of attention of enquiring about other houses, sometimes through different channels and at various times. A couple of information books of the Hope & Company firm dating from the end of the eighteenth century are preserved in the Amsterdam city archive. The oldest contains 317 pages with inform ation on other business firms all throughout Europe. The Bonifas brothers of Lisbon wrote that the firm of Anselmo José da Cruz 'est sans contredis une des 1eres de cette capitale pour sa richesse, bonne correspondence x la consideration qui lui est generalement due'.[113]

From the same source, it becomes clear that the Hopes asked several merchants for information on the same firm, but also that a firm who was under enquiry could later also be asked to provide information. It suggests that such information was not always used to find out about the reputation and trustworthiness of a potential new business contact, but also to be kept updated on the commercial reputation of already established correspondents. It shows that traders remained prudent in whom they trusted, and that trust was never an established aspect of a commercial relationship. It was verified, checked and if necessary, questioned. At other times, the information was asked in order to set up new correspondents, and it stands beyond doubt that in 1757, when David and Joseph Ximenes wanted to trade in diamonds on the Antwerp market, they had asked their contacts for information. The person they turned to was Joseph Salvador, and he in turn not only provided what was asked, he recommended them to who he thought would be the right person, James Dormer:

> Sir, by recommendation of one of your good friends in this town, we have taken the liberty of valuing ourselves of your favours, being informed of your intelligence in the branch of diamonds, x in order to make a beginning we send this day by the way of Amsterdam a pacquet of the same ... x on recieving advice of the disposal of this parcell, shall continue remitting you other parcells successively not doubting of your vigilence x care that youll obtain for us the best advantage possible regarding our Interests as your own, on which termes we offer you our service for whatever you should have ocasion[114]

If a trial or response was satisfactory, correspondence could develop itself into a permanent affair. This fragment shows how reputation was used in a wider sphere than that of already existing privileged relations. It was a form of social capital circulating in the larger merchant community, by means of correspondence.[115] This system of recommendation not only helped merchants to satisfy their trading wants, it also had an indirect beneficial effect regarding the trustworthiness of the person introducing them to each other. Although the Ximenes firm was not involved in the Dormer network, this kind of connection helped to strengthen the ties between Salvador and Dormer, both network members. By introducing a firm to Dormer, Salvador also offered Dormer a potential profitable new correspondence. Secondly, he vouched that the Ximenes firm was trustworthy, and as such put his own reputation on the line.

A trade correspondence was not always used to recommend traders: sometimes, the bad reputation of a merchant would reach others by means of business letters. When a transaction in which the house of Pels was involved with a merchant who turned out to be unreliable, the former commented on that merchant's behaviour in a letter to Dormer, saying that 'le caractere de Mr Compton etant assez connu'.[116] If one's reputation was not very well known, or bad, other merchants would remain careful in their dealings with them. The return of good information, about business but also about other merchants, was a sign that the person giving it could be trusted.[117]

Personal information was not limited to potential trading partners. When the Cliffords sent Dormer a letter of recommendation for a Mr John Hopkins in 1750 they also regretted the fact that Mr Hopkins had left their firm to pursue a business of his own. Hearing that Dormer was in London, they took the liberty of writing him a letter in which they asked him if he could inquire among his acquaintances in England and Flanders if they knew a

> propper person who understands both English x French x able to carry on the correspondence in both languages ... in short a person fitt for any business in a counting house ... and if he understood Spanish trade it would not be less agreable pray excuse this liberty, which in ease we were not persuaded of your good nature x friendly nets towards us, we should not presume to do[118]

As in several examples before, the importance of correspondence in business is again very central. This quote is an example of how reputation was a negotiable characteristic. If Dormer was able to suggest a possible employee for the Cliffords, he would enhance his reputation with them, and this could serve him not only in his direct relationship with the Cliffords, to whom he would have rendered a commercial service, but also to interesting contacts that the banking firm had.

Owing to the international nature of the cross-cultural diamond trade network, the concrete transactions that took place in them also warranted the circulation of information. Berthon & Garnault sold diamonds on Dormer's behalf in Lisbon, and they were always looking for good buyers. In times when the payments underlying commodity trade were often made on credit, ranging from a couple of weeks to several months, it was crucial to establish the reputation of a potential buyer in general, and his creditworthiness in particular. This information was often sent to Dormer when his Lisbon agents concluded a sale. Examples are numerous in their mutual correspondence. One purchaser was referred to as 'an honest man (or at least that passes for such)'.[119] Two other buyers were described as 'esteemed to be good and Punctual, and we hope they will prove so'.[120] Buyers did not belong to the network, although they could be returning customers, and this type of information circulation again links the network to outsiders through reputation, while at the same time enhancing the reputation of Berthon & Garnault, for it was their responsibility to come up with reliable buyers. Sometimes they used professional brokers, whose intermediation can be considered as another institutional solution to the problem of trustworthiness and reputation. Because it would take much more effort for Berthon & Garnault to make enquiries on every single buyer, they put their trust in brokers, who they knew through repeated dealings with them, thus creating a part of reputation based on passed conduct, while another part of reputation comes from the fact that they were professionals, which implies that they were trusted enough within the business community allowing them to be professionals in the first place.

Remittances and Credit: The Financial Function

The above-mentioned functions of commercial correspondence show how, in the daily life of traders, social and commercial relationships become intertwined. This implies that a personal aspect of a relationship can exist without having necessarily a functionalist meaning in commerce. Nevertheless, social mechanisms were behind a substantial amount of a trade relationship based on correspondence. Perhaps the best proof for this interwovenness of personal, social and commercial aspects can be found in one of the most common types of transaction that was discussed in Dormer's correspondence: the remittance. Turgot wrote that commerce existed by the virtue of credit and the long-distance character of international trade is necessarily based on a system of promise and delayed payment.[121] This meant that creditworthiness was of vital importance, especially when dealing with buyers whose reputation was not already known. As Dormer's sales agents in Lisbon, Berthon and Garnault had to make sure that clients would be able to fulfil the agreed method of payment within due time. 84 per cent of the monetary value of diamonds sold by them was paid on credit.[122] One particular passage in a letter they sent is very revealing in that regard, and also shows that creditworthiness was verified through information from others:

> it is well that you had noted the sale of the 4 Papers of your Diamonds which we sold to Pedro Affonço Ribeira, and hope with you that he will be punctual in the payment since said sale no opportunity for making any more has offer'd, there is a great many goods in town and hardly any money, so that good People dont care to engage until they know little more or less what to depend on of the Rio fleets arriving, and as this is not to arrive before January from the middle forward they differ ingaging doubtfull

> buyers there are enough, but we dont want to give em your goods and then be dunning of them years and years for the payment, we know People that some of them owe to that have debts of some years standing, and they give them an excellent character, but as it is to entice others to sell them, and endeavour by that means to be paid themselves, we dont trust to any of their informations, on the other hand whilst we have your goods in hands they are safe, so shall continue in our old scheme of endeavouring to sell when at trust only to such who have a very good reputation, both of honesty and punctuality.[123]

Reputation and information mechanisms worked on two levels. The privileged network relationship that existed between Berthon and Garnault caused the former to trust the judgement of the latter regarding potential buyers, and this was a practice that could sustain Berthon & Garnault's reputation as a reliable firm. Secondly, Berthon and Garnault turned to contacts in the wider commercial community with regard to creditworthiness of buyers. Their reputation, but also the one of their informers, was also put to the test and at times, they refused offers based on reputation alone. In 1752 a buyer had made a good offer for a parcel of diamonds, and he had an honest name. Unfortunately for him, he also had the reputation for being very slow in paying. Berthon and Garnault decided to decline the offer.[124]

When payment was received, usually after one, three, four or six months, Berthon and Garnault still had to find a way to send the profits to the network members for whose interest the diamonds had been sold. Financial remittances could be made in different ways. On one occasion, Berthon and Garnault accepted two gold bars from a buyer, which they sent via London to Dormer as a form of payment.[125] Much more common was remitting profits through bills of exchange. In its most classic form, a bill of exchange was a contract of payment between four parties. The drawee, also called the remitter, bought a bill in one place from the drawer. The latter, generally a merchant-banker, drew for that amount of money on a correspondent in a second place, the payer. This party was to pay out the bill to the payee to whom the bill was sent by the drawee. When the bill was paid out, it was often destroyed and at the end, the drawer was indebted to the payer. According to Larry Neal, the development of banks such as the Amsterdam Wisselbank in 1609 allowed for a settlement of this debt by bank account transfers.[126] When they made a remittance to Dormer, Berthon & Garnault often did so in the forms of bills of exchange drawn on Amsterdam by a Lisbon correspondent of theirs, as is shown by the following bill:[127]

> A Lisbonne le 1° juillet 1755 Pour #1000 a 47½
> A Uzance Payez par cette seconde de change (la Premiere ne l'etant) a l'ordre de Monsieur Jaques Dormer, La Somme de Mil Cruzades
> a Quarante Sept & demy gros par Cruzade, valeur receue de Messieurs Berthon & Garnault que passeres suivant lavis de
> messieurs vos tres humbles et tres obeissantes serviteurs
> Messieurs George Clifford & Fils Perochon Firth & Girardot
> George Jean & Henry
> Amsterdam

The term 'usance' refers to the stipulated time by which the bill had to be paid out and this was determined by commercial custom.[128] Most bills that Berthon & Garnault bought to make a remittance contained the names of merchants they were well acquainted with, and it is no surprise that many names on the bill were those of merchants belonging to either the foreign nation of English merchants in Lisbon or other Huguenot traders active in Lisbon. The names of firms such as Perochon, Dodd, Firth & Company or G. Lang and P. J. Hasenclever return frequently on bills.[129] Peter Garnault's daughter was married to Hasenclever.[130] Such direct social ties fortified Berthon and Garnault's belief in the bills, and enhanced the sense of trust between them and Dormer. This was not unimportant, as bills could be protested by the payer, meaning he refused to pay the bill.[131] In this manner, a network counted on each member's abilities to bring trustworthy outside elements in when necessary and Berthon and Garnault's choice of drawers added to their trustworthiness and reputation within the network. Sometimes, Berthon and Garnault sent bills to Dormer of which they were the drawers and that were to be paid out in Amsterdam, by contacts of Berthon and Garnault there.[132] This made their financial involvement larger as they now were temporarily in debt with the Amsterdam payer.

Within the network, a lot of bills that were to be paid out to Dormer were drawn on Amsterdam and not on Antwerp. The classic scheme of two places was not often observed in bills of exchange, but this was not really a problem as long as the payer and the payee, whose cities were often different, did maintain a good correspondence. When Dormer received the bill issued by Perochon, he sent it to Clifford who answered after reception of the bill that it was a good one and that Dormer's account with them would be credited.[133] Instead of making a remittance, a merchant could also allow for others to draw on him, something that occurred regularly between Salvador and Dormer: 'I Confirm my desire of your Remitting or permitt Mess.rs Aron David x Joseph Fernandes Nunes of Amst.m to draw on you f20 a 22000, as may be most Convenient to both of you'.[134] Dormer not only received remittances from Lisbon, he had to make regular transfers of money to London in order to pay Salvador for joint sales. The endorsement had made the bill of exchange a negotiable commodity. If he wanted to assign a bill to another party, a payee had to write an endorsement at the back of the bill. He still held financial responsibility towards the new payee, who could be unacquainted with the payer.[135]

Thanks to the negotiability of bills of exchange, merchants tried to find the most advantageous way to make remittances, depending on exchange courses between different cities. A merchant living in London but with good connections in Amsterdam could desire to receive bills in a certain currency in either city. As every merchant, Joseph Salvador kept informed on exchange rates and specified to Dormer what type of remittance he desired: 'With regard to remittances I must leave messrs Nunes and you to Settle it ... I want the money in Holland but if it will turn better to account to remit it on Bills for this Place you may remit me'.[136] When the rate was good, bills drawn on other cities such as Paris were also used.[137] The fact that merchants looked out for the best opportunity to remit made the timing of a money transfer important: 'sometime about the middle of next month I shall Expect remittances for all the Sales [of diamonds] as I think the Exchange will then be most advantageous I Shall beg you to watch the opportunity and remit me'.[138]

The use of bills of exchange and the different timing between the conclusion of a transaction, payment for a transaction and the transfer of the profits caused a separation between commodity trade and the underlying financial transactions. When diamonds were sold in Lisbon, Dormer received a sales account and adjusted his current account with Berthon & Garnault accordingly. The timing thereof was determined by the moment a sale was concluded and the travelling time of letters between Lisbon and Antwerp. When actual payment was made a while later by the buyers to Berthon & Garnault, they prepared a remittance. In May 1750, the Frenchmen sold 49 carats of brilliants to a mister Gonçalves, who 'being very good no doubt will be punctual.'[139] He promised to pay within the month and Berthon & Garnault confirmed to Dormer that they would make a remittance in the future. Two weeks later Gonçalves paid the amount due, 1,217$650 *reis*, and Berthon & Garnault sent Dormer a bill worth 1,200$000 *reis* that was drawn by P. Lang and P. J. Hasenclever of Lisbon on Jacob Le Clercq in Amsterdam.[140] The difference in amount is not explained by subtracting commission and other costs made by Berthon & Garnault, as some remittances were slightly higher than the value of the sale but is explained by the separation of commodity trade and financial activity. Profits were not transferred to Dormer, but a payment was made to him, a payment that was achieved by proceeds of a transaction. This difference is fundamental in understanding relationships between correspondents. It adds routine and continuity to the relationship, and also exposes its underlying self-interested basis: the purpose of a correspondence often was the regular transfer of remittances.

4 COMPETITION FROM AN ASHKENAZI KINSHIP NETWORK

The previous chapter introduced a cross-cultural diamond trade network. The merchants who were active in this circuit had chosen to do business together and to that purpose they created privileged relationships with each other. They shared a certain intimacy in commerce and expected a certain level of loyalty from one another. High competition was one of the reasons why long-lasting informal structures were set up between traders, to avoid dealing with different faces for every transaction. It was Dormer who had tried to align himself ever more closely with Salvador in the hope that his commercial circle could gain from Salvador's involvement in the Brazilian monopoly. They were aware of competitive organizations that were active in the diamond trade.

In the course of the eighteenth century, Ashkenazi merchants started to form a serious commercial threat to established diamond merchants. They often relied on kinship networks and it is commonplace to say that the Ashkenazim were a more closed religious community than the Sephardim, who had come to London and Amsterdam earlier. Dormer was involved in a regular correspondence with a number of Ashkenazi firms, with whom he traded in diamonds, bullion and bills of exchange. Although he felt a certain loyalty towards the Salvador firm and others, he also looked out for his own self-interest. Traders who were active in a human web of privileged relations based on trust, intimacy and friendship did not see these relations as an impediment to the establishment of a similar type of relation with merchants who were not only outside such a network, but who were direct competitors of it.

The correspondence between Dormer and the Ashkenazi firms in Amsterdam was another form of cross-cultural interaction. Religious differences were easily overcome in trade, and the Ashkenazi community was not so rigidly closed to outsiders and conservative as is sometimes suggested. The juxtaposition between Sephardic merchants, cosmopolitan, wealthy and open on the one hand and Ashkenazi traders who were poorer, more conservative and less adapted to their host society on the other, lacks nuance to say the least. The particular mechanisms of the commercial world, based on personal relationships, provided a solid basis for daily interaction that proved to be the most practical and concrete expression of tolerance. A good way to analyse the historical experience of different diasporas is not a comparison based on financial wealth, but a study of the type of networks merchants were involved in. Although it is true that Ashkenazi business ties relied to an important extent on kinship networks, the commercial relationship between Dormer and different Ashkenazi diamond traders shows that they were also actively constructing connections outside their own community, and that they were not that different from the internationally-oriented Sephardic traders.

Ashkenazi Diamond Merchants in Amsterdam

The Limits of Comparison

In recent years, a substantial body of literature concerned with the Sephardic community of Amsterdam has been generated. Most of the contributions to publications that give a general survey of Jewish history and culture in the Low Countries have focused on the Portuguese community of the Netherlands, and especially Amsterdam. The story of the Sephardim, their social presence and struggle for acceptance in the Low Countries, their commercial activities and their contribution to international trade is well-researched. As was pointed out by Jozeph Michman, one of the largest remaining gaps in the history of Dutch Jewry is the absence of an academic body concerned with the Ashkenazi Jews who had arrived from Eastern Europe, mainly Germany and Poland. Social customs, spiritual life as well as their economic activities are all aspects that so far have not received the attention they deserve.[1]

According to Michman, the main reason for this lacuna is an insufficient knowledge of Hebrew and Yiddish.[2] A second reason is the higher historical agency attributed to the Sephardim. When considering the involvement of Jewish merchants in international trade, Sephardic businessmen take a very prominent place. Jonathan Israel, for instance, one of the main academic voices in Jewish diaspora history, has highlighted the role played by Dutch Sephardic Jews in the development of the Atlantic.[3] Only one out of ten essays in a recently published volume on Jewish diasporas across the Atlantic deals with Ashkenazi Jews. This has led Natalie Zemon Davis to remark in the epilogue of the collection that 'comparison of trading Diasporas and New World settlement patterns could fruitfully be extended to them'.[4] The difference in historical attention given to the two different Jewish diasporas becomes even more striking when considering the fact that around 1720, the Ashkenazim overcame the Sephardim in demographical numbers. A large immigration in the first half of the eighteenth century caused their numbers to expand exponentially, from around 4,300 in 1715 to 13,200 in 1735, making their community in the Dutch Republic much larger than that of the Sephardim.[5]

The Ashkenazi diaspora is often analysed in unfavourable comparison with the Sephardim, and has often suffered from the stereotypical portrait of a less integrated, more traditional and much poorer community. The Ashkenazim from Eastern Europe had arrived later than the Jews from the Iberian Peninsula, who had already managed to develop a small upper class of wealthy and acculturated merchants and bankers. The Jewish community was to a large extent self-regulating and initially the Ashkenazim lived within the same quarter as their co-religionists. Well-to-do Jews of Iberian descent were afraid that their status of relative freedom could be damaged by newcomers and the Ashkenazi poor were supported by Sephardic charities. Ashkenazim were also regularly employed in menial positions in Sephardic households or trade firms. The Jewish community in Amsterdam did not only see newcomers as a threat because of their social status or demographical numbers, but also in their appearance. While Iberian Jews already had been exposed longer to non-Jewish communities, either in Spain, Portugal or France before coming to Amsterdam, the Ashkenazim had remained more traditional in their religious and social customs. Jewish life was difficult in Eastern Europe and often confined within traditional communities.[6] The perception of difference between Ashkenazim and Sephardim, particularly from a visual point of view, can be observed in the etchings that Bernard Picart made in 1723 of Jews and Jewish life.[7] A greater reliance on tradition was also expressed in the observation that the Ashkenazim had a stricter obedience to the praxis of Jewish faith. It would be a mistake to assume that by the time the Ashkenazim migrated to Amsterdam *en masse*, the Sephardim had become an assimilated group. First, the Sephardim were still very much a separate community, living in a particular area of the city, with their own leaders and rules. Part of the hailed tolerance of Amsterdam was exactly the fact that the Jewish community was allowed to exist *as a community*. This understanding, built on day-to-day experience, was threatened by the new migrations from Eastern Europe, or that was at least the perception by members of both the host society and the Sephardic community.

From 1628 onwards, a higher influx of immigrants from Eastern Europe, due to the consequences of the Thirty Years' War, accelerated the founding of a separate Ashkenazi community. They had established their own congregation in 1635 and their own synagogue in 1671. Nevertheless, they remained economically dependent on the Sephardim who, by the middle of the eighteenth century were no longer able to support the Ashkenazi community financially. At that time, the Ashkenazim had become more numerous and two different diaspora entities had developed, each with their own social and communal life.[8] One of the most noticeable differences between the two groups was language, a difference that affected culture in general. The Sephardim often spoke Portuguese and Spanish amongst each other, but also knew Hebrew. The verbal language of Ashkenazim was Yiddish, spoken in different Eastern European dialects. A new dialect developed in Amsterdam, a Judaic-Dutch version of spoken Yiddish, difficult to understand for Eastern European Jews outside Holland and similar to Dutch.[9]

The Ashkenazim whose businesses are researched in this chapter were already second-generation immigrants whose parents came from Germany.[10] The language of the business letters the Ashkenazim of Amsterdam sent to Antwerp was Dutch. Yet they remained attached to the Hebrew language. Their wills were made in Hebrew and afterwards translated by a notary.[11] This shows that in the eighteenth century, a certain amount of success goes together with sufficient language skills to overcome all technical communication problems. Linguistic problems were more due to social circumstances than to different cultural background. More and more Ashkenazim were able to climb up the social ladder. They became strong competitors to Sephardic traders, not in the least in the diamond trade. At the end of the eighteenth century, several Ashkenazi trading and banking houses managed to achieve the same economic and social status as Sephardic firms.[12] Throughout most of the eighteenth century, however, class differences continued to play a role. In writing about prostitution in Amsterdam, Lotte van de Pol has concluded that there was a very visible social divide between the two communities in that Sephardic men often kept mistresses, while their Ashkenazi counterparts could be found at lower-class brothels.[13]

A difference in class does not justify the difference in historical attention.[14] Jewish merchants arriving at substantial financial success were a minority. The problem that this analysis is biased on Sephardim is different from the problem that the majority of the Jewish population has not been a subject for historical study at all. According to Todd Endelman, the Jewish poor have remained outside history as passive bystanders.[15] Both problems overlap in the false assumption that Ashkenazi traders were mostly active as peddlers or petty traders and were of much lesser historical importance than Sephardic merchants. A second problem with the history of Jewish diaspora in Western Europe is a focus on the emancipation movement, which has led to a simplified discourse on pre-nineteenth-century Jewish history. In a number of countries, a movement of Jewish emancipation had started towards the end of the eighteenth century, which eventually led to equality in a legal sense. The classical argument is that emancipation came after a period of social mobility.[16] This theory has as a consequence that all interaction previous to this age of change is placed on a meritocratic basis with regard to an event that was to take place later. Sonnenberg-Stern is correct to question this narrative, and she has a strong argument in considering the Ashkenazim as a group that eventually became more acculturated in everyday life because there were less social conventions for them to cross than for the wealthier Sephardic merchant-bankers. This argument, however, does not fundamentally change the problem of seeing the history of Jewish migration as an evolutionary path leading to equality.

A changed evaluation of the emancipation movement should lead to greater attention to Eastern European Jewry. This chapter will analyse the dealings of a number of interconnected Ashkenazi firms. As merchants, they were perhaps not representative of their entire community, but an analysis of their activities will show the shortcomings of studying the Ashkenazi diaspora in a comparative framework with the Sephardim and solemnly in terms of social difference, integration and commercial merit.

Ruben Levy & Company, a Family Firm in a Kinship Network

Ruben Levy gave his name to a firm that was established in Amsterdam. An absence of source material means that almost all concrete information with regard to their firm comes from their correspondence with Dormer. The number of letters they sent him, 382, gives the Levy firm a prominent place amongst the different correspondents of Dormer. The amount is much smaller than the correspondence with the Salvadors or the Cliffords, but surpasses the correspondence of other network members such as the Nunes' firm or Berthon & Garnault.[17] The Levy firm consisted of three partners: the brothers Ruben and Jacob Elias Levy and their cousin Jacob Norden, who was also related to them by marriage. They were active in diamond trade, but also in the commerce in bullion and bills of exchange.[18] Two of their main partners in Amsterdam, Alexander Norden and Salomon Norden & Company, also maintained a correspondence with Dormer.

The Norden family shared close kinship ties with the Levy firm. Jacob and Alexander Norden were brothers.[19] Alexander Norden called Salomon Norden & Company his brothers as well, and Ruben Levy referred to that firm as his brothers-in-law.[20] These claims match the family tree, as it seems likely that Salomon Norden's oldest son Assur was a partner in the firm, and that he was the brother and brother-in-law to who reference was made. A closer look at genealogical material shows that the Norden and Levy families shared kinship ties with two other Ashkenazi families who were relevant in the diamond trade: Salomons and Keyser.[21] Alexander Norden was the son of Salomon Norden (of Salomon Norden & Company) and Telts Levy Hamburger. The last name indicates that she came from Hamburg, something that also explains the adoption of the non-Jewish name 'Norden', indicating 'coming from the north'.[22] They had ten children, of whom Levy and Ruben Salomons are the most important in revealing family ties and diamond trade activities.[23] Their sister Frida Norden had married Ruben Levy. From the will of Levy Salomons it can be derived that the original family name of the Nordens was Salomons.[24] In fact, Norden and Salomons are two names for the same family, with an Amsterdam branch that changed to the name Norden, something that is confirmed by the will of Solomon Ruben Norden wherein he indicated that in England the family members stayed with the name Salomons while those in Amsterdam adopted the name Norden.[25] The name Salomons returns frequently in lists of Jewish tax payers in the German cities of Hamburg and Altona.[26] The fact that Alexander Norden had married a woman from Hamburg further suggests that the family had their roots in Germany.

The frequent use of the same first names makes it somewhat difficult to identify the correct persons, and the knowledge that these people lived and died in the right time frame does not in itself prove that the Nordens and Levys mentioned in the database are in fact the same Nordens and Levys who conducted business with Dormer. One thing that helps is that the first names of Alexander and Ruben, unlike Salomon and Jacob for instance, were not that common. The fact that Ruben Levy mentioned two weddings to Dormer in 1745 confirms that the individuals in the database were the same individuals who corresponded with Dormer.[27] In June, Ruben Levy mentioned that the daughter of his brother Jacob Elias was to marry that month. The genealogical database contains records of a marriage in 1745 of a Judith Jacob Levy Hamburger, daughter of Jacob Eliaser Leizer Levy Hamburger. The following month, Ruben Levy announced the wedding between his son and another daughter of Jacob Elias Levy. The database contains a record of a marriage in 1745 between Levy Ruben Levy, son of Ruben Levy, and Eva Levy, daughter of Jacob Elias Levy.[28] The last name Levy, also written as Levi, was uncommon in the Ashkenazi community, which makes the task of identification easier.[29]

Merchants belonging to the Levy, Salomons and Norden families did not all live and work in Amsterdam. They had family members who were established in London and who were active in the diamond trade with India. Gedalia Yogev has mentioned a number of them as important Ashkenazi diamond traders of London.[31] Their direct involvement with India can be traced in the court minute books of the English East India Company, which include names such as Elias Levy, Samuel Hartog Levy, David Levy and Samuel Andries Levy.[32] A 1749 guide of London traders included different Levys, and one of them, Elias Levy, was a neighbour of Francis Salvador in Lime Street.[33] Ruben Levy mentioned Samuel Levy Junior and David Levy once to Dormer, and he described them as 'being amongst the most prestigious merchants in our nation'.[34]

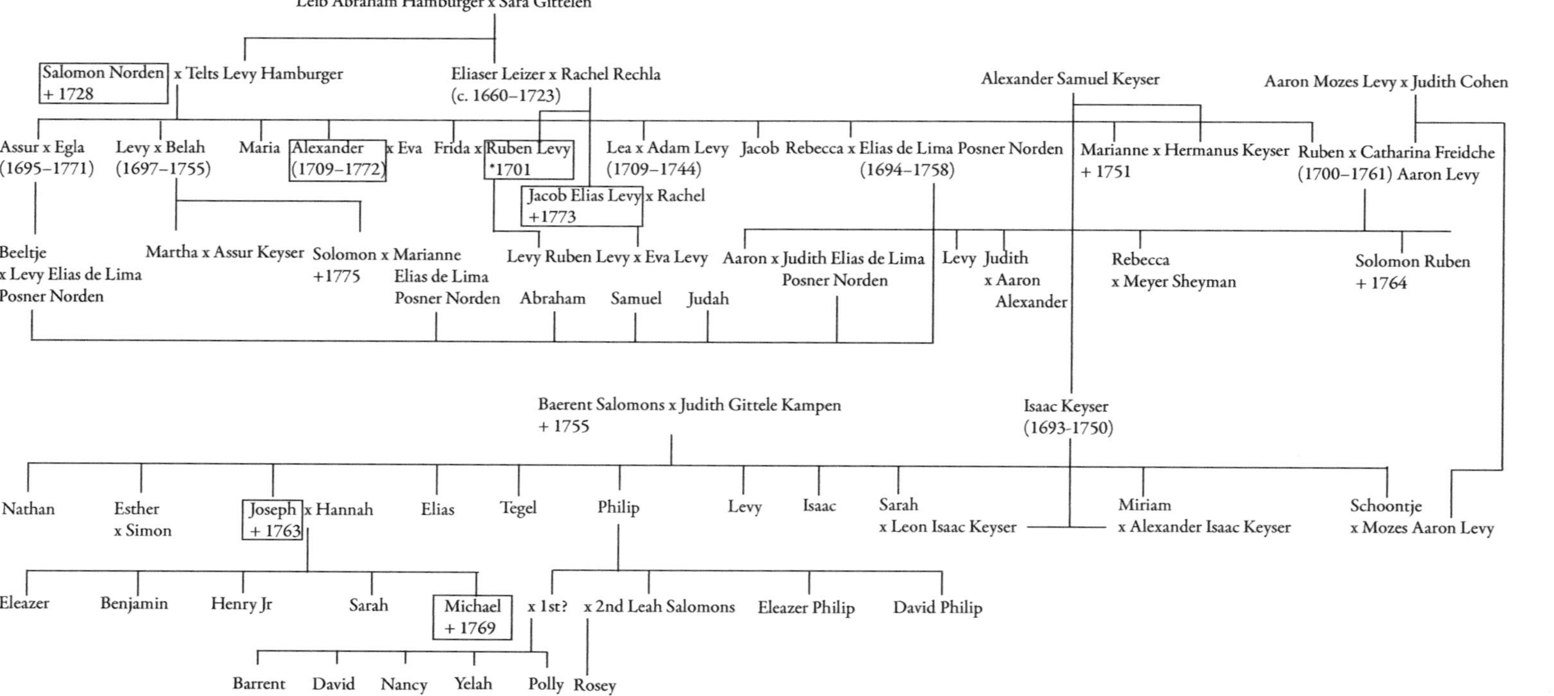

Figure 4.1: Family tree of Levy, Salomons and Norden families.[30]

The Nordens of Amsterdam also had relatives in London. The brothers Aaron and Solomon Norden were active in the 1760s in the diamond-coral trade.[35] They were the sons of Ruben Salomons. This merchant was a brother of Alexander Norden and related by marriage to Ruben Levy. In diamond trade, Ruben had formed a partnership with his brother Levy Salomons. The will of Levy Salomons shows that he lived with his wife in London and that he was born in Amsterdam in 1697. He was the second oldest son of Salomon Norden and Telts Levy Hamburger, after his older brother Assur who was born in 1695. None of Salomon Norden's sons died young and the migration between Amsterdam and London, which was characteristic of all the families studied here, can be attributed to the impossibility of making all the sons partners in a firm. Out of Salomon Norden's five sons, one had established his own firm, while two had founded another firm as partners and a fourth had become partner in the Ruben Levy firm. It was interesting to have correspondents in other cities who were close relatives. It meant contact with a valuable and trustworthy correspondent with whom ties did not need to be constructed, since they were already there. Even if a son sent abroad wished to be ambitious or malevolent, the fact that he arrived within a well-established diaspora community where he was very likely to find uncles, friends or business relations of his father made it harder for him to cheat. Beyond direct kinship ties, but intertwined within them, there was also a strong element of communal control.[36] This was strengthened by the high degree of intermarriage within the international Ashkenazi community, sometimes even within the same family. Daughters in particular often married Ashkenazi merchants of a different city and moved accordingly. Most families had members on both sides of the channel and a large intermarried Ashkenazi community had developed in London and Amsterdam.

The firm of Levy and Ruben Salomons delivered rough diamonds to their relatives in Amsterdam. A testimony from them shows that Salomon Norden & Company frequently employed the Salomons brothers as their agents in London. They sent rough diamonds to Amsterdam and sold polished stones and jewels in London.[37] The partnership worked successfully and Levy Salomons left a considerable amount of wealth at the time of his death in 1765. To his wife he left £500 and the interest on £6,000 bank annuities that he possessed. His only son received most of his estate and was to continue his father's merchant affairs.[38] In total, Levy Salomons possessed bank annuities worth £14,000, which was a substantial amount. Towards the end of the eighteenth century, London's upper income group earned approximately £200 per year, about 2 or 3 per cent of its total population; the middling classes, 16 to 21 per cent of the population, earned between £80 and £130 per year.[39] The interest of the annuities gave his wife a yearly income of £240, which placed her in the highest income group.

Salomons' daughter received £320 a year on interests, also placing her in that group.

Levy's younger brother Ruben Salomons had married Catharina Freidche Aron Levy, daughter of the Hamburg-born Aaron Moses Levy and Judith Cohen. She had a brother who was seven years younger and who married Schoontje Salomons, the daughter of another prominent member of the Salomons family, Baerent Salomons. He had four sons who were all active in the diamond trade. Baerent's son Joseph was in contact with Dormer and they were also connected to Ruben Levy and Alexander Norden in business. Two of Joseph's sons, Michael and Henry, both wrote to Dormer about diamond sales between 1756 and 1758.[40] Michael lived in London, but Henry, who acted as an agent for his father, lived in Amsterdam, at least for a while, as he instructed Dormer to contact him at the house of the widow of Baerent Salomons.[41] The date and place of birth of Baerent Salomons remain unknown, but his will was proved in September 1755.[42]

Through marriage, the Salomons and Norden families were also related to the prominent Keyser family. Two daughters of Baerent married two sons of Isaac Alexander Keyser (1693–1750). According to Gedalia Yogev, he was a London broker selling silver to the East India Company that was used to purchase diamonds in India.[43] Not much else is known about the Keyser family. According to the genealogical database, Isaac Keyser had eight children, and most of them moved to London to become successful bankers. Different Keysers were related to the Norden and Salomons families: Assur Keyser was a cousin and business partner of Aaron Norden, son of Ruben Salomons and a brother-in-law of Solomon Norden, Ruben's brother Levy's son. Solomon's will also made mentioned of the fact that Lyon Keyser, a nephew, was to receive £500 and a friend of the family, Levy Cohen, was to receive £50.[44] Assur Keyser and Lyon Keyser remain unknown with regard to their position in the Keyser family, but it is clear that there were links to that family through Baerent Salomons as well as through Levy and Ruben Salomons, further complicating the interconnectedness of these different Ashkenazi families. A brother of Isaac Keyser, Hermanus Keyser, married Marianne Miriam Norden, a sister of Levy and Ruben Salomons. The marriage ties to different members of the Keyser family is further proof that these Ashkenazi families, settled in both London and Amsterdam, became connected in many more ways than just one inter-family marriage.

The strong intermarriage between different Ashkenazi families suggests that they relied on their kin in matters of business. This was true, but at the same time it did not exclude commercial relationships with others, as is shown in the correspondence between Ruben Levy and Alexander Norden with Dormer. The Englishman also worked on occasion and on commission for other family members.[45] It also did not mean that the life of Ashkenazi merchants only took place within an international diaspora community. Ruben Levy, Alexander Norden and the other Ashkenazi correspondents of Dormer did not only consider themselves to be Jews; they also thought of themselves as patriots: proud inhabitants of Holland. When the *stadhouder* returned to Amsterdam in 1747, the inhabitants of the city illuminated their houses as a sign of joy. Ruben Levy expressed his happiness and wrote that he was also busy lighting his house.[46] Two months later the *stadhouder*, Prince of Orange and Nassau, was to be officially installed in the town of Utrecht. For that occasion, Alexander Norden decided to travel there, so he could be a witness to the events.[47] The period in which the correspondence between Dormer and the Ashkenazim took place was a period in which the Ashkenazi diaspora was still fully developing itself. A lot of movement was still taking place, with people moving from Amsterdam to London and *vice versa* and some future wives that came from Germany and had not grown up in Amsterdam.[48] The Ashkenazi merchants mentioned in this chapter were mostly second-generation migrants whose parents had come from Eastern Europe at the end of the seventeenth and the beginning of the eighteenth century, and that makes this period particularly interesting. It becomes more than a narrative of assimilation; it becomes a story that focuses more on the different new possibilities offered to people that were in-between different cultures. They were not Dutch citizens, but they were not born in Eastern Europe either.

External Relationships: Ruben Levy and James Dormer

Dormer maintained a correspondence with three Ashkenazi firms in London that was less intensive than most of the ones he maintained with network members. Salomon Norden & Company sent him 42 letters between 1743 and 1758; Alexander Norden sent 23 between 1743 and 1747. The most intensive was the correspondence with Ruben Levy & Company, who sent 372 letters between 1743 and 1752. The majority of the business discussed in that correspondence was financial. Dormer was active as a small banker and acted regularly as payer for bills issued by Ruben Levy and others. In 1744, Jacob Elias Levy had drawn on Dormer and the bill was in the hands of either Alexander Corvers or the widow M. A. Donckers, in whose place Corvers stayed. Dormer was asked to send his servant to Donckers's house, to inform the owner of the bill that Dormer would pay it.[49] No commission fee was mentioned in the letters sent to Dormer for his financial services to Levy. This was most likely because it was included in the exchange. The church and Christian scholars had not been very enthusiastic with regard to financial transactions and usury was officially forbidden. There were certain ethical rules with regard to credit and merchants were used to hiding their profits within the exchange rate.[50] It was important for Levy to inform Dormer in time that he had drawn on him, because if Dormer protested the bill, the reputation of the Levys would be harmed as they could not ensure international payment to the persons they owed money. They explicitly instructed Dormer that if bills were presented to him by benevolent merchants, he should pay them out, even if he had not received advice before.[51] The need for information is perfectly understandable. A bill could be forged and a signature could be falsified.[52] If he paid somebody carrying a false bill, he would have to take the loss.

Bills originally served as payment for commodity trade, with merchants being financed by merchant-bankers, but in reality, the distinction between the two is not always easily made. A large merchant-banker such as George Clifford & Sons very often served as payer and drawer, but it has been mentioned in the previous chapter that, in their financial relationships, merchants often acted as payer for each other in a reciprocal way. The same was the case for Levy and Dormer was allowed to draw on them if necessary. In early 1746, Dormer owed the firm of Andries Pels & Sons in Amsterdam an amount of money and Ruben Levy informed him that he could draw on him on a short term of eight days with Andries Pels & Sons as the payee.[53] Dormer must have anticipated this answer, as a letter from Pels addressed one day before Levy's suggestion confirms that they had received a letter from Dormer informing them of the fact that Ruben Levy was ordered to make a payment to them on Dormer's behalf.[54] Dormer's assumption suggests that his drawing on Ruben Levy was a common practice between them. Then, however, things went wrong. Andries Pels wrote that he had talked with Ruben Levy, who claimed to have had no news from Dormer about a payment.[55] Dormer was not pleased at all and wrote an angry letter to Amsterdam. Ruben Levy explained the misunderstanding. A writer of the Pels' firm had tried to talk to Ruben Levy at the Amsterdam Exchange. It was instead his companion Jacob Norden that had a conversation with him, and the writer asked him whether his firm had received an order to pay Pels. Norden answered that Dormer had not specified an exact amount, but that Pels could specify an amount at will, 'unlimited shall we give for you [James Dormer]'. The writer misinterpreted that response and returned with a bad message to his masters.[56] Things were settled by a payment of Ruben Levy to Andries Pels of f2,800 in bank money and the sending of a remittance of f2,000.[57]

Problems were solved, but Dormer's rapid assumption could seriously have harmed different reputations. In a world that relied so heavily on information that merchants at times even wrote more than one letter per day to each other, it did not look good when an acquaintance claimed that he was without news from you. Secondly, Andries Pels had to wait for money that was promised to him because his debtor did not get in contact in time with his correspondent. But the reputation of the Levys was also at stake. A merchant who asked a contact in a foreign city to make a payment on his behalf relied on the fact that it would be done without problems. The whole correspondence could be at stake. Dormer's angry letter apparently upset the Levys and Pels was asked to write Dormer a letter on their behalf. He wrote Dormer that they had come to see him and that they admitted that Jacob Norden had expressed himself in an ungracious manner. Pels wrote further that they were known as very honest, 'we even believe that that quality makes them find credit in general beyond that they seem to be great experts in their commerce'.[58] Ruben Levy quickly wrote to Dormer and expressed the desire that the incident would not hurt their harmonious correspondence. He also added that Dormer was free to end the correspondence if he took any displeasure in it.[59]

A second common financial operation between Levy and Dormer was the negotiation of bills of exchange. Because of a difference in exchange rates on foreign places between Antwerp and Amsterdam, it could be profitable for an Amsterdam merchant to send a bill to Antwerp. Levy could endorse a bill to Dormer, which enabled him to cash it himself or to negotiate it on the market.[60] Dormer's commission for acting as Levy's agent selling and cashing bills in Antwerp was specified at ⅓ per cent of the value of the bill, the usual fee the Levy firm paid to their correspondents.[61] Most of the bills that were sent to Antwerp were in pounds sterling to be paid out in London. Apart from bills drawn on London, Ruben Levy also sent bills on places in Brabant and Flanders, mostly Brussels, Gent or Bruges. Table 4.1 shows the different Amsterdam payers of the London bills received by Dormer and gives their share of the total monetary value of bills issued in London.

Table 4.1: Remittances by Ruben Levy & Company to James Dormer on London firms.[62]

Payer in London	Value of bill (£:shillings:pence)	Percentage of total value
Levy Salomons	9330:5:0	21
Other family members	2982:10:7	7
Other Ashkenazim	1093:19:9	2,5
Sephardim	2599:14:4	6
Other merchants	12136:11:4	27
Muilman	3260:0:0	7,2
Unknown	12997:4:0	29,3
Total	44401:4:4	100

Direct relatives of Ruben Levy counted for 28 per cent of the total value of the bills. Ashkenazi traders with whom no kinship ties can be confirmed make up 2.5 per cent. Other (non-Jewish) merchants provided 34.2 per cent and in 29.3 per cent of the cases, the firm was not mentioned in the letters by Ruben Levy. The total group of Jewish firms forms the largest source of the remittances, 36.5 per cent, a bit more than one-third of the total. The large share of family members can be explained by the fact that it is probable that Levy had received a number of bills related to commodity trade, possibly polished diamonds that were sent to his London contacts. Ruben Levy also bought a lot of bills at the exchange that were issued by the biggest bankers such as George Clifford and Thomas and Adrian Hope.[63]

It is important with regard to the relationship between Dormer and Levy that Levy could trust the payers in London. If they refused payment to Dormer, or to another merchant to whom he sold the bills, their reputation would suffer substantially. Both merchants were aware of this, and Dormer especially sometimes had reserves towards bills sent to him. He expressed doubts with regard to some endorsements, which was insulting to Levy especially when he had received an endorsed bill by a close relative. When Dormer questioned a bill endorsed by Salomon Norden, Levy wrote that if they needed money, they did not need endorsements, neither within nor outside the Jewish community and that they had traded for 28 years with Antwerp, without problems.[64] It is possible that the information was given to Dormer by one of his agents, Bernardus van Merlen, a member of the cross-cultural diamond network. Two weeks after Levy wrote his letter van Merlen informed Dormer that Jacob Levy was coming to Antwerp and that he probably would complain a great deal about him.[65]

On several occasions, Ruben Levy had to assure that the payers carried a good reputation; mister Barbanel was as good as Andries Pels in Amsterdam, Jacob Pereira was the richest Jew and David Levy was one of the foremost merchants of the Jewish nation in London. Other bills were drawn on the biggest bankers in London.[66] The letters containing these descriptions were in fact angry and disappointed responses to Dormer's official reserve, based on the fear that the bills would be protested in London. Ruben Levy accused Dormer of acting against 'all merchant's style' and suggested that jealous traders had led Dormer to be disrespectful.[67] A couple of days later, Ruben Levy addressed a letter to Dormer but the content was specifically intended for his wife. He asked excuse for the strong language that was used, but he also made it clear that their honour was at stake, something that was serious enough to send Jacob Levy to Antwerp on a Sunday night to resolve the issue, although there was stormy weather.[68] The problem was solved by Dormer's willingness to take the bills and Levy asked for the matter not to be left behind. Levy could probably permit to lose Dormer as a correspondent, but he could not afford to be labelled by him as untrustworthy. If Dormer publicly doubted the payability of the bills Levy sent him, he questioned Levy's commercial judgement at the bourse where he bought his bills, and he also questioned Levy's contacts in London who were often members of the same kinship network. A business correspondence kept two merchants in contact with each other, but the international financial system based on the bill of exchange kept a whole world together.

A third type of financial transaction was less risky with regard to commercial reputation and was in fact a commodity trade. For a period of two years, between July 1744 and May 1746, Dormer and Levy were engaged in a regular trade in bullion. It is remarkable that during this period, transactions involving precious stones between the two firms had come to a standstill. The specie trade seems to have been an attempt to make use of the correspondence, and not let it dry up, when the market for diamonds was not good. Dormer did not have much experience in that branch of commerce and the fact that he turned to his Ashkenazi correspondents is logical considering their historical presence in bullion trade.[69] In 1749, a group of merchants in Amsterdam petitioned against a new resolution that forbade the payment of a commission fee to merchants who delivered precious gold and silver to be coined. Among the merchants signing the petition were the names of Hermanus Keyser, a brother-in-law of Alexander Norden, Isaac Alexander Keyser, Salomon Norden & Company, Baerent Salomons, Benjamin & Samuel Symons, Philip Salomons and Alexander Salomons.[70] Amsterdam had become the undisputed centre for the world trade in precious metals after the peace between Spain and Holland in 1648, and the Amsterdam Bank of Exchange played an important role in this success.[71] Although that position was increasingly challenged during the eighteenth century, ships sailing from Cadiz to Texel, an island in the north of Holland, carried almost 50 million guldens between 1740 and 1749.[72]

In the bullion trade, the firm of Ruben Levy & Company acted as agent for Dormer in Amsterdam supplying Dormer with specie. Besides Levy, Dormer also traded with a number of related Ashkenazi families in Amsterdam. Alexander Norden also sent coins to Dormer, and several bags were sent to Antwerp in which both the firms of Ruben Levy and Salomon Norden had a share. Levy had written to Dormer that 'with dito [Salomon Norden & Company] we buy together a lot of gold and silver and also diamonds'.[73] At first, shipments took place in Rotterdam and initially, Dormer preferred to use his acquaintance there, the firm of Joan Osy & Son, but Ruben Levy proposed to work with an acquaintance of his, Ezechiel Salomons, member of the considerable Ashkenazi community there.[74] At first, Dormer expressed his doubts about this new agent, but Ruben Levy vouched for his friend.[75] The ties between Levy and Ezechiel Salomons were so good that the latter did not ask a commission to the Levys.[76] It indicates that the level of trust in kinship networks was generally higher than in cross-cultural networks, since the former implied a stronger sense of obligation.[77]

On one occasion, a dispute arose between Levy and Dormer about the commission charged by the former. The Levys had sent a sack of ducats and charged a commission that was too high according to Dormer. Ruben Levy answered that they sold cheaper to him than other merchants who shipped bullion to Antwerp, and that buyers of specie did not make difficulties for the prices that the Levys charged them. So they informed him that they would comply with his last order and after that stop with the shipments, putting an end to their bullion transactions.[78] For the Ashkenazim, Dormer was an outsider and of minor importance in their bullion trade and Levy was of opinion that he did Dormer a favour. Only a few times, the Levy firm asked Dormer to supply them with French pistols and guineas bought in Antwerp and destined for relatives in London. Levy's remark that they had other suppliers for bullion in Antwerp confirms Dormer's minor importance for the Ashkenazim.[79] In August 1748, the Levys wrote that they were no longer interested in receiving specie from Antwerp.[80] The bullion trade between Levy and Dormer dried out quickly, but their correspondence did not. Commerce in precious metals might have given some profit to both firms, but its real importance lied perhaps in the ability to maintain business between the two parties: 'Sir we have in some time not had the honour to try something of importance with you, so this is only not to let our correspondence with you come to a standstill.'[81] Dormer's financial activities with the Ashkenazim did not really put him in a difficult position towards other contacts. As a banker, exclusivity was not an issue, and the negotiation of bills of exchange had become common in the eighteenth century. Although Dormer and Salvador did some transactions in bullion, the trade volume was so low that this was not considered to be an important trade for either one of them. More risky was Dormer's involvement with the Ashkenazim in the diamond trade, as an agent for them in Antwerp.

Competing Circuits of Commerce

Ashkenazi Diamond Traders

It is not surprising that Dormer wanted to trade in diamonds with the Ashkenazim. The Englishman had shown great ambition in that branch of business and a substantial amount of Ashkenazi traders in Amsterdam were successful diamond traders. In 1746, Ruben Levy wrote to Dormer that he had been active for twenty-eight years in the diamond business.[82] Initially, the Sephardim who were involved in this trade did not have much competition from Eastern European merchants, but that had changed towards the end of the seventeenth century. Around that time, three Ashkenazim in Amsterdam were mentioned in documents as independent diamond dealers, employing others, among them also an Eliaser Levy.[83] Half a century later, several Ashkenazim could rival Sephardic diamond traders in commercial success in Amsterdam and in London. It is in the diamond trade that the Ashkenazi business organization based on family ties across the channel becomes the most visible. It was also in this business that the firms of Levy and Norden were the most direct competitors of the Sephardim of London and Amsterdam. Dormer's involvement with both the Ashkenazi family network and the cross-cultural diamond trade network was rather particular and proves that the pursuit of self-interest was a prime motive, even if it meant trading against one's most loyal commercial partners. In the cross-cultural diamond trade network, Dormer was an important member. He was not a member of the family-based Ashkenazi network, but he was nonetheless involved in an intense correspondence with the firms of this circuit, discussing regular trade in rough and polished diamonds.

Ashkenazi diamond merchants were involved in three manners with Dormer. First, they supplied him with rough diamonds. This only happened for partnership sales Dormer made with Bernardus van Merlen and the diamonds were probably bought or negotiated by van Merlen in Amsterdam. About 17 per cent of the monetary value of all diamonds purchased and registered in Dormer's diamond books were supplied by Ashkenazi firms. This is less than half the supply sent from London by the Salvadors but it is still a significant amount when considering that the Ashkenazim were competitors to Salvador and other network members. About 79 per cent of this number came from Ruben Levy & Company and Salomon Norden & Company. Only on one other occasion was Dormer supplied with diamonds by another Sephardic merchant, Gomes Dias. This brings the share of supplies coming from Jewish merchants to 57 per cent, a high number that clearly indicates Jewish importance in the international diamond trade but also downplays the idea that Jews controlled that trade entirely.

A second involvement of Ashkenazim was that Dormer sold them, on behalf of different partnerships, polished diamonds. These sales were mostly conducted by van Merlen in Amsterdam but merchants such as Jacob Elias Levy also came to Antwerp to buy precious stones. The monetary value of these sales is hard to calculate as they were often expressed in money used in Holland ('Hollands Courant') and exchange and discounts are often calculated on a group of sales occurring at the same time and in the same place, but to different buyers. By far most of the sales were concluded with merchants of the Ruben Levy & Company firm and a few parcels were sold to Alexander Norden. The fact that Dormer only traded with a handful of Ashkenazi firms who were intermarried is also clearly visible in his activities as an agent working on commission. He only sold diamonds on a commission of 1.5 per cent for three Ashkenazi firms: Ruben Levy & Company in Amsterdam and Michael and Joseph Salomons in London.[84] The diamonds sold on behalf of Ruben Levy & Company were rough diamonds and the total value of different sales amounted to only f8713:2:0. He only concluded one sale for Joseph Salomons, for two parcels of rough diamonds weighing 242 and 274 carats, which Dormer sold for f8877:4:0. The diamonds had been sent to him via his son Henry Salomons Junior in Amsterdam. Michael Salomons was another son, and in 1757, 1758 and 1759 Dormer and his son made a few transactions for him by selling Brazilian diamonds, rough stones and yellow diamond dust for a total of f62912:8:0 Brabant money.

These numbers are low and do not reflect the true scope of Dormer's relationship with the Ashkenazi diamond merchants. Market prices fluctuated and different types of diamonds were in different demand.[85] Diamonds often circulated between markets and most of the precious stones sent to Dormer to be sold were returned because the Englishman did not manage to conclude a deal. Ruben Levy sent a total of 3016.5 carats to Antwerp to be sold on commission by Dormer, who only managed to sell 843.25 carats, which is a relative share of 28 per cent. 72 per cent was either sent back to Amsterdam or given in person to a member of the Levy firm, mostly Jacob Norden. This seems a very high percentage, and it indicates that commerce was definitely not always a matter of smooth and regular operations benefiting both parties. It also indicates that merchants were very patient over periods of years, and were not quickly tempted to completely abandon trades once they had become established. It also shows that, by calculating profits or analysing successful sales, the true scope of a relationship can remain underestimated. A lot of effort was put in sending diamonds abroad, testing the market, looking for buyers, and diamonds remained in Dormer's hands for months before they were sent back. Although his activities were past their zenith in 1758, it can never be known whether Dormer's correspondence with Michael, Joseph and Henry Salomons could have revived his diamond affairs. Michael had lived in India and the activities of these merchants in the diamond trade were considerable.

Similar unsuccessful attempts in the diamond trade are found in Dormer's sending of diamonds to Amsterdam, trying to sell them to Ruben Levy. In 1746, Dormer sent several small packages of rose diamonds and brilliants to Holland. The first of these, containing 47.75 carats of rose diamonds, was quickly sent back after arrival. The price was too high and the Levys were not interested.[86] The other diamonds were subject to a great deal of negotiation. Dormer had obtained them from a merchant who was interested in buying 436 carats of rough diamonds from Ruben Levy only if he could use some parcels of polished diamond as payment, in truck, a practice that was not at all uncommon. The Levys were more reluctant, and preferred money instead of other stones, especially because some of the diamonds could not serve them at all. Between 22 September and 14 October, various letters were sent back and forth to negotiate this deal. Finally, the Levys did sell their diamonds for money, although at a lower price than they had set initially.[87]

It is not clear what happened with the polished stones. Ruben Levy wrote that they would conclude the transaction and 'keep the made good for us'.[88] This suggests that they kept (and paid for) the polished diamonds, but no mention can be found in the correspondence or in the diamond books thereof. Since the terms of payment with regard to their 436 carats rough stones were not very clearly expressed, the possibility remains that the polished stones were in the end included in the same transaction. Transactions in which polished stones were used as payment for rough diamonds did occur, but it seems that merchants generally preferred money. The Levy firm was interested in the purchase of polished stones as a separate product and on one other occasion they did agree to a possible change operation wherein their uncut stones would be traded against polished diamonds. The fact that polished rose diamonds were sent from Antwerp confirms the idea that this type was more frequently available in Antwerp than in Amsterdam or London.[89]

The various attempts of Ruben Levy to sell his diamonds in Antwerp through Dormer, notwithstanding its limited success, is proof that a running business correspondence that showed its profitability in the past was not something one was willing to give up easily. Regular remarks in the letters confirm this. Sometimes an unsuccessful transaction could still be valuable, since traders could see the efforts one was prepared to take for another. Since they almost certainly had more than one single contact in important places, it seems likely that the Levys knew the current prices for different kinds of diamonds at the Antwerp market, and indeed they expressed a few times their wonder that apparently Dormer was not able to sell when the prices were high.[90] The fact that members of the Levy firm travelled regularly to Antwerp in person enabled them to monitor Dormer's actions with regard to their diamonds in person. And although he returned most of the precious stones being sent to him, the Levys never really expressed a desire to completely stop this non-too-lucrative branch of their business. The fact that Dormer earned a commission on sales for the Levys is mentioned very clearly in the letters. Obviously, this was an incentive for Dormer to try his best, at least if the fee was good. If Dormer was able to make good deals, he would attract acquaintances of the Levys who might be interested in trying to include Dormer in their operations. It was a combination of self-interest, someone else's interest and the possibility to confirm a reputation with an acquaintance and establish a new one with somebody else. On the other hand, paying Dormer for his efforts, even if they did not maximize the profits, would ensure the Levys that the business connection they had with Antwerp could be maintained. As such, it seems that sometimes they set a price and in the end agreed to sell at a lower one, so that Dormer could have his commission and the Levys could have their profit.[91] Commission sales could, however, never compete with the role Ruben Levy and other Ashkenazim played as suppliers of diamonds for Dormer and his partners.

Rough diamonds arrived in Amsterdam, but it seems probable that Ruben Levy and others, because of their good kinship contacts across the channel, sent Dormer diamonds that they had obtained from London. On one occasion in 1743 they mentioned that they were expecting stones from Lisbon.[92]

It is unlikely that Ashkenazim who had come from Eastern Europe had extensive Portuguese business contacts with regard to the diamond trade and it is a good guess to assume that Levy received these diamonds through illegal channels. Portuguese sailors are known to have smuggled diamonds into Amsterdam and Ruben Norden is mentioned in literature as a trader who grew rich from contraband trade.[93] Still, most diamonds that the Ashkenazim sold came from London, and a substantial amount of them had arrived there through business with India. A lot of Ashkenazi diamond traders had personal representatives operating in India, a link that needs further research to establish the exact scope of the Ashkenazi network. Research on the Jewish community in India confirms once more the scientific focus on Sephardic merchants. Although their number was higher than that of the Ashkenazim, the latter did have a substantial representation in India.[94] A certain Moses Salomons received permission from the East India Company to settle in India as a free merchant.[95] Samuel Moses had received such permission as well, although it is not clear if he went to Fort St George to stay there or whether he had only planned one voyage. It was merely specified that he could go out 'on the usual Terms in the Diamond Trade'.[96] Sometimes, merchants in London provided their co-religionists in Asia with more than commercial products and in 1748 Assur Isaac Levy asked and received permission to send a parcel of books in the Hebrew language to Bombay, for a total value of twenty pounds sterling.[97] Requests to send Hebrew books return a few times in the Company's court books and are clear proof of the presence of Ashkenazi traders in Bombay, Fort St George and also Cochin.

Whether the Norden and Levy firms who were in business with Dormer had such direct business links with India remains an open question. Their family members are found in the court minute books of the English East India Company, amongst the merchants who asked the Company for permission to send silver or precious stones to Bombay or Fort St George in India in order to buy diamonds. Amongst these relatives was the firm of Levy and Ruben Salomons, who were amongst the biggest exporters of silver in their extended family. Table 4.2 gives the value of products sent to India by members of the Norden and Salomons families in exchange for diamonds between 1743 and 1758.

Table 4.2: Shipments to India to purchase diamonds, 1743–58.[98]

London firm	Silver (ounces)	Pearls and precious stones (£)	Coral (£)
Levy & Ruben Salomons	187,000	11,670	625
Henry & Peter Muilman & Joseph Salomons	24,000	110	0
Nathan Salomons	29,320	0	0
Michael Salomons	4,000	0	0
Aaron Norden & Salomon Norden Jr	26,000	0	0
Total	270,320	11,780	625

Apart from silver, pearls and precious stones such as rubies or emeralds, coral was a highly demanded product for export to India.[99] It seems more than likely that a lot of the diamonds they obtained were sent to Amsterdam, where they came into the hands of Dormer's Ashkenazi contacts. Nathan and Joseph Salomons were sons of Baerent Salomons, while Michael was a son of Joseph. Michael Salomons had started writing to Dormer in 1756, and from his first letter it is clear that he wanted to start a regular correspondence. Although Michael's father maintained a small correspondence with Dormer, it seems that he had a different agent in Antwerp at the time.[100] Michael wrote that he wanted to trade on the Antwerp market through Dormer, he himself not being acquainted with the buyers there, and that he would

> allow you [Dormer] as my father Mr Joseph Salomons allowes Mr J. B. de Clerq at your place, that is 1% comission & 1% delivadro & if you encourage me, you may depend I shall do largely with you, as I have as much opportunity to get all sorts of diamands as anney [any] one in the trade, therefore anney sorts of diamands there is a demand at your place advice me, & you may depend I shall send you the said sort, as I do at present largely in diamands & send to A'dam.[101]

In October 1754, the court books of the East India Company mentioned a Joseph Moses, free merchant leaving for Fort St George in India, who asked permission to take Michael Salomons with him as a menial servant.[102] The Moses family was another Ashkenazi family with family ties to the others.[103] It is possible that Joseph Salomons had sent one of his younger sons to India in the service of an acquaintance to work in the diamond trade, and that when Michael Salomons came back to London he wanted to enter himself in the diamond business, looked for a contact in Antwerp and wrote to Dormer. Another son of Joseph, Henry Salomons, had started to write Dormer in 1758 but the correspondence was very short-lived because the Englishman died unexpectedly later that year. A remarkable name found in Table 4.2 is that of Henry and Peter Muilman. These bankers resided in London, but were originally Dutch and Henry Muilman was a director in the South Sea Company.[104] The books demonstrate that they often purchased diamonds from India in partnership with Joseph Salomons. Not much more is known about their relationship with Salomons, but the latter appointed Henry Muilman as one of the executors of his will, and assigned a payment of two hundred pounds sterling to Muilman for his efforts.[105] Their partnership in shipments with Joseph Salomons indicates that Dormer's involvement with the Ashkenazi network was not an isolated case.

In spite of these recurrent relationships with non-Jewish entrepreneurs, the Ashkenazim who corresponded with Dormer were not really interested in developing a strong reciprocal relationship with Dormer. They operated within a kinship circuit, the network of Ashkenazi families of London and Amsterdam, and they needed a commercial agent in Antwerp in order to include that city's market in their business. At the time, there was no real Jewish trading community in Antwerp, and if Ruben Levy and others wanted to be active on that market, they needed Christian correspondents. Furthermore, the Ashkenazim never had the historical ties to the Brabant city that the Portuguese Jews had. When Ashkenazi migration reached high levels, Antwerp had already lost its economic dominance. It was therefore logical that more Eastern European Jews came to more tolerant cities such as Amsterdam or London. This made several traders in precious stones look for correspondents in Antwerp, showing that that city might have lost its predominant position in the diamond business to London and Amsterdam, but that it still played an important role in international diamond trade networks.

Trust, Intimacy and Mobility

It has been shown that in the diamond trade, Ashkenazi businessmen did have contacts outside kinship and religious relations, but that they chose to rely to a large extent on a diaspora network that existed between Amsterdam, London and India. This meant that they were direct competitors of other commercial circuits, including the cross-cultural trade network in which Dormer was involved. Although he remained an outsider to Ashkenazi kinship circuits, the correspondence between Dormer and Ruben Levy was of a comparable intimate nature as the letters written between Dormer and the Salvador firm. Ruben Levy was not as close a friend of Dormer as Joseph Salvador was, but the letters written by him reveal a similar creation of familiarity. He wished Dormer and his family happy Christmas and New Year, and he frequently expressed his concerns when Dormer was ill with a fever.[106] There was, however, a difference in personal contact. When Jacob Elias Levy went to Antwerp, credit or lodging was not asked from Dormer. Instead, gratitude was expressed for Dormer's polite attitude towards Jacob Levy.[107] No personal favours were asked or given, and not a single letter that Ruben Levy sent to Dormer remained silent on concrete transactions between Dormer and Levy – bills of exchange, diamonds and bullion trade.

Still, there are signs that the Levys considered Dormer to be more than just a correspondent. In 1745, two daughters of Jacob Elias Levy were to be married. In June, Ruben Levy wrote Dormer that 'since we consider you amongst our best friends, we ask you to give us the honour to be present with your loved one and family during our joy and honour it with your presence to assist in celebrating'.[108] Marriages were very important events within the diaspora, and expense was not spared, which was one of the reasons why the leaders of the Ashkenazi community in Amsterdam decided to regulate the spending allowed on marriages and similar festivities in 1747.[109] This shows that the invitation sent to Dormer was perhaps not all that exceptional, as it was decided that no more than thirty families could attend the festivities, with the exemption of Portuguese Jews and foreigners who could be invited beyond that number.[110] Dormer did not attend the wedding, but his absence did not do the relationship with Levy any harm, and not much later, the Englishman was invited to the marriage of the second daughter of Jacob Elias Levy and the son of Ruben Levy.[111] The fact that, although Dormer's relationship with Levy was different on a personal level than the one he maintained with Joseph Salvador, many similarities can be found in the intimacy of the correspondence, suggests that mercantile relationships became increasingly standardized in manners.[112]

The commercial relationship between Dormer and Levy was fortified by meetings in person that allowed for direct contact and oral agreements. Jacob Elias Levy, associate and brother of Ruben Levy, travelled on a regular basis between Amsterdam and Antwerp, as well as Jacob Norden, although his affairs in Antwerp seem to have been restricted to financial transactions. Often transactions that had been discussed in letters developed into something concrete when Jacob Levy came to Antwerp to talk things through with Dormer. In 1744, he travelled at least six times to Antwerp, sometimes to conduct financial transactions, but mostly to buy polished rose diamonds.[113] On one occasion, Ruben Levy wrote specifically that his brother had the intention to travel to Antwerp, but that he decided not to leave Amsterdam because 'if we don't have an occasion for made good [polished diamonds] than it is not worth the trouble to travel there [Antwerp] from our house'.[114] This type of remark occurs at various times in the business correspondence. In 1746 for instance, Ruben Levy required an answer from Dormer whether it was worthwhile for them to travel to Antwerp, because the market seemed rather bad at the time the letter was written.[115] This means that Dormer was an important information channel for the Levys and that they trusted his advice.

The absence of this type of contact in the relationship Dormer maintained with his fellow network members is striking, and provides one of the most important differences between them and the Ashkenazim. The latter's mobility was even seen as a serious threat to the diamond business of others. Francis Salvador expressed such fear in a letter written to Dormer in the beginning of 1746:

> Those people from Amsterdam [the Ashkenazim] make Trucks for polished diamonds and they have brothers cousins and nephews they send to all the fairs and courts of Germany which we cannot do ... I will send you by my next the prices of small roses and brilliants as you desire, but beg you send me none except it be some trifles to try the market, since our German Jews run from one end of the town to another which I can not do, nor any of my family.[116]

This seems to confirm the image of established and wealthy Sephardim feeling threatened by dynamic Ashkenazi newcomers. The reference to the German fairs is particularly interesting, since the Levys frequently sent family members to the Leipzig fairs. This passage suggests that they sold diamonds there. According to literature, Ashkenazi traders had a tradition of dealing in finished products and jewels, which were sold and bought at fairs.[117] The Leipzig fairs were held three times a year, for two to three weeks, and although trade fairs had lost importance since the Renaissance, they continued to play an important role in commerce, also in linking the Atlantic economy with Eastern Europe.[118] These fairs attracted a wide range of merchants arriving from all over Europe. The spring and fall fairs of 1752 had attracted 6,451 visitors for several weeks.[119] Herbert Bloom cites a number of 484 Jewish visitors at the Leipzig Easter fair of 1756, and that ten came from Holland. Dutch Jews started to frequent the Leipzig fairs regularly after 1675, with firms often visiting at least one of the fairs each year, and the number of Dutch Jews sometimes outnumbering the number of Dutch Christian traders that travelled to the fair. English Ashkenazim also travelled to Germany. The synagogue of the London Ashkenazi community had a rule that persons who travelled frequently to the continent were not to be elected for administrative offices. Several merchants were mentioned in this context that had acquired passes for the Leipzig fairs.[120] 2,496 were mentioned to have visited the fair of 1756, a number in accordance with the 6,451 mentioned for the three fairs of 1752.[121]

Jacob Elias Levy and Jacob Norden both undertook voyages to the fairs in Leipzig. Norden visited the spring fairs of 1744 and 1745.[122] The transactions that they conducted in Germany remain unknown but secondary literature shows that many of the Dutch Jews came to purchase Silesian linen, destined to be shipped to St Eustatius.[123] Books of the Dutch East India Company make it clear that Ruben Levy & Company did trade in textiles, as the books for the years 1724 to 1728 mentioned Ruben Levy selling cotton cloth for a total amount 10,125 guilders.[124] The letters to Dormer remain vague on the nature of trade that had taken place in Germany. After coming back from the spring fair of 1744, Levy just expressed his happiness that the Leipzig fair had been reasonably advantageous for them and that he had bought many different goods.[125] A letter written the following year indicates that Ruben Levy used the Leipzig fair as one of his main sources of gold and silver, as he wrote to Dormer in June 1745 that he had sent him 650 ducats and that the coins were purchased by his partner at the Leipzig fair that year.[126]

The larger personal mobility of the Levy firm was a vital difference with the cross-cultural network. It might indicate that the level of trust maintained within that circuit was never reached by Dormer and Levy. The English merchant was not a member of the Ashkenazi network and he had no direct contacts with the Ashkenazi suppliers in London. Rationally, he could suspect that if problems were to arise, their interdependent family ties would prove to be stronger than the ties he had with them. This problem did not exist in the cross-cultural network, which was not based on kinship ties. In its diversity, it was less likely that some merchants would actively seek disadvantage of others. Secondly, Dormer acted mainly as the Antwerp correspondent of Levy, Norden and Salomons. This meant an important feature of the cross-cultural trade network was absent in Dormer's relationship with the Ashkenazim: reciprocity. The forging of trustworthy ties between him and the Ashkenazim might have required face-to-face encounters.

The visits of Jacob Levy should be seen as an active attempt to construct a more trustworthy relationship and the absence or much more sporadic nature of similar visits in the cross-cultural network show that the latter's organization worked. If Salvador was to visit Antwerp regularly to achieve the same, the use of the network, so carefully crafted, would be partially obsolete. This does not mean that business was consciously organized to build a trustworthy relationship. The difference between personal visits as a consequence of lack of trust or as an attempt to built trust is largely theoretical. Both ideas imply a lack of trust, and persons were not purely rational economic individuals taking a stagecoach to Antwerp with the concrete idea of building trust. It is a reaction that is both rational as well as sentimental, deriving from a problem of trustworthiness. The combination of rationality and feeling as the trigger of action is vital since otherwise, network analysis based on trust would be an artificial construction.[127]

The fact that the relationship between Dormer and the Ashkenazim relied less on an established trustworthy relationship is shown by the fact that at times, Ruben Levy specifically mentioned his good reputation in order to ensure his English correspondent in Antwerp that he worked with honest merchants ('Eerlijke Cooplieden').[128] This did not prevent for some commercial disagreements from occurring. In February 1746, Dormer was angry over a transaction in coins involving the firm of Andries Pels. The Englishman was of the opinion that he had given orders to the Levys to act as agents between him and Pels, while the Levy firm did not know anything about the transaction. Ruben Levy wrote that he was surprised by Dormer's anger, and that in his opinion the firm did not make any mistake. He expressed the desire to continue a harmonic relationship, but also wrote that Dormer was 'free to say whether he didn't take satisfaction with their correspondence but it would thank God not be disadvantageous to them'.[129] The affair remained without consequences, but Ruben Levy's letter is an indication that the loyalty between the two merchants was not particularly high and if at that time Dormer would have decided to abandon the correspondence, the Levys would have accepted it. A second friction took place only two months later. Dormer was suddenly reluctant to trade in bills given by the Levys and the Nordens and seemed to have lost his confidence in their creditworthiness. Levy answered that they had bought gold, silver and diamonds for many years, and that they had sent large parties of diamonds to previous correspondents. According to Levy, Dormer must have received information from jealous individuals.[130] Ruben Levy was quite upset. He had been trading for many years with Dormer without difficulty, and during those years 'you [Dormer] didn't know us as much as the tenth part as now'.[131] Ruben Levy stretched that Dormer knew them well, knew their practices and sincerity, and he was not amused that jealous and malicious traders could change his opinion. The message is quite clear: Dormer should have known better, in a relationship in which trust was based on a belief in personal reputation through experience. Again, the affair did not have consequences. As quickly as the trouble had started, business was resumed as usual. Levy's strong reaction in both affairs, especially in the second case, is logical. If Dormer had a problem with trading in their bills of exchange because of certain information he had received, the problem could expand rapidly. A merchant's reputation was one of his more valuable assets, and the Levys obviously knew that Dormer had different correspondents to whom he might spread harmful information regarding the business mentality of the Levys.

Competition and Loyalty

Different merchants involved in the cross-cultural trade network, or at least close to it, saw the Ashkenazi kinship networks as rivals and they complained about their way of doing business. In 1749, Abraham van Moses Lopes Suasso observed the low price at which Jacob Elias Levy was selling diamonds.[132] He wrote to Dormer that 'nous ne sommes pas surpris, puisque nous savons leur manière d'agir et nous ne doutons point qu'après que ces messieurs seront partis vous pourrez avec beaucoup plus de facilité vous défaire de notre partie au prix que nous vous l'avons limité'.[133] In a letter written two months later, Suasso referred again to the low selling prices and wrote that everything would change if those 'messieurs' [the Levys] would stop to sell 'à des prix si honteux'.[134] The Suasso firm was not the only one to complain. Thomas and Adrian Hope also mentioned difficulties with Jacob Levy: 'we know him very well and are not unacquainted with ye nature of ye trade of ye Jews both in your parts and here, but we have never seen instances of their being Dupes, or Knaves, to their own prejudice'.[135] The business practices of Jacob and Ruben Levy remained a source of concern for them, and on different occasions Thomas and Adrian wrote that they did not understand the secret of the Levys, referring to their low prices. More merchants expressed their worries about the firm of Ruben Levy. In 1753, Isabella de Coninck, who was working for Dormer in Amsterdam after her husband died, wrote that nobody in Amsterdam dared to sell to Ruben Levy & Company, and she called them people full of 'alteration'. She did not even want to write the things Ruben Levy did to ruin the trade, but assured Dormer that she would tell him in person when she would come back to Antwerp.[136]

Not only were the Ashkenazi firms seen as undermining the market, they were clearly labelled as belonging to a different trade circuit. The Hopes remained determined to beat the competition: 'les Levys ... ils ne pouront pas lutter contre nous'.[137] Francis Salvador called them 'our German Jews', all brothers, cousins and nephews, and he felt threatened by their dynamism and family ties. For many merchants, the Levy family was not very reputable, and was involved in another network that competed with theirs. It is also clear that there was a divide on cultural and religious differences, since Francis Salvador had made a clear distinction between German Jews and other Jews, although he still used 'our' to indicate some affiliation. The fact that Dormer traded with Ruben Levy questions his loyalty to the network and the question arises whether Dormer's partners knew of his involvement with Ruben Levy and other Ashkenazi firms. Although network membership was based on a certain notion of insiders and outsiders, it did not stop merchants from conducting business with others. Loyalty had its boundaries, and although individual self-interest was not the only motive for commerce, it still remained one of the most important elements.

Dormer's involvement with the Levys poses a question of confidentiality. Once, Dormer complained to Joseph Salvador about Jacob Levy, and Salvador wrote back: 'I observe what you mention about Jacob Levy spoiling the trade of diamonds at your place you will now find that my thoughts were right.'[138] This poses the question whether Dormer was in the end more loyal to the network he belonged to, or whether he just wanted to keep his correspondence with Levy undisclosed. Secrecy was an important feature of the diamond trade, with its high level of contraband trade. At different times, Ruben Levy wrote to Dormer that his brother was to come to Antwerp, and he asked at the same time to keep the news secret.[139] One time, Ruben Levy had sent diamonds to Antwerp so that Dormer could sell them and he specified that he had to keep it secret from Isabella de Coninck. If she asked about the diamonds, Dormer had to say they came from London.[140] Secrecy was not only important in order to benefit best from particular information or certain opportunities. A merchant's reputation was partially based on his commercial behaviour. This also meant reliability on a technical level, something that was particularly important in the diamond trade.[141] A loyal and trustworthy merchant that was careless or neglectful in his calculations would soon lose his reputation. In 1744, Ruben Levy & Company sent two parcels of diamonds to Dormer to be sold by him for Levy's account on the Antwerp market. Not much later, Jacob Elias Levy came to Antwerp personally, and since the diamonds (54 carats in total) were still unsold, Dormer handed them over to Jacob, who sold them to a customer in Antwerp himself. He neglected to weigh them again after he had received them from Dormer, and apparently 2 carats were missing. Ruben Levy asked Dormer whether he had weighed the stones after reception from Amsterdam. They also asked to read the particular passage of the letter concerning these diamonds to Isabella de Coninck, Dormer's agent but to keep it secret beyond that.[142] Nobody liked to be known as careless, or as a merchant who would lose merchandise, especially not when one was dealing in diamonds, a valuable commodity that was sold in small portions. Precision in calculations was important, not only to prevent commercial loss, but also to prevent loss of reputation.

Trust and loyalty implied that trading partners were supposed to respect demands for secrecy, but Dormer breached the confidentiality that Ruben Levy had asked for. In 1749 there seems to have been a particularly fierce competition between the Levys and the cross-cultural network, and both parties tried to undersell each other. Dormer became worried and wrote to Francis Salvador that he could not sell at the same low prices as Ruben Levy, and that the trade he did in partnership with Salvador would suffer. Salvador had to send several letters to assure him that the Levys would not choose to sell at a loss, and that their activities would not be that harmful to their business, although Dormer's letters made him worry.[143] When he had loyalty to give, it was given to network members, although it did not mean that Dormer extended this loyalty to concrete business affairs. Loyalty did not stop him from trading directly with the competition, at times when it was beneficial to him.

It is remarkable that Dormer could so easily separate his different contacts, and write bad news about one to the other. Self-interest was a stronger motivator than loyalty simply for loyalty's sake. One of the defining characteristics of merchants as it can be distilled from the letters they wrote to each other was that, since their profits per transaction were not very high, they constantly looked for opportunities, and wished to keep possible trade channels with other merchants open whenever possible, especially when these channels had proved to be successful in the past and provided them with information. Business was uncertain, as were supply and demand, and it was absolutely vital to receive regular updates with regard to commercial but also political facts that could influence trade opportunities, so that risks resulting from a one-time short-term profitable venture did not win out against the long-term idea. In a system of personal relationships where trust was so important, one's reputation was not risked easily to pursue purely one's own interest in the short run. These theoretical findings seem to be in accordance with the practical evidence found in the many letters that were sent to Dormer, and long-term interest was definitively one of the main pursuits of a merchant.

Dormer's double loyalty demonstrates that long-term interest was not the only motivation. At times, traders did pursue their short-term self-interest, and by this they were risking their longer commitments. Dormer breached Levy's demand for confidentiality, and he also breached the loyalty he had in the circuit involving the Salvadors. He complained about Levy to Salvador, but did not mention the fact that at times he acted as his agent for diamond sales in Antwerp. If it was revealed to Salvador that Levy was a regular correspondent of Dormer, and if Levy knew that Dormer did not always keep things confidential, the reputation of the Englishman might have suffered a great deal. In a world that relied on cooperation, reciprocity and mutual interest, the importance of a moral aspect to commercial reputation is very real and it makes it all the more remarkable that Dormer was tempted to break certain codes in order to pursue his own interest. But if we see his complaints to Salvador as a genuine description of his own feelings, rather than a purely calculative attempt to play different groups against each other so he could draw the benefits from that, the story becomes more understandable. Perhaps he did not consider Ruben Levy as entirely reputable. Different merchants in the cross-cultural network did not consider them totally honest, and Francis Salvador expressed very negative feelings towards them, perhaps most clearly demonstrated by his use of the word *smous*, a word that was used against Jews which also meant swindler.[144] The use of this negative word by Salvador is particularly interesting. It could be that it was only directed to Ashkenazi Jews, and that Salvador wanted to make a clear distinction between them and the (in his eyes) more reputable religious group to which he belonged. In considering the Levys not completely honest, Dormer perhaps would feel relieved from the moral obligation to be honest with them. Honesty and loyalty should go both ways and perhaps Dormer felt that this was not the case in his involvement with an extensive kinship network. Although this might explain his attitude towards Ruben Levy & Company, it fails to explain why he put his loyalty towards the cross-cultural diamond network in jeopardy. It stands beyond doubt that in Dormer's eyes Salvador's reputation was entirely good. It seems that long-term commitment was up to a point combinable with short-term self-interest. After all, in carefully analysing mechanisms at work in eighteenth-century trade relationships, one should not forget that merchants were not always rational. Not all their actions would be directed towards a conscious construction of trust. This personal agency was only one of the factors at work. And there was no full transparency. As long as Salvador did not know the extent or exact nature of the relationship between Dormer and Levy, the former's reputation remained unaltered in Salvador's eyes.

5 THE EMBEDDEDNESS OF MERCHANTS IN STATE AND SOCIETY

Most of the merchants that belonged to the cross-cultural diamond trade network belonged to a group of outsiders. Dormer came from England to settle first in Flanders, than in Brabant. A similar trajectory was taken by the Cliffords, who settled in a country in which the majority shared their religion. They did not have structural difficulties in integrating in a new society and did not have to overcome religious differences. Dormer gained entry into the local nobility, possessed a house in Antwerp and a small castle a little outside of town. Francis Mannock had experience as an English merchant abroad, when he operated out of Cadiz for a few years. The Salvador and Nunes families, as well as Paul Berthon and Peter Garnault, were outsiders who had a harder time settling abroad, because of their embeddedness within a religious diaspora. The strong attachment of Joseph Salvador and other Sephardic merchants to the Jewish diaspora and religion had consequences with regard to their relationships with the host society within which they had settled. This rang also true for the members of the Levy, Norden and Salomons families with whom Dormer maintained a correspondence.

Because of their attachment to an international community, diaspora merchants are often considered in the light of their contribution to forms of globalization. If worldwide integration is thought of as occurring through personal connections and interdependencies across the globe, it is of crucial importance not only to study these international personal relationships, but also to analyse the different societies within which global actors were embedded. Otherwise, international human webs such as diasporas cannot possess the necessary agency to bring about the large-scale interconnectedness that is a characteristic of globalization. The search for a place in English and Portuguese society by respectively the Salvador family and the Berthon & Garnault firm shows that they were aiming at more than the giving up of their diaspora identity for membership of a host society. One could feel Jewish as well as English, and one could also be a French Huguenot and an English merchant at the same time. Especially for merchants, who were often operating on an international scale, it seems that many aspects of daily life regarding eighteenth-century identity were the same for the person experiencing them, whether he was an Ashkenazi Jew, Sephardic Jew or Huguenot. Adaptation was not a process in which terms were dictated by the host society and the integration of foreigners in early modern societies was a process that took place by reciprocal interaction. Acknowledging this leaves the possibility of globalization through international human networks open.

Merchants Between Diaspora and Society

The Threat of the Outsider

Merchants were considered to be a different group with a separate identity and, historically, societies often have reacted towards them with hostility. This can be partially explained by the perceived threat to social tissue posed by distinctive immigrant groups. Societies are based on a certain social division or hierarchy. Such organization comes from a variety of elements, but historically religious systems have often played an important role.[1] These not only serve to justify the way in which a society is organized and the rules it adopts, but also contributes to social cohesion by group identification that is also expressed in daily practice, tradition, rituals and customs. Certain practices serve not only to fortify social cohesion and suggest cultural unity, but also to confirm an order. The foreigner in his appearance alone could be looked at as a threat to order. Dress codes or other ornaments could imply status, connected with a certain position in society. Such external elements were sometimes exclusive and tied to specific rules. Not everybody could appropriate the symbols of a certain class, and foreigners were often seen as upsetting social order. This was subject to debate in the eighteenth century and a commentary appearing in the *London Chronicle* of 1773 stated that if certain dress codes could be adopted freely, it would lead to the forgetting of 'those necessary Distinctions that arise from Age, Rank, or Profession'.[2] Such comments are seen as expressions of experiencing social change, and were directed at a more commercialized society, who were perceived to be 'undermining the integrity and reliability of familiar categories of social distinction'.[3] A resistance to social mobility or possible evolutionary effects caused by contacts with outside elements would be a logical reaction from the side in control.

A second motive for the negative perception of foreigners in local societies was their common association with commerce. Throughout history, trade has often been seen as a negative activity, driven by negative feelings. The idea that the political participation of citizens was hard to reconcile with commercial activities was to become popular again in seventeenth- and eighteenth-century republicanism.[4] Charles Davenant, writing at the end of the seventeenth century, had adopted a negative attitude towards trade: 'Trade, without doubt, is in its nature a pernicious thing; it brings in that wealth which introduces luxury; it gives rise to fraud and avarice, and extinguishes virtue and simplicity of manners'.[5] Luxury can be seen as the desire to show one's wealth by possessing goods that are not needed. As such, it conflicted with the sin of pride, and could also disturb the language of hierarchy adopted by society, as demonstrated in fashion. Not everybody could dress the same way, and privilege was something that money could not always buy.[6] The pursuit of luxury was perceived as harmful in different ways: demonstrating sin, corrupting society and upsetting the social order that was based on hierarchy. Social inequality has often been justified in religious terms, especially in the *Ancien Régime*, and what was perhaps originally a divine ordering of society should not be challenged by egoistic, wealth-seeking individuals.[7]

The idea of social advancement based on a selfish search for financial profit was considered problematic by certain thinkers who started to see the rise of a commercial society in light of the destruction of an older society that was based on other values. This line of thought is shared by conservative thinking, as it was developed as an important criticism of thinkers holding onto the ideals of the Enlightenment. Selfishness was destructive to the community and the tradition of seeing personal gain as detrimental to others and to society has a long history that goes back to ancient thinkers, and that has been revived by conservative thinkers, such as Justus Möser in the eighteenth century, who saw the particularity of Osnabrück society, where he lived, as threatened by arrival of international commerce.[8] This community feeling is connected to the idea of social order. Christianity did not simply justify society's structure as the will of God without further explanation; there were rules to be followed. In a scheme of moral categories of acts, commerce was connected to avarice, the search for wealth and luxury, also connected to the cardinal sin of pride. These condemnations did not even need the argument of damage done to fellow man; the pursuit of profit in itself was already sufficient for some to be hostile to commerce.[9] Negative characteristics of trade were applied to become negative characteristics of a merchant, and because of the importance of religion in shaping early modern societies, they sometimes became attached to other religions that were already seen as threatening and has contributed to the stereotyping of non-Christian religions.[10]

The eighteenth century saw the rise of theories that relied on self-interest and passion as human character traits that contributed to the foundation of society, rather than destroying it, and offered a different view on trade.[11] Eighteenth-century thinkers inspired their theories on their own perception of changes in society and the development of self-interest as a pillar of society indicates a growing commercialization of society, something that was equally hinted at by public opinion that still doubted the presence of foreign merchants. The two most common objections of public opinion with regard to outsiders, their identification as strangers and their association with commerce, determined the dialogue between diaspora movements and the host society. This dialogue did not take place in one direction and did not lead to a simple assimilation. In his work on migration, Patrick Manning wrote about Creole societies that were culturally mixed and that had developed new hierarchies based on race, religion, ethnicity and legal status.[12] Society was in constant motion, and hence hierarchy was up to some point always under a certain negotiation. It is in this sense that the embeddedness of outsiders within a host society is of vital importance when considering global change that was brought about by international and cross-cultural commercial networks. It shows how traders belonging to these networks managed to tie regions and societies closer together, not only by developing a cosmopolitan outlook but also by integrating locally in a manner that changed both their host society as well as themselves. It is well put by Dror Wahrman that London in the eighteenth century counted so many different strangers that they became familiar figures.[13]

Joseph Salvador was a merchant and a prominent member of London's Sephardic community. His biography can be read in a traditional way. His family had come to London and set up a business that gained considerable wealth in the diamond trade with India. There are no signs that Salvador had turned his back on the Jewish faith, as for instance Samson Gideon had done, the most noteworthy financier of mid-eighteenth-century England. The desire for acculturation that motivated wealthy Jews in their social behaviour seems an underlying factor in different literature on Anglo-Jewry.[14] For Lucy Sutherland, Gideon was the example *par excellence* of an integration combined with an abandoning of the diaspora:

> About this time, [1742] Gideon had set his foot on the social ladder he meant to climb. Like so many who achieved wealth in the eighteenth century, he formed the ambition of using it to found a family which could take its place among those of the landed classes. In his case, and in the circumstances of the time, this meant ultimately the cutting himself off from his religion and from the associates of his past.[15]

It seems that two different mechanisms, which were active in two different spaces, played a complementary role. The acculturation-idea of Jewish wealthy merchants seems to suggest that a strong community feeling within Sephardic Jewry existed, but that the members of the diaspora that became successful left that community. Since literature on diaspora emphasizes trade, it suggests a mere teleological reading of the diaspora: that it is used to achieve wealth, and is left behind once wealth is achieved. It reduces human relationships to a means and does not correspond with the multiple positions diaspora merchants were able to take in society, locally as well as internationally.

Joseph Salvador as a Member of the Anglo-Jewish Elite

Francis Salvador belonged to a family that had fled Portugal for fear of religious persecution.[16] Members of the family first went to France, before settling in London and Amsterdam. Around 1670, members of the Salvador family that carried the last name Jessurun Rodrigues can be found in Rouen, in connection with other Sephardim.[17] Around that time, they changed the family name, and 'subsequent generations of the Rodrigues family assumed different family names depending on the name of the patriarch. Thus the children of Salvador Rodrigues alias Josua Jessurun Rodrigues adopted the family name Salvador'.[18] Around the turn of the century, different Salvadors already lived in London and some figured amongst a group of Jewish money-lenders to the British King for the payment of Dutch troops in Flanders.[19] One of Joseph's grandchildren was the first family member to be baptized. He even became a reverend and changed his name to John Lovell. This departure from the Jewish community remained an exception and as members of the Sephardic diaspora, the Salvadors were firmly attached to other families in Amsterdam and London by marriage.

Perhaps the strongest kinship ties were maintained within the Mendes da Costa family. A brother of Joseph Salvador's grandfather had married a Rachel Mendes da Costa and Francis Salvador, Joseph's father, married a Mendes da Costa as well.[20] In 1738, at the age of twenty-two, Joseph had married Rachel Lopes Suasso, daughter of Isaac Antonio Lopes, third Baron Suasso.[21] Salvador wrote to Dormer that 'I have taken your Example and got married'.[22] The Lopes Suasso family belonged to Amsterdam's Sephardic Jewish aristocracy. Born and raised in Bordeaux as a second-generation immigrant from Portugal, Antonio Lopes Suasso had settled in Amsterdam in 1653, where he married Rachel de Pinto. His business affairs in diamonds, precious stones, bullion and Campeche wood made him a prosperous man and by 1674 he was probably the wealthiest member of the Sephardic community in Amsterdam. He died in 1685 and was succeeded by his only son Francisco, the grandfather of Joseph Salvador's wife. He supported the Prince of Orange in the 1688 invasion of England and granted him a significant loan.[23] Both men enjoyed a close relationship, and according to Swetschinski, 'until William's death in 1702, Don Francisco remained a welcome and appreciated courtier in London and in The Hague'.[24] The grandmother of the wife of Joseph Salvador belonged to one of the most prominent Sephardic families. The de Pinto family was of high standing in Amsterdam and had business connections with Joseph Salvador who acted as a London agent for Isaac de Pinto, who lived in Amsterdam and was a pensioner of the Dutch East India Company.[25] De Pinto was an economic thinker who published treaties on money circulation and credit, and even found himself in a controversy with Voltaire regarding the Jewish religion.[26]

Joseph's sister Sarah married Moses Franco. The Franco family was one of the families that gained a lot of financial success in the diamond-coral trade through Leghorn.[27] Another sister of Joseph, Abigail, married Jacob Pereira de Paiba. Different members of that family worked in London in the diamond trade as brokers.[28] If one is to believe what Joseph Salvador wrote to Dormer in 1741, one of his sisters, the eldest, was going to marry a marquis. In that year, Salvador asked Dormer to buy textiles for 'the marquis who is going to marry my Eldest Sister'.[29] The youngest sister of Joseph, Rebecca, had married Moses da Costa, a merchant who was active in the Anglo-Indian diamond-coral trade.[30]

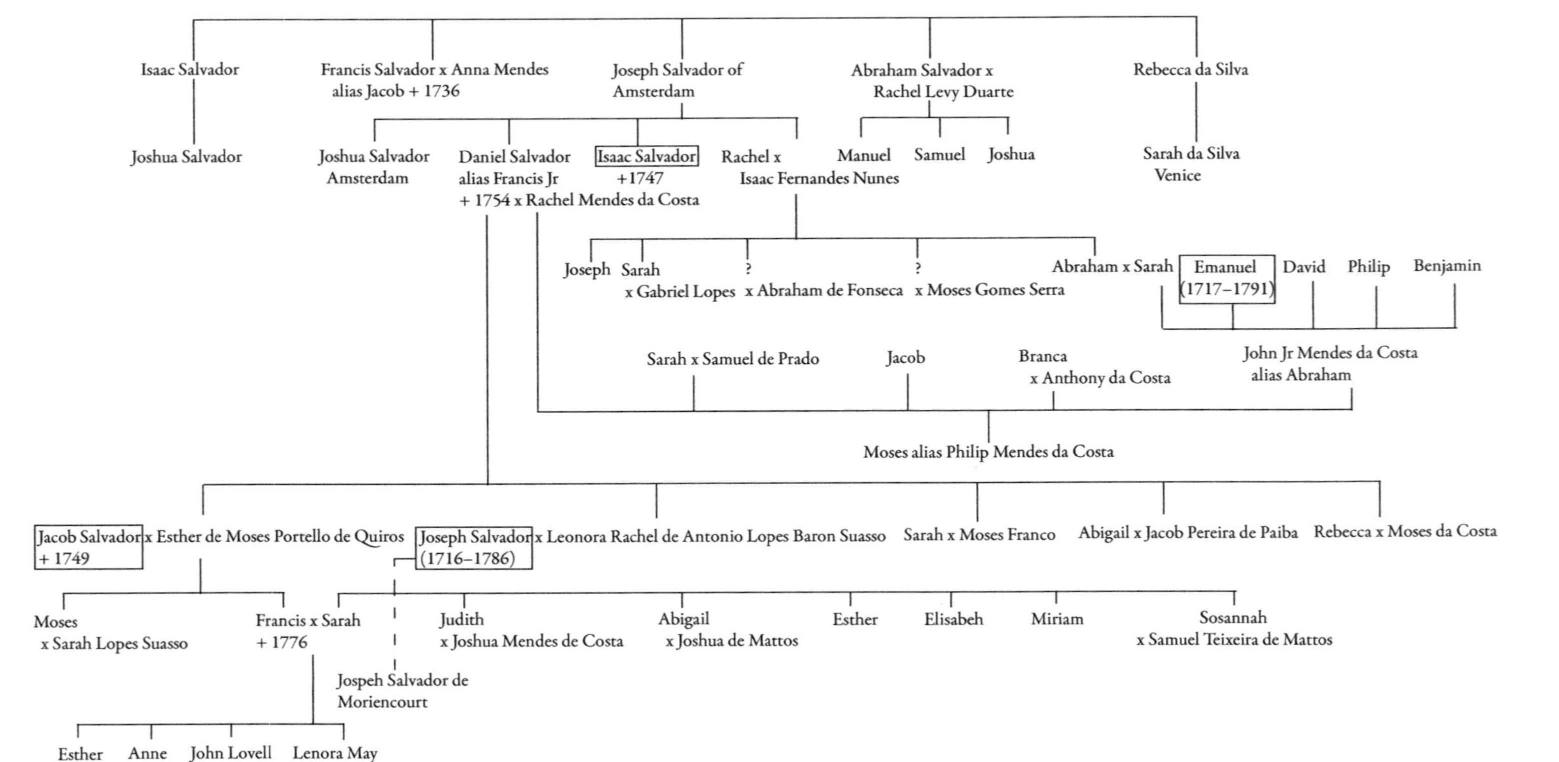

Figure 5.1: Salvador family tree.[31]

By marriage, the Salvadors were strongly linked to the foremost Sephardic families in England and Holland. Joseph's only brother Jacob married Esther Portello de Quiros. After the early death of her husband, she married a second time, with Abraham Prado. They lived in Twickenham, as did Jacob's oldest son.[32]

The marriage patterns of the children of Jacob and Joseph Salvador are no different. Three of Joseph's daughters married within the Jewish community. Judith married Joshua Mendes da Costa and Susanna married a member of the Teixeira de Mattos family. The Teixeira de Mattos family was part of Amsterdam's Jewish elite and was also married within the Lopes Suasso family.[33] Jacob's son Francis married Joseph's daughter Sarah and their three children were baptized in 1780, together with their mother.[34] Jacob's other son Moses married again a Lopes Suasso. Born a year before the early death of his father, Moses married in 1771 in The Hague, where different members of the Lopes Suasso family also resided, and stayed there. The Dutch King William I made him a member of the gentry in 1821 and he was part of the commission that drafted the first constitution of the Netherlands.[35] A last marriage worth mentioning here is that of Joseph's niece Sarah, the daughter of Rebecca Salvador and Moses Mendes da Costa, with Ephraim Lopes Pereira, second Baron d'Aguilar. His name is mentioned a couple of times in letters to Dormer, all in relation to a tobacco contract that interested Dormer.[36] The example of d'Aguilar's father, an English denizen born in Portugal, was used by Gideon in his hopes to gain a noble title.[37]

The wedding patterns of three subsequent generations of Salvadors bore striking similarities: there was always a Salvador who married a Mendes da Costa, and there was also always a Salvador who married with a member of a prominent family that resided in Amsterdam. This recurrent pattern points to a strategy that was adopted by the different families, a strategy that fortified connections within Anglo-Jewry as well as with the important Jewish community of Amsterdam. David Katz has already traced the extraordinary level of intermarriage within London Jewry. Evidence shows that this level was also maintained across the channel.[38] The kinship ties based on marriage were used in business transactions of these families, as was for instance the case for Baron d'Aguilar but also for the firm of Aaron and David Fernandes Nunes.

Joseph Salvador was not only tied to the Sephardic community by kinship relations. He also used his position as a successful merchant to become a prominent and active member within the Jewish community in London. He was installed as a community leader, a *Parnas*, in 1746, and in 1761 he was a member of a committee of the Portuguese-Jewish synagogue in London to look into public affairs that might interest the Dutch and English Jewish communities.[39] According to Endelman, the well-to-do Sephardim often performed acts of charity,[40] and Joseph Salvador was no exception. Maurice Woolf claims that he was concerned in the founding of a communal hospital, the *Beth Holim*.[41] And when a

Jewish man who travelled across Europe to collect money for the poor of Hebron stopped in London, he was told to pay a visit to Joseph Salvador: 'We do not know what you can do, but if you are wise, behold Señor Joseph Salvador, who is one of the Parnassim, is going to the waters; he is very clever and whatever he says is done immediately.'[42] Apparently, Haim David Azulai, as the traveller was called, was granted a meeting with Salvador who proved to be a great help. David Katz mentioned another event that could not stress more the prominence of Joseph Salvador within the Jewish community. This event had to do with the ascension to the throne of George III. The Sephardic community wished to pay their respects, and apparently, on 11 December 1760, Joseph Salvador was given the honour of meeting the new queen and the Duke of York, together with a representative of the Great Synagogue and a representative of the Hambro Synagogue.[43] It was after this occasion that a permanent body was formed, the Board of Deputies of British Jews, of which Joseph Salvador was the president between 1766 and 1789.[44]

Joseph Salvador and other members of his family were firmly rooted in the international Sephardic diaspora. This was less the case in the personal sphere, as Todd Endelman confirms in his study on Anglo-Jewry: 'although many wealthy Jews personally strayed from the path of traditional Judaism, they still maintained strong institutional ties to Jewish life'.[45] Different from other successful Jewish merchants such as Samson Gideon, Joseph Salvador never turned his back on his faith. The rhythm of correspondence the Salvadors had with Dormer was influenced by the Shabbat. As detailed in Chapter 3, in May 1758, Joseph Salvador sent a letter to Dormer in which he expressed his desire to buy a painting for a room he was furnishing. His only instruction for Dormer was as follows: 'I am likewise deprived the use of the History of the New Testament & d° by the forms of my Religion.'[46] Perhaps these seem only details that convey almost nothing about Salvador's personal relationship with his religion, but the fact that he writes these remarks almost invisibly, between letters that otherwise are concerned with technical matters of trade or with a list of possible paintings and furniture he wished to purchase for a new room in his house, signifies something. It seems to suggest that for Salvador, his faith was not really something that was up for discussion, but that it was rather an element in his life that was there since his birth and that he saw as an integral part of himself.

Joseph Salvador as a Member of English High Society

Joseph Salvador maintained good relationships with various prominent figures in the English government and in the East India Company, and was firmly connected to several members of the English government as a financer and an advisor. His father Francis Salvador had been one of the subscribers to a loan that was raised in the light of the Austrian succession war in 1742, for an amount of £10,000 of a total loan of £321,000.[47] He was one of two Jewish subscribers, the other one being Samson Gideon. After the death of Francis Salvador, Joseph continued financing activities, and the sums increased. In April 1757 he raised £82,000 for the government, and he was involved in the large loan later that year of £3,000,000. He contributed a sum of £44,500, from himself and friends abroad. Other members of his family are to be found on the list as well. His wife subscribed £1,000, the Baron d'Aguilar £10,000 and his sister Rebecca £3,000.[48] Joseph also lent considerable funds to the East India Company during the early 1750s.[49]

The participation in loans shows the financial success of Joseph Salvador, something that helped him to gain access to a privileged segment of English society. It seems that Salvador's social status rose with the establishment of his contacts in the upper strata of English politics, for the *London Evening Post* of 10 July 1753 wrote about an event taking place at Salvador's country house: 'A few days ago, Mr. Salvador, the rich Jew who married the daughter of Baron Suasso, gave a grand entertainment at his seat at Tooting in Surrey to a great number of noblemen and gentlemen, members of both Houses of Parliament'.[50] It is unclear when Salvador purchased this estate, perhaps it was already in the family before him, but it seems that the year before this social event, he had expanded his country seat by buying land for £1,700. A couple of years later, in 1757, Salvador built a new house in the city. He settled in White Hart Court, Bishopsgate, where one of his neighbours was Baron d'Aguilar.[51] The fact that he built a new residence in 1757 might indicate that Salvador's financial problems in the 1750s had not at all driven him to poverty. The common reading of his merchant career is that he did very well in trade, but that especially after the Lisbon earthquake of 1755, his most successful days were over.[52] Surely, he had lost financially by the 1755 event, but his assets still seemed to have been more than sufficient.

The retreat of successful Jews to their country houses has been considered to be proof of their physical separation from the mass of the Jewish community.[53] As such, it would almost be the completion of the trajectory a wealthy Jew undertook in order to become accepted by English high society. His new neighbours were other successful individuals, mostly non-Jewish. The refashioning process, in which well-to-do Jews acculturated themselves to the practices of the upper class in England – dress, language, manners, recreations, diet, education and literature – now found a spatial expression in the country house. Having escaped from the urban boundaries of their own diaspora, some Sephardim were even noted to fill their houses with 'explicitly Christian paintings'.[54] The symbolical entry of Christian art into the personal intimacy of the Jewish household suggests a successful acculturation, but there are different indications that many Jewish merchants did the opposite. Joseph Salvador took great care in buying art that was not regarded as offensive to his religion.[55] Using inventories of several well-to-do Jewish merchants living in Rembrandt's Amsterdam, Michael Zell shows that other Sephardim possessed Old Testament paintings that were in accordance with their faith.[56]

Next to his country house, Joseph Salvador still owned a house in the city, where he had Jewish neighbours. At least in his case, the country house was not the evolutionary outcome of a process that drove wealthy Jews away from their community into the company of the non-Jewish elite. It was rather part of a dual setting, his town residence and his country estate, in which each of the two buildings can be considered to be a symbol of Salvador's participation in two different communities: the international Sephardic diaspora on the one hand and the English higher class on the other. In both communities, connections play a key role. In the Portuguese-Jewish community, human relationships were a means to strengthen the community, a logical incentive of a diaspora that tried to find its place within a host society. Those connections found expression in intermarriage but also in trade partnerships. Relationships were also of vital importance when regarding higher society, especially for someone who could be regarded as an outsider. It stands beyond doubt that Salvador possessed relationships that made an entry into the higher circles possible, such as Robert Clive.[57]

The idea that a wealthy individual seeking entry into one sphere had to give up membership of another holds no ground with regard to Joseph Salvador. The webs of human interaction that he constructed allowed him membership of both. It is difficult to see in the experiences of a group of wealthy Jewish merchants, of whom some left Judaism but others did not, the proof that an entire diaspora acculturated. Access to high circles was restricted to the lucky few, and the mass of Jewish individuals did not get it, just like the mass of the English population. It shows an integration process by a group of merchants who had achieved commercial success. The fact that it was a minority amongst Jewish population does not make that process unimportant. Their successful integration, which was not a process of assimilation, contributed to later developments that led to the emancipation period in the early nineteenth century and the establishment of equal rights for all Jews. Because they had the means to gain entry into the circles were policy-makers also resided, they managed to contribute to change without abandoning their Jewish culture and heritage. Although financial success might have given Salvador a way into English high class, it also made him vulnerable. He became somewhat of a celebrity in mid-eighteenth-century London and he became associated with the luxurious lifestyle of the rich and famous. He went to see plays at theatres, although he claimed he did not go much.[58] Eventually, Joseph Salvador's lifestyle caused trouble for him. According to Todd Endelman, the upper-class way of life that wealthy Sephardim embraced did not just entail physical changes, such as country houses, fashion and art, but also led to the acceptance of a code of sexual behaviour that was freer than was permitted by Jewish law and custom.[59]

Joseph Salvador had adopted some of the looser mores that were kept in the higher circles in which he moved. He was openly linked with three different women, and one of them bore him an illegitimate son. The mother of this child, the Comtesse de Moriencourt, belonged to the aristocracy in the Low Countries.[60] Their son Joseph Salvador Moriencourt served later in the British Royal Navy, where he became a lieutenant on the *Princess Royal*. He retired as an officer in command on 30 January 1816.[61] Joseph Salvador recognized his son and he was included in his last will. His natural son, as he was described in the will, was to receive the interest of £500 per year for expenses, until he turned twenty-one. At his birthday, he was to receive the remainder of the £500, a rather modest sum.[62] Little else is known about the countess and her son, but she seems to have been an acquaintance of the secretary of the French ambassador in London, le Comte de Guines. Through the countess, the secretary implicated Salvador in a plan that speculated on a conflict between England and Spain regarding the Falklands. Tort hoped to make a profit on the stock market by speculating on a war, and desired Salvador's assistance. Since the Lisbon earthquake and his failure of securing the Brazilian diamond contract, Salvador had lost a lot and accepted.[63] But the plan failed and resulted in further financial losses for Joseph, who even went to France trying to recover his money from the secretary.[64]

His second affair proved damaging to both his wealth and reputation. He became involved with the 'fashionable courtesan' Mrs Margaret Caroline Rudd.[65] Born in 1745, she married an English soldier when she was seventeen. They went to England, where she seems to have eloped with another soldier after spending her husband's small patrimony. It is unclear how she lived the following years, but it is commonly assumed that she became a courtesan and she was said to have a relationship with Joseph Salvador, who was thirty years older.[66] In the 1770s she lived with Daniel Perreau, with whom she had three children. Perreau and his brother were accused of forgery in 1775, and Caroline Rudd offered to testify in court against them in order to save herself. Her offer was not accepted, and she went on trial as well. The brothers were found guilty and hanged in 1776, but Mrs Rudd was freed of all charges. She eventually married and her date of decease is unknown, but her husband remarried in 1798.[67] By that time, she was no longer involved with Salvador, but the high publicity given to the Perreau affair also led to the revelation of her affair with Salvador. Their affair was considered publicly as that of Rudd playing Salvador to gain money and jewellery from him, and 'all accounts played with the comic vein of the tale of an unscrupulous courtesan ensnaring the whily Jewish financier'.[68] In his biographical text on Salvador, Maurice Woolf mentioned a poem that appeared in the *Gentleman's Magazine* in 1775, directed to Mrs Rudd, containing the verse 'Come thou, whose arts our doting sex adore, Comfort of Rudd and choice of Salvadore!'[69] Different letters of Salvador denying an intimate relationship with

Mrs Rudd found their way to the papers.[70] They did not stop the *Bath Journal* to write in March 1775 that

> A celebrated Female Adventurer whose history is such a fashionable subject, had address enough to persuade an Israelite in the city, that she had it in her power to effect a match between him and one of the princesses of Mecklenburgh Strelitz[71]

Although Mrs Rudd was not at all an anonymous character in eighteenth-century London, the third woman that was linked with Salvador was by far the most notorious. Kitty Fisher was one of the most famous courtesans of the eighteenth century and even Casanova mentioned her in his memoirs, stating that he was not interested in having her, because she did not speak French, although others claimed she spoke French with great fluency. She was born around 1738 and died in Bath in 1767. She appears in different memoirs and poems, and a portrait of her is preserved in the *National Portrait Gallery*.[72] Salvador's relationship with Miss Fisher is not entirely clear. Maurice Woolf described her as his former friend and David Katz only mentions that he was involved with her. It is known that, after Kitty died, Salvador sued her widower to recover a sum that he had lent to her four years earlier.[73]

Endelman used the examples of Caroline Rudd and the Countess of Moriencourt show that there is explicit evidence for the hypothesis that well-to-do-Jews 'had adopted the sexual morality of the English upper class'.[74] This aspect of acculturation cannot serve to demonstrate the idea of a conscious adaptation to high society behaviour in order to be accepted by that society. The acculturation thesis that is expressed by different authors on Anglo-Jewry is presented as a desire for acceptance, motivating different actions of the individuals that looked for membership of high society, to the extent that some, like Samson Gideon, were prepared to give up their ties with the Sephardic community in order to achieve the sought acceptance. Such a teleological reading of social ascendancy might have been true for some, and surely has its place in a diaspora history that was stigmatized by anti-Semitism, but historical reality sometimes paints a more complex picture.

The forces opposing Salvador's entry into the higher strata of society remain unknown, but they existed beyond doubt. It seems an obvious matter that a selective circle of the 'rich and famous' would fight newcomers – Jews but others also. This does not mean that the English upper class can be seen as one body, wherein everyone knows everyone else, that took a uniform stand against individuals trying to find their way in. Different opinions reigned, and different standpoints were taken. The fact of the matter is that Joseph Salvador, and to some extent perhaps already his father, had entered high society, by achieving wealth and by establishing connections with other members of the upper class. Salvador owned a country house, knew men of the government and had affairs with notorious courtesans. Nevertheless, he never left Judaism behind, and his respectable status in the English upper class did not interfere with his social status within the Portuguese-Jewish community or vice versa. He was firmly rooted in both spheres through a web of human relationships, and if they influenced each other, it was in a fortifying manner, as is for instance indicated by his meeting with the new queen as a representative of the Sephardic community. The thesis of acculturation as an inevitable process that was linked with modernity seems not to hold ground for Joseph Salvador. It has been pointed out by Marshall Sahlins that 'the individual in particular and society in general confront each other over an empty social space'.[75] In not placing Salvador and others like him in an opposite position confronting a potentially hostile society, this danger is averted. As such, the historical dialogue between Salvador and the upper classes is not placed in an *empty* space. On the contrary, it takes place in a space that is constructed by reciprocal human interaction, not only in Salvador's direct position in the web of human interaction within a particular segment of society, but also in the public opinion shown in the attention by other parts of that society through journals for instance. Abandoning that space as the arena in which the individual and the global meet is one answer to the call for a 'greater attentiveness to human activity in the construction of historical spaces'.[76] As a consequence, the issue of Salvador's position in host society is valued on terms that can be analysed, namely the frequency and the nature of different relationships between individuals.[77]

Diaspora, Commerce and the State

The Search for Nationality

Joseph Salvador had created a position for himself in English society based on commercial success and social capital. He had friends in the government and he was a successful diamond merchant with international connections. Yet, where he stood was not entirely his own merit. He belonged to a diaspora that had left the Iberian Peninsula long before he was born, and the arrival of Sephardic Jews in England had begun before the eighteenth century. There were reasons why many Jews chose to settle in London and Amsterdam. They arrived in a relatively tolerant society, where they were allowed to live without fear of persecution from an inquisition. This did not mean that public opinion on them was univocally positive and the discussion about the position of Jewish immigrants in English society was still undecided in eighteenth-century England. The fact that the Jewish community was perceived as relying strongly on international trade was an important factor in this debate and has often been a cause to further label foreign presence as negative.[78] There was, however, a growing tendency to consider the identification of foreigners with trade as a positive element.

For thinkers who had a negative opinion about commerce as a socially corrosive force, trade could be better tolerated in society if it was to a large extent in the hands of foreigners, who could act as commercial agents. It kept business from society's subjects, as many members of diaspora movements could not gain official citizenship, and governments sometimes offered special protection to foreign merchants.[79] With the development of a more positive stand about trade and a growing tendency to identify society with the state, a utilitarian standpoint towards strangers was developed that contributed to the debate about their naturalization. Commercial expansion between the sixteenth and eighteenth centuries has often been studied in a competitive national framework.[80] Although the particular case study used in this book shows that nations are not always the best categories to use for large-scale historical analysis, a growing contemporary perception of the state has to be taken into account when considering the context within which the merchants of the cross-cultural diamond trade network lived and worked. Economic thinkers in the seventeenth and eighteenth centuries were increasingly concerned with state policy towards trade, indicating a growing awareness of rivalry between different states as an important factor in commerce. This dimension is visible in the coining of the term 'political economy'.[81] It also finds expression in the use of the prefix 'political' in different writings that were also about commerce.[82] There was the strong idea that commerce was best regulated by the state and that an enlightened ruler should direct a lot of his attention towards commerce.[83] This was also reflected in different economical and political writings of the time.

For Daniel Defoe, naturalization of foreigners would advance trade, bring wealth and good to the state.[84] Sir Josiah Child explicitly addressed the people who were against naturalization of the Jews. Against the arguments that they were 'penurious people, living miserably', he pointed out that 'they are like to encrease trade, and the more they do that, the better it is for the Kingdom in general, though the worse for the English merchant, who comparatively to the rest of the people of England, is not one of a thousand'. He also pointed out that 'The trifier they live, the better example are they to our people; there being nothing in the world more enducing to enrich a kingdom than thriftiness'.[85] One of the oldest documents relating to the Salvador family is a document from 1717 and written in Latin. It is a warrant for a letter of denization of different merchants, amongst them John and Jacob Mendes da Costa and Francis Salvador.[86] One could become such an adopted subject by acquiring a letter patent from the English Crown.[87] Although the status of a denizen is difficult to define, it appears he had some but not all of the privileges of an English subject. One of the limitations was that a denizen could not inherit real property. A later document, which is not dated but that is concerned with the same matter, mentions about Francis Salvadors and others that

> They have for several years past removed Themselves with their Estates & Effects to London, where They have ever since resided; That, being aliens, They are desirous to settle Themselves in his Majesty's Kingdom under the Protection of the Laws, and

> His Majtys mercifull Government, your Pet pray your Majesty to grant Them Them Letters Patent of Denization for their greater Encouragement to settle & trade here, and to enable Them to purchase and enjoy such Privileges & Estates in His Majty's Kingdom, as Denizens may have by Law.[88]

Another warrant for denization bears the name of Isaac Salvador, a brother of Francis, and was issued in November 1730.[89] It is not sure whether the merchants subject to this petition gained the denizen status, although it seems probable. It shows a desire of several Jewish immigrants to gain a legal status that would allow them to settle definitively in their new country. Joseph Salvador, however, had never known another home country than England and he considered himself not only a Sephardic Jew, but also an Englishman. When he discussed political matters with Dormer, he did so as an English subject: 'I am sorry we dont agree in our Political sentiments I hope we shall again in wishing the restoration of Esteem and Freindship between our Sovereigns'.[90] And although his cousin Francis, who was married to his daughter Sarah, died in 1776 in the struggle for American Independence, Joseph Salvador himself stayed loyal to the King: 'the contumacious behavior of the Americans and their daring declaration of Independency has determin'd me to exert the little talent I have in the national cause under his majestys auspices among whose Friends I have always thought it an honour & my duty to be rank'd'.[91] Similar patriotic feelings were expressed to Dormer by Ruben Levy.[92]

Salvador's sentiments made him an activist in the struggle for citizenship rights for Jews. He was accepted in certain strata of society, but legally, he was not on equal footing with his friends. He was not allowed to vote or to be elected to public office. In 1753, public outcry broke out over a law called the Jew Bill. It was a parliamentary act granting the naturalization of Jews and was to benefit particularly foreign-born Jews.[93] The passing of the bill caused a clamour in London, and pamphlets were spread by opponents and supporters of the law. Two texts in favour of the Jew Bill were written under the pseudonym of 'Philo Patriae'. Their authorship is commonly attributed to Joseph Salvador, also because a lot of the arguments used in favour of a legal Jewish presence in England seem to come from the direct experience of the Salvadors.[94] The pamphlet indicated that it was written by a merchant, and writes about the utility of Jews in trade and compares their situation in England with that of other nations, especially Holland.[95] If Joseph Salvador was truly the author of the two pamphlets, it proves his allegiance to the Jewish community, as well as his idea that that community was not an isolated island in the city of London, but a social group that could change with time and become totally integrated into English society. There is even the strong suggestion that it was in fact Joseph Salvador who had come up with the idea for the Jew Bill and that his good contacts with the government allowed it to pass through parliament.[96] This further supports the idea that Joseph Salvador was influential within as well as outside Sephardic circles, and that for him different spheres in society overlapped. The bill and pamphlets were obviously written out of concern for the Jewish diaspora, but also out of a patriotic feeling, something that is reflected in the name Salvador adopted to sign his texts. Joseph Salvador seems to have had a third reason to write his pamphlets, which had to do with the inability for foreign-born Jews to possess land:

> Old Mr. S— [Francis Salvador], being an Alien, had two Sons; the eldest [Joseph] was born before the Father's Denization; the younger [Jacob] died and left Sons. By the Law, should these Sons inherit a landed Estate, and die Minors, their Uncle [Joseph] cannot inherit the landed Estate, the Right of Inheritance reverting to an Alien, e're it arrives at him; now this the Law does not allow.[97]

The problem was that Joseph's brother had inherited land from his father and that there was a risk the land was to be escheated to the Crown as *bona vacantia*.[98] Joseph probably could not have inherited it since he was born before his father was made a free denizen. In spite of efforts made by the author of these pamphlets and others, the bill was repealed after parliamentary election in 1754 and the whole episode was quickly forgotten, without a legal change in the status of Anglo-Jewry.[99] Perhaps the fact that the bill did not pass in the end, and that some uncertainty remained in existence with regard to Jewish land possession, made Salvador consider the purchase of lands outside England, thinking it would be a more secure investment. He finally decided to buy land in South Carolina, where he spent the last year of his life.[100]

Several historians have considered the Jew Bill controversy of 1753 and 1754 as an important element in the shaping of British identity and have argued that 'the vociferous nature of public opinion on this matter certainly speaks to concerns about internal and external threats to national identity'.[101] In its public denunciation of the Jew Bill, many Christians not only showed an opinion on Jewish presence in England, but also on themselves. It is an example of how the century-long debate on Anglo-Jewry has not exclusively followed a line of growing tolerance, but that more complicated negotiations took place in the public space. According to Dana Rabin, it is not a coincidence that the debate regarding the Jew Bill was surrounded with such strong opinions from opposing parties as England was at the time very much concerned with imperial ambitions on a worldwide scale: 'the task of empire necessitated some change in these older perceptions of those defined as others'.[102] Jewish presence in England was far from new, but the granting of naturalization to Jews could lead to a much larger incorporation of other groups already present in the empire. The public debate surrounding the Jew Bill was to do with Christian self-perception with regard to identity in a world that was becoming more global, also because of international trade. John Hanway, an English merchant, published a series of letters that were specifically against the naturalization of Jews. They were addressed to J. S., most likely Joseph Salvador, and were a response to his pamphlets. One of the elements that disturbed Hanway the most was Salvador's suggestion that successful Jewish merchants could leave the country if the Jew Bill was revoked. Salvador had written that the Jews had enhanced English wealth by their commercial activities, and that naturalization was a logical consequence. Hanway replied by writing that a merchant was driven by the pursuit of wealth, the fear of God and the love of his country. Salvador had claimed that members of his family had been naturalized in France, and Hanway wondered how this would make him better than his current situation in England made him. For Hanway, Salvador had an obligation to the country that had offered him more opportunities than others could have. In spite of the fact that he argued against naturalization, he also wanted Jewish merchants to stay and be part of English society.[103]

In daily life and in public, the debate regarding foreigners was not one-dimensionally positive or negative, and reality encompassed the notion that the relationship between foreigners and host society only circled around assimilation. The process of integration, both in practice as in legality, as it was experienced by Joseph Salvador, shows a complex interplay of sentiments and considerations that changed the diaspora community as well as the host society, and both parties linked identity to nationality. This was not only the case for the two Jewish diasporas in England but extended to other migratory movements.

The Huguenot Diaspora

It is no surprise that Hanway took offence to Salvador's suggestion that his family was better treated legally in France than in England. Discussions on the naturalization of foreigners already existed in the seventeenth century.[104] This discussion was not always a matter of religion, as it also included debates on the status of Protestant immigrants. Berthon & Garnault, the firm that was Dormer's contact in Lisbon, were originally French Huguenots. Their families had left France for England and Holland out of fear of persecution, after the Edict of Nantes was revoked in 1685. Both families came originally from the town of Châtellerault, not far from Poitiers. Several members of the Berthon family were mentioned amongst a series of refugees who ended up settling in England or the Dutch Republic.[105] A Paul Berthon was born in Châtellerault, in 1674.[106] This origin is confirmed in his last will, originally written in French, which was customary amongst the members of the Berthon family.[107] He fled France as a child, around 1685, and he ended up in London. It seems that he was married twice, to a Magdalena Davall in 1703 and to a Martha Martineau, the daughter of a merchant, in 1716. The will of the latter can also be found in the National Archives.[108]

Berthon did not have any children from his second marriage, but three sons were mentioned in Martineau's will, children of Berthon's previous marriage with Magdalena Davall. The sons were John, Michael and Paul Berthon.

The latter is the Paul Berthon who had established a firm with Peter Garnault in Lisbon.[109] He was born in 1705 and settled in Lisbon at an unknown time. It is not clear from the archival material why certain Berthon family members relocated so quickly again to a Catholic country such as Portugal, but it could be attributed to commercial considerations. It seems that different members of the Berthons who went to London passed through Lisbon first. An old article in the *Oxford Dictionary of National Biography* mentions a St Pol le Berthon, the marquis de Châtellerault, who had fled to Lisbon in around 1685. His son went to London.[110] Although it is not certain, this son could very well have been directly connected to Paul Berthon the elder. It would explain the fact that John Paul Berthon, when writing his family tree, described Paul Berthon the elder as 'Saint Paul Berthon whose Godfather's surname was Saint Paul'.[111] In its marriage pattern, the Huguenot diaspora was not very different from the Sephardic and Ashkenazi migratory movements and Paul Berthon married the daughter of a man who also had French origins, John Sauret, a silk weaver living in London. The marriage between his daughter, Jane, and Paul Berthon was contracted on 16 July in 1727 and John Sauret paid three hundred pounds sterling for it.[112] It is not clear whether the marriage took place in London or Lisbon. The marriage produced five children, but one died as an infant. The four surviving children were all sons: John, Paul, Daniel and Peter. Peter and Paul both settled in London, and it was Peter Berthon who wrote later to the widow of Dormer.[113] John remained in Lisbon, and in his mother's will reference is made to his firm in Lisbon, since some of the sums that were to be paid out to other children had come from dividends from the Lisbon firm, in which Jane Sauret, John's mother, was officially involved.[114] It is clear from the wills that most of the Berthons mentioned here were merchants. An exception was Michael Berthon, brother of Paul Berthon, who was an engraver.[115] As merchants, who were also mostly married to children of other merchants, they remained socially a distinguishable group. But with later generations, they became increasingly English and less French. Indeed, Daniel Berthon, a grandson of Paul Berthon of Lisbon, lived in London and had found employment in the Treasury Office of the United East India Company.[116]

The Garnault family can also be traced back to Châtellerault, and their history is very similar to that of the Berthon family. Different Garnaults fled to Amsterdam and London, where many of them were active as merchants. The father of Peter Garnault of Amsterdam had been a minister of the Holy Gospel in the Reformed Church of Magdeburg and his sister was married to somebody in Berlin.[117] The links of Peter Garnault of Lisbon, one of the merchants considered in this chapter, to the rest of the Garnaults is difficult to establish. The pedigree that was composed by Wagner contains correspondence confirming this problem. The will of Aymé Garnault mentions a son named Peter Garnault, and Michael Garnault as a brother. Aymé and Michael had another brother, also named Peter. The will of Michael Garnault mentions a cousin Mary Girardot. One of the bills of exchange sent to Dormer by Berthon & Garnault was issued by the firm of Perochon, Firth and Girardot, and it would not be the first time they sent bills that were issued by firms with marriage ties.[118] It is possible that Peter Garnault of Lisbon was directly related to Aymé or Michael Garnault. What does seem certain is that Peter Garnault was in London before he left for Lisbon, since he married there in 1728, to a woman named Mary.[119] His own will only mentioned his wife, children some of his friends. His wife was called Mary Garnault and the wives of his sons are not mentioned. Elizabeth, his only daughter, was married to the Protestant merchant Peter Jacob Hasenclever, a personal friend of Garnault and originally from the Rheinland in Germany.[120] This link with Germany is interesting and can also be found in the marriage of John Berthon, a son of Paul Berthon in Lisbon, who married Ann Giese. The link with German Protestants is interesting and shows that Huguenot marriage policies were expanded to a larger Protestant community.

The families of Berthon and Garnault belonged to the international Huguenot diaspora that had decided to flee from a Catholic country ruled by a Catholic king. While Jewish immigrants hoped to find a tolerant government in their new country, Huguenots could hope to find co-religionists and a government that shared their dislike of the French royals. As a consequence, Huguenot migration to Protestant countries such as England and its North American colonies and the Dutch Republic has too often been labelled as a successful process that quickly led to assimilation. In different historiographies, Huguenots were considered to be 'ideal immigrants' and different scholars pointed out their fast adaptation into a new society.[121] The history of Huguenot migration has also be considered in light of mutual change brought about by an integration that was more than simple assimilation, a similar argument that has been made for the Jewish diasporas. It has been argued that the Huguenots brought with them a different culture and language that made the host society richer, and they were even called 'England's cultural intermediaries par excellence'.[122] Initially Huguenots received benefits that were not given to other minorities, in the form of financial assistance. Many Huguenots were in need of financial aid and the foreign churches that were already present in England made it easier to apply to the government or other institutions for assistance. In twenty-one years between 1696 and 1727, £15,000 was given yearly to the Huguenot population.[123] This aid stands in contrast with the measures that were taken by the Jewish community to relieve their own poor. Both Jewish communities were heavily self-reliant and the Ashkenazi poor were at different times transferred to England's colonies in the New World by Sephardim.[124]

The image of the Huguenot diaspora as a group that quickly assimilated without problems by a welcoming host society that even assisted them financially requires nuance, because religion was not all that mattered in debates regarding foreigners. The public debate in England at the end of the seventeenth and beginning of the eighteenth century centred on questions of politics and ideology as well.[125] A recent article on the Huguenots argues that they maintained a French identity and that their discontent was focused against the king, something that could very well go hand in hand with a nationalist feeling.[126] It was also thought that fear for religious persecution was not the prime motivation for all Huguenot immigrants and that a number of Catholic Frenchmen had left France under false pretences. The fact that this was an issue in the eighteenth-century debate regarding the status of French immigration into England confirms that nationality was an issue. The question of whether England should assist or welcome a group of refugees that had left France when the government was not good for them but who surely hoped to return when the government and its attitude towards Protestantism would change again was put publically on the table. The perception of Huguenots as a distinct group with a separate identity tied to France was further confirmed by the high degree of intermarriage within the Huguenot community.[127] Parallel to the Jewish experience, the twofold identity that was perceived to exist in the French Huguenot community created public doubts about the loyalty of new subjects with regard to their host society. Aymé Garnault, whose will is mentioned above, had been a jeweller in Paris before he settled in London. He still considered himself a Parisian resident when he was in England.[128] This was, however, not the case for Paul Berthon and Peter Garnault. They did not stay long in England but went to Lisbon to set up a commercial partnership, as Protestant merchants in a Catholic country. Notwithstanding, they shared with Joseph Salvador the idea of a belonging to a new country. They left England feeling part of it.

Berthon and Garnault within the English Factory of Lisbon

The origins of the partnership between Berthon and Garnault are not clear, and neither is the exact date when they chose to form a business together. It is clear from the letters they wrote that their social world in Portugal was very much connected with the existing body of English traders in the city: the Lisbon Factory. This organization was one of the most important trading communities of Lisbon, owing to the privileged nature of trade between England and Portugal. In the second half of the seventeenth century, in 1654, Portugal signed a treaty with England that was to last for more than 150 years, the *Treaty of Peace and Alliance*, which granted English merchants trading privileges in Portugal and the colonies.[129] Another alliance was signed in 1661 and sealed by the marriage of Catharina, daughter of D. João IV, with Charles II of England. The treaty confirmed the 1654 treaty and granted trading privileges to the English in Brazil.

It also included the concession of Bombay by the Portuguese. In spite of these treaties, the English representative in Portugal stated in 1683 that the English trading community was in a very bad condition.[130] In the very beginning of the eighteenth century, the Spanish War of Succession had broken out. In 1703, D. Pedro signed two Anglo-Portuguese treaties, a defensive one and a commercial one. The latter became famous under the name of the English envoy, John Methuen. It once more established the privileged position of England and its merchants with regard to Portuguese commerce, including the colonies. The period after the signing of the Methuen Treaty was one of the most flourishing for Anglo-Portuguese trade.[131]

It was also in this period that an official English mercantile body was organized. In 1711, fifty-nine English commercial houses signed a memorial that confirmed the foundation of the English Factory in Lisbon. Most merchants were active in trade with the Portuguese colonies, Newfoundland and the Mediterranean. Besides the favourable commercial treaties, the fact that Portuguese merchants did not actively pursue commerce in these regions on a large scale left an open space of opportunity for Englishmen, who were active in the textile trade, grain, wine, general shipping and finance.[132] This commercial organization was also recognized by Portuguese authorities and the British consul-general had official authority over the mercantile body. Merchants also had the right to practise the Protestant religion. It is said that the Factory had its own chapel and a burial ground, although it has also been argued that the only authorized religious gatherings took place in the house of the consul.[133] There were, as can be expected, troubles and quarrels between the Portuguese government and the English traders, most notoriously about the right to carry arms and the smuggling of bullion. Officially, it was forbidden to export precious metals out of the country. Yet this was a common practice amongst the English traders for sending their revenues to London. The Portuguese were aware of this, and at times did not allow it, leading to some arrests of ship captains and merchants. Yet these disputes were always resolved, the English traders never gave up their practices and in general, the relationship between Portuguese officials and English traders worked well.[134]

The English Factory was held in high regard and membership was crucial for an English trader active in Lisbon. The mercantile body could exert pressure on the Portuguese government and it was supported by the official diplomatic English channels. Membership of the Factory was valuable and a candidate had to be English and a merchant of good reputation. In addition, a yearly tax had to be paid, which was calculated as a percentage of the total volume of trade imports of a particular merchant. The revenue obtained was used in charity benefiting the English community of Lisbon.[135] Contemporary sources show that different members of the English Factory had a Huguenot background. It seems logical to assume that these merchants, or their parents, had been naturalized, otherwise they could not belong to the nation of English merchants in Lisbon, and it seems that they did belong to the commercial body. An uncompleted list compiled in 1803 mentioned acceptance of Peter Berthon in 1759, resident of London, and John Garnault in 1764, resident of Lisbon, where he died in 1815.[136] Peter Berthon must have been one of Paul Berthon's sons, the one writing to Dormer's widow, and John Garnault was almost certainly one of the two sons of Peter Garnault, and most likely the one to be his father's partner in the Lisbon firm after he had parted ways with Paul Berthon in 1756.[137] They were not the only merchants with a Huguenot background that appear within the English body of merchants. Several French names appear as signatories of Factory documents in the 1740s and 1750s, such as Auriol, Perochon and Le Sueur. Born in England, Berthon and Garnault considered their firm English, and when writing to Dormer about general issues, they identified themselves with the other English merchants. When writing to Antwerp about commercial privileges, they wrote that 'we English have more than any of them'.[138]

Merchants belonging to the English Factory could count on support from officials. As a state, England was interested in commerce and protecting groups of their subjects organized abroad formed a part of this interest. English treaties with Portugal had stipulated that disputes involving English and Portuguese merchants were allowed to be heard by a special judge conservator. Around the time of Berthon & Garnault, one of these judges was Ignacio da Costa Quintela, belonging to one of the families that became so heavily involved in the diamond administration in Lisbon around the same time.[139] He died in 1752 and it was his successor who had to deal with an affair regarding diamonds sold by Berthon & Garnault the following year. Patricio dos Santos Curado, their Portuguese buyer, had made a first payment three months late and tried to escape further payments. Berthon and Garnault threatened him in two ways: they were to 'expose his character', and would have him 'judicially notified'.[140] These are clear references to the two possible threats a merchant could make: the loss of commercial reputation and the initiative towards litigation. The combined threat worked well: Curado paid two weeks later and all troubles were forgotten. One month later they sold to him again, and this time Curado turned out to be a worse payer than before. When they went to his house to settle the debt, Curado was preparing to go to the countryside for recovery. Curado's illness caused feelings of sympathy, and at this point, legal procedures were only mentioned as a necessity if Curado was to die, in order to recover the debt.[141] But although Curado's health improved, no payments were made and Berthon and Garnault decided to apply legal means. The threat that had worked before now seemed insufficient, and in late August Curado received news that he had to appear before the special judge in ten days.[142]

Berthon and Garnault were adamant in their decision to press charges, but their initiative also showed the weakness of the legal option. After all, the outcome of such a trial was very uncertain, considering the international nature of the line of credit: a Portuguese buyer indebted to an English merchant in Antwerp through a French Huguenot firm whose commercial interests were defended within the framework of the body of English traders in Lisbon. The jurisdiction of the Portuguese judge with regard to disputes with English merchants was not clearly defined. Dos Santos Curado did not recognize the judge's jurisdiction over this affair. Berthon and Garnault employed a lawyer, but wrote to Dormer that the laws of the country were against them. The judge ignored Curado's refusal to appear, but the latter appealed against the order.[143] Berthon and Garnault continued to press the debtor, and in June 1755 an agreement was reached, because Curado feared that his goods would be sequestered. Berthon and Garnault were content, since they had received an official sentence against Curado. They wrote that he might still try to avoid payment, but that it would not hinder them. The use of words in letters describing this affair to Dormer is very interesting as it is highly emotional. It shows a great deal of frustration: 'we go gaining but little ground, but some we do, and hope that shall at last go winding to the end, and chastise our chap in the manner he deserves'.[144] It shows that feelings played a role next to rational calculation in commercial decision-making by cooperating merchants and that emotions materialized in correspondence between traders.[145]

Berthon and Garnault did not only turn to the English Factory for commercial or legal help. Since the English community in Lisbon was quite small, it was more than a commercial body. Members found each other in the practise of their Protestant religion, but also socially. Connections were never motivated on a single basis, and the families of the English merchants must have been connected on a social level as well as on a commercial level. As such, it would not only shape the world of English residents, but also that of visitors of various kinds. They turned to the English nation in Portugal not only for advice, but also for leisure and for credit.[146]

Berthon and Garnault were commercially and socially embedded in the English community of Lisbon. Children of Paul Berthon of Lisbon were mostly married into English families, such as Sibley, Hammond and Lewis. The famous writer Henry Fielding (1707–54), who wrote the novel *Tom Jones*, left for Portugal in 1754 trying to recover from ill health. He was joined by Margaret Collier for the voyage, who was a known correspondent of Samuel Richardson, another English writer. The wife of Paul Berthon is at times mentioned in this correspondence, when she wrote to Richardson about the earthquake of 1755. Collier had already left Portugal by that time, but she was worried about the friends she had there: 'I see the public newspapers pretty constantly, and have watched earnestly for some account amongst the English who got on board ships, and are coming to England, for the name of Stubbs, or Berthon, and others, but am not yet satisfied'.[147] Richardson answered the following January that Mrs Berthon and her family were safe, surprising his correspondent that he had kept up a personal correspondence with Mrs Berthon, 'so excellent a woman'.[148] The answer of Miss Collier implied that Mrs Berthon corresponded directly with Samuel Richardson, which was true.[149] It is very logical that the social circle that was attended by Fielding and Collier in Lisbon was at least partially composed of the well-to-do merchants of the English Factory and their families, such as Berthon.[150] Fielding's visit to Lisbon and the correspondence of Mrs Berthon with Samuel Richardson show that, like the Salvadors in London, merchants did not exclusively move around in commercial circles. They showed interest in the world around them. It also shows the acceptance of Berthon and Garnault in the English world; they were now seen by English visitors as fellow countrymen, having experience in a foreign country and the best contacts one could have in going abroad. It is this type of connection that is very important in Anderson's theory of a nation as an imagined community. Berthon and Garnault imagined themselves as being part of English community, and in a way they belonged to two diasporas: that of the Huguenots, which was both religious and commercial, and that of the English, which was purely commercial in origin but extended itself into a wider sphere.

It is interesting to note that the English presence in Portugal, a Catholic country, has not really been studied in terms of religious interaction. Practical difficulties with regard to religion were mentioned in monographs about Anglo-Portuguese relationships, but the fact that both countries had forged a special relationship seems to be sufficient to discard more serious questions of religion and commerce in this aspect. Part of this neglect might be due to a biased point of view. England in the eighteenth century was a powerful nation, and histories of its commercial relationship often depart from the starting point that England was superior and its relations were weaker nations. As such, the history of Anglo-Portuguese commerce has been reduced to England reaping Portugal's benefits in the form of Brazilian gold and diamonds, making the island rich and partially financing its industrial revolution later on, leaving Portugal only with architectural remains that it once possessed access to sources of great material wealth.

Studies on diaspora relations often take the form of a strong host society and a weaker community of religiously persecuted migrants. The image that has arisen from analysing the integration of the Salvador family in the beginning of this chapter already challenges this overly simplified relationship. Rather than trying to become accepted in a strong nation, they became a constructional part of it. This type of diaspora relationship is inversed when regarding the English merchants in Lisbon: the host society becomes the weak partner of the dual bond, and the migrant community becomes the stronger part, backed up by beneficial treaties and a diplomatic body. The English migrants in Lisbon possessed important agency with regard to their surrounding society. At a time when commerce was regarded as one of the tools for enhancing a nation's power and national wealth, the nation of English traders can also be seen as a body of representatives. In writing about the 'nation française' in Lisbon, Jean-

François Labourdette remarked that the *raison d'être* of the French traders in the Portuguese capital was to be engaged in French commerce, and to allow for its prosperity and expansion. As such, it was their duty to maintain a distinct French nationality. In the French case, merchants were at risk of confiscation of their goods if they breached their social isolation, and it was forbidden for them to officially engage in relationships with Portuguese women.[151] It seems likely that similar terms existed for the English traders, although the difference in religion made such obligations less necessary. It shows a preoccupation of the state with commerce. Although the individual traders surely had more personal motives, the inclusion of them in official state policy distinguishes them from other diaspora merchants. Yet this distinction is not simply one of a national trade diaspora versus a religiously inspired diaspora. Dormer was English, and has been studied as a member of a trade diaspora.[152] But he was also a Catholic, and married into the Brabant gentry. He did not send his profits to England, and his business cannot be considered to be an English business abroad.

Assimilation within Portuguese society was never an issue, although many merchants arrived in Lisbon never to leave it again. Their motivation had always been commercial; religion was rather a counter-motivation and a practical nuisance for an optimal relationship with the Portuguese hosts. Logically, the bulk of interaction between the English traders and the Portuguese was commercial. They were interested in trade, not in ascending in Portuguese society. The letters from Berthon and Garnault show that the idea of a weak host society and a strong body of migrants has its historical roots. Although the firm was established in Lisbon for a while, and their familial life took place in the Portuguese capital, it seems that they were not at all interested in the country they were living in, and they maintained a feeling of superiority.

In the letters they sent to Dormer, they described Portuguese merchants and officials often in emotional and pejorative terms. Surely this partially originated from the need to maintain a strong image towards their correspondent in Antwerp, but these passages occur all too frequently to discard them as small outcries of frustration in a number of particular trade transactions.[153] It seems that, apart from commerce, the members of the English Factory in Lisbon and other Portuguese cities such as Porto remained isolated socially and culturally from the surrounding society, an isolation that must have been easy to adopt considering the nature of a port city such as Lisbon and the privileged position of the English traders there. This isolation stands in contrast with the social acceptance by some of the English and Dutch merchants that were closely involved in the diamond contract, whose experiences show that there was a form of social integration into Portuguese high society.[154]

Berthon and Garnault considered themselves to be English, but they had not forgotten their French heritage and they maintained good commercial contacts with France and French firms. Between 1717 and 1755, twenty-four ships that arrived from France in Lisbon were assigned to them, making them an average-size firm.[155] One of their French correspondents was the house of Begouën, established in Le Havre in 1729.[156] When Salvador and Dormer had thought of a plan to buy diamonds belonging to the French captain La Bourdonnais, Berthon and Garnault kept Dormer informed about meetings between the captain's wife with French merchants and officials, indicating that they had information contacts with the French trading nation in Lisbon.[157] As a commercial body, traders from France did not benefit from the same privileges as the English, but their community was recognized legally by Portugal and its organization, headed by the French consul, operated on very similar terms as the English one.[158] Officially, it was a Catholic nation, but many French merchants already established in Lisbon in the seventeenth century were Huguenots, and a policy of tolerance was adopted within the French nation. It was easier for Huguenots to participate in the meetings of the French nation than for sons of mixed French-Portuguese marriages. Most of the French Protestant merchants operated nevertheless under the protection of either the Dutch Republic or England, and a certain number of Huguenots had become members of the English trading nation, and some, such as Auriol and Perochon were amongst the largest trading firms in Lisbon.[159]

This tolerant mentality between Protestants and Catholics was also reflected in the fact that, especially after the 1755 earthquake, many associations existed between French Catholic traders and foreign houses of Protestant origins, often English, Dutch or from Hamburg and founded by Huguenots. A good example is the house of the Bonifas brothers. Paul, the older brother, was a Huguenot and member of the English trading nation. He was a personal friend of Peter Garnault.[160] His younger brother Philippe was Catholic and a member of the French trading nation, and married to the Catholic daughter of an English merchant.[161] A tolerance in commerce between merchants of different religions can be found after 1755, when Berthon and Garnault were flexible with regard to payments of creditors who had lost much of their belongings in the earthquake.[162]

6 TRADE, GLOBAL HISTORY AND HUMAN AGENCY

The previous chapter has demonstrated how merchants belonging to international diasporas tried to find a place in a new host society. The human interaction that resulted from this brought about change and led to reflections on identity, both from the point of view of the merchants in question and from individuals and groups from the host society. An important aspect of this negotiation was the fact that the foreigners in question were traders. Globally dispersed but religiously and culturally united to some extent, diasporas have proven to be useful stones in the construction of a global historical space and hence in any hypothesis regarding forms of early modern globalization, by challenging other criteria for space-building such as the national state: 'Jews allow us to see how a focus on nation-based Atlantics can sometimes obscure the actual experience of life in the early modern Atlantic.'[1]

In working on a set of merchants active in international trade, David Hancock has attributed a number of characteristics to them. One of the adjectives he used was 'integrative'.[2] This is a key element when analysing the influence of people on the cohesion of the place where they live and work. Atlantic history has been defined as 'the powerful "covering idea" that the entire Atlantic world was integrated'.[3] It is a description that firmly shows the belief that the Atlantic isn't simply a geographical area defined by water, but a paradigm for the integration of the whole world after 1800, and that as such it can be seen as a precursor to globalization, or one of the steps towards growing global interconnectedness.[4] And human agency is a central element in sustaining this claim. It is in their integrative abilities, both geographically and operationally, that Hancock's merchants were exponents of a more global history. The integration is not only shown by diverse commercial activities, linking different trade routes, geographical areas and commodities with each other, but also by connecting people, in different circuits. These connections were made through trade but also through interactions in different societies. These interactions added to a change in mentality that was already brought about by a widening eye on global commercial opportunities. It is in this aspect that networks, and particularly cross-cultural ones, are the key stone in the formation of a growing global world. Hancock's argument that merchants were integrating a global space is valid for the cross-cultural trade network as well, and perhaps especially for Francis and Joseph Salvador.

Globalization through Commerce

Business in the West Indies

According to Maurice Woolf, the Salvadors were active in the Spanish and Portuguese trade, and probably also in the contraband trade from Jamaica to Spanish territories.[5] Evidence confirms these claims. Francis Salvador was said to have correspondents in Lisbon.[6] In 1740, Joseph Salvador sent diamonds to Dormer and asked him to sell them on behalf of Salvador and his partners Medici and Niccolini of Lisbon, who were proprietors of half the parcel.[7] Three years before, a request had been sent by a number of London merchants who had interests in Lisbon to the Duke of Newcastle, regarding a problem one of these merchants, Richard Yates, had experienced with the drawing of bills of exchange on correspondents in Lisbon. Francis Salvador was one of the sixty-eight merchants signing the request.[8] Fifteen years later, Joseph Salvador was one of the signers of a letter directed to Lord Tyrawly, who had been a 'Minister Extraordinary and Plenipotentiary' at the Court of Portugal. There had been problems regarding English bullion exports, and Tyrawly was sent to Lisbon. After he had left for London in 1752, a group of Lisbon traders, including Joseph Salvador, sent him a letter in which he was thanked for his efforts.[9]

In 1755, Dormer received a letter from Salvador in which he informed him about the earthquake that had taken place in Portugal. Joseph wrote about 'the Melancholly news we had already received that all the Citty was entirely destroy'd Except the Mint, but Could not Calculate how many People had perish'd in this Calamity' and mentioned to Dormer that 'for my part I shall be a Considerable looser'.[10] From this letter, it seems that Salvador had considerable interests in Lisbon. It has been a common reading of his career that the Lisbon earthquake was one of the events that would eventually ruin Joseph Salvador, one of the reasons that made him retire later to his estates in South Carolina.[11] In June 1756 he sent Dormer a letter in which he expressed his desire to sell his share in Dormer's insurance company, since 'this Lisbon misfortune has lessend my Cash so that I should be glad to sell my actions'.[12] That the disaster in Lisbon had left quite a mark on Joseph Salvador becomes clear when he compared the difficulties of a Cadiz firm in repaying Salvador a considerable amount of money with the 1755 event: 'my Concern herein is very Considerable and tis to me a Second Earthquake'.[13] Their involvement in the Brazilian diamond contract demonstrated a further commercial interest with the Portuguese colonies.[14]

According to Woolf, the Salvadors acted as London agents for English merchants in Cadiz.[15] Letters sent to Dormer imply that they were more than agents, and that they traded on their own account. After 1745, Joseph Salvador included Dormer in different commercial operations through Cadiz. In November 1750, the Salvador firm and the Dormer firm took a share on the *Superbe* that was to set sail from the Spanish port to Veracruz.[16] The English firm of Tyrry acted as intermediaries in Cadiz and they bought goods on Salvador's and Dormer's accounts. The ship and its cargo were secured for the outward and the homebound voyage, and news of its arrival in Veracruz reached London in July 1751.[17] The ship was expected back in Cadiz the following October or November, and Joseph Salvador was hoping for good returns. Unfortunately, the vessel shipwrecked:

> this serves to advise you the melancholy News we have received this Day of the Loss of our Ship the Superbe coming from La VeraCruz in a Place called Conill 5 Leagues from Cadiz in a great Storm, she sitts in a Flatt in hard Sand all her upper works are washed away by the great Sea.[18]

The nature of the freight was not mentioned apart from the letter sent in January, when silver was mentioned, which was probably the proceeds of the goods sent. Salvador estimated that the cargo was worth 70,000 pagodas, and the involved traders hoped to save some of their share: in August the Tyrry firm informed the Salvadors that 'if they have good Weather they are in hopes of Dyving all the money up'.[19]

In the meantime, another enterprise was being set up, this time involving a ship called the *Purissima Concepcion*, which was to sail to Spanish America. The Salvadors were already purchasing goods to be put on board the vessel, mostly bulk goods, 'few woollens & no fine Linnens'.[20] In 1753, Salvador's friends at Cadiz had bought a Genovese ship and the Salvadors were again purchasing cargo, indicating to Dormer that there was place on the ship for goods from his country. It seems to have been a regular undertaking for the Salvadors, but perhaps not for Dormer:

> as several of the old Concerned are Dead and remov'd there is room to Introduce some new and as you formerly told us you had some money'd Friends we tender you an Interest of £3000 but must Desire an answer as soon as possible that we may give you an order for the Goods we want.[21]

When the voyage of the *Purissima Concepcion* was delayed for several months, and new capital had to be searched, the Salvadors wrote to Dormer that it was not unusual, and that the same 'was practis'd in former voyages.'[22] The firm of Francis & Joseph Salvador was in full control regarding the cargo, while the Tyrry firm supplied the ship. Dormer informed the Salvadors that other merchants in Antwerp claimed to have a share in the enterprise, but Joseph Salvador answered him that such a thing was impossible, for 'they Cannot have it but by our Hands'.[23] Dormer and Salvador never saw profits from the trip, as the Tyrry firm went bankrupt. There were suggestions to go to court in London, but the merchants never ressorted to legal means.[24] It is interesting to note that at some point, the Salvadors had started to complain that the Tyrry firm 'have not of late been so regular in their Correspondence nor so pontual in their advises'.[25] Through the Salvador firm, Dormer supplied goods to other firms in Cadiz, for instance to the French merchants Magon and Le Fer Frères. Some of these goods were sent to them by way of the Salvadors, others were not.[26] One of Dormer's other contacts was established through Francis Mannock. He had worked in Cadiz for a few years and was in close contact with the English firm of Mannock & Ryan. An account of the firm is preserved about a shipment of lace to Cadiz to be sent to Veracruz. Dormer was involved as a partner for a quarter, next to a merchant from Gent named Jacques Brame and Francis Mannock. The latter was involved for half the value of the shipment.[27] A year earlier, Jacques Brame had asked Dormer for advice regarding parcels of rough diamonds he had received from Goa that he wanted to sell in London, Amsterdam or Antwerp.[28] Dormer also had different previous experience in sending textiles to the West Indies. In 1751, he received a letter from Curação about the sale of lace that had arrived there three years earlier.[29] In the early 1750s, Dormer had sent a number of boxes of lace to Bermuda. There was a problem with the returns, and Salvador contacted William Popple, a former governor of Bermuda.[30] It turned out to be a long-lived affair and, against advice from the Salvadors, Dormer intended to begin a lawsuit trying to recover his money. The affair was discussed between Salvador and Dormer in several letters during the following years but it seems the affair was not resolved by the time of Dormer's death.[31]

Another type of textile that Dormer sent across the Atlantic was ticks. These were textiles that were made of flax, and were generally used to cover mattresses. Their production took place on the countryside of Brabant. The town of Turnhout, about 40 km from Antwerp, was known for its tick production.[32] In the 1740s and 1750s the trade in ticks was suffering from foreign competition, as well as from import restrictions issued by the England, the country that imported the most. A guild of tick manufacturers existed and the head of the guild, Robert Jannesone, was an acquaintance of Dormer and his most important supplier.[33] Most of the ticks wherein Dormer was involved were sent to England. Dormer acted as an agent in this business, and referred to Jannesone as the most important supplier to his English correspondents.[34] Apart from this English business, Dormer also sent ticks for his own account to Berthon & Garnault in Lisbon, who acted as Dormer's agents in this trade the same manner they did in the diamond trade, with the difference that Dormer only delivered textiles on demand. Diamonds were regularly sent to Lisbon and many were eventually sent back to

Antwerp, when time had passed without a successful sale. Diamonds were easy to send, since they were small, and the additional freight costs were also small, so no great loss would be made in the return journeys.[35] Other commodities were not so easy to return, and Dormer only sent ticks to Lisbon when Berthon and Garnault asked for it. Between 1752 and 1756, 423 ticks were sent to Lisbon and 370 of those were bought by one firm, that of Francisco José & Manoel Lopes. For the remaining fifty-three ticks, no buyer was mentioned in the letters sent to Dormer. The Lopes firm sold to shopkeepers in Lisbon, but was also an important supplier for the Brazilian market.

It is difficult to determine the amount of ticks delivered by Dormer that were eventually sold in Brazil. Different extracts from letters sent by Berthon & Garnault point to a certain routine, suggesting it was a recurrent operation involving delivery by Dormer, agency by Berthon & Garnault and export by the Lopes firm. In 1753, Berthon and Garnault let Dormer know that a shipment of ticks had arrived and that they would warn 'Manoel & joseph Lopes que cette marchandise est icy afin quils tachent sy possible encore de la charger sur la flotte'.[36] A similar comment was made the following year. Lopes demanded specific types of ticks, and Berthon & Garnault informed Dormer and added that they wished that 'they were already on the way, for as the going of the Rio fleet may be sooner then the king had determin'd it, and that tis there Fran.co Joseph Lopes wants to send them, he'l soon be impatient not to see them arrive'.[37] It is clear from evidence that the Lopes firm made their demands at a moment that they anticipated the departure of the Rio fleet. At least on one occasion Dormer was unable to send ticks before the fleet had left the port of Lisbon.[38] Most of the shipments were made via Amsterdam, and Dormer used another one of his contacts in the diamond trade to arrange transportation, the firm of George Clifford & Sons. Dormer had many correspondents in Amsterdam, and it is interesting to note that a huge firm such as that of George Clifford performed such tasks.

No information is given on a more exact destination in Brazil. In several areas, such as the diamond district in Minas Gerais, the local elite were fond of European imports, particularly textiles. Local production systems also existed and the relation between local emerging production and imports from Lisbon is not clear, and it has been argued that exports from Portugal started to suffer from domestic Brazilian competition.[39] The Brazilian demand for European textiles was also determined by fashion and taste. Although ticks in general were white with blue stripes, some variety did occur, mostly in size, and the Lopes firm clearly specified what kind of ticks they wished. As it was also the case with diamonds, taste was different at different markets. Ticks with red stripes for instance were not popular in Lisbon, although they were sold in Cadiz.[40] The quality also should not be too high, for they would not find buyers in either Portugal or Brazil.[41] A good price was important, and as such there was a rigid competition from Hamburg, that produced cheap common ticks, and England, from where ready-made mattresses were shipped that did not require ticks.[42] A cheap price became even more important in the aftermath of the 1755 earthquake which ruined many merchants. The earthquake caused a great rupture in the lines of credit: many debtors could no longer pay since they had lost everything, and it created a chaos wherein uncertainty reigned.[43] Francisco Lopes had lost all of his goods and was ruined. It was on account of Lopes's good reputation that they asked Dormer to help him and he was characterized as someone who was 'beginning his world a new and being honest and industryous'.[44] An agreement was later reached with his creditors giving him four years to recover the large debts people in Brazil owed him, as well as smaller debts from shopkeepers in Lisbon.[45]

Some of Dormer's other activities also point to a relatively large interest in the Iberian Peninsula. As an insurer, a lot of the sea insurances underwritten by Dormer's company were for voyages to Spain. Including Portugal and the colonies, this share amounts to almost half the total of sea insurances (48.4 per cent). Other important destinations of insured ships were France (20.8 per cent), England and Ireland (14.8 per cent) and the Bay of Biscay (10 per cent).[46] Dormer had also acted as an underwriter for sea voyages on his own account, twice before the Company came into existence, and several times after as well. In 1752 and 1754, he insured three voyages between Emden and China, including return. In 1757, he insured risks for a total of twenty-three voyages as a private insurer.[47]

The Salvadors and the India Trade

The above examples make it clear that different merchants belonging to the cross-cultural diamond trade network were involved in the sending of different textile commodities to the West Indies, Spanish and Portuguese colonies. Part of the return cargo was in silver and this was often connected with trade in Indian diamonds.[48] The Salvador firm had experience in the silver trade.[49] In 1749, Dormer wanted to set up a trade in gold and silver with them, but the Salvadors hesitated. They expressed their surprise when Dormer informed them about the high demand in Antwerp.[50] A year later, they changed their mind but demanded care: 'now if Silver is really wanting in your Place the best would be sincerity between us for if anyone can Do it tis we'.[51] As was the case with the diamond trade, it seems that Dormer fully realized the experience of the Salvadors in different branches of commerce, and he tried to set up different enterprises with them. The Salvador firm was able to attain large quantities of that commodity, perhaps through their American interests that they had with the Tyrry firm in Cadiz. In discussing a general scheme with Dormer, they wrote that 'we can help them to any sum of ounces from 1000 to Ten million & it is according to what Quantities they want & in what manner, that the Price can be fixed'.[52] One month later, they gave Dormer a better insight into their affairs regarding silver, showing that they were active in the trade, for they wrote that between 17 September and 2 October they had received 250,000 ounces of silver from India, and that they had already sold them in Amsterdam.[53]

The activities of the Salvadors in the silver trade interested the East India Company. In 1749 a contract was signed between the British East India Company, Samson Gideon, Francis Salvador, John Bristow and David Pratviel. The three merchants promised to deliver three million ounces of silver, in pieces of eight, to the Company, through the intermediation of Gideon, who in fact bought it on the Company's behalf from Salvador and his companions.[54] A large amount of the silver the Salvadors got from the Spanish Americas was not sold in Europe. They used it to finance diamond purchases in India. The Salvador family had been active in the trade in precious stones with India since the beginning of the eighteenth century, and many of Dormer's diamond supplies came through this channel.

The question of how the Salvadors received their Indian diamonds is interesting. On several occasions, they bought parcels of diamonds at public sales in London.[55] They also used specialized Sephardic brokers to buy diamonds for them, such as Abraham de Paiba.[56] There is a great deal of evidence showing that Francis Salvador had privileged connections in India and did not need to resort to public sales.[57] According to letters sent to Dormer, a lot of the diamonds that were destined for the Salvadors arrived in London on ships used by the East India Company. They held consignments of diamonds on those ships:

> The Warwick a Ship from the East Indies we know was Arrived at St. Helena x we Expect her Daily to Arrive here this Ship brings in Register of Diamonds about 190,000 Pagodas, we fear the Goods are Very Dear x bad, we should be glad to know in Particular what Sorts will be Saleable with you for as we have a large Consignment to ourselves we may perhaps be able to do something either for your Account of for our Account in halves[58]

The Salvadors bought a shipping space and used that to send silver, coral and jewellery to India for returns in rough diamonds. Part of the commodities destined to go to Asia was purchased through Dormer, such as some silver but polished stones also. The 20.875 carats of rose diamonds that Dormer sold to Francis Salvador in 1747 might have shipped to India, although it is also possible that they were sold in London.[59] In India, local representatives for the Salvador firm arranged the sale of arrived goods and the purchase of rough diamonds. The Salvadors had kinship ties with merchants living in India. According to Walter Fischel, who studied the Jewish merchant colony in Madras in the late seventeenth and early eighteenth centuries, a Salvador Rodrigues came to India in 1681. He travelled to Golconda in 1686, where, still according to Fischel, he started to work for the English East India Company. Rodrigues was a business partner in Madras of Daniel Chardin and the Jewish merchant travelled to the mines in Golconda to buy diamonds for their partnership.[60] He was apparently still in Golconda in 1694.[61] This Salvador Rodrigues was identified as Isaac Salvador, a brother of Francis.[62] These are not the same Francis and Isaac that were Joseph's father and uncle, but belonged to an older generation. The family tree of the Salvadors shows that they were brothers of Joseph Salvador's grandfather, something that explains the use of the name Rodrigues.[63] According to a journal of a diamond merchant preserved in the Amsterdam city archive, two brothers of Salvador Rodrigues lived in Amsterdam. One brother, Joseph, was a diamond polisher and another one, Abraham, was a jeweller.[64] The partnership with Chardin shows that, like the Salvadors in London, family members working in India were involved in trade operations that expanded beyond the kinship network. Kinship remained very important nonetheless and different members of the da Costa family were involved in the diamond business with the Salvadors.[65] It is not entirely clear whether the Salvadors had other relatives in Asia but according to Edgar Samuel, Salvador Rodrigues had integrated very well: 'he lived with Hindu mistresses and the children they bore him, spoke Telugu, wore Indian costume and ate a strict vegetarian diet'.[66] There is no evidence to support this description, but a Salvador Rodrigues Junior appears once on an account of 1727 made between Francis Salvador and a partner of him in some diamond ventures.[67] A Joseph Salvador was buried in Calcutta in June 1789 and he was described a poor inhabitant.[68]

Different Sephardic families related to the Salvadors by marriage also had relatives working in India. Fischel mentioned a Solomon Franco, born in Leghorn and buried in Madras in 1763.[69] He was active in India at the same time that the Salvadors were very active in the diamond trade. Later, Joseph Salvadors sister was married to someone of the de Paiba family, of which many members were diamond traders and brokers. Through this marriage, the Salvadors might be connected to Mosseh Pereyra de Paiba, a merchant who went to India to set up business in diamonds in 1685.[70]

Beyond kinship relations, the Salvadors had other representatives, such as Richard Benyon, an English merchant residing in Madras.[71] Salvador conducted some partnership business with Edward Fenwicke in diamonds, and they both corresponded with Benyon, acting as their agent in Madras. Around 1726, Salvador and Fenwicke stopped that collaboration to work with Nathaniel Turner. The agent in Madras received silver and gold thread from Salvador and Fenwicke, who included careful instructions about the diamonds to be bought with it.[72] Further research is necessary to establish the exact nature of contacts the Salvador firm had in India. It is clear that they had kinship as well as non-kinship relations with merchants in India, and that they served Francis and Joseph Salvador's interests in the diamond trade. It was very convenient to have a direct, personal correspondence with somebody in India to take care of their business there. Because merchants had to receive permission from the East India Company, it is possible to determine the amount of goods they sent to India by using the court minute books of the Company. Table 6.1 shows the different goods shipments by the Salvador family to India between 1730 and 1758. Phineas Serra was Joseph Salvador's attorney, and because he might have acted on his account, he is included. Since Jacob Salvador was partner in the firm of his father, shipments in his name belong to the Salvador firm, as well as shipments made in the name of Francis and Joseph Salvador. Because Isaac was a brother of Francis and his diamond business was often done in partnership with Francis, his activities have also been included in the table. A part from the usual commodities used in the Indian diamond trade, the sending of ostrich feathers was mentioned, although only one time.[73]

Table 6.1: Shipments to India by the Salvador firm, 1730–58.[74]

Commodity	Isaac Salvador	Jacob Salvador	Joseph Salvador	Francis Salvador	Phineas Serra
Total silver (£)	0	10,200	0	0	3,200
Total coral (£)	64,328	145,035	57,500	0	14,100
Gold and silver (£)	0	0	2,250	0	0
Jewels (£)	0	3,000	500	300	0
Coral, emeralds and silver (£)	0	0	10,000	0	0
Ostrich feathers (£)	0	0	25	0	0
Total value (£)	64,328	158,235	70,275	300	17,300
Silver (ounces)	10,000	0	0	0	600

The rough diamonds that came back in return were sold by the Salvador firm at different markets, and Dormer and other members of the cross-cultural diamond trade network played an important role in this.[75]

One particular phrase in the letters sent by the Salvador firm to Antwerp suggest that the Salvadors not only bought shipping space, but that they also owned ships that sailed to India: 'The Lapuring from Fort S:t Davids belonging to this Comp.y arrived safe at Lisbon She brings but 2 Parcells of Diamonds.'[76] It is unclear whether Salvador meant his company or the East India Company, although when he referred to the latter he often wrote 'our Company'. It was not all that rare for a merchant to possess a share in a ship that was bought in a partnership, especially before a real specialization in ship-owning had begun.[77] It seems realistic to assume that the Salvador firm owned several ships or at least shares in them and that they were chartered to the East India Company. It was not uncommon for the East India Company to charter ships. This was regular practice each year until the Seven Years' War.[78] For this purpose, a charter party was signed between a merchant, a ship owner and a captain. In the first half of the eighteenth century, different entries of charter parties signed by Francis and Joseph Salvador can be found.[79] The Salvadors were sometimes referred to as merchants of London, but on different occasions the formula 'the following owners were now approved of to sign charterparty'.[80] Ten different ships were mentioned in charter parties involving the Salvadors. Research shows that it was very uncommon for an individual to be called a 'ship owner', and that such individuals were simply referred to as merchants. It was common for these merchants to possess ships, but very often on a partnership basis. Having a share in a ship was common practice, as opposed to owning a vessel entirely. A certain Thomas Hall had a share in eighteen different ships at the time of his death in 1748.[81] Specialization in ship owning occurred at a later date, making it surprising for one merchant to own that many vessels, besides being active as a merchant in different commodities and regions. It is possible that Salvador owned the largest share and therefore was authorized to sign for the other owners as well, since at times a merchant would only possess one sixteenth of a share in a vessel, and it must have been practically difficult to always get all sixteen signatures of the different shareholders. For some of the parties Francis and Joseph Salvador signed charterparties with, it can be proved that they were in the Company's service at the time, such as John Folson. The use of charterparties for voyages to India created a shipper's group that managed to exercise a monopoly power over ships suitable for the East India trade. This group of ship-owners managed to gain a significant influence by using their large East India stocks in the election process for directors.[82] Taking into account the influence that Joseph Salvador held for a while in the East India Company and considering the fact that he was not a director of the Company, as is sometimes mentioned in literature, it is very plausible to assume that he was part of this power group within the Company.

The Salvadors and the New World

Apart from regular business relationships that connected the Salvador firm to different countries in Europe but also to India and Brazil, they also had a connection with North America since the 1730s. In the period between 1720 and 1735, the amount of Sephardim coming to London increased due to a renewed inquisitorial activity on the Iberian Peninsula. The London Sephardic community consisted of about 1,000 people in 1720, with 1,500 additional immigrants arriving in the fifteen years that followed. During the same time, Ashkenazi immigration further caused an expansion of the number of Jewish habitants of London. Many of these new immigrants were poor refugees and the community leaders were responsible for their well-being. This often meant a form of charity offered by well-to-do Sephardic traders and bankers who had established themselves in London earlier. A number of Sephardim who had managed to build successful careers and integrate to a certain extent into London's well-respected higher circles considered these newcomers a threat to a balance in daily life between Jews and their host society. They feared that the level of tolerance might decrease if a new mass of immigrants arrived who possessed significantly lesser financial means.[83] In addition to charity and support, some Sephardim decided to give financial aid to groups of newcomers so that they could travel to the New World to settle. In 1732 the British Crown issued a charter for the colonization of Georgia, and money was raised to send about forty persons to Savannah.[84] The plan was executed by three leading figures in London Sephardic Jewry, Anthony da Costa, Alvaro Lopes Suasso and Francis Salvador.[85] This plan, at least partially intended to relief pressure on London's Jewish community, was the only involvement of Francis Salvador with North America.

Twenty years later, Joseph Salvador decided to purchase land in South Carolina. It was a typical investment for a well-to-do eighteenth-century London merchant and Salvador had extra reasons. The controversy concerning the Jew Bill must have been a decisive moment. The difficulties of inheriting land within the Jewish community in England, especially when foreign-born Jews were involved had made him fight for citizenship rights.[86] When the bill did not make it, Joseph Salvador started to think of other means to invest his money. Four weeks after the Lisbon earthquake, on the 27 November 1755, a year after his father had died, Salvador bought a tract of land 100,000 acres from John Hamilton in South Carolina.[87] During the following years, he bought more adjacent lands and sold other parts. The acts that show this activity are preserved in ninety-one different entries in the South Carolina archives.[88] These are long, technical texts that explain little about the nature of the estate, or what Salvador was doing with it. There seem to have been plans to establish a plantation, although these intentions never seem to have materialized fully.[89] In 1764, the American merchant and planter Henry Laurens sent a letter to Richard Oswald, a slave trader later known for his role as peace commissioner at the Paris Treaty of 1783.[90] Oswald was interested in buying land, and Laurens replied to him that 'Your view of establishing a Farm, plantation & Vineyard in our back settlements are commendable, Generous' but also added that it was by no means an easy enterprise, citing the example of Salvador:

> There is a large almost wholly-unoccupied Tract of about 100.000 Acres of fine Land at the place commonly called *Ninetysix* formerly run out & I believe granted to one Hamilton, now the property or within the claim of Mr. Joseph Salvador & Co., which at present is a *nuisance,* as it lies vacant & hinders the establishment of a great many useful settlers.[91]

Richard Oswald seems to have been a personal acquaintance of Joseph Salvador, as he proposed to Charles Jenkinson to introduce Oswald to him.[92]

Perhaps Salvador decided to buy land in the Americas as a security. His losses due to the Lisbon earthquake might have made him realize that wealth could perish quickly, and that it was dangerous to have no financial protection. Landownership could make up for that. If it was an investment, Salvador did not need to be there himself, and there are no records showing that he moved to South

Carolina. He moved to the New World at the very end of his life. He arrived in 1784 and died two years later. The first family member that settled there was his son-in-law Francis Salvador, who was also the son of his deceased brother Jacob. He arrived in Charleston in 1773 and sources indicate that his departure for Northern America was due to personal misfortunes. He purchased some lands of his own in 1774, partially from his uncle, and settled in a place called Coroneka, close to his uncle's estate.[93] It is not clear to what extent he was looking after the possessions of Joseph Salvador, but it seems probable that he had some responsibilities with regard to his uncle's estates. Francis Salvador came to North America at a time when the revolutionary spirit was already strong, and a year after his arrival, he was elected a member of the first General Assembly of South Carolina. He was very active in the American movement for independence. He was a member of two provincial congresses in 1775 and 1776 and of various committees. When hostilities started in Carolina between Americans and the English, Francis Salvador decided to fight. In July 1776, the British fleet had arrived off Charleston, and Cherokee Indians supporting the British troops made several raids in South Carolina. Salvador was involved in an expedition against the Cherokees from which he would never return. He was shot on 1 August and scalped by Indians.[94] His uncle only arrived in South Carolina eight years later and no trace can be found in his surviving correspondence about his nephew's involvement in the independence movement. Joseph Salvador had chosen the English side and three months after Francis's death, he wrote about 'the contumacious behavior of the Americans and their daring declaration of Independency'.[95]

Salvador started selling parts of his estate in the 1770s, mostly to family members such as his sister Rebecca, Francis Salvador and the stepfather of Francis, Abraham Prado. It is suggested that he lived the last years of his life on the money that he earned with these sales.[96] Joseph Salvador's last will shows that he did not possess much at the end of his life. It was not uncommon for merchants to grant their remaining family members annuities, government annuities in particular. Salvador did not seem to have those. Three of his daughters were given 1,000 pounds sterling in cash. His daughter Judith, who was married, was to receive £100 to give to anybody she wanted. She was to receive a small annuity of £50 per year. Some other family members and the will's executors received small sums, and his three unmarried daughters were to divide the remainder of the estate. Some money was also given to the Jewish community. The Portuguese synagogue in London was to receive £100, and the same amount was given to the Portuguese synagogue in Charleston. It was far more uncommon to grant a sum to the other Jewish community. It would not occur often that an Ashkenazi merchant left money to the Portuguese congregation or the other way around. The two different communities in Charleston were probably quite close, and Joseph Salvador paid £20 to the German synagogue there.[97]

It is possible that Salvador's purchase of lands in South Carolina was a pure investment. The absence of evidence that he turned it to practical use further confirms this hypothesis, although it is interesting to note that in 1768, Salvador had mentioned to Charles Jenkinson his retirement to the New World.[98] This suggests that he had other intentions with the land he bought as well. Some of the correspondence he maintained with Emanuel Mendes da Costa hint at plans Salvador had with his lands.[99] Joseph Salvador had asked Mendes da Costa, as a naturalist, his advice regarding his estates. The scientist replied extensively and specifically pointed to the possible economical value of his lands:

> Your situation (as from) great navigable rivers or the sea makes that any mineral or metallic works cannot be expected or wrought to any profit ... You should seek the nature of the rocks on beds of stone within the country, for should any prove of the lime stone kind, they will be extremely useful to break & burn into lime prove a valuable manure, of excellent service to you in number of cases ... Let your agents be also attentive to all deep diggings or openings of the Earth, to search for clays markes x that may be useful for making bricks, pottery & various other occonomical uses[100]

This passage suggests that Salvador did not own a territory suited to establish a plantation, but wild lands that he thought perhaps could be searched for natural resources. Perhaps these could be used in agricultural and industrial enterprises, to make a profit. It seems that at the end of his life, when his most successful years in trade were long behind him, Joseph Salvador had not given up his interest in precious stones. He must have asked Mendes da Costa about the possibility of finding them on his lands, because the latter gave him an extensive answer that implied the possibility that valuable commodities could perhaps be found on his territories:

> The rivers on their descent or towards the sea at seasons or periods, allways swell, considerably then roll as torrents at those periods or seasons especially the sands of them (whose sources are known to be far inland, or up in the country) should be collected, washd & sifted to get the particles of the Gold x precious stones from their sands that they often roll down, with their torrents from the upper lands or mountains as is the case with the lavaderos of gold in New Spain and the Rubies & other precious stones in Ceylon & Pegu in the East Indies proper tryals of those circumstances might be made at certain intervals & seasons which perhaps would prove of consequence & gain. The Apalachian Mountains (which divide Carolina from Florida in South America) as the celebrated Mr Catesby informd me, are full of mineral & metallic veins it is not unlikely some of the Carolina rivers may take their source from them or in those very mountains – your agents should therefore have dams made high upon inland on them and where the waters roll least rapid.[101]

The reference to other areas where precious stones were found, in Asia and New Spain are interesting and it is revealing to see a combined interest in science and trade. However, the letter was never sent to him. Before Mendes da Costa mailed it, he received the news that Joseph Salvador had died in Charleston, on 29 December 1786. It is extraordinary that the last remarks that Mendes da Costa intended to make to Salvador show that the latter remained interested in precious stones, and that apparently he wanted to turn his lands in Coroneka to an active use. The old merchant spirit had not vanished completely, and the bitter remarks that Salvador made to Jenkinson regarding his misfortunes in the 1760s seem to have changed in ambitious reflections regarding the possibilities of his American estates. Salvador's correspondence with da Costa shows an interest in precious stones that goes beyond the purely commercial aspects. Because of the importance of technical expertise in determining the value of precious stones, merchants needed to possess knowledge about diamonds, rubies and emeralds, their qualities and their supposed rareness.[102]

The Perception of the World: Mentality and Globalization

A Cosmopolitan and Commercial Mind

The international connections in business maintained by Dormer, Joseph and Francis Salvador, Berthon and Garnault and other merchants who belonged to the cross-cultural trade network hint at the classical view of commerce as a carrier for globalization. Although this is undoubtedly true, it can be argued that the efforts made by merchants to send their textiles across the Atlantic and to buy rough diamonds from the Golconda mines in exchange for Brazilian diamonds polished in Amsterdam, Spanish silver and Mediterranean coral in itself is not enough to proclaim these traders as agents of globalization. It has been argued that the volume of commerce that was sent across trade routes was simply not sufficiently high to consider an early modern globalization.[103] Salvador's investments in North America and his subsequent physical move to South Carolina is in itself not enough to make him a cosmopolite. David Hancock has called the merchants he analysed 'citizens of the world' and he found them to be opportunistic and global. 'Opportunistic' refers to general commercial behaviour: the search for opportunities and the openness to grasp new possibilities. By using the adjective 'global', Hancock referred to the adoption of Hancock 'a particularistic framework for understanding the ways in which merchants worked and prospered'.[104] Both terms have to do with a way of thinking. A merchant that, out of self-interest, looks for new business opportunities is not automatically an agent for globalization. He can become one if his scope of possibilities becomes larger. One of the most important aspects of commercial thinking was the regard for possibilities. A vast amount of ink was spilled just to describe market fluctuations, and to discuss the best destination for parcels of diamonds. Precious stones were sent from London to Antwerp, from Antwerp to Lisbon, back to Antwerp, to Amsterdam and then perhaps back to London again, and sometimes their physical appearance changed in the meantime.[105] The commercial world of Dormer, Salvador and others was a world of possibilities, and they had to keep their eyes open in order not to miss them. A lot of the diamonds that circulated were never sold, and a lot of the commercial opportunities merchants suggested to each other never materialized. In that sense, the correspondence that the merchants who were active in the cross-cultural diamond trade network sent to each other can be considered to be a window of their world. A careful analysis of their letters shows that this window became increasingly global. Enough examples have been given throughout this book to show that traders kept each other informed of a variety of events, both political as well as commercial, that encompassed a great part of the world. In 1737, Francis Mannock hoped to come visit Dormer in Antwerp, but '[I] am detaind by the great demand of Corn in Spain from whence an Express last week bro.t an account of the Barly Cropps being utterly perished & the wheat in almost the same Condition, South France wants it'.[106] A few months later, Mannock wrote about a scarcity of corn that had reached Barcelona.[107] A part from the many references to fleets from India and Brazil that were bringing diamonds, different correspondents of Dormer also referred to other fleets that were not that relevant for their activities in precious stones: 'Two of our China Ships are arrived in Ireland who had a very narrow escape from being taken by 4 m: of war upon the Coast of Africa'.[108] Berthon and Garnault equally wrote to Dormer about the rhythm of ships that arrived in the Lisbon harbour: 'The Pernambuco fleet whoze loading consists of sugars and dry'd and Tanned Hydes, and as usual hardly any money is arrived, as did also at the same time a China ship from Macao, her cargo consists of Plain & wrought silks China & Teas'.[109] At times, Joseph Salvador even informed Dormer of events that seemed entirely unrelated to their commercial affairs: 'I am sorry to tell you tis said the King of Prussias Ship is lost in the Ganges as to the Particulars I shall make it a Point to enquire them.'[110] A whole lot of other information is regularly found in the letters, from political events such as wars ('you will see by the publick news what passes in Scotland the disadvantage of the Kings Troops was owing to the Dragoon's ill behaviour & were the same that caused the defeat of General Cope'), to economical news ('Dear Sir, This serves to acquaint you that the Banck of England having made a call upon their stock of 10 p cent for which they give capital at par to the proprietors').[111] Apart from dry information, merchants often discussed these events in their letters. The biggest space taken up in correspondence was of course given to commercial discussions about prices of commodities, the conditions of certain markets or the availability of supplies. Political discussions about conflicts between nations were also frequent:

> You are right in your conjectures that I wrote you by the mail that was taken I should fear your flag will not be much respected should the french as your auxiliaries raise contributions in Hanover I know so many and Powerful enemies bear hard on us att present but we are in a state not to fear them time will come when the continent must repent what they are now a doing and particularly your Queen nor will it be the least surprise to me should I before the End of the next Campaign See France Supporting her Enemies and carrying them to the Walls of Vienna she may apply when too late to us for Peace[112]

None of the quotations from the above paragraphs were unique and they give a good insight into the world as it was perceived by merchants from a commercial point of view. It goes without saying that the commercial angle sought by merchants forms a serious limitation to an analysis of the world traders considered themselves to be living in, but it forms a strong indication that merchants were used to look at a lot of different situations in a lot of different regions, and that they wanted to share their findings with a certain number of correspondents. The commercial correspondence of the merchants studied in this book reveals an awareness of a world that was becoming more global and it is in this sense that the term cosmopolitanism has often been used to describe merchants active in international trade. It is important to fully comprehend between the difference of an eighteenth-century cosmopolite as someone who is aware of the world surrounding him and an eighteenth-century cosmopolite who is defined as such by a historian from the twenty-first century.

It is important to analyse the eighteenth-century world as it was seen by historical agents, as it makes it possible to study how their image of the world influenced their behaviour. A number of historians working on the emergence of modernity in the late eighteenth and nineteenth century have stressed the importance of the perception of the world by historical actors. For Chris Bayly, growing self-awareness is connected to modern society; for Hodgson a shift in one's way of looking at the world is crucial.[113] By making historical awareness an important element of historical change, both authors give human agency a central place in historical developments. A similar line of reasoning can be found in Frederick Cooper's analysis of empires in world history, when he attributes to people living in empires the quality to be able to think like an empire.[114] In a similar sense, merchants living in a world that was becoming more interconnected had started to think in a global way, which is what David Hancock meant when he attributed the adjective 'global' to the merchants he analysed.[115]

There are a number of advantages in giving the concept of awareness, both of the self and of others, a central place in global history. It avoids the risk of a concept such as early modern globalization to become an anachronism and it allows taking historical limitations into account without the need for abandoning the hypothesis of an early modern globalization. It is the awareness of an interconnected world in the minds of humans who were living in it that can be used as a concept to study forms of pre-industrial globalization in world history. In its attention to cultural specificities, an analysis of awareness avoids that global history becomes a forum dealing exclusively with looking for a modern and often Eurocentric definition for non-modern but global historical developments.[116] A great deal of world history aims at challenging Eurocentric viewpoints and lines of questioning. In comparing Europe with other regions in the world, several historians have discarded the idea of Western European exceptionalism with regard to modern economic progress. The development of modernity as based on economic development has often relied on the singularity of specific circumstances in Western Europe.[117] Uniqueness of elements does not only require that they are present somewhere, but also that they are absent elsewhere. Different scholars have successfully argued that features such as government support for free trade or merchant organization are found outside Europe in a comparable manner. Frédéric Mauro has pointed to the similarities between merchants of the Indian Ocean and traders of the West regarding issues of commercial organization and attempts to achieve prestige and cultural influence.[118] Wang Gungwu has written that 'long-distance overseas trade for the Chinese was no different than for other trading peoples ... merchants developed their skills in a relatively free officially backed trading atmosphere.'[119]

In bringing the self-awareness of groups, individuals and networks to the forefront, and by analysing how different perceptions of the self and the other helped to shape the world, human agency is added to the history of globalization. The danger of opposing regions or cultures and comparing blocs such as empires or civilizations is averted in this manner. In other areas, other scholars have already used the idea of awareness by historical actors to connect their agency to the global, as was done for instance by Nader Sohrabi when he wrote about the Young Turk Revolution of 1908 in the Ottoman Empire.[120] His conclusion may be seen as an important incentive for future research in other areas:

> In conclusion, what the Young Turks knew about other revolutions mattered. Keeping an eye on global revolutions and another on local outbreaks and repertoires, they devised a unique strategy of action that made them part of the wave of constitutional movements at the beginning of twentieth century. Their action transformed the Empire, and with it, the course of modern Turkish history.[121]

The Young Turks were self-aware but also had a perspective on the world. Bayly's self-awareness and Hodgon's way of looking at the world are two coins of the same medal. Self-perception is changed through contact with others. For Margaret Jacob, cosmopolitan meant 'the ability to experience people of different nations, creed, and colors with pleasure, curiosity, and interest'.[122] A consequence of such experiences is that it also leads to self-perception. A consciously positive mentality cannot be attributed to everyone engaged in cross-cultural contact. It is also not sufficient to see cosmopolitan individuals as both cause and consequence with regard to a world that became more interconnected on a global scale. For her, a cosmopolite is 'best defined as a citizen of the world'.[123] This implies a self-awareness that leads to a certain identification of a cosmopolite with the world surrounding him, an identification that can be both positive and negative and that is not exclusive. It is not a coincidence that Jacob found that cosmopolitanism started to develop after a national or local identity had been firmly fixed.[124] The experiences of different diaspora merchants in settling in new host societies have shown that both an internationally rooted as well as a locally constructed identity could coexist. These were not rigid, but depended on context and on negotiation.[125] The term 'embedded cosmopolitanism' might best describe the complementary character of a cosmopolitan, outward-looking mentality of many diaspora merchants and an inward-looking position, following from a desire for belonging, even if the society wherein acceptance was sought was not univocally outward-looking itself.[126] It is this combination that allows for expanding cross-cultural human relationships as foundations for the development of worldwide interconnectedness.

Commerce is one of the aspects of human activity that have played a large role in the expansion of cross-cultural interaction. Thomas Doerflinger, who studied the merchant community of Philadelphia around the time of American independence, underlined that economic development is more than a physical achievement. It is also a cultural expression and a social process.[127] The importance of social embeddedness and cultural influence with regard to commerce has been analysed in the first and third chapters of this book, and it has been suggested that it allows for the use of the concept 'commercial society.'[128] This is visible in the mechanics underlying cross-cultural trade networks. It means that global history cannot limit itself to the economical, for different spheres were very much linked. It is both the interplay of different social and commercial circuits, and the interaction between individuals that growingly took place on transnational and intercultural terms that account for a growing interconnectedness. Cosmopolitanism and cross-cultural interaction both rely on interaction with the stranger. The fact that this interaction was taking place suggests a certain ethics. For Margaret Jacob, the cosmopolitan aspect of commerce implied a politeness that was not always there.[129] For Kwame Anthony Appiah, cosmopolitanism contains the notion that people have obligations to others, and that these 'stretch beyond those to whom we are related by the ties of kith and kind, or even the more formal ties of a shared citizenship'.[130] This notion existed within the international mercantile community within which formal and informal rules and organizations were developed within which cross-cultural trade could reside. As it has been demonstrated above, commercial relationships between people not sharing a similar background or kinship ties did take place on a basis of routine. Merchants knew what to expect from one another, and they had developed a common language within which to understand their cooperation, through correspondence and through the use of trust through reputation and creditworthiness.[131] The expansion of such language to include larger parts of the world can also be witnessed in the development of trade manuals.[132] The commercial ethics that was developed in these written texts had a strong origin in self-interest but was nevertheless an expression of how the commercial world was expanding through the development of growing international connections that became more based on routine and less on chance.

Between merchants, expectations and ethics did not limit themselves to trade exclusively. For Immanuel Kant, hospitality toward strangers is an important aspect of cosmopolitan behaviour.[133] Merchants often offered such hospitality to each other, but also to mutual acquaintances and it is no surprise that Joseph Salvador, when passing by in Flanders, asked Dormer for an introduction to some of his friends for the purpose of leisure:

> Our Joseph Salvador Proposes Going thro' Flanders to Holland Purposely to wait on you he will depart hence in may and hope to reach your Parts ere June your Stile he may perhaps Stop att Lisle Ghent or Brussells so Shall be oblig'd to you for a Recomendatn. To your Friends in those Parts he does not want money or Trade but such as Can Shew him the Places or Introduce him into Company Drink a Glass of Wine or Play a Game att Cards and assures you he Shall ever honour any of Mr. Dormers acquaintance.[134]

A Scientific Interest in the Natural World

The awareness of merchants with regard to the outside world was not restricted to commercial opportunities alone. On 15 March 1759, Joseph Salvador was made a fellow of the Royal Society.[135] According to David Katz, 'Salvador craved public recognition and social status, his route being a fellowship in the Royal Society.'[136] A scientific interest was an important aspect of the sociability of bourgeois culture in the eighteenth century.[137] For Salvador, this could mean two things. He either wanted to use a scientific interest to advance within English high society, or his acceptance in English high society had ignited a certain intellectual curiosity in him. Surely Salvador's presence in a certain social class made him adopt some of the mores and interests of that class, but considering the extent of Salvador's interest in science, his membership of the Royal Society can also be attributed to other reasons: one being genuine scientific interest, the other related to the Jewish community and financial matters.[138]

There were other Jewish members in the Society, and one of them was Emanuel Mendes da Costa. Elected a fellow in 1747, da Costa was a natural historian, a conchologist and a collector of fossils. In the 1760s he was an internationally known scientific figure and he corresponded with acclaimed figures such as Linnaeus.[139] In 1763, da Costa became the Society's clerk, museum keeper, librarian and housekeeper, a job that came with a salary of £50 each year and the provision of a room in Crane Court, in the buildings of the Society. In 1767 it was discovered that da Costa had committed fraud in collecting membership payments.[140] The episode led da Costa to be expelled from the Royal Society. He even was imprisoned in King's Bench, where more debtors spent their time, and remained there for five years.[141] He never recovered from his time in prison and he died in poverty in 1791.[142] Salvador was a cousin of Emanuel Mendes da Costa through marriage, and da Costa's father was John Mendes da Costa, who is mentioned on a warrant for a letter of denization in 1717 next to Francis Salvador, Joseph's father.[143] Da Costa was one of the supporters of Joseph's entry in the Society, and when da Costa became responsible for the fees of the new fellows, Joseph Salvador was one of two men who provided a bond of £1,000 in total as financial security, a sum that he paid to the Society when da Costa's fraud was discovered.[144]

Joseph's role in the Society did not restrict itself to financial support for his cousin. He had a genuine interest in science and his admission letter mentioned him as 'a Gentleman worthy that honour and as versed in several parts of Literature'.[145] An inquiry made about certain books by Salvador demonstrates more a professional interest than one in literature, for it features books on German government and French finance, some of Montesquieu's works in French, 'Works of Mr Rollin, [other] than his Histoires Anciennes & his belles lettres.'[146] Salvador also wanted to improve his notions of Spanish, and he asked his cousin for 'Mariana's history of Spain in Spanish, Ustariz on commerce in Spanish, Ulloa's voyages to measure a degree in Spanish.'[147]

Joseph Salvador co-proposed the admission of five new fellows. Naphtali Franks was 'a person conversant in Botany and other branches of Literature, and likely to prove a valuable and Useful member'.[148] The Franks family was one of the most important Ashkenazi families active in England and North America. Naphtali maintained business contacts with his brother in Philadelphia and was active as a diamond trader in London.[149] David Riz was described as 'greatly conversant in Mechanics & Natural Philosophy',[150] Marie Joseph Louis d'Albert d'Ailly Picquigny was skilled in mathematics, experimental physics and chemistry,[151] and a John Baptist Elie de Beaumont promoted philosophical knowledge.[152] The specialties of William Cracraft of London were not indicated.[153] It is worth noticing that from the three individuals whose specialty is known, two of them were skilled in natural science.

Salvador's interest in science is also confirmed when looking at the life of a Jewish scientist who never received a fellowship of the Royal Society. Israel Lyons, who died in 1775 when he was only thirty-six years old, grew up in Cambridge, published a mathematical study when he was only nineteen and lectured on botany at Oxford. He worked on a Nautical Almanac for the Astronomer Royal and was chosen as the astronomer on the 1773 voyage toward the North Pole.[154] He published *A Treatise of Fluxions* in 1758. This mathematical work had earned him a promising reputation in scientific circles, since it was published when Lyons was only nineteen. The list of subscribers of this work includes many prominent figures from Cambridge, professors and professors to be, but also future bishops.[155] A number of members from the London Sephardic Community are featured on the subscription list. The Sephardic subscribers were almost all related to Joseph Salvador. Next to Salvador himself, Baron d'Aguilar, married to Salvador's niece, was on the list, as well as Phineas Serra, Salvador's attorney, Moses Franco, Salvador's son-in-law, and Abraham de Paiba, related to the husband of Joseph's sister Abigail.[156] The reason for the presence of Joseph Salvador and a group of individuals that were interconnected with him within the Sephardic community must have been more than an attempt to support a member of the same community, for Lyons was an unorthodox Ashkenazi Jew, and the Ashkenazi and Sephardic communities in London, although not without mutual contacts, were two different social groups.[157] Perhaps Joseph Salvador was genuinely interested in Lyons's work, and tried to spread his enthusiasm to family members.

In January 1785, Salvador had settled in South Carolina, and he sent Mendes da Costa a description of the land and its inhabitants. He wrote about the natural environment, the animals that lived there and the habits of the people. The letter becomes particularly interesting when Joseph Salvador described an astronomical observation he had made at a place called Cross Creek: 'I saw a small bearded comet having no instrument in the place all I could do was to observe her course with the eye she seemd to me to be about 18 degrees to the south ward of Capricorn.'[158] It seems that Salvador intended to publish his observation, for Emanuel Mendes da Costa answered him that his description of the phenomenon was 'not sufficiently complete as to demand publication'.[159] Two decades before, Salvador had already expressed an interest in astronomy. When he was in Paris in 1763, Mendes da Costa sent him a letter relating the latest news regarding the Royal Astronomer, the same Society that had given Israel Lyons the task of writing a Nautical Almanac.[160] The following year, somebody sent Salvador a letter in which he described a solar eclipse that had taken place that year.[161] It is unknown whether Salvador had obtained membership of the astronomical society, but he was at least active in two other scientific circles. In 1785, Salvador wrote three small letters to the clerks of three societies, ordering that the books he possessed as member of each circle should be given to his cousin, so that he could send them to South Carolina via Joseph's son Joshua. Apart from the Royal Society, he addressed letters to the clerks of the Society of Arts and Manufactures and the Society of Antiquaries.[162]

These requests imply that Salvador knew he would not be returning to England, that he possessed a certain amount of scientific literature, and that he considered these books to be important enough to be sent to him in the New World. Membership of different scientific circles was more than a vehicle with which attain social status and acceptance: it was the expression of a personal interest in science, an interest that he had elaborated in London and that he took with him when he went to settle himself in South Carolina at the end of his life. Perhaps this interest was better developed because in London he had moved in circles where such an interest was not at all atypical, but that does not mean it that it was not always already there.

Salvador's interest in science was shared by another merchant in the cross-cultural diamond trade network. George Clifford was very interested in botany, zoology and horticulture, and he was a patron and benefactor of Linnaeus, who stayed at his estate between 1736 and 1738. Linnaeus greatly admired the gardens of Clifford's estate at Hartekamp. He made a catalogue of the gardens under the title *Hortus Cliffortianus*.[163] Clifford was more than a wealthy benefactor; he shared with Salvador a genuine interest in scientific matters. The specimens he had in his garden and tropical houses contained exotic birds and plants and seeds originating from all over the world, Virginia as well as the East Indies. It is a good example of interaction and awareness. Scientific networks have been studied as another type of early globalization, and it can be said that both Salvador and Clifford belonged to such networks, by correspondence, by membership of scientific organizations and, in Clifford's case, by exchange circuits between botanists and garden owners.

Agency through Position

The international scope of the commercial activities undertaken by Francis and Joseph Salvador and other merchants in the cross-cultural trade network contributed to a change in mentality. Commercially, their activities remained rooted in the self-interested search for profit, but this self-interest was applied to social relationships that maintained a form of expectation of commercial ethics that had to be taken into account. Socially, most of the merchants active in the diamond network were outsiders and they were all looking for a place in a new and sometimes hostile society. The position they managed to find in society and in international trade was linked with awareness and self-perception. From the sometimes negative public opinion towards these merchants it is clear that this reflection on the self and on the world was not restricted to the traders themselves. Others had an opinion on them. The acceptance of foreign merchants in socially and commercially distinct environments did not only depend on them and their capacity to adapt. It also had to do with the image that others held of them. They were known to the public, and Salvador's sexual escapades had even reached the papers. It seems to have become increasingly difficult for wealthy diamond merchants who were internationally active to remain totally anonymous at a time when the curiosity of the public was expanding as well:

> On Tuesday last came to Town a Jew, who has been nine Years in India a Diamond-hunting, and 'tis said has gain'd a great Estate by that Pastime; He left here, when he went for India, a Wife and nine Children; his Wife then going with a Tenth; all of whom he has found in good Health.[164]

Some of these merchants were also known by the government, and the Salvadors were taken interest in by policy makers of different countries. In the 1730s, Francis Salvador was in control of the family business, and the success of his firm did not go unnoticed by Portuguese representatives in London. They were looking for advice regarding a severe price crisis in the European diamond market caused by the discovery of diamonds in Brazil a decade earlier.[165] Because of the dominant position at that time of London as an import centre for Indian diamonds, the Portuguese turned their attention to experienced traders in the British capital for their advice.

The Portuguese ambassador, an uncle of Sebastião José de Carvalho e Melo, was explicitly requested by the King to consult Francis Salvador, 'q entre os da Sua Nação fazia huma das primeiras figuras por cabedal, por credito, e por Inteligencia'.[166] He advised to the Portuguese ambassador the arrangement of the diamond trade in the form of a trade monopoly. The Portuguese government did not immediately follow this advice, but they did install a mining monopoly. In 1738, the advice of Francis Salvador was sought for a second time. The Portuguese settlement on the island of Salsete, off the coast of Bombay, was threatened by an invasion of the Marathas. The same year, Pombal was named Portuguese minister at the court in London and he asked the English government for ships to be sent to the island for its defence. Negotiations with directors of the East India Company followed and they took place at Salvador's house in London.[167] Salvador's good connections with the Company were named as the reason for his role as intermediary.[168] Failure of the talks about Salsete fortified Pombal's idea that Portugal should take care of itself and that a Portuguese East India Company should be established, the *Companhia geral do Oriente*.[169] In trying to resolve their problems in Salsete, Portuguese officials decided to buy ships in the English capital that could be sent to India. Pombal was asked to consult Portuguese merchants in London on the different options and letters were sent back and forth regarding the *nau de guerra* Cumberland. In February 1740 the news was spread that Francis Salvador had bought the Cumberland for the Portuguese government and that the ship was to sail to Macao.[170] Later, Cardinal da Motta, who was the prime minister, asked Pombal whether Salvador was interested in buying another vessel on behalf of the Portuguese. Eventually, other ships parted from Lisbon to the Coromandel Coast but Pombal was thanked for his efforts and efficiency in purchasing a ship in London.[171] The reliance of Portuguese officials on a merchant whose family had left Portugal a century earlier for fear of persecution is noteworthy, and a third affair between Portuguese officials and Francis Salvador in London was the most peculiar one. After his arrival in London, Pombal deplored the state of his official residence. Soon enough, he asked permission to move to another, more expensive, residence. In November 1740 the decision was made to rent another house, that included a chapel to celebrate Catholic mass, and Francis Salvador paid the deposit.[172] He also financed several repairs to the chapel that were made in the following years.[173] Problems arose when Salvador had difficulty getting his money back. John Bristow, a good acquaintance and business partner of Salvador in later years, eventually lent money to the Portuguese officials in London.[174]

The advisory and financial rendered by his father to the Portuguese government were matched by Joseph's activities in favour of the British government. The development of the British Empire relied on the 'monied interest', a group of men that were 'closely and habitually concerned with that machinery for creating and mobilizing credit which had been taking shape since the late seventeenth century'.[175] It is argued that this group of men not only helped to tie the city of London together, but also the British Empire, by a series of entangled relationships.[176] Joseph Salvador was a financial advisor for the government, and he maintained correspondence with the Duke of Newcastle, who was prime minister from 1754 to 1756 and 1757 to 1762. He also frequently provided Charles Jenkinson, future Earl of Liverpool with advice when he was undersecretary of state during the governments of Lord Bute and Lord Grenville, with whom Salvador also had direct contacts. In December 1758, Salvador sent a plan to the Duke of Newcastle regarding a lottery to raise considerable funds for the government. He did not mention a possible subscription of himself.[177] In the following years, Salvador continued to give financial advice and in 1778 he worked on a plan inspired by Necker's idea to raise money for the French government. He made it clear that he could engage for a sum of money, but that he preferred an advisory role.[178]

Salvador also played a prominent role in a dispute within the East India Company in the 1760s. The conflict polarised around Robert Clive and Laurence Sulivan. The origins of this conflict between these two men lied in the problem of remitting fortunes that were made in India by company servants. Sulivan complained that the drafts that were made on the Company were so high that damage was done to its credit. Clive supported a reply from the Bengal servants of the Company who disagreed with Sulivan.[179] Matters came to a head in 1763, after Sulivan and his faction won the elections for new directors. Clive possessed the revenue rights of a district in Bengal. One of the first things Sulivan did after his successful election was the suspension of Clive's *jagir* payments in Bengal.[180] Joseph Salvador saw a possibility of a restoration for Clive when armed Company forces were defeated in Bengal in 1764. Clive had already proven his military worth at the Battle of Plassey in 1757 and Salvador proposed a scheme in which Clive was to return to Bengal as commander-in-chief and governor, and in which his *jagir* income was returned to him. The plan also included an attempt to secure the election of new directors that would be favourable to Clive and his faction.[181] Salvador talked his plan through in private meeting with Clive and other members of the Company that stood on his side, such as Mr Rous.[182] He also tried to win government support through Lord Grenville, who had replaced Lord Bute as the head of the administration.[183] A motion supporting Salvador's plan was accepted in March 1764 and new Company elections took place exactly one month later. The vote was tied and Salvador thought that reconciliation between Clive and Sulivan might be better for the Company.[184] Sulivan withdrew and Rous, a member of Clive's faction, became the new chairman of the general court of directors. At that point, Clive seemed to be quite confident in the success of the rest of the plan, others, including Joseph Salvador were more cautious: 'I propose going up to attend the General Court & shall use my utmost endeavors to fix things on a solid basis for I am apprehensive these disputes if not stoppd will give the administration much trouble in future.'[185] In May of that year, the debates about the *jagir* ended with a favourable decision for Clive, who was to receive the revenues for another ten years. He departed for India on 4 June 1764.[186] Classic theories of the British Empire that analyse the role of the East India Company with regard to military expansion and growing territorial control over the Indian subcontinent, picture Clive as a stereotypical 'empire-builder'.[187] Clive emerges as a history-maker but the plan of Joseph Salvador and its success however shows that there is a much more complex reality behind such a straightforward reading of historical agency. Clive's actions in India depended on a wider set of interactions. In this context, imperial agency becomes something that might find its public expression in the actions of 'great men', and as such it might be seen as 'constituted by a cultural order of which it [agency] is an idiosyncratic expression'.[188]

These episodes of different involvement of Francis and Joseph Salvador in government affairs show how position affects agency. Inspired by Raymond Aron, Marshall Sahlins connected agency with position, defined as a 'place in a set of relationships, whether institutional, conjunctural, or both'.[189] According to Sahlins, one's position can enable individual agency. In the case of Francis Salvador, and subsequently in the case of his son Joseph, his position as a well-to-do Jewish merchant in London put him in a position that gave him agency, institutionally as well as conjuncturally. It complements the idea of self-awareness with an appreciation by others. The interest taken in Francis and Joseph Salvador came from the status attributed to them. They were thought of as well-connected and intelligent, and were asked to give their opinion with regard to imperial policy, finance, conflicts in India and diamond trade in Brazil. The cosmopolitan outlook of the Salvadors was appreciated as such by people holding different positions in society, and this allowed for merchants such as Francis and Joseph Salvador agency in the creation of a more globalized early modern world.

CONCLUSION

This book has attempted to answer two questions. The first one is a specific historical question: How did international, cross-cultural commerce take place in the first half of the eighteenth century? The second question is more general: How did a growing evolution of international and cross-cultural trade contribute to globalizing movements? If many of the claims about global trade made in large-scale histories are to be taken seriously, two questions need to be addressed regarding the concrete and durable organization of trade and the best methodology of analysis.

This book has departed from a concrete case study, that of a cross-cultural commercial network active in the diamond business, and it has advocated the use of network analysis as a good methodological tool to study commercial history. In such analysis, the point of departure is micro-historical, and focuses on the organization of horizontal human relationships. In this focus, relationships within mono-cultural groups or trade diasporas have not been at the centre of analysis. All too often, large-scale histories have remained limited to a comparison between different groups, different regions or different cultures, especially when trying to answer the question of differing paths towards modernity or economic progress.

In focusing instead on cross-cultural relationships, human interaction becomes fundamental in explaining the world. This avoids a history of early globalization that is built on a comparison of difference and inequality. It suggests that merchants were very capable, by the nature of their profession, to overcome cultural barriers and to construct long-lasting relationships with traders from very different backgrounds. Analysing the internal organization of a cross-cultural circuit of trade has put the question of trust on the table. Without the ability to rely on other merchants or without the reliance on personal judgement about the future behaviour of other network members, a structural and regular business network could not have existed. In the absence of an international law-enforcing framework, informal mechanisms were needed in order for these merchants to be able to cooperate without meeting eye-to-eye, in a regular and long-lasting manner. This was achieved by the incorporation of routine.

The circulation of information, the reciprocal state of relationships and the creation of a sense of familiarity between correspondents were the main components of the generation of trust amongst merchants. These informal mechanisms were not only created in a functional way, corresponding to a commercial need, but were embedded in a social and cultural framework. All of these elements made a merchant's reputation, and this was a commodity that was applicable beyond the confines of the network.

Self-interest and an open vision assured that loyalty within networks was not limitless. Dormer cooperated with a number of intermarried Ashkenazi firms who were severe competitors of his partners in the cross-cultural diamond trade network. This relationship demonstrates that trade networks and their internal organization were not de-attached structures. Next to an insertion in a socio-cultural environment, of which they took certain elements such as friendship and applied them to business, they were also embedded in an informal and international commercial society. Thanks to this embeddedness, mechanisms of trust and credit can be used in the construction of more privileged relationships. Further research is needed to assert the importance of other types of commercial organization and their connection with a larger and informal business community. The role of business correspondence also deserves further research. Part of the reason why personal characteristics such as reputation and creditworthiness were so important was because no internationally accepted legal system existed that allowed for a speedy and cheap resolution of commercial conflicts. The development of a legal framework that was more apt to deal with an internationally-expanding commerce can shed more light on the role played by formal and informal agreements in the international business community. It should also not be forgotten that a lot of commercial correspondence has been preserved exactly because of their legal use in cases of bankruptcy.

Business correspondences started generally with a demand for information. Most of the firms for whom Dormer worked on commission became acquainted with the English merchant through recommendation. The Salvadors in particular made various efforts to mention Dormer to merchants who were interested in the diamond trade. In this manner, merchants built a portfolio of correspondents, residing in different cities, with whom a mutually beneficial relationship was maintained. Sometimes a correspondence proved to be a dead end, but sometimes it evolved into a web with other traders involved, a network. Merchant society was not a community in which everybody knew everybody else. However, intensive webs of correspondence and extensive strings of credit were able to overcome problems of uncertainty. The notion of the stranger was an acceptable one, as long as they could prove their trustworthiness. Dealing with unknown merchants was followed according to certain commercial custom that relied on international reputational mechanisms. In trade, strangers became familiar through informal habit.

The high amount of reciprocal credit operations that can be distilled from Dormer's correspondence is remarkable. More research is needed on the way in which connections based on credit tied the international mercantile community closer together. The evolution of the bill of exchange as a negotiable commodity is very important in this regard, since it shows how the familiar and the unfamiliar became connected. In the eighteenth century, the establishment of financial interdependencies through credit was already well on its way in contributing to more global interdependencies. The breakdown of the strings of credit between Brazilian diamond miners and Portuguese and foreign merchants in Lisbon had profound consequences on both sides of the Atlantic. A new law in August 1753 tried to isolate the diamond district in Minas Gerais from the surrounding colony. It brought about social change in the mining society that had developed itself in Brazil ever since the first discoveries of diamonds in the 1720s. Additional research should focus not only on the role of credit played in the long-distance relationships between traders, but also on different solutions put forward by different cultures to solve problems of credit. Bills of exchange worked as a method of payment because they were internationally accepted. Although their functioning was partially based on a certain legal enforceability, it seems to have been more important that their acceptance was widespread. One of the questions that need to be addressed is about the boundaries of the bill of exchange and its relation with regard to other credit systems as adopted in other societies and cultures, such as Hinduism, Islam and the Chinese civilization.

It is important to note that in studying a trade network, the analytical unit is the collective body of merchants, not necessarily the most successful or largest ones, since it is not just about individual performance or economic success. In its group aspect, this book has been inspired by the 'history from below'-school. The image of merchants arising from this book is a multiple one. Their careers cannot be restricted to those of wealth-seeking, self-interested individuals. The best example is that of Joseph Salvador. He combined the India trade with commerce in Brazilian diamonds, sent voyages to Spanish America, and had different ideas regarding imperial difficulties such as the problems of Lord Clive and the East India Company in Bengal. His mentality, connections and business enterprises all had integrative effects regarding the bigger world around him. He was firmly embedded in different social and professional circles, and his position in these circles gave him different forms of agency. Within the Sephardic community, he was known as a philanthropist. He made different contributions, varying from relieving the poor to projects related to education and health care. He was a *parnas* of the Portuguese-Jewish Synagogue and was consulted as one of the community's leaders. The Salvador firm was, through business links and intermarriage, firmly rooted in London's Sephardic community, with a very important extension to Amsterdam. He was a practising Jew but felt loyalty to the British Empire. His communal attachments perhaps found their way out when his involvement became clear in the promotion for the Jew Bill in 1753. His scientific interests had made him a fellow of the Royal Society and through connections he had in the upper echelons of the British government, he became part of a group of decision-makers that was located at the very centre of the empire. As such, he was more than an outsider who sought social acceptance outside the diaspora. Merchants were aware of the difficulties that came with the label of being a foreigner. It is a vital observation to make that all of the merchants involved in the cross-cultural diamond trade network experienced a sense of detachment. Almost all of them had started as foreigners searching for acceptance in sometimes hostile societies. Yet, the belonging to an international diaspora is not sufficient to attribute these merchants with fundamental historical agency with regard to an early modern globalization. It did give them an outward-look, and a mindset that was cosmopolitan and international. These characteristics were further fortified because of their profession. As merchants, they constantly had to keep their eyes open for fruitful business opportunities. The means through which the vision of possibilities in traders' eyes was transmitted were the letters they wrote to one another. Seen in this way, business correspondence sent around within a network not only worked as a way of maintaining internal integration, but also served as a vehicle to interact with the outside world, and as such an analysis of these letters is a reflection upon the state of awareness and the seizure of possibilities as experienced by the concerned merchants. This also meant that merchants who regularly cooperated with traders from different backgrounds were aware of differences but did not consider them to be harmful to trade. They rather made efforts to overcome cultural, social or religious differences with their correspondents by informing themselves of the habits of others. In the trade in bills of exchange, for instance, Jewish participation was seen by contemporaries as so important that Christian merchants made calendars indicating the Shabbat:

> because of the multiplicity of the transactions with the Jews of Amsterdam and their daily negotiations and commerce, it is necessary for the Christians to know at what time on Fridays the Jewish Shabbat begins and when it ends on Saturdays. We therefore drawn up this neat schedule of Shabbat times for the entire year [1753].[1]

On an organizational and public level, there were still signs of inequality, with laws in use forbidding Jews to be part of the guilds, but perhaps on an individual level, of day-to-day interactions, tolerance with regard to Jews was not really an issue. There was equality, and although it was very clear for Dormer that he was trading with Jewish merchants and that such religious difference had consequences with regard to the pace of their business, it was never questioned.

Next to the component of worldly awareness in business, the traders studied in this book all felt loyalty to different host societies. Berthon and Garnault were socially part of the body of English traders in Lisbon, and both the Salvador and Levy families were patriots, who considered England and Holland, respectively, as their home. James Dormer had married into local gentry and some of the members of the Clifford family became important members of the Amsterdam city administration, some of them even became major figures. It is exactly through the notion of shared loyalties, to international diasporas and networks of trade, but also to a host society, that growing global interdependency can be sustained. The awareness the merchants in the cross-cultural network possessed was cosmopolitan. In this manner, the dialogue between action and thought was crucial when thinking about globalization. It is not possible to know whether a particular frame of mind shaped their concrete actions in the world of trade, or whether their activities as merchants helped to create a particular psychology that can be seen as a contributor to a globalization current. It also does not really matter, and it is most likely that both aspects enhanced each other. A cosmopolitan outlook caused by international trade connections did not conflict with a desire to belong to a local society. This opened some possibilities and closed others. It kept the eyes of merchants open to the outside world, without being dettached from the place where they lived. As such, they can be seen as embedded cosmopolites. The wife of Paul Berthon had written to her son staying in London that 'now indeed I regard myself as a Citizen of the World'.[2]

This self-awareness found confirmation in the opinion made about these merchants by outsiders. They were seen as people who knew what was going on in other parts of the world, and their character and abilities put them in an advisory role with regard to international issues. They were not only citizens of the world in their own eyes, but also in those of others, and it is this mentality that caused change in, and was affected by, growing global interaction through human-shaped networks. The merchants that have been the subject of this book might have been exceptions in the eighteenth-century world, but their presence contributed to change with regard to the society that surrounded them and forced societies to develop new ways of thinking about identity, the self and interaction with the other, politically, legally, socially, culturally and commercially. The combination of the cosmopolitan outlook and membership of international networks of diaspora merchants with the search for a position in local society offers a solution for the paradox that the same merchants who managed to integrate remote regions were not really embedded in those regions. The change brought about by merchants active in cross-cultural trade networks did not remain limited to them. Their active search for local acceptance forced societies to re-think their organization and the discussion on the position of foreigners took an important place in eighteenth-century public debate. Discussing change in mentality brought about by international trade asserts the importance of culture, and the role it plays deserves further study. An anthropologist has put it this way: 'the claim is not that culture determines history, only that it organizes it'.[3]

This book has called for human interaction across boundaries as a basic explanatory factor in accounts of early modern globalization. The idea of an early modern integration through commerce might be disputed on hard economic terms, but the growing amount of successful cross-cultural interactions and the change it incited in societies can be labelled as a form of globalization. More research is needed to demonstrate the change brought about in other societies. Network analysis relies heavily on social and cultural elements, and these were far from universal. Through a study of the reciprocal interaction between societies and outsiders on a worldwide scale, a more global history of globalization will be possible. Further analysis on the influence of international trade on societies as a whole, and not just on the creation of a cosmopolitan mercantile mentality in individuals, might show that in the eighteenth century, the minority of internationally active merchants was not the only group to have developed a more global frame of mind.

At the same time, this monograph has attempted to offer a historical narrative based on cross-cultural interaction instead of inter-cultural comparison, and in doing so, it has tried to avert the dangers of prejudice regarding technological, organizational or mental superiority of one cultural group over another. Cultures change; they are not timeless essences imposing their framework on individuals. Human action has contributed greatly to such change, especially when it was cross-cultural. In this sense, this book has hoped to avoid Eurocentric notions with regard to accounts of early modern globalization, in spite of the fact that the merchants studied in this book were European. Rather than developing a discourse in which the role of Europe is denied, this book has aimed to answer the call made by Dipesh Chakrabarty to 'provincialize' Europe.[4] In arguing for a history of globalization, a historian cannot limit him- or herself to the idea that a global phenomenon only has a right to exist when it is directly applicable to the world as a whole. Tendencies of growing interdependence on a worldwide scale must have started with co-existent forms of local integration. The centrality of human interaction in the process of worldwide integration is vital. This means that globalization should be seen as a movement arising from within human communities and that man should be seen as a social animal, looking for interaction with others. If that is a natural tendency, different patterns of interdependence can occur at the same time but in different places. In this manner, the history of globalization becomes also a history of how varying types of regional human interaction became increasingly connected on a global scale.

More focused histories of interaction within a specified area, such as the Atlantic, the Indian Ocean or the space of the Silk Road deserve to be incorporated in a world history that is conceived as a history of global interconnectedness.

In discarding the idea of a geographically centralized origin of globalization, the emphasis on human interaction becomes ever more important. World history is not a history of the evolutionary path towards a unified world, in which one region has succeeded in imposing its culture on the regions with which it has interacted. Different cultures that were engaged in mutual contact in the Indian Ocean, for instance, were not waiting on European arrival to start a form of local integration based on networks of trade and information exchange. Many interdependencies between different people and different cultures were already taking place, creating a local pattern of integration that became attached, also through European action, to a wider world. Multiple integrative movements at different places all have to take into account a human propensity to cooperate with people who were fundamentally different. Historical network analysis can play an important role in future research regarding various large-scale interdependencies that might or might not include a European contribution. A methodological cadre that departs from social and cultural specificities allows better for an analysis of cross-cultural dialogue than an analysis that departs from a universal image of man as self-interested and rational. Such an analytical framework also corresponds better with our present-day reality in which Western economical and political dominance is increasingly considered a thing of the past. This book has analysed merchants who were all European. The historical development of networks of European merchants can be rightfully considered to be an important contributor to interconnectedness on a large scale, but it was not a unique development that was absent in other regions. A larger focus on the role played by different people might allow for a global history in which European developments can be analysed next to historical phenomena in other regions that played an equally crucial role. Concretely, this means that other types of commercial interaction should be included in histories of commodity trade. One of the challenges posed to historians researching international diamond trade, for instance, will be the investigation of networks of Indian entrepreneurs selling precious stones in Persia, China and the Mogul Empire. It is only by including these other circuits that the full role played by international commerce in the development of globalization can be asserted.

NOTES

The following abbreviations have been used throughout the notes:

AdB/DG	Archief de Bergeyck, Beveren, Deelarchief Goubau
AHU/CUMG	Arquivo Histórico Ultramarino, Lisbon, Conselho Ultramarino Brasil/ Minas Gerais
AHU/MAMG	Arquivo Histórico Ultramarino, Lisbon, Manuscritos Avulsos de Minas Gerais
APM/SC	Arquivo Público Mineiro, Belo Horizonte, Seção Colonial
BL/BCD	Burney Collection Database, British Library
BNA/PRO	British National Archives, Kew, Surrey, Public Records Office
BL/IOR	British Library, India Office Records
BL/LP	British Library, Liverpool Papers
BL/NP	British Library, Newcastle Papers
BL/TP	British Library, Tyrawly Papers, Correspondence of Lord Tyrawly when ambassador in Portugal
BNL/CFGM	Biblioteca Nacional, Lisbon, Códices e Fundo Geral dos Manuscritos
BNL/PBA	Biblioteca Nacional, Lisbon, Colecção Pombalina
FAA	Felixarchief Antwerpen
FLRU/RFP	Fondren Library Rice University, Richardson Family Papers (1714–1802)
GAA	Gemeentearchief Amsterdam
GAA/PIGA	Gemeentearchief Amsterdam, Archief van de Portugees-Israëlitische Gemeente te Amsterdam
HLL	The Huguenot Library University College London
LMA	London Metropolitan Archives
NA/SP	National Archives, Kew, Surrey, State Papers
NEHA	Dutch Economic Historical Archive in Amsterdam
ODNB	*Oxford Dictionary of National Biography*
RS	Archives of the Royal Society
SCDAH/PRCB	South Carolina Department of Archives & History, Public Register Conveyance Books (Charleston Deeds)
SCHS	South Carolina Historical Society Charleston
TdT	Arquivo Nacional da Torre do Tombo

Introduction

1. See for instance W. J. Baumol, 'Entrepreneurship: Productive, Unproductive, Destructive', *Journal of Political Economy*, 98:5, part 1 (October 1990), pp. 893–921, for an analysis of how the role of entrepreneurs in society depends on the payoffs offered by society with regard to productive economic activities. See D. S. Landes, *The Wealth and Poverty of Nations: Why Some are So Rich and Some So Poor* (New York: W. W. Norton & Company Inc., 1999); E. L. Jones, *The European Miracle: Environments, Economies and Geopolitics in the History of Europe and Asia* (Cambridge: Cambridge University Press, 1981).
2. See for instance K. Pomeranz, *The Great Divergence: China, Europe, and the Making of the Modern World Economy* (Princeton, NJ: Princeton University Press, 2000).
3. For a general critique of a Eurocentric approach, see J. M. Blaut, *Eight Eurocentric Historians* (New York: Guilford Press, 2000). A. G. Frank, *ReOrient: Global Economy in the Asian Age* (Berkeley, CA: University of California Press, 1998), pp. 1–51 provides an outline of a non-Eurocentric methodology.
4. M. Hodgson, *Rethinking World History: Essays on Europe, Islam, and World History*, ed. E. Burke III (Cambridge and New York: Cambridge University Press, 1993), p. 315.
5. J. de Vries, 'Connecting Europe and Asia: A Quantitative Analysis of the Cape-Route Trade, 1497–1795', in D.O. Flynn, A. Giráldez and R. von Glahn (eds), *Global Connections and Monetary History, 1470–1800* (Aldershot: Ashgate, 2003), pp. 35–106, on p. 37.
6. A. Greif, *Institutions and the Path to the Modern Economy: Lessons from Medieval Trade* (Cambridge and New York: Cambridge University Press, 2006), p. 124.
7. M. Granovetter, 'The Strength of Weak Ties', *American Journal of Sociology*, 78:6 (May 1973), pp. 1360–80; and M. Granovetter, 'Economic Action and Social Structure: The Problem of Embeddedness', *American Journal of Sociology*, 91:3 (November 1985), pp. 481–510.
8. The most common examples are those of the Jewish, Huguenot, Greek and Armenian diasporas. See for instance E. R. Seeman, 'Jews in the Early Modern Atlantic: Crossing Boundaries, Keeping Faith', in J. Cañizares-Esguerra and E. R. Seeman (eds), *The Atlantic in Global History 1500–2000* (Upper Saddle River, NJ: Pearson Prentice Hall, 2007), pp. 39–59; R. L. Kagan and P. D. Morgan (eds), *Atlantic Diasporas: Jews, Conversos, and Crypto-Jews in the Age of Mercantilism, 1500–1800* (Baltimore, MD: The Johns Hopkins University Press, 2009); I. B. McCabe, G. Harlaftis and I. P. Minoglou (eds), *Diaspora Entrepreneurial Networks – Four Centuries of History* (Oxford and New York: Berg, 2005); M. Rozen (ed.), *Homelands and Diasporas: Greeks, Jews and their Migrations* (London and New York: I. B. Tauris & Co, 2008); J. Israel, *Diasporas within a Diaspora: Jews, Crypto-Jews and the World Maritime Empires (1540–1740)* (Leiden: Brill, 2002); and J. Israel, *European Jewry in the Age of Mercantilism, 1550–1750* (Oxford: Clarendon Press, 1985). For more specific references to the different Jewish diasporas and on the Huguenots, see Chapters 4 and 5, pp. 208–9, nn. 15–16, p. 216, n. 17 and p. 221, nn 121–2.
9. See for instance F. Trivellato, *The Familiarity of Strangers – The Sephardic Diaspora, Livorno, and Cross-Cultural Trade in the Early Modern Period* (New Haven, CT; London: Yale University Press, 2009), pp. 132–52 for an analysis of the link between marriage policy and business association.

10. F. Trivellato, 'Juifs de Livourne, Italiens de Lisbonne, hindous de Goa. Réseaux marchands et échanges interculturels à l'époque moderne', *Annales: Histoire, Sciences sociales*, 58:3 (May–June 2003), pp. 581–603, on pp. 582–4.
11. A. O. Hirschman, *The Passions and the Interests – Political Arguments for Capitalism before Its Triumph* (Princeton, NJ: Princeton University Press, 1977), pp. 51–2.
12. A. D. Kessler, *A Revolution in Commerce: The Parisian Merchant Court and the Rise of Commercial Society* (New Haven, CT; London: Yale University Press, 2007), p. 106. See also A. D. Kessler, 'Enforcing Virtue: Social Norms and Self-Interest in an Eighteenth-Century Merchant Court', *Law and History Review*, 22:1 (Spring 2004), pp. 71–118.
13. I. Ben-Amos, 'Gifts and Favors: Informal Support in Early Modern England', *Journal of Modern History*, 75 (2000), pp. 295–338, on p. 295.
14. G. Jones and K. E. Sluyterman, 'British and Dutch Business History', in F. Amatori and G. Jones (eds), *Business History around the World* (Cambridge: Cambridge University Press, 2003), pp. 111–45, on p. 131.
15. L. Bernstein, 'Opting Out of the Legal System: Extralegal Contractual Relations in the Diamond Industry', *Journal of Legal Studies*, 21 (January 1992), pp. 115–57; and B. D. Richman, 'How Community Institutions Create Economic Advantage: Jewish Diamond Merchants In New York', *Law & Social Inquiry*, 32:2 (Spring 2006), pp. 383–420.
16. For cross-cultural partnerships noted in records of the East India Company, see above, pp. 46–7.
17. Trivellato, *The Familiarity of Strangers*.
18. S. Chapman, *The Rise of Merchant Banking* (London; Boston, MA; Sydney: George Allen & Unwin, 1984), pp. 1–5.
19. E. Meel, 'De firma James Dormer tussen traditie en vernieuwing: een Englishman abroad in het achttiende-eeuwse handelskapitalisme te Antwerpen' (PhD dissertation, Katholieke Universiteit Leuven, 1986), pp. 219–27.
20. Ibid., pp. 162, 223.
21. K. Degryse, 'De Antwerpse fortuinen: kapitaalsaccumulatie, -investering en –rendement te Antwerpen in de 18[de] eeuw', *Bijdragen tot de Geschiedenis*, 88:1–4 (2005), p. 87.
22. L. Kooijmans, *Vriendschap en de kunst van het overleven in de zeventiende en achttiende eeuw* (Amsterdam: Bert Bakker, 1997), pp. 326–7.
23. Chapman, *The Rise of Merchant Banking*, p. 3.
24. D. Hancock, *Citizens of the World: London Merchants and the Integration of the British Atlantic Community, 1735–1785* (Cambridge: Cambridge University Press, 1995), p. 4.
25. M. Jacob, *Strangers Nowhere in the World: The Rise of Cosmopolitanism in Early Modern Europe* (Philadelphia, PA: University of Pennsylvania Press, 2006), p. 67.
26. For the insertion of cosmopolitan diaspora merchants in the specific society of the port city, see D. Cesarani, *Port Jews – Jewish Communities in Cosmopolitan Maritime Trading Centres, 1550–1950* (London; Portland, OR: Frank Cass, 2002); and D. Cesarani and G. Romain (eds), *Jews and Port Cities 1590–1990: Commerce, Community, and Cosmopolitanism* (London: Mitchell Vallentine & Co., 2005).
27. I. B. McCabe, 'Trading Diaspora, State Building and the Idea of National Interest', Presented at Interactions: Regional Studies, Global Processes, and Historical Analysis, Library of Congress, Washington DC, 28 February to 3 March 2001, p. 1, online at http://www.historycooperative.org/proceedings/interactions/mccabe.html [accessed 17 June 2009].

28. F. Trivellato, 'Images and Self-Images of Sephardic Merchants in Early Modern Europe and the Mediterranean', in M. Jacob and C. Secretan (eds), *The Self-Perception of Early Modern Capitalists* (New York: Palgrave Macmillan, 2008), pp. 49–74, on p. 67.

1 Models for Trade and Globalization

1. G. Ingham, 'Some Recent Changes in the Relationship Between Economics and Sociology', *Cambridge Journal of Economics*, 20:2 (March 1996), pp. 243–75, on p. 246.
2. J. Maloney, 'Marshall, Cunningham, and the Emerging Economics Profession', *Economic History Review*, new series, 29:3 (August 1976), pp. 440–51, on p. 442.
3. New economic history has attempted to reconcile history with classical economic theory by considering it applied neoclassical economics. See N. Lamoreaux, 'Economic History and the Cliometric Revolution', in A. Molho and G. S. Wood (eds), *Imagined Histories – American Historians Interpret the Past* (Princeton, NJ: Princeton University Press, 1998), pp. 59–84 or T. J. Hatton, K. H. O'Rourke and A. M. Taylor (eds), *The New Comparative Economic History – Essays in Honor of Jeffrey G. Williamson* (Cambridge, MA; London: MIT Press, 2007).
4. For an overview of limitations with regard to market capitalism today and alternatives, see A. Shipman, *The Market Revolution and its Limits – A Price for Everything* (London; New York: Routledge, 1999).
5. See above, p. 34.
6. S. Holmes, *Benjamin Constant and the Making of Modern Liberalism* (New Haven, CT; London: Yale University Press, 1984), p. 67.
7. P. Force, *Self-Interest before Adam Smith: A Genealogy of Economic Science* (Cambridge: Cambridge University Press, 2003), pp. 48–90.
8. G. Clark, *A Farewell to Alms – A Brief Economic History of the World* (Princeton, NJ; Oxford: Princeton University Press, 2007), p. 183.
9. A. Hirschman, 'Rival Interpretations of Market Society: Civilizing, Destructive, or Feeble?', *Journal of Economic Literature*, 20:4 (1982), pp. 1463–84, on p. 1473.
10. See above, pp. 21–2.
11. A multi-disciplinary approach is advocated by J. R. Holton, *Economy and Society* (Abingdon: Routledge, 1992); and M. Bevir and F. Trentmann, 'Markets in Historical Contexts: Ideas, Practices and Governance', in M. Bevir and F. Trentmann (eds), *Markets in Historical Contexts – Ideas and Politics in the Modern World* (Cambridge: Cambridge University Press, 2004), pp. 1–24. Bevir and Trentmann address the need to historicize economic behaviour.
12. E. L. Jones, *Cultures Merging – A Historical and Economic Critique of Culture* (Princeton, NJ, and Oxford: Princeton University Press, 2006), p. 3. For a call to bring culture back into economics, see S. Gudeman, *Economics as Culture: Models and Metaphors of Livelihood* (London; Boston, MA: Routledge & Kegan Paul, 1986). A good example of a socio-cultural analysis of an economical topic is D. Valenze, *The Social Life of Money in the English Past* (Cambridge: Cambridge University Press, 2006).
13. E. Rothschild, *Economic Sentiments: Adam Smith, Condorcet, and the Enlightenment* (Cambridge, MA; London: Harvard University Press, 2001), p. 44.
14. See above, p. 20. See also above, p. 87, for ethics in trade and p. 166 for ethics in relationships with others.
15. A. Sen, *On Ethics and Economics* (Oxford: Blackwell, 1987), p. 31.
16. M. Sahlins, *Stone Age Economics* (London: Tavistock Publications: 1974), especially ch. 1, 'The Original Affluent Society', pp. 1–39; and Marcel Mauss's *Essai sur le don. Forme*

et raison de l'échange dans les sociétés archaïques in M. Mauss, *Sociologie et anthropologie* (Paris: Presses Universitaires de France, 1950).

17. Carrier, J. G., *Exchange and Western Capitalism since 1700* (London; New York: Routledge, 1995) and Offer, A., 'Between the Gift and the Market: The Economy of Regard', *Economic History Review*, New Series, 50:3 (August 1997), pp. 450–76.
18. J. A. Schumpeter, *History of Economic Analysis*, ed. E. B. Schumpeter (New York: Oxford University Press, 1954), p. 186.
19. As in Schumpeter's famous list; the introduction of a new good, of a new method of production, the opening of a new market, the carrying out of a new organization or the conquest of a new source of supply in raw materials. J. A. Schumpeter, *Theorie der wirtschaftlichen Entwicklung* (Leipzig: Duncker & Humblot, 1911), pp. 100–1.
20. Ibid., pp. 126–39.
21. Ibid., pp. 123–7.
22. J. Goody, *Capitalism and Modernity – The Great Debate* (Cambridge: Polity Press, 2004), p. 92.
23. S. Bowles and H. Gintis, 'The Revenge of Homo Economicus: Contested Exchange and the Revival of Political Economy', *Journal of Economic Perspectives*, 7:1 (Winter 1993), pp. 83–102, on pp. 96–7.
24. R. M. Solow, 'Economic History and Economics', *American Economic Review*, 75:2, Papers and Proceedings of the Ninety-Seventh Annual Meeting of the American Economic Association (May 1985), p. 328.
25. M. Sahlins, *Apologies to Thucydides – Understanding History as Culture and Vice Versa* (London; Chicago, IL: University of Chicago Press, 2004), p. 4.
26. R. Grassby, *The Idea of Capitalism before the Industrial Revolution* (Oxford: Rowman & Littlefield Publishers, 1999), pp. 6–14.
27. T. Veblen, *The Vested Interests* (1919; New York: Viking Press, 1964), p. 1.
28. G. Simmel, *The Philosophy of Money* (London: Routledge & Kegan Paul Ltd, 1978), pp. 443–4.
29. Ibid., p. 444.
30. J. Mokyr, 'The Intellectual Origins of Modern Economic Growth', *Journal of Economic History*, 65:2 (June 2005), pp. 285–351, on p. 336.
31. This citation comes from E. Bonnot, *Commerce and Government Considered in their Mutual Relationship* (1776), trans. S. Eltis (Indianapolis: Liberty Fund, 2008), p. 50.
32. See for instance P. J. Zak (ed.), *Moral Markets: the Critical Role of Values in the Economy* (Princeton, NJ; Oxford: Princeton University Press, 2008), in particular an essay by Robert C. Solomon entitled 'Free Enterprise, Sympathy, and Virtue' on pp. 16–41 and the articles in part V: 'Values and the Economy', pp. 259–337. See also E. Hadas, *Human Goods, Economic Evils: A Moral Approach to the Dismal Science* (Wilmington, NC: ISI Books, 2007); E. S. Phelps (ed.), *Altruism, Morality, and Economic Theory* (New York: Russell Sage Foundation, 1975).
33. On trust in the framework of network analysis, see above, pp. 28–33. On the concrete establishment of trust between merchants, see Chapter 3, above, pp. 81–91.
34. Granovetter, 'Economic Action and Social Structure', pp. 481–510. On the idea of embeddedness in Polanyi's work and his tension between embedded economies and disembedded market economies, see K. Gemici, 'Karl Polanyi and the Antinomies of Embeddedness', *Socio-Economic Review*, 6:1 (January 2008), pp. 5–33.
35. On a positive view on different approaches to new institutional economics, including Williamson's transaction cost economics, see R. Richter, 'The New Institutional

Economics: Its Start, its Meaning, its Prospects', *European Business Organization Law Review*, 6:2 (June 2005), pp. 161–200.

36. O. E. Williamson, *Markets and Hierarchies: Analysis and Antitrust Implications – A Study in the Economics of Internal Organization* (New York: Free Press, 1975), pp. 21–6. See also L. H. G. Slangen, L. A. Loucks and A. H. L. Slangen (eds), *Institutional Economics and Economic Organisation Theory* (Wageningen: Wageningen Academic Publishers, 2008), pp. 212–72.
37. D. North, *Institutions, Institutional Change and Economic Performance* (Cambridge, Cambridge University Press, 1990), p. 3. See also D. North, 'Institutions', *Journal of Economic Perspectives*, 5:1 (Winter 1991), pp. 97–112.
38. A. Greif, 'Institutions, Markets, and Games', in V. Nee and R. Swedberg (eds), *The Economic Sociology of Capitalism* (Princeton, NJ and Oxford: Princeton University Press, 2005), pp. ix–xxxi.
39. Ibid., p. xiii.
40. Oliver Williamson's *Markets and Hierarchies* is an example of this line of reasoning.
41. See above, pp. 14-15.
42. This was the opinion of Edmund Burke. E. Burke, *Reflections on the Revolution in France, and on the Proceedings in Certain Societies in London Relative to that Event. In a Letter Intended to have been Sent to a Gentleman in Paris. By the Right Honourable Edmund Burke* (London: printed for J. Dodsley, 1793).
43. P. A. David, 'Why are Institutions the "Carriers of History"?: Path Dependence and the Evolution of Conventions, Organizations and Institutions', *Structural Change and Economic Dynamics*, 5:2 (1994), pp. 205–20.
44. This is the general critique given by Granovetter to this school of economics. Granovetter, 'Economic Action and Social Structure', pp. 482, 487–9.
45. P. Lewis and E. Chamlee-Wright, 'Social Embeddedness, Social Capital and the Market Process: An Introduction to the Special Issue on Austrian Economics, Economic Sociology and Social Capital', *Review of Austrian Economics*, 21:2–3 (September 2008), pp. 107–18, on p. 108.
46. R. Swedberg, *Max Weber and the Idea of Economic Sociology* (Princeton, NJ: Princeton University Press, 1998), p. 145.
47. Swedberg, *Max Weber and the Idea of Economic Sociology*, pp. 120–5.
48. Y. Slezkine, *The Jewish Century* (Princeton, NJ: Princeton University Press, 2004), p. 54.
49. G. Marshall, *In Search of the Spirit of Capitalism: An Essay on Max Weber's Protestant Ethic Thesis* (London: Hutchinson, 1982), p. 12.
50. G. Marshall, *Presbyteries and Profits: Calvinism and the Development of Capitalism in Scotland: 1560–1707* (Oxford: Oxford University Press, 1971). Marshall's arguments remind one of the difficulty in establishing economic history as a 'hard science', see above, pp. 18–19.
51. Swedberg, *Weber and the Idea of Economic Sociology*, p. 8.
52. Ibid., p. 130.
53. Lewis and Chamlee-Wright, 'Social Embeddedness, Social Capital and the Market Process', p. 109.
54. M. Granovetter, *Getting a Job: A Study of Contacts and Careers* (Chicago, IL: University of Chicago Press, 1995), p. 65.
55. N. Lamoreaux, D. M. G. Raff and P. Temin, 'Beyond Markets and Hierarchies: Toward a New Synthesis of American Business History', *American Historical Review*, 108:2 (April 2003), pp. 404–33.

56. A well-known critique came from Thorstein Veblen, who belonged to the early institutionalist school of economics. T. Veblen, 'Why is Economics Not an Evolutionary Science?', *Quarterly Journal of Economics*, 12 (July 1898), pp. 373–97. The idea that other forms of rationality play a role in economic action is advocated in B. G. Carruthers, 'Homo Economicus and Homo Politicus: Non-Economic Rationality in the Early 18th Century London Stock Market', *Acta Sociologica*, 37:2 (1994), pp. 165–94.
57. F. Braudel, *Civilisation matérielle, économie et capitalisme : XVe–XVIIIe siècle*, 3 vols (Paris: Armand Colin, 1979).
58. C. Markovits, *The Global World of Indian Merchants 1750–1947; Traders of Sind from Bukhara to Panama* (Cambridge: Cambridge University Press, 2000), pp. 4–9.
59. Besides Claude Markovits, publications include P. D. Curtin, *Cross-Cultural Trade in World History* (Cambridge; New York: Cambridge University Press, 1984), Trivellato, *The Familiarity of Strangers*; Trivellato, 'Juifs de Livourne, Italiens de Lisbonne, hindous de Goa', pp. 581–603; D. Hancock, 'L'émergence d'une économie de réseau (1640–1815)', *Annales: Histoire, Sciences sociales*, 58:3 (May–June 2003), pp. 649–72. Part of that issue is devoted to merchant networks, and contains a collection of essays edited by Anthony Molho and Diogo Ramada Curto. See also G. Dahl, *Trade, Trust, and Networks: Commercial Culture in Late Medieval Italy* (Lund: Nordic Academic Press, 1998); and M. Fusaro, *Reti commerciali e traffic globali nell'età moderna* (Bari; Roma: Laterza, 2008). Some relevant publications by Avner Greif are: *Institutions and the Path to the Modern Economy*; 'Contract Enforceability and Economic Institutions in Early Trade: The Maghribi Traders' Coalition', *American Economic Review*, 83:3 (June 1993), pp. 525–48; and 'Reputation and Coalitions in Medieval Trade: Evidence on the Maghribi Traders', *Journal of Economic History*, 49:4 (December 1989), pp. 857–82. See also M. Schulte-Beerbühl, *Deutsche Kaufleute in London: Welthandel und Einbürgerung (1660–1818)* (München: Oldenbourg, 2007), pp. 14–17.
60. The Brazilian diamond trade was for a while arranged on a monopolistic basis, see above, pp. 50–7.
61. It should not be assumed that this natural trust is always sufficient as explanation. See, pp. 29–30 and pp. 84–8.
62. See above, pp. 96, 149–50. See also Chapter 5, throughout.
63. See above, p. 29. For the role played by the merchant Joseph Salvador as a leading member of the Sephardic Jewish community in London, see pp. 129–30.
64. Trivellato, 'Juifs de Livourne, Italiens de Lisbonne, hindous de Goa', p. 583.
65. Curtin, *Cross-Cultural Trade in World History*, p. 3. In this sense, the concept of network can include other types of classical historical agency, such as the trading companies or diaspora networks. K. Ward, *Networks of Empire – Forced Migration in the Dutch East India Company* (Cambridge: Cambridge University Press, 2009). For the concept of trust in a mono-cultural network, see S. Aslanian, 'Social Capital: "Trust" and the Role of Networks in Julfan Trade: Informal and Semi-Formal Institutions at Work', *Journal of Global History*, 1:3 (November 2006), pp. 383–402.
66. Trivellato, *The Familiarity of Strangers*, p. 8.
67. Trivellato, 'Juifs de Livourne, Italiens de Lisbonne, hindous de Goa', pp. 583–91, analyses the difficulty of defining informal and cross-cultural networks.
68. See Chapter 4 above, pp. 104–9, 119–22.
69. Markovits, *The Global World of Indian Merchants 1750–1947*, p. 132. See also S. Subrahmanyam (ed.), *Merchant Networks in the Early Modern World* (Aldershot; Brookfield, VT: Variorum, 1996), including essays on Italian merchant organization in early Tudor London, the Wangara of the Central Sudan, Chulia Muslim merchants in South East Asia and Bahian merchants in Brazil.

70. For a discussion on different concepts of trust in economic behaviour and its relevance, see O. E. Williamson, 'Calculativeness, Trust, and Economic Organization', *Journal of Law and Economics*, 36 (April 1993), pp. 453–86; R. Craswell, 'On the Uses of "Trust": Comment on Williamson, "Calculativeness, Trust, and Economic Organization', *Journal of Law and Economics*, 36 (April 1993), pp. 487–500; and M. Perelman, 'The Neglected Economics of Trust: The Bentham Paradox and its Implications', *American Journal of Economics and Sociology*, 57:4 (October 1998), pp. 381–9.
71. Trivellato, 'Juifs de Livourne, Italiens de Lisbonne, hindous de Goa', p. 582.
72. See for instance Amalia Kessler's monograph on the Parisian merchant court. Kessler, *A Revolution in Commerce*. See also P. R. Milgrom, D. C. North and B. R. Weingast, 'The Role of Institutions in the Revival of Trade: The Law Merchant, Private Judges, and the Champagne Fairs', *Economics & Politics*, 2:1 (March 1990), pp. 1–23; E. Moglen, 'Commercial Arbitration in the Eighteenth Century: Searching for the Transformation of American Law', *Yale Law Journal*, 93:1 (November 1983), pp. 135–52; and G. Bossenga, 'Protecting Merchants: Guilds and Commercial Capitalism in Eighteenth-Century France', *French Historical Studies*, 15:4 (Autumn 1988), pp. 693–703.
73. Greif, 'Contract Enforceability and Economic Institutions', p. 530.
74. It was this problem of information that was the basis for the foundation of Transaction Cost Economics. See above, p. 187, n. 35.
75. For a good overview on different applications of trust, not only in commerce, but also in friendship, society, government and the creation of order, see D. Gambetta (ed.), *Trust: Making and Breaking Cooperative Relations* (Oxford; New York: Basil Blackwell Ltd, 1988) or E. L. Khalil (ed.), *Trust* (Cheltenham; Northampton, MA: Edward Elgar, 2003). See also B. A. Misztal, *Trust in Modern Societies: The Search for the Bases of Social Order* (Cambridge: Polity Press, 1996); R. Hardin, *Trust & Trustworthiness*, Russell Sage Foundation Series on Trust, 4 (New York: Russell Sage Foundation, 2002); and U. Frevert, *Does Trust Have a History?* Max Weber Lecture Series (European University Institute, MWP – LS 2009/01).
76. A concrete application of this definition, and how commercial trust resided within a particular cross-cultural network will be developed in Chapter 3 above, pp. 81–91.
77. F. Trivellato, 'Merchants' Letters across Geographical and Social Boundaries', in F. Bethencourt and F. Egmond (eds), *Cultural Exchange in Early Modern Europe*, vol. 3: Correspondence and Cultural Exchange in Europe, 1400–1700 (Cambridge: Cambridge University Press, 2007), pp. 80–103. For the use of manuals with regard to the writing of letters, see R. Chartier, A. Boureau and C. Dauphin, *Correspondence: Models of Letter-Writing from the Middle Ages to the Nineteenth Century* (Princeton, NJ: Princeton University Press, 1997).
78. A good example is the richness of the still largely unexplored Insolvente Boedelskamer in Antwerp.
79. For ideas about merchant culture and the circulation of correspondence, see F. Trivellato, 'A Republic of Merchants?', in A. Molho, D. R. Curto and N. Koniordos (eds), *Finding Europe: Discourses on Margins, Communities, Images ca. 13th–18th Centuries* (New York; Oxford: Berghahn Books, 2007), pp. 133–58. Merchant culture also relates to ideas of a 'social imaginary of the market', the universe of potential partners in commerce. L. Spillman, 'Enriching Exchange: Cultural Dimensions of Markets', *American Journal of Economics and Sociology*, 58:4 (October 1999), pp. 1056–9. See also F. Angiolini and D. Roche (eds), *Cultures et formations négociantes dans l'Europe moderne* (Paris: Éditions de l'école des hautes études en sciences sociales, 1995).
80. A. Silver, 'Friendship in Commercial Society: Eighteenth-Century Social Theory and Modern Sociology', *American Journal of Sociology*, 95:6 (May 1990), pp. 1474–1504, on p. 1482.

81. H. Mizuta, 'Moral Philosophy and Civil Society', in A. S. Skinner and T. Wilson (eds), *Essays on Adam Smith* (Oxford: Clarendon Press, 1975), pp. 114–30, on p. 120.
82. For friendship between merchants, see A. Silver, '"Two Different Sorts of Commerce" – Friendship and Strangership in Civil Society', in J. Weintraub and K. Kumar (eds), *Public and Private in Thought and Practice* (Chicago, IL: University of Chicago Press, 1998), pp. 43–74. See also above, p. 185, n. 22.
83. Goody, *Capitalism and Modernity*, pp. 25–6.
84. P. Dimaggio, 'Cultural Aspects of Economic Action and Organization', in N. J. Smelser and R. Swedberg (eds), *Handbook of Economic Sociology* (Princeton, NJ: Princeton University Press, 1994), pp. 22–57, on p. 38.
85. J. de Vries, 'The Limits of Globalization in the Early Modern World', *Economic History Review*, 63 (August 2010), pp. 710–33, on pp. 714–16.
86. D. Acemoglu, S. Johnson and J. A. Robinson, 'The Rise of Europe: Atlantic Trade, Institutional Change, and Economic Growth', *American Economic Review*, 95:3 (June 2005), pp. 546–79.
87. L. Neal, *Rise of Financial Capitalism: International Capital Markets in the Age of Reason* (Cambridge: Cambridge University Press, 1990); and R. Austen and W. D. Smith, 'Private Tooth Decay as Public Economic Virtue: The Slave-Sugar Triangle, Consumerism, and European Industrialization', in J. E. Imkori and S. Engerman (eds), *The Atlantic Slave Trade* (Durham, NC: Duke University Press, 1992), pp. 183–203.
88. W. Bernstein, *A Splendid Exchange – How Trade Shaped The World* (London: Atlantic Books, 2008) is a good example.
89. See for instance H. V. Bowen, *Elites, Enterprise, and the Making of the British Overseas Empire, 1688–1775* (London: Macmillan, 1996); and N. Robins, *The Corporation that Changed the World: How the East India Company Shaped the Modern Multinational* (London: Pluto Press, 2006) on the English East India Company; J. Black, *Trade, Empire and British Foreign Policy, 1689–1815: The Politics of a Commercial State* (London: Routledge, 2007); J. Adams, *The Familial State: Ruling Families and Merchant Capitalism in Early Modern Europe*, Wilder House Series in Politics, History, and Culture (Ithaca, NY: Cornell University Press, 2005); J. Israel, *The Dutch Republic: Its Rise, Greatness, and Fall 1477–1806* (Oxford: Oxford University Press, 1995).
90. This view of agency is a Marxist one. See K. Marx, 'Das Kapital, Band I: Kritik der politischen Ökonomie', in K. Marx and F. Engels, *Werke*, Band 23 (Berlin: Dietz Verlag, 1962), pp. 11–802.
91. J. C. van Leur, *Indonesian Trade and Society* (Den Haag: W. Van Hoeve, 1955), pp. 270–2.
92. Two collections of essays about global trade that attempt to move away from such bias, not necessarily by questioning eventual European triumph, but by taking non-European points of view are J. D. Tracy (ed.), *The Rise of Merchant Empires: Long-Distance Trade in the Early Modern World 1350–1750* (Cambridge; New York: Cambridge University Press, 1990) and J. D. Tracy (ed.), *The Political Economy of Merchant Empires: State Power and World Trade 1350–1750* (Cambridge; New York: Cambridge University Press, 1991).
93. D. O. Flynn and A. Giraldez, 'Path Dependence, Time Lags, and the Birth of Globalisation: A Critique of O'Rourke and Williamson', *European Review of Economic History*, 8 (2004), pp. 81–108, on p. 83.
94. de Vries, 'The Limits of Globalization', p. 711.

95. For instance F. Braudel, *La méditerranée et le monde méditerranéen à l'époque de Philippe II*, 2 vols (Paris: Armand Colin, 1949); P. Horden and N. Purcell, *The Corrupting Sea – A Study of Mediterranean History* (Oxford: Blackwell, 2000); J. P. Greene and P. D. Morgan (eds), *Atlantic History – A Critical Appraisal* (Oxford: Oxford University Press, 2009); H. Prabha Ray and E. A. Alpers (eds), *Cross Currents and Community Networks: The History of the Indian Ocean World* (Oxford: Oxford University Press, 2007), or journals such as the *Journal of Pacific History*, which was founded in 1966. A good starting point with regard to debates regarding historical spaces is the collection of articles in a special issue of the *American Historical Review*, 111:3 (June 2006), AHR Forum: Oceans of History, including the introduction by Kären Wigen and essays by P. Horden and N. Purcell ('The Mediterranean and "the New Thalassology"', pp. 722–40), A. H. Games ('Atlantic History: Definitions, Challenges, and Opportunities', pp. 741–57), and M. K. Matsuda ('The Pacific', pp. 758–80).
96. Different scholars rely on the idea of different national Atlantics. See essays by Jan de Vries on the Dutch Atlantic, Daviken Studnicki-Gizbert on the Spanish Atlantic Empire or Claudia Schnurmann on Atlantic Trade and American identity in P. A. Coclanis (ed.), *The Atlantic Economy during the Seventeenth and Eighteenth Centuries: Organization, Operation, Practice, and Personnel* (Columbia, SC: University of South Carolina Press, 2005). See also the collections of essays in honor of Ian K. Steele about different contexts of the British Atlantic. N. L. Rhoden (ed.), *English Atlantics Revisited* (Montreal; Kingston; London; Ithaca, NY: McGill-Queen's University Press, 2007).
97. B. Bailyn, *Atlantic History: Concept and Contours* (Cambridge, MA: Harvard University Press, 2005), p. 48.
98. K. Wigen, 'AHR Forum – Oceans of History: Introduction', *American Historical Review*, 111:3 (June, 2006), pp. 717–21.
99. The aspect of routine is crucial when considering international trade in order to maintain a notion of globalization through commerce. See above, p. 27.
100. Braudel, *La méditerranée et le monde méditerranéen à l'époque de Philippe II*, vol. 1, p. 253.
101. Bailyn, *Atlantic History*, p. 44.
102. One only has to refer to Fernand Braudel and the tradition of the *Annales* to see that this is by no means a new debate. See also D. Brewer, 'Lights in Space', *Eighteenth-Century Studies*, 37:2 (Winter 2004), pp. 171–86, in which he distinguishes different historical spaces in the eighteenth century, social, geographical, epistemological, physical, colonized and esthetical. He argues that 'spatial analysis ... must account for this overlapping multiplicity of eighteenth-century spaces' and that analysis should be historical, by considering the space *of* the eighteenth century as well as different historical spaces *in* the eighteenth century (p. 184).
103. See for instance Ward, *Networks of Empire*. This monograph fits in a newer dynamism through its emphasis on networks, but also continues to rely on top-down issues of power, sovereignty and the historical influence of the Dutch East India Company through the concept of forced migration. Works that offer a new theoretical approach to imperial and colonial history in this regard include F. Cooper, *Colonialism in Question – Theory, Knowledge, History* (Berkeley, CA: University of California Press, 2005) and S. Akita (ed.), *Gentlemanly Capitalism, Imperialism, and Global History* (Basingstoke: Macmillan, 2002).
104. J. Bentley, 'Cross-Cultural Interaction and Periodization in World History', *American History Review*, 101 (June 1996), pp. 749–70.

105. Israel, *Diasporas within a Diaspora*, p. 1.
106. Generally, this discourse is also valid for non-commercial networks, but in the light of this book, the attention goes to commercial circuits.
107. The meaning of the term society is difficult to establish, and it is not always clear where its boundaries are. The relationship between a host society and a diaspora will be analysed in the fifth chapter of this book, using the idea of different memberships. See Chapter 5 above, pp. 123–48.
108. Goody, *Capitalism and Modernity*, p. 48.
109. See above, Chapter 5, pp. 123–4.
110. J. Boulton, 'Microhistory in Early Modern London: John Bedford (1601–1667)', *Continuity and Change*, 22:1 (May 2007), pp. 113–41, on p. 113.
111. C. Ginzburg and C. Poni, 'The Name and the Game: Unequal Exchange and the Historiographic Marketplace', in E. Muir and G. Ruggiero (eds), *Microhistory and the Lost Peoples of Europe* (Baltimore, MD: John Hopkins University Press, 1991), pp. 1–10, on p. 5.

2 A Short History of the Diamond Trade

1. S. Tolansky, *The History and Use of the Diamond* (London: Shenval Press, 1962), pp. 13–17 discusses biblical references to diamonds.
2. G. Lenzen, *The History of Diamond Production and the Diamond Trade* (New York: Praeger Publishers, 1970), pp. 1–8, 15–25.
3. Ibid., pp. 21, 35–41.
4. N. Gross (ed.), *Economic History of the Jews* (New York: Schocken Books, 1975), p. 158.
5. Lenzen, *The History of Diamond Production*, pp. 60–1.
6. Ibid., pp. 71–5.
7. J. H. van Den Hoek Ostende, Review of 'Asscher, S., *Diamant, Wonderlijk Kristal* (Bussum: Unieboek, 1975)', *Amstelodamum – Maandblad voor de kennis van Amsterdam*, 63:1 (January–February 1976), p. 24.
8. Lenzen, *The History of Diamond Production*, p. 85.
9. K. Hofmeester, 'Diamonds as a Global Luxury Commodity', in B.-S. Grewe, *Luxury in Global Perspective: Commodities and Practives, 1600–200*, International Studies in Social History (New York; Oxford: Berghahn Books, forthcoming).
10. Lenzen, *The History of Diamond Production*, p. 72; and J. Mokyr (ed.), *Oxford Encyclopedia of Economic History*, 5 vols (Oxford: Oxford University Press, 2003), vol. 3, p. 202.
11. Lenzen, *The History of Diamond Production*, p. 86.
12. J. Denucé, 'Het Huis Affaytati', *Antwerpsch Archievenblad*, 2:4 (1929), pp. 218–24.
13. Index 1548, IB1581, FAA, loose document.
14. J. C. Boyajian, *Portuguese Trade in Asia under the Habsburgs, 1580–1640* (Baltimore, MD: Johns Hopkins University Press, 2008), p. 135.
15. J. Everaert, 'Soldaten, diamantairs en jezuïeten – Nederlanders in Portugees-Indië voor 1590', in R. Van Gelder, J. Parmentier and V. Roeper (eds), *Souffrir pour Parvenir – De wereld van Jan Huygen van Linschoten* (Haarlem: Uitgeverij Arcadia, 1998), pp. 80–94, 182–4, on pp. 87–91.
16. J. Verberckmoes and E. Stols, *Aziatische omzwervingen – het levensverhaal van Jacques de Coutre, een Brugs diamanthandelaar 1591–1627* (Berchem: EPO, 1988), pp. 194, 242–3.
17. See above, pp. 47–9.
18. For a summary of different sources, see Hofmeester, 'Diamonds as a Global Luxury Commodity'.

19. For a letter from 1615 confirming this, see P. van Dam, *Beschryvinge van de Oostindische Compagnie*, Tweede Boek, Deel II (Den Haag: F. W. Stapel, 1932), pp. 174–5. The letter is entitled 'Berigt raeckende den handel in diamanten tot Sensier, soo oock meede van de peerlen, sooals dat in 't jaer 1615 is opgestelt.' [Translation: 'Message touching the diamond trade with Sensier, including the [trade in] pearls, as it is compiled in the year 1615.']
20. M. Mehta, *Indian Merchants and Entrepreneurs in Historical Perspective* (Delhi: Academic Foundation, 1991). For Shantidas Zaveri, see pp. 91–114, for Virji Vora see pp. 53–64.
21. 'Henrick Brouwer, Antonio van Diemen, Dr. Pieter Vlack, Philips Lucasz. and Jan van der Burch to the Heren XVII of the V.O.C.', Batavia, 15 August 1633, in W. P. Coolhaas (ed.), *Generale Missiven van Gouverneurs-Generaal en Raden aan Heren XVII der Verenigde Oostindische Compagnie*, Deel I: 1610–1638 (Den Haag: Rijksgeschiedkundige Publicatiën, 1960), p. 390.
22. Boyajian, *Portuguese Trade in Asia*, pp. 134–5.
23. For examples of diamond trade, see ledger Paolo du Jon, 1622–1632, IB1737, FAA, f. 32. See also J. Denucé, 'De Familie Wallis-Du Jon, De Familie van Lamoraal, Graaf van Egmond', *Antwerpsch Archievenblad*, 2:3 (1928), pp. 1–18
24. For da Vega and the Inquisition, see Boyajian, *Portuguese Trade in Asia*, pp. 181–2.
25. 'Pieter de Carpentier, Jacques Specx, Dr. Pieter Vlack and Antonio van Diemen to the Heren XVII of the V.O.C.', Batavia, 3 February 1626, in W. P. Coolhaas (ed.), *Generale Missiven van Gouverneurs-Generaal en Raden aan Heren XVII der Verenigde Oostindische Compagnie*, Deel I: 1610–38, pp. 186–7. Atchin was a region on the island of Sumatra.
26. 'Joan Maetsuyker, Carel Hartzinck, Arnold de Vlaming van Oudtshoorn, Nicolaes Verburch and Dirck Jansz. to the Heren XVII of the V.O.C.,' Batavia, 16 January 1658, in Coolhaas (ed.), *Generale Missiven van Gouverneurs-Generaal en Raden aan Heren XVII der Verenigde Oostindische Compagnie*, Deel III: 1655-1674 (Den Haag: Rijksgeschiedkundige Publicatiën, 1968), p. 201.
27. R. Challe, *Journal d'un voyage fait aux Indes Orientales (1690–1691)*(Paris: Mercure de France, 1979), pp. 369–71.
28. Van Dam, *Beschryvinge van de Oostindische Compagnie*, p. 177.
29. L. C. D. Van Dijk, *Neerland's vroegste betrekkingen met Borneo, den Solo-Archipel, Cambodja, Siam en Cochin-China* (Amsterdam: J. H. Scheltema, 1862), p. 2.
30. 'Letter of John Saris to the Right Worshipful the East India Company', Bantam, 4 December 1608, in F. C. Danvers, *Letters Received by the East India Company from its Servants in the East, Transcribed from the 'Original Correspondence' Series of the India Office Records*, vol. 1: 1602–13 (London: Samspon Low, Marston & Company, 1896), pp. 20–3.
31. Radicaale Beschrijving van't Eyland Borneo en de Postvatting te Banjermasjing (1757), Nationaal Archief Den Haag, V.O.C., No. 4885, unnumbered.
32. 'The diamond mine was closed for the merchants, the King had worked for his own account', 'Pieter de Carpentier, Jacques Specx, Dr. Pieter Vlack and Antonio van Diemen to the Heren XVII of the V.O.C.', Batavia, 3 February 1626, in Coolhaas (ed.), *Generale Missiven van Gouverneurs-Generaal en Raden*, Deel I: 1610–38, p. 186.
33. 'also, the English liberties seem to carry more capital than ours', 'Henrick Brouwer, Antonio van Diemen, Dr. Pieter Vlack, Philips Lucasz. and Jan van der Burch to the Heren XVII of the V.O.C.', Batavia, 15 August 1633, in Coolhaas (ed.), *Generale Missiven van Gouverneurs-Generaal en Raden*, Deel I: 1610-38,Lenzen, *The History of Diamond Production*, p. 91
34. Lenzen, *Th e History of Diamond Production*, p. 91
35. T. R. de Souza, 'Goa-Based Portuguese Seaborne Trade in the Early Seventeenth Century', in *Indian Economic & Social History Review*, 12:4 (1975), p. 438.
36. G. Yogev, *Diamonds and Coral: Anglo-Dutch Jews and Eighteenth Century Trade* (Leicester: Leicester University Press, 1978), pp. 82–3.
37. Ibid., pp. 83–5.
38. Ibid., p. 88.

39. Boyajian, *Portuguese Trade in Asia*, pp. 138, 217.
40. J. C. Boyajian, *Portuguese Bankers at the Court of Spain, 1626–1650* (New Brunswick, NJ: Rutgers University Press, 1983), pp. 117–20.
41. The Salvador firm for instance had shipments arriving in England through Christian partners at least in the 1680s and 1690s, a practice that they used to a much lesser extent from the turn of the century onwards. See above, Chapter 6, pp. 155–7.
42. Yogev, *Diamonds and Coral*, pp. 85, pp. 94–5.
43. Agreement between Sir Robert Nightingale acting for George Drake, and Anthony da Costa acting for Joseph James Osorio, connected with their partnership at Fort St George in the diamond trade, December 1721, L/AG/50/5/5, BL/IOR.
44. For the trade in coral, see Trivellato, *The Familiarity of Strangers*, pp. 224–50. For the use of coral in jewellery, see M. Pointon, *Brilliant Effects: A Cultural History of Gem Stones and Jewellery* (New Haven, CT; London: Yale University Press, 2009), pp. 107–12, 127–44.
45. Yogev, *Diamonds and Coral*, p. 102.
46. Ibid., p. 91; E. Samuel, 'Gems from the Orient: The Activities of Sir John Chardin (1643–1713) as a Diamond Importer and East India Merchant', *Proceedings of the Huguenot Society*, 27:3 (2000), pp. 351–68, on p. 354.
47. M. Pointon, 'Jewellery in Eighteenth-Century England', in M. Berg and H. Clifford (eds), *Consumers and Luxury: Consumer Culture in Europe 1650–1850* (Manchester: Manchester University Press, 1999), pp. 120–46, on p. 120. See also the 1716 quote from a London newspaper above, p. 58.
48. D. van der Cruysse, *Chardin le Persan* (Paris: Fayard, 1998) is a good biography of Chardin. Jean Chardin wrote a diary in which he described not only his affairs but also his voyages into Persia. J. Chardin, *Travels in Persia 1673–1677* (New York: Dover Publications, 1988)
49. For the involvement of the Salvador family in the Indian diamond trade, see above, Chapter 6, pp. 154–8.
50. Van der Cruysse, *Chardin le Persan*, pp. 275–6.
51. Samuel, 'Gems from the Orient', pp. 354–6.
52. See in this regard also the relationship between Lord Clive and Joseph Salvador, Chapter 6, pp. 172–3.
53. D. Jeffries, *A Treatise on Diamonds and Pearls* (London: C. & J. Ackers, 1751), p. 66.
54. Israel, *Diasporas within a Diaspora*, p. 37.
55. Jeffries, *A Treatise on Diamonds and Pearls*, p. 101.
56. Yogev, *Diamonds and Coral*, p. 142.
57. See above, pp. 61–2.
58. Yogev, *Diamonds and Coral*, p. 114. See above, pp. 53–7, for the importance of Christian merchants in the Brazilian diamond trade.
59. Yogev, *Diamonds and Coral*, pp. 125–6. For a practical example of the German activities of an Ashkenazi diamond trade network, see above, Chapter 4, pp. 116-17.
60. Yogev, *Diamonds and Coral*, p. 136.
61. Ibid., p. 264.
62. D. M. Swetschinski, 'The Portuguese Jewish Merchants of Seventeenth-Century Amsterdam: A Social Profile' (PhD dissertation, Brandeis University, 1980), p. 303.
63. Yogev, *Diamonds and Coral*, pp 169–75. For a more general overview, see P. J. Marshall, *East India Fortunes: The British in Bengal in the Eighteenth Century* (Oxford: Clarendon Press, 1976).
64. C. R. Boxer, *A Idade de Ouro do Brasil (Dores de Crescimento de uma sociedade Colonial)* (São Paulo: Nova Fronteira, 1963), pp. 49–58; A. J. Antonil, *Cultura e Opulência do Brasil* (1711), ed. A. P. Canbrava (São Paulo: Editora Nacional, 1967), pp. 119–23.
65. Bernardo Fonseca Lobo is mentioned in an anonymous manuscript narrating the history of the Brazilian diamond monopolies. 'História Chronológica dos Contratos da Min-

erassão dos Diamantes dos Outros Contractos de Extracsão delles dos Cofres de Lisboa para os Paizes Estrangeiros dos Abuzos em que todos laborarão, e das Providencias com que se lhe tem occorrido ate o anno de 1788' (hereafter 'História Chronológica'), BNL/CFGM, códice 746, f. 2r. See also below, p. 197, nn. 88, 100. Further information on Lobo can be found in J. F. dos Santos, *Memórias do Distrito Diamantino da Comarca do Sêrro Frio* (Rio de Janeiro: Itatiaia, 1956), p. 60.

66. Dos Santos, *Memórias do Distrito Diamantino da Comarca do Sêrro Frio*, p. 61. In his history on the diamond trade, Augusto de Lima Junior attributes the discovery to a worker in Lobo's gold mine. A. de Lima Júnior, *História dos Diamantes nas Minas Gerais* (Rio de Janeiro: Dois Mundos, 1945), pp. 19–20.
67. 'Matricula dos escravos adventicios e recuperados lojas vendas e officios que pagáo pro racta', APM/SC, Registo de escravos, vendas e licenças em Tejuco (1735–84), códex 51.
68. The letter was copied in 'Bando do Governador da Capitania, D. Lourenço de Almeida, designando o Dr. Antônio Ferreira do Valle e Mello Ouvidor do Serro do Frio, encarregado do governo de todas a forma minerar diamantes naquela comarca', 24 June 1730, BNL/PBA, cód. 4530, ff. 280–81.
69. Francisco da Cruz to Francisco Pinheiro, 3 August 1729, in L. Lisanti (ed.), *Negócios Coloniais*, 5 vols (Brasília: Ministério da Fazenda; São Paulo: Visão Editorial, 1973), vol. 1, p. 322.
70. Lord Tyrawly to the Duke of Newcastle, Lisbon, 2 May 1732, NA/SP, 89/37, ff. 166–8.
71. This letter was included in 'Condicoes para o estabelecimento do commerco dos diamantes, 1734', AHU/CUMG, cx. 28, doc. 73, f. 22r. Andries Pels and Sons was one of the richest merchant-banking houses at the time. See J. G. Dillen, *Van Rijkdom en Regenten. Handboek tot de economische en sociale geschiedenis van Nederland* ('s Gravenhage: Martinus Nijhoff, 1970), pp. 456–7, 472–3.
72. The same year, different European firms made proposals to the Crown with regard to trading monopolies, but none were accepted. 'Condicoes para o estabelecimento do commercio dos diamantes, 1734', AHU/CUMG, cx. 28, documents 71, 73, 74.
73. 'Carta do Conde de Sabugosa', 16 January 1733, AHU/CUMG, cx. 23, document 4.
74. 'Condicoes para o estabelecimento do commercio dos diamantes, 1734', AHU/CUMG, cx. 28, document 73, ff. 6r–8v. The six were Gomes Antonio Vas Coimbra, Batholomeu Miguel Vienne, Francisco de Bellagoarda, Antonio Vanpraet, Guillerme Mauman and Noé Hounaye. A separate offer was made by a certain Belchior do Rego, but was equally refused.
75. J. F. Furtado, *Chica da Silva e o contratador dos diamantes: o outro lado do mito* (São Paulo: Companhia das Letras, 2003), p. 33.
76. V. M. T. Valadares, 'Elites mineiras setecentistas: conjugação de dois mundos (1700–1800)', 2 vols (PhD dissertation Universidade de Lisboa, 2002), vol. 1, p. 373.
77. Furtado, *Chica da Silva e o contratador dos diamantes*, pp. 74–9.
78. 'Escritura de sociedade feita entre João Fernandes de Oliveira e Francisco Ferreira Silva, caixas e administradores da companhia de diamantes', 20 June 1739, AHU/MAMG, cx. 41, document 55.
79. 'Condizóes para a extracáo dos Diamantes aprovada pello Senhor General Gomes Freire de Andrada', 20 June 1739, APM/SC, códex. 1, 'Registros de alvarás, cartas patentes, provisões, confirmações de cartas patentes, sesmarias e doações (1609–1799)', ff. 173r–77r.
80. Furtado, *Chica da Silva e o contratador dos diamantes*, p. 82.
81. Requerimento de Manuel Nunes da Silva Tojal e José Ferreira de Veiga, 05/05/c.1751, AHU/MAMG, cx. 58, doc. 3, f. 1.
82. P. T. de A. Paes Leme, 'Nobiliarquia Paulistana', *Revista do Instituto Histórico Geográfico Brasileiro*, 34:1 (1871), p. 209, '*Gomes Freire, que protegia a João Fernandes*'.
83. 'História Chronológica', f. 51r.

84. Dos Santos, *Memórias do Distrito Diamantino da Comarca do Sêrro Frio*, p. 104. For diamond mining in Goías, see D. P. R. Vasconcelos, *Breve descrição geográfica, física e política da capitania de Minas Gerais* (1807), ed. C. M. J. Anastasia (Belo Horizonte: Fundação João Pinheiro, 1994), p. 238.
85. 'Termo de obrigaçáo, que assignáo todos os Interessados no terceiro Contrato dos Diamantes', in 'História Chronológica', ff. 179r–81v. See also J. F. Furtado, 'O labirinto da fortuna: ou os revezes na trajetória de um contratador dos diamantes', in E. Nodari, J. M. Pedro et al., *História: fronteiras*, 2 vols (Florianópolis: XX Simpósio Nacional da ANPUH, 1999), vol. 1, p. 312.
86. 'Carta do ouvidor a informar o rei dos excessos cometidos pelo contratador dos diamantes Felisberto Caldeira Brant e das diligencias feitas sobre o assunto', 1752, AHU/MAMG, cx. 58, doc. 110. In August, another letter was sent in which all Brant's infractions were summed up. 'Carta de Sancho de Andrade Castro e Lançóes expondo ao Rei os fundamentos da queixa de que formulava contra o contratador Felisberto Caldeira Brant', 5 August 1752, AHU/MAMG, cx. 60, doc. 29.
87. 'Oficio do governador de Minas José Antonio Freire de Andrada para o secretario da marinha e ultramar Diogo de Mendonça Corte Real', 6 September 1752, AHU/MAMG, cx. 60, doc. 56.
88. This text can be found in another anonymous manuscript, 'Deducçaó Compendiosa dos Contractos de Mineraçaó dos diamantes; dos outros contractos da Extracçaó delles; dos cofres de Lisboa para os Payzes Estrangeiros; dos perigos em que todos laboravam e das Providencias, comque a elles occorreo o senhor Rey Dom Jozeph para os conservar, S.d.' (hereafter 'Deducçaó Compendiosa'), BNL/PBA, cód. 695 (ff. 306–80), f. 318v–319v. This text is almost identical as códice 746, and there is textual evidence that suggests that both manuscripts were originally written by the marquis de Pombal. See for instance below, p. 197, n. 100.
89. 'Condizóes para a extracáo dos Diamantes aprovada pello Senhor General Gomes Freire de Andrada', 20 June 1739, APM/SC, códex. 1, ff. 173r–77r.
90. Berthon & Garnault to James Dormer, Lisbon, 22 December 1750, FAA, IB1652.
91. Berthon & Garnault to James Dormer, Lisbon, 7 March 1752, FAA, IB1652.
92. Berthon & Garnault to James Dormer, Lisbon, 28 August 1753, FAA, IB1652.
93. 'Deducçaó Compendiosa', f. 320v.
94. 'Deducçaó Compendiosa', ff. 320v–22v. Berthon & Garnault described this turn of events in detail to Dormer in Berthon & Garnault to James Dormer, Lisbon, 30 January 1753, FAA, IB1652.
95. 'Ordem Régia ao Ouvidor do Serro do Frio sobre abertura de Devassa contra descaminhos praticados pelo contratador de Diamantes, Felisberto Caldeira Brant', 22 February 1753, BNL/CFGM, mss. 71, no. 8.
96. Furtado, 'O labirinto da fortuna: ou os revezes na trajetória de um contratador dos diamantes', p. 317.
97. Berthon & Garnault to James Dormer, Lisbon, 24 April 1753, FAA, IB1652.
98. Berthon & Garnault to James Dormer, Lisbon, 15 May 1753, FAA, IB1652.
99. Berthon & Garnault to James Dormer, Lisbon, 31 July 1753, FAA, IB1652.
100. 'Deducçaó Compendiosa', f. 324r, '[oito dias] em que pude estár fechado no Meu Gabinete sem ser interrompido.'
101. K. Maxwell, *Marquês de Pombal, paradoxo do iluminismo* (São Paulo: Editora Paz e Terra, 1996), p. 95. For Pombal's attempt to nationalize Portuguese trade with Brazil, and to loosen Portugal's dependence on English traders, see K. Maxwell, 'Pombal and the

Nationalization of the Luso-Brazilian Economy', *Hispanic American Historical Review*, 48:4 (November 1968), pp. 608–31.

102. 'Deducçaó Compendiosa', f. 323v. 'Os lugares delles haviam ser substituidos por outros tantos Commerciantes Estrangeiros para vendessem as Suas Fazendas per si mesmos com huma insuperavel arrogancia.'
103. 'Deducçaó Compendiosa', f. 323.
104. Decreto Real de 11 August 1753, TdT, Col. Leis, Maço 4, N°144.
105. F. de C. Brandão, *História Diplomática de Portugal, uma cronologia* (Lisbon: Ministério dos Negócios Estrangeiros, 1984), p. 144.
106. W. Stechow, 'De Tempel der Kunst of het Kabinet van den Heer Braamcamp', Review Article, *Art Bulletin*, 44:2 (June 1962), pp. 151–2.
107. L. M. E. Shaw, *The Anglo-Portuguese Alliance and the English Merchants in Portugal, 1654–1810* (Aldershot; Brookfield, VT: Ashgate, 1998), p. 89; P. G. M. Dickson, *The Financial Revolution in England – A Study in the Development of Public Credit 1688–1756* (Aldershot: Gregg Revivals, 1993), p. 289.
108. 'A narrative of the reasons, which constrained the underwritten Bristow's, Warde & Company to the Committee of the Factory (no minister or consul from His Majesty being then resident here) for their assistance and support in so critical a situation', Lisbon, 22 June 1752, British Library, add. 23634 (Tyrawly Papers; Correspondence of Lord Tyrawly when ambassador in Portugal, 1752–7), ff. 86–7. See also ff. 104–5. For the relationship between Pombal and Bristow, see above, p. 172.
109. A copy of the contract of 10 August 1753 can be found in 'História Chronológica', ff. 230v–3v.
110. Paul Berthon to James Dormer, Lisbon, 1 March 1757, FAA, IB1651. Joshua van Neck was a very considerable Anglo-Dutch merchant and financer and was one of the main subjects of Charles Wilson writing about Anglo-Dutch finance. C. Wilson, *Anglo-Dutch Commerce and Finance in the Eighteenth Century* (Cambridge: Cambridge University Press, 1966).
111. 'as ordens de lançar olhos sobre todos os Negociantes Opulentos da Bolça de Londres, de escolher tres ou quarto, em que concorrem as majores cabedaes, e mais establecida reputaçaó', Deducçaó Compendiosa, ff. 338r–9r.
112. John Bristow died in 1768, without settling his debts. Shaw, *The Anglo-Portuguese Alliance*, p. 89.
113. For David Purry, see F. Brandt, *Notice sur la vie de Mr le Baron David de Purry, suivie de son testament et d'un extrait de sa correspondance particulière* (Neuchatel: Imprimerie de C.-H. Wolfrath, 1826).
114. For a copy of the contract, see 'História Chronológica', f. 238r.
115. 'Deducçaó Compendiosa', f. 340v; 'grandes e conhecidos talentos' and 'corporaçaó dos Hebreos'
116. Yogev, *Diamonds and Coral*, pp. 114–19.
117. 'Deducçaó Compendiosa', f. 347r: 'Em razaó de ser Negociante da Praça de Lisboa que pela commua opiniaó tinha accumulado os mayores Cabedaes pecuniarios.' See also 'Processo relativo a arremataçao dos contratos dos Diamantes e suas contas', 1751, AHU/MAMG, cx. 58, doc. 111, f. 1v.
118. 'História Chronológica', ff. 239v–44v.
119. Maxwell, *Marquês de Pombal, paradoxo do iluminismo*, pp. 44–57.
120. D. de A. Affonso and R. D. T. Valdez, *Livro de oiro da nobreza: apostilas à resenha das famílias titulares do reino de Portugal*, 3 vols (Braga: S.n., 1934), vol. 3, p. 350.

121. The ambassador wrote in his diary that the son of Gildemeester was consul for Holland at the time and that his father had opposed the marriage on the basis of a difference in religion. Marquis de Bombelles, *Journal d'un ambassadeur de France au Portugal (1786–1788)*, ed. R. Kann (Paris: Presses Universitaires de France, 1979), pp. 129–30.
122. 'Letras sobre o contrato dos Diamantes que há para pagar, e dias dos seus vencimentos', 1770, BNL/PBA, cód. 691, f. 18.
123. 'Regimento para os administradores do contrato dos diamantes', 1771, BNL/PBA, cód. 691, ff. 1–11. The period of the Royal Extraction has been analysed by Júnia Ferreira Furtado in J. Furtado, *O livro da capa verde: o regimento diamantino de 1771 e a vida no Distrito Diamantino no período da real extração* (São Paulo: Annablume, 1996).
124. 'Recibos dos lapidarias da fabrica de lapidar diamantes do Campo Pequeno, 1806–1807, Núcleos extraídos do conselho da fazenda, junta da direcção geral dos diamantes', livro IV, TdT.
125. For all the measures taken, including a government loan, see 'Decreto de 17 de dezembro 1771 autorizando suprimento por empréstimo aos diretores e Caixas da Administração do contrato de diamantes', BNL/PBA, cód. 691, f. 15; 'Decreto do estabelecimento da Administração dos Diamantes', 12 July 1771, Livro de Registo Geral da Direcção do Negocio dos Diamantes em Lisboa, f. 1r, TdT.
126. In the 1770s, gold and diamond production in Minas Gerais had started to decline. V. Alexandre, *Os sentidos do império* (Porto: Afrondamento, 1993), p. 25.
127. 'História Chronológica', f. 8r.; A. Boyd (ed.), *The Journal of William Beckford in Portugal and Spain 1787–1788* (Stroud: Nonsuch Publishing, 2006), p. 91.
128. D. Rabello, *Os Diamantes do Brasil na rêgencia de Dom João (1792–1816): um estudo de dependência externa* (São Paulo: Editora Arte e Ciência, 1997), p. 177.
129. For the loans made in London with Baring Brothers & Company and in Amsterdam with Hope & Company, see M. G. Buist, *At spes non fracta: Hope & Co. 1770–1815; Merchant Bankers and Diplomats at Work* (The Hague: M. Nijhoff, 1974), pp. 383–427. See also H. Bernstein, *The Brazilian Diamonds in Contracts, Contraband and Capital*, Atlantic Studies on Society in Change, 54 (Lanham, MD: University Press of America, 1988). For an overview of Brazilian diamond trade between 1792 and 1816, see Rabello, *Os Diamantes do Brasil.*
130. Buist, *At spes non fracta: Hope & Co.*, p. 384.
131. See for instance correspondence between the Hope firm and merchants in Turkey, such as 'Vander Schroets & Co. to Thomas & Adrian Hope', Constantinople, 2 January 1768, no. 735.111, GAA, or different transactions in 'Balance Book Hope & Co.' (1762–1790), no. 735.592, GAA.
132. *Saturday's Post* (London), 2 (6 October 1716), BL/BCD.
133. See above, p. 42.
134. Pointon, *Brilliant Effects*, p. 4. This book provides a very good analysis of diamonds, used in jewellery as well as individual stones, next to other gems from a cultural point of view.
135. See above, p. 193, n. 3.
136. For Alexander Hume and his brother, see Degryse, 'De Antwerpse fortuinen', p. 39.
137. Degryse, 'De Antwerpse fortuinen', pp. 81–5. See also J. Denucé, 'James Dormer en de Keizerlijke en Koninklijke Verzekeringskamer te Antwerpen', *Antwerpsch Archievenblad*, 2:4 (1929), pp. 225–62.
138. B. Blondé, 'Conflicting Consumption Models? The Symbolic Meaning of Possessions and Consumption amongst the Antwerp Nobility at the End of the Eighteenth Century', in B. Blondé, N. Coquery, J. Stobart and I. Van Damme (eds), *Fashioning Old and New – Changing Consumer Preferences in Europe (Seventeenth-Nineteenth Centuries)*, Studies

in European Urban History (1100–1800) (Turnhout: Brepols Publishers, 2009), pp. 61–79. His wife owned, with other family members, a small castle not far from Antwerp called Courtewalle, where Dormer spent his summers. The archive there possesses the four diamond books in which Dormer registered his accounts of the diamond trade and that have been used here for the first time. For a full reference see below, p. 204, n. 62. See also the list of manuscript sources, p. 233.

139. Meel, 'De firma James Dormer tussen traditie en vernieuwing', pp. 236–8. He also made his highest relative profits in the diamond trade, although Karel Degryse attributes this to one large transaction in 1754, which cannot be found in Dormer's diamond books wherein he kept his diamond activities. Degryse, 'De Antwerpse fortuinen', p. 83. For a closer look on his ambitions in the diamond trade, see Chapter 3 pp. 72–6.
140. For some of Dormer's other business ventures, see above, p. 80, on his insurance firm and pp. 150–4 on his activities in colonial trade with Veracruz and Brazil.
141. Degryse, 'De Antwerpse fortuinen', p. 146.
142. Meel, 'De firma James Dormer tussen traditie en vernieuwing', pp. 358–60.
143. Ibid., p. 413.
144. Ibid., pp. 524–32.
145. 'Diamond Book N°1' (1744–1752), AdB/DG, no. 1084, f. 95v.
146. For more information regarding the Salvadors, see the last two chapters of this book, pp. 126–39 and pp. 150–74.
147. Meel, 'De firma James Dormer tussen traditie en vernieuwing', p. 342.
148. Francis Salvador to James Dormer, London, 9 Septmeber 1737, FAA, IB1741.
149. For a detailed description of the diamond trade network and the role played by its different members, see the following chapter, pp. 68–72.
150. *Middlesex Journal or Chronicle of Liberty* (London), 276 (Saturday 5 January 1771), BL/BCD.
151. See above, pp. 54–7.
152. Curtin, *Cross-Cultural Trade in World History*, pp. 8–9
153. For the rhythm of the different Brazil fleets, see A G. R. Russell-Wood, *Society and Government in Colonial Brazil, 1500–1822* (Aldershot, Ashgate Variorum: 1992), p. 199.
154. 'Francis & Joseph Salvador to James Dormer', London, 17 June 1746, FAA, IB1741.
155. 'Berthon & Garnault to James Dormer', Lisbon, 1 July 1755, FAA, IB1652.
156. 'Berthon & Garnault to James Dormer', Lisbon, 8 September 1750, FAA, IB1652.
157. 'Berthon & Garnault to James Dormer', Lisbon, 8 September 1750, FAA, IB1652.
158. 'Aaron & David Fernandes Nunes to James Dormer', Amsterdam, 23 November 1741, FAA, IB1723.
159. See above, p. 79. See also pp. 110–12 for Dormer's relationship with Ashkenazi firms as their Antwerp agent.
160. O. Prakash, *European Commercial Enterprise in Pre-Colonial India*, The New Cambridge History of India, II.5 (Cambridge: Cambridge University Press, 1998), p. 242.
161. 'Berthon & Garnault to James Dormer', Lisbon, 22 June 1751, FAA, IB1652.
162. 'Berthon & Garnault to James Dormer', Lisbon, 13 December 1757, FAA, IB1652.
163. 'Berthon & Garnault to James Dormer', Lisbon, 17 December 1754, FAA, IB1652.
164. Jeffries, *A Treatise on Diamonds and Pearls*, p. 30.
165. 'Francis & Joseph Salvador to James Dormer', London, 6 July 1738, FAA, IB1741.
166. 'Francis & Joseph Salvador to James Dormer', London, 11 April 1743, FAA, IB1741.
167. For instance in 1748. 'Francis & Joseph Salvador to James Dormer', London, 12 April 1748, FAA, IB1743.

168. 'George Clifford & Sons to James Dormer', Amsterdam, 07 September 1747, FAA, IB1662.
169. 'Aaron & David Fernandes Nunes to James Dormer', Amsterdam, 27 September 1742, FAA, IB1723.
170. 'Thomas & Adrian Hope to James Dormer', Amsterdam, 05 March 1750, FAA, IB1701.
171. 'Berthon & Garnault to James Dormer', Lisbon, 6 August 1754, FAA, IB1652.
172. 'Berthon & Garnault to James Dormer', 24 June 1749, FAA, IB1652.
173. 'Thomas & Adrian Hope to James Dormer', Amsterdam, 03 August 1747, FAA, IB1701.
174. 'Berthon & Garnault to James Dormer', Lisbon, 21 October 1749, FAA, IB1652.
175. 'Aaron & David Fernandes Nunes to James Dormer', Amsterdam, 5 June 1758, FAA, IB1723.
176. 'Francis & Joseph Salvador to James Dormer', London, 25 May 1753, FAA, IB1742.
177. 'B. E. van Merlen to James Dormer', Amsterdam, 18 April 1746, FAA, IB1717. The letter is written in Dutch and the original quote mentions 'de turcken'.

3 A Cross-Cultural Diamond Trade Network

1. E. Rothschild, 'An Alarming Commercial Crisis in Eighteenth-Century Angoulême: Sentiments in Economic History', *Economic History Review*, new series, 51:2 (May 1998), pp. 268–93, on p. 269.
2. This table is based on the correspondence preserved in the City Archive in Antwerp (FAA). Four letters of Joseph Salvador and 2 letters of Francis Mannock have been preserved at the Dutch Economic Historical Archive in Amsterdam (NEHA).
3. M. Woolf, 'Joseph Salvador 1716–1786', *Transactions and Miscellanies of The Jewish Historical Society of England*, 21 (1962–7), pp. 104–37, on p. 137.
4. 'Ntre couzyn x commun amis Mr Joseph Salvador', 'Aaron & David Fernandes Nunes to James Dormer', Amsterdam, 28 July 1755, FAA, IB1723. For other references to the Salvador firm see above, p. 200, n. 146.
5. 'Diamond Book N°1' (1744–52), AdB/DG, no. 1084, f. 5.
6. No family connection can be established with Isabella, but Jan de Coninck Senior and his son had gained considerable wealth working in Antwerp as financial brokers and money changers. Degryse, 'Antwerpse fortuinen', p. 144.
7. 'Ruben Levy & Co. to James Dormer', Amsterdam, 14 April 1746, FAA, IB1708. For Dormer's commercial relationship with a number of intermarried Ashkenazi firms in Amsterdam, see Chapter 4, pp. 95–122.
8. The few preserved letters written by van Merlen came from Amsterdam and evidence in Dormer's diamond books about sales clearly shows that van Merlen worked in the Dutch capital. He also sent packets of diamonds to Dormer, saying that the latter had to give them to van Merlen's housewife, indicating that he had a residence in Antwerp. 'B. E. Van Merlen to James Dormer', Amsterdam, 18 April 1746, FAA, IB1717.
9. This is clearly indicated in the diamond books, for instance in an entry on 25 January 1748, 'Diamond Book N°2' (1747–50), AdB/DG, f. 14r., which mentions 'given to Bernardus Edmundus van Merlen the following parcell diamonds recd from mr F Salvador taken from f°41 to polish for 1/2 profit'.
10. J. –F. Labourdette, *La nation française à Lisbonne de 1669 à 1790 – Entre Colbertisme et Libéralisme* (Paris: Fondation Calouste Gulbenkian Centre Culturel Portugais, 1988), p. 40. For more on Berthon and Garnault, see Chapter 5, pp. 139–48.
11. See above, pp. 144–5.

12. J. de Vries and A. van der Woude, *Nederland 1500–1815: de eerste ronde van moderne economische groei* (Amsterdam: Balans, 1995), p. 174.
13. The Clifford family archive in the Netherlands was destroyed in a fire during the Second World War. Some documents, mainly genealogical, were donated by a member of the family in the 1960s to the city archive of Amsterdam. Archive Clifford Family, GAA, no. 236 (1738–1934).
14. One of the reasons Dormer sent diamond to London and Lisbon through Amsterdam and Rotterdam was the closure of the river Scheldt, making it impossible to send them from Antwerp.
15. See above, pp. 91–4. A particular example of a remittance through the Clifford firm is the bill of exchange drawn on them. See above, p. 92.
16. Degryse, 'Antwerpse fortuinen', p. 142; H. Houtman-De Smedt, 'Charles Proli, Antwerps zakenman en bankier, 1723–1786. Een biografische en bedrijfshistorische studie', *Verhandelingen van de Koninklijke Academie voor Wetenschappen, Letteren en Schone Kunsten van België, Klasse der Letteren*, 45:108 (1983), pp. 34–6.
17. A letter copy book of the firm, containing letters written between 1749 and 1804 mentions trade in tobacco, cacao and sugar, NEHA, Special Collections no. 188, Firm Joan Osy & Son. See also A. Wegener-Sleeswijk, 'La relation problématique entre principal et agent dans la commission: l'exemple de l'exportation des vins vers les Provinces-Unies au XVIIIe siècle', in S. Marzagalli and H. Bonin (eds), *Négoce, Ports et Océans, XVIe-XXe Siècles: Mélanges Offerts à Paul Butel* (Bordeaux: Presses Universitaires de Bordeaux, 2000), pp. 29–60, on p. 34.
18. For a short time they were Dormer's transport agents with regard to operations in bullion taking place between Dormer and a number of Ashkenazi firms, until they were replaced by a Jewish contact in Rotterdam. See above, p. 108.
19. See above, p. 74.
20. 'I observe your general plan of this trade & that you would have us engage together for account in halves'. 'Francis & Joseph Salvador to James Dormer', London, 10 January 1746, FAA, IB1742.
21. See G. W. Forrest, 'The Siege of Madras in 1746 and the Action of La Bourdonnais', *Transactions of the Royal Historical Society*, 3rd series, 2 (1908), pp. 189–234.
22. 'Francis & Jacob Salvador to James Dormer', London, 6 October 1747 and 13 October 1747; 'Francis & Joseph Salvador to James Dormer', London, 20 October 1746, FAA, IB1743.
23. 'Francis & Jacob Salvador to James Dormer', London, 8 December 1747, FAA, IB1743.
24. 'Francis & Joseph Salvador to James Dormer', London, 9 February 1748, FAA, IB1743.
25. 'Francis & Jacob Salvador to James Dormer', London, 24 November 1747, FAA, IB1743.
26. 'George Clifford & Sons to James Dormer', 21 December 17417, FAA, IB1662 and 22 January 1748, FAA, IB1663.
27. 'We observe what you write about ye projected engagement in diamonds, x how far you have succeeded in it, which is rather more than we expected'. 'George Clifford & Sons to James Dormer', Amsterdam, 30 April 1750 and 07 July 1750, FAA, IB1663.
28. 'Francis & Joseph Salvador to James Dormer', London, 27 Decmber 1751, FAA, IB1741.
29. This comment shows that the Salvadors maintained good commercial contacts with Lisbon, and that a trade monopoly in Brazilian diamonds already was considered before the 1753 crisis.
30. On the establishment of a monopoly in the trade in Brazilian diamonds, see above, pp. 52–5.
31. 'Francis & Joseph Salvador to James Dormer', London, 20 July 1753, FAA, IB1742.
32. 'Berthon & Garnault to James Dormer;, Lisbon, 14 August 1753, FAA, IB1652.
33. 'George Clifford & Sons to James Dormer', Amsterdam, 8 October 1753, FAA, IB1663.
34. 'Francis & Joseph Salvador to James Dormer', London, 28 September 1753, FAA, IB1742.

35. 'we are sorry for the loss of your friend dhr van Merlen'. 'George Clifford and Sons to James Dormer', Amsterdam, [8] January 1753, FAA, IB1663.
36. See different documents belonging to the 'Requête du Sr. James Dormer Contre Les Lapidaires de la ville d'Anvers' (1753), AdB/DG, no. 1089. See also D. Schlugleit, 'De Strijd om de Ambachtsregelingen in het Diamantvak te Antwerpen in 1754', *Bijdragen tot de Geschiedenis*, Nieuwe Reeks, 22:9 (1931), pp. 42–9.
37. 'Francis & Joseph Salvador to James Dormer', London, 3 December 1753, FAA, IB1742.
38. Berthon & Garnault to James Dormer, Lisbon, 19 February 1754, FAA, IB1652.
39. Denucé, 'James Dormer en de Keizerlijke en Koninklijke Verzekeringskamer te Antwerpen', pp. 258–59.
40. Entry on 19 September 1754 in 'Diamond Book N°4' (1752–62), AdB/DG, no. 1087, f. 21.
41. 'Francis & Joseph Salvador to James Dormer', London, 23 September 1754, FAA, IB1742. For Dormer's insurance company, see above, p. 80.
42. 'Joseph Salvador to James Dormer', London, 6 January 1755, NEHA, Special Collections, no. 159, 'James Dormer'. The letter was written on an official document that was also signed by Savador's attorney, Phineas Serra, to establish the name change of the firm.
43. 'Joseph Salvador to James Dormer', London, 15 December 1755, NEHA, Special Collections, no. 159, 'James Dormer'. For the Lisbon earthquake, see J.-P. Poirier, *Le tremblement de terre de Lisbonne* (Paris: Odile Jacob, 2005). For narratives based on contemporary sources, see T. E. Braun and J. B. Radner, *The Lisbon Earthquake of 1755 – Representations and Reactions* (Oxford: Voltaire Foundation, 2005); and J. Nozes and M. L. Machado de Sousa, *O Terramoto de 1755 Testemunhos Britânicos – The Lisbon earthquake of 1755 British Accounts* (Lisbon: The British Historical Society of Portugal, 1990). Detailed information of the consequences of the earthquake for the English merchants in Lisbon can be found in various letters sent by the wife of Paul Berthon to England. 'Letters of Jane Berthon regarding the Lisbon earthquake' (1755), FLRU/RFP, ms 279.
44. 'Deducçaó Compendiosa', ff. 308v–11v and 338v–9r. See also p. 55.
45. 'Paul Berthon to James Dormer', Lisbon, 01 March 1757, FAA, IB1651.
46. For Salvador's decline in the 1760s and 1770s, see above, pp. 131, 133, 160.
47. 'Pierre Garnault & Fils to James Dormer', Lisbonne, 14 September 1756, FAA, IB1690; and 'Paul Berthon to James Dormer', Lisbon, 11 January 1757, FAA, IB1651.
48. 'Joseph Salvador to James Dormer', London, 7 July 1758, FAA, IB1744. The same year, different letters of Joseph Salvador mention his dealings with the Brazilian diamond contractors.
49. According to Erika Meel, Joseph Salvador also made the funeral arrangements. Dormer was buried in the church of Great Missenden, northwest of London. Meel, 'De firma James Dormer tussen traditie en vernieuwing', pp. 168–9.
50. This is shown by Dormer's transactions in diamonds with a number of Ashkenazi non-network firms. See above, Chapter 4, pp. 109–22.
51. See above, pp. 24–8.
52. 'there is no shipping arriv'd this last week from amstm so of consequence have no letters from Messrs Geo: Clifford & sons', 'Berthon & Garnault to James Dormer', Lisbon, 03 February 1750, FAA, IB1652 and 'we have received ... a letter from Berthon and Garnault', 'George Clifford and Sons to James Dormer', Amsterdam, 17 December 1750, FAA, IB1663.
53. Meel, 'De firma James Dormer tussen traditie en vernieuwing', pp. 763–91.
54. 'Berthon & Garnault to James Dormer', Lisbon, 17 June 1749, FAA, IB1652.
55. 'Francis & Joseph Salvador to James Dormer', London, 22 January 1753, FAA, IB1742.

56. 'Isabella de Coninck to James Dormer', Amsterdam, 03 August 1753, FAA, IB1717 in which she wrote that she will talk to Dormer in person about the trade in Amsterdam when she comes back.
57. 'George Clifford and Sons to James Dormer', Amsterdam, 06 November 1747, FAA, IB1662. They wrote that they had given two parcels of diamonds that they had received to van Merlen.
58. 'George Clifford and Sons to James Dormer', Amsterdam, 23 July 1753, FAA, IB1663.
59. For the system of remittances, see above, pp. 91–4.
60. For reciprocity in commercial relationships, see above, pp. 81–4.
61. See Chapter 4, pp. 109–22.
62. The percentages have been calculated by analysing all sales transactions in diamonds noted in Dormer's four diamond books. Diamond Books N°s 1–4 (1744–62), AdB/DG, nos. 1084–7. The different sales identifications correspond to the merchants on whose behalf a sale was made. In the case of Dormer making a commission sale, the different merchants have been grouped together as one category.
63. Meel, 'De firma James Dormer tussen traditie en vernieuwing', pp. 423–8.
64. 'Berthon & Garnault to James Dormer', Lisbon, 12 November 1754, FAA, IB1652.
65. 'Francis & Joseph Salvador to James Dormer', London, 14 Decemeber 1754, FAA, IB1156, Akten en Briefwisseling over de Opstart en Liquidatie van de Keizerlijke Assurantiekamer, Compte de Vente, Anvers, 10 March 1756.
66. For other activities connected with network members, see above, pp. 150–4.
67. 'Joseph Salvador to James Dormer', London, 10 December 1756, FAA, IB1743.
68. 'Joseph Salvador to James Dormer', London, 06 January 1755, NEHA, Special Collections, no. 159, 'James Dormer'. For Samson Gideon, see above, p. 126.
69. 'Joseph Salvador to James Dormer', London, 21 February 1755, FAA, IB1743.
70. For more evidence of Dormer's efforts to work with network members, see above, p. 204, n. 66.
71. See the following chapter, pp. 109–22.
72. For the importance of commercial correspondence in networks, see Trivellato, 'Merchants' Letters across Geographical and Social Boundaries', pp. 80–103; and S. Aslanian, '"The Salt in a Merchant's Letter": The Culture of Julfan Correspondence in the Indian Ocean and the Mediterranean', *Journal of World History*, 19:2 (June, 2008), pp. 127–88. The articles in this volume not only focus on business letters, but also analyse the more general meaning of correspondence. See also above, p. 190, nn. 77, 79.
73. 'David & Joseph Ximenes to James Dormer', London, 18 October 1757, FAA, IB1762.
74. 'George Clifford & Sons to James Dormer', Amsterdam, 10 August 1747, FAA, IB1662.
75. For reciprocity in credit relationships, see above, pp. 83, 105.
76. Greif, 'Reputation and Coalitions in Medieval Trade', p. 872.
77. 'George Clifford & Sons to James Dormer', Amsterdam, 16 April 1750, FAA, IB1663.
78. James Dormer once complimented Andries Pels & Sons regarding a letter of recommendation they sent with a Mr Le Theorier. 'Andries Pels & Sons to James Dormer', Amsterdam, 21 May 1744, FAA, IB1729.
79. 'Francis & Joseph Salvador to James Dormer', London, 10 September 1742, FAA, IB1741.
80. 'Francis & Jacob Salvador to James Dormer', London, 6 October 1747, FAA, IB1743.
81. See above, p. 154.
82. 'Berthon & Garnault to James Dormer', Lisbon, 27 January 1756, FAA, IB1652.

83. It was put explicitly in 'Berthon & Garnault to James Dormer', Lisbon, 16 March 1756, FAA, IB1652: 'that a Consideration or rather a Charitty would be well placed w.th he poor Man has nothing left him, but the character of the honest man we've experienced in him, its true we always held him as such, mais quelquefois Loccazion fait Le Larron, and finding it but to often so with the generallity of theze People, we praize the Man now, thô in want, for doing us justice'.
84. Kooijmans, *Vriendschap en de kunst van het overleven in de zeventiende en achttiende eeuw*, p. 327, 'degenen die konden worden aangesproken om bepaalde doelen te bereiken of problemen op te lossen'.
85. 'Joseph Salvador to James Dormer', London, 21 November 1737, FAA, IB1743
86. 'Francis Mannock to James Dormer', Cadiz, 23 October 1731, FAA, IB1710. Remark the word 'intimacy'.
87. Kooijmans, *Vriendschap en de kunst van het overleven in de zeventiende en achttiende eew*, p. 327.
88. 'Aaron & David Fernandes Nunes to James Dormer', Amsterdam, 28 December 1741, FAA, IB1723.
89. 'Aaron & David Fernandes Nunes to James Dormer', Amsterdam, 19 June 1749, FAA, IB1723.
90. 'Paul Berthon to the widow of James Dormer', Lisbon, 05 December 1758, FAA, IB1651.
91. See references above, on p. 204, n. 72.
92. 'Francis & Joseph Salvador to James Dormer', London, 20 February 1747, FAA, IB1743.
93. 'Joseph Salvador to James Dormer', London, 14 September 1744, FAA, IB1743.
94. See also p. 83.
95. 'Aaron & David Fernandes Nunes to James Dormer', Amsterdam, 3 July 1747, FAA, IB1723.
96. 'Aaron & David Fernandes Nunes to James Dormer', Amsterdam, 2 August 1751, FAA, IB1723.
97. 'as well as for your kind injunction to accept your offer of lodging in your house', 'Francis Mannock to James Dormer', Brussels, 22 January 1741, FAA, IB1710.
98. 'Francis Salvador to James Dormer', Lille, 6 September 1737, FAA, IB1741.
99. 'Francis & Joseph Salvador to James Dormer', London, 10 January 1747, FAA, IB1743.
100. Greif, 'Reputation and Coalitions in Medieval Trade', p. 858.
101. N. Luhmann, 'Familiarity, Confidence, Trust: Problems and Alternatives', in Gambetta (ed.), *Trust: Making and Breaking Cooperative Relations*, pp. 94–107, on p. 95.
102. In the same essay, Luhmann pointed out the importance of a familiar world and symbolic events: 'Trust and confidence are placed in a familiar world by symbolic representation, and therefore remain sensitive to symbolic events which may suddenly destroy the basis for their existence.' I would add that symbolic events might not only destroy, but also contribute to the basis for their existence. The latter is more important here, since we are concerned with the establishment of trust, not with its destruction, which can obviously occur. Luhmann, 'Familiarity, Confidence, Trust: Problems and Alternatives', p. 96.
103. This notion of familiarity with merchants coming from different communities is both needed for and generated by cross-cultural trade. See also Trivellato, *The Familiarity of Strangers*, the title of which points directly to the central issue of trust in cross-cultural trade.
104. Greif, 'Reputation and Coalitions in Medieval Trade', p. 858.
105. 'Joseph Salvador to James Dormer', London, 12 May 1758, FAA, IB1744.

106. 'Joseph Salvador to James Dormer', London, 18 August 1738; 1 September 1738; and 6 September 1757, FAA, IB1743.
107. 'Joseph Salvador to Joseph Xavier Thompson', London, 27 October 1758, FAA, IB1744.
108. See the following chapter, pp. 120–2.
109. See references above on p. 204, n. 72.
110. See above, pp. 20–4.
111. See for example the rhythm of the Brazil and India fleets, Chapter 2, pp. 62–4.
112. Berthon & Garnault to James Dormer, Lisbon, 9 March 1751, FAA, IB1652.
113. 'Information Booklet' (1778–87), GAA, Archive Hope & Co., no. 735.1404, p. 16 (2 January 1781).
114. 'David & Joseph Ximenes to James Dormer', London, 15 July 1757, FAA, IB1762.
115. Francesca Trivellato acknowledges the important role of correspondence with regard to reputation and information. For Markovits, information and knowledge formed the lifeblood of a network. Both authors thus agree on the importance of information and correspondence as a way to divulge it. It was one of the founding mechanisms to make a network operative, not only as a way to distribute knowledge, but also as a mechanism connected to network membership. Trivellato, 'Juifs de Livourne, Italiens de Lisbonne, hindous de Goa', p. 596; and Markovits, *The Global World of Indian Merchants 1750–1947*, p. 156.
116. 'Andries Pels & Sons to James Dormer', Amsterdam, 14 December 1744, FAA, IB1729.
117. The case in which a bad reputation of a third merchant is given is especially interesting, since it creates a certain intimacy of complicity between the traders sharing that information. The third party is seen as bad, creating more opportunity for the two others to build a positive relationship between them.
118. 'George Clifford & Sons to James Dormer', Amsterdam, 14 July 1750, FAA, IB1663.
119. 'Berthon & Garnault to James Dormer', Lisbon, 10 June 1755, FAA, IB1652.
120. 'Berthon & Garnault to James Dormer', Lisbon, 02 March 1751, FAA, IB1652.
121. A. R. J. Turgot, *Mémoires sur le prêt à intérêt et sur le commerce des fers* (Paris: Chez Froullé, 1789).
122. This number has been derived by analysing all transactions mentioned in the correspondence between James Dormer and Berthon & Garnault, FAA, IB1652.
123. 'Berthon & Garnault to James Dormer', Lisbon, 12 September 1752, FAA, IB1652.
124. 'Berthon & Garnault to James Dormer', Lisbon, 6 June 1752, FAA, IB1652.
125. 'Berthon & Garnault to James Dormer', Lisbon, 16 September 1749, FAA, IB1652.
126. Neal, *Rise of Financial Capitalism*, pp. 5–9. Besides Neal's explanation of the bill of exchange, see also C. P. Kindleberger, *A Financial History of Western Europe* (London: George Allen & Unwin, 1984), pp. 39–40; G. Poitras, *The Early History of Financial Economics, 1478–1776 – From Commercial Arithmetic to Life Annuities and Joint Stocks* (Cheltenham; Northampton: Edward Elgar, 2000), pp. 228–66; R. de Roover, *L'évolution de la Lettre de Change XIVe–XVIIIe* siècles, Affaires et gens d'affaires, 4 (Paris: Librairie Armand Colin, 1953).
127. 'Perochon, Firth & Gerard to George Clifford & Sons', Lisbon, 1 July 1755, AdB/DG, no. 1111 (Bankactiviteiten, Wissels & Secundas).
128. R. de Roover, 'What is Dry Exchange? A Contribution to the Study of English Mercantilism', *Journal of Political Economy*, 52:3 (September 1944), pp. 250–66, on pp. 252–3.
129. Some examples can be found in 'Berthon & Garnault to James Dormer', Lisbon, 19 June 1753; 20 November 1753; and 26 February 1754, FAA, IB1652.
130. On the family link between Garnault and Hasenclever, see above, p. 141.

131. See for example the Brazilian diamond crisis in 1753, above, p. 000.
132. See for instance 'Berthon & Garnault to James Dormer', Lisbon, 22 February 1752 and 20 January 1756, FAA, IB1652.
133. 'George Clifford & Sons to James Dormer', Amsterdam, 1 September 1755, FAA, IB1664.
134. 'Joseph Salvador to James Dormer', London, 13 May 1757, FAA, IB1743.
135. Neal, *Rise of Financial Capitalism*, p. 7; and H. van der Wee, 'Monetary, Credit and Banking Systems', in E. E. Rich and C. Wilson (eds), *The Cambridge Economic History of Europe*, vol. 5: The Economic Organization of Early Modern Europe (Cambridge: Cambridge University Press, 1977), p. 328.
136. 'Joseph Salvador to James Dormer', London, 20 May 1757, FAA, IB1743.
137. 'Joseph Salvador to James Dormer', London, 28 April 1756 or 1 October 1756, FAA, IB1743.
138. 'Joseph Salvador to James Dormer', London, 17 September 1756, FAA, IB1743.
139. 'Berthon & Garnault to James Dormer', Lisbon, 12 May 1750, FAA, IB1652.
140. 'Berthon & Garnault to James Dormer', Lisbon, 26 May 1750, FAA, IB1652.
141. J. Smail, 'Credit, Risk, and Honor in Eighteenth-Century Commerce', *Journal of British Studies*, 44:3 (July 2005), pp. 439–56, on p. 445. Smail advocates the treatment of credit not as an abstract factor of production or consumption but as an aspect of a merchant's everyday life. He also incorporates it into a discourse of commercial virtue. For a case study linking credit and reputation, see N. Zahedieh, 'Credit, Risk, and Reputation in Late Seventeenth-Century Colonial Trade', in O. U. Janzen (ed.), *Merchant Organization and Maritime Trade in the North Atlantic, 1660–1815*, Research in Maritime History, 15 (St John's: International Maritime Economic History Association, 1998), pp. 53–74. See also J. Hoppit, 'The use and abuse of credit in eighteenth-century England', in D. C. Coleman and N. McKendrick (eds), *Business life and public policy: essays in honour of D.C. Coleman* (Cambridge: Cambridge University Press, 1986), pp. 64–78. Credit has been mostly analysed in the framework of consumer credit, see for instance R.-M. Gelpi and F. Julien-Labruyère, *The History of Consumer Credit: Doctrines and Practices* (London: MacMillan, 2000). For a socio-cultural analysis of credit, see C. Muldrew, *The Economy of Obligation: The Culture of Credit and Social Relations in Early Modern England* (Basingstoke: Macmillan, 1998).

4 Competition from an Ashkenazi Kinship Network

1. See for instance C. Brasz and Y. Kaplan (eds), *Dutch Jews as Perceived by Themselves and Others*, Proceedings of the Eighth International Symposium on the History of the Jews in the Netherlands (Leiden; Boston; Köln: Brill, 2001). In this work, five out of six contributions regarding the eighteenth century deal exclusively with Sephardic Jewry. See also J. Israel and R. Salverda (eds), *Dutch Jewry: Its History and Secular Culture* (Leiden; Boston, MA; Köln: Brill, 2002). Nine essays in this volume deal with the early modern period, four of those focus on the Portuguese community, three are more general and only two have a topic related to the Ashkenazim. There is a recent tendency to include Jewish communities outside of Amsterdam. For an account of historical sources with regard to Ashkenazi communities in four towns, including the Hague, see S. Litt, *Pinkas, Kahal and the Mediene – The Records of Dutch Ashkenazi Communities in the Eighteenth Century as Historical Sources* (Leiden; Boston, MA; Köln: Brill, 2008).

2. J. Michman, 'A Decade of Historiography of Dutch Jewry', in *Dutch Jewish History iii* – Proceedings of the Fifth Symposium on the History of the Jews in the Netherlands, Jerusalem, November 25–8, 1991 (Assen:, S.n., 1993), p. 11.
3. J. Israel, *Dutch Primacy in World Trade, 1585–1740* (Oxford: Oxford University Press, 1989).
4. N. Zemon Davis, 'Epilogue', in Kagan and Morgan (eds), *Atlantic Diasporas – Jews, Conversos, and Crypto-Jews in the Age of Mercantilism, 1500–1800*, pp. 213–17, on p. 217.
5. H. P. H. Nusteling, 'The Jews in the Republic of the United Provinces: Origins, Numbers and Dispersion', in Israel and Salverda (eds), *Dutch Jewry: Its History and Secular Culture*, p. 54. For a fuller account of Ashkenazi migration to Amsterdam and its causes, see Y. Kaplan, 'Amsterdam and Ashkenazic Migration in the Seventeenth Century', in M. P. Beukers and J. J. Cahen (eds), *Proceedings of the 5th International Symposium on the History of the Jews in the Netherlands – The Netherlands and Jewish Migration, the Problem of Migration and Jewish Identity*, Studia Rosenthaliana Special Issue, 23:2 (Fall 1989), pp. 22–44.
6. K. Sonnenberg-Stern, *Emancipation and Poverty: The Ashkenazi Jews of Amsterdam 1796–1850* (London: Macmillan Press Ltd, 2000), pp. 30–2.
7. S. Baskind, 'Bernard Picart's Etchings of Amsterdam's Jews', *Jewish Social Studies: History, Culture, Society*, 13:2 (Winter 2007), pp. 40–64. See also S. Baskind, 'Distinguishing the Distinction: Picturing Ashkenazi and Sephardic Jews in Seventeenth- and Eighteenth Century Amsterdam', *Journal for the Study of Sephardic and Mizrahi Jewry*, 1:1 (February 2007), pp. 1–13.
8. Sonnenberg-Stern, *Emancipation and Poverty*, p. 32.
9. Y. Kaplan, 'The Jews in the Republic until about 1750: Religious, Cultural, and Social Life', in J. C. H. Blom, R. G. Fuks-Mansfeld and I. Schöffer (eds), *The History of the Jews in the Netherlands* (Oxford; Portland: Littman Library of Jewish Civilization, 2002), pp. 44–163, on pp. 151–2. One of the few studies devoted to the social life of the Ashkenazim deals with the Yiddish theatrical tradition. See H. Berg, 'Thalia and Amsterdam's Ashkenazi Jews in the Late 18th and Early 19th Centuries', in Israel and Salverda (eds), *Dutch Jewry: Its History and Secular Culture*, pp. 191–211.
10. For a history of German Jewry, see A. Elon, *The Pity of it All: A History of Jews in Germany, 1743–1933* (New York: Metropolitan Books, 2002).
11. Many of these wills are preserved in the British National Archives, Kew, Surrey, Public Records Office (BNA/PRO). Most of these wills were originally written in Hebrew and then translated by an official translator. The wills that have been consulted were used in their translated version.
12. See in this regard the rising competition from Ashkenazi merchants in the diamond trade, Chapter 2, p. 49. Yogev, *Diamonds and Coral*, pp. 183–274 analyses an important Ashkenazi firm, the Prager brothers, between 1760 and 1796.
13. L. van De Pol, 'Amsterdam Jews and Amsterdam Prostitution, 1650–1750', in Brasz and Kaplan (eds), *Dutch Jews as Perceived by Themselves and Others*, pp. 173–85.
14. Part of this difference is due to the fact that higher classes have left more historical material than the anonymous lower class. Sonnenberg-Stern, *Emancipation and Poverty*, p. 15.
15. T. M. Endelman, *The Jews of Georgian England 1714–1830: Tradition and Change in a Liberal Society* (Ann Arbor, MI: University of Michigan Press, 1999), p. 166.
16. For France, see P. Cohen Albert, *The Modernization of French Jewry: Consistory and Community in the Nineteenth Century* (Hanover, NH: Brandeis University Press, 1977) and for Germany see M. Richarz, *Jewish Social Mobility in Germany During the Time Emancipa-*

tion 1790–1871, Leo Baeck Institute Yearbook XX (London: Secker and Warburg, 1975), pp. 69–85. For England, see Endelman, *The Jews of Georgian England 1714–1830*.

17. See Table 3.1 on p. 68.
18. For more on their concrete activities in commerce, see above, pp. 104–22.
19. 'Alexander Norden to James Dormer', Amsterdam, 13 November 1744, FAA, IB1721.
20. 'Alexander Norden to James Dormer', Amsterdam, 14 December 1745, FAA, IB1721; and 'Ruben Levy & Co. to James Dormer', Amsterdam, 4 April 1746, FAA, IB1708.
21. The genealogical data that is used in this relies to a great extent on the information that can be found in an online database published by Akevoth, the genealogical department of the Center for Research on Dutch Jewry at the Hebrew University of Jerusalem. The web site is located at http://shum.huji.ac.il/~dutchjew/genealog/ashkenazi/index.htm [accessed 18 March 2011] and is a reliable source. Their data comes mainly from Jewish archives in Amsterdam that were originally written in Yiddish and tombstones on Jewish cemeteries.
22. A suggestion made to me by Prof. John M. Efron, Koret professor of Jewish history at the University of California at Berkeley.
23. See above, pp. 102–3.
24. 'constituted by the oath of Solomon Salomons otherwise Norden', 'Will of Levy Salomons', 01 March 1765, BNA/PRO, Prob 11/907. The dates used in reference to different wills refers to the date a specific will was proved, not when it was written. The fact that it was common to change wills later would create a confusion if dates of writing were to be used to refer to wills.
25. 'my uncle Levy Norden who is tailed in the English tongue Levy Salomons', 'Will of Salomon Reuben Norden', 2 June 1764, BNA/PRO, Prob 11/899.
26. Altona was a town close to Hamburg that was incorporated in the latter city in 1937. The lists of tax payers were printed in M. Grunwald, *Hamburgs deutsche Juden bis zur Auflösung der Dreigemeinden 1811* (Hamburg: Alfred Janssen, 1904), pp. 189–205.
27. See above, pp. 115–16.
28. 'Ruben Levy & Co. to James Dormer', Amsterdam, 24 June 1745; 05 July 1745, FAA, IB1707.
29. The name does occur in different countries, and in the period between 1643 and 1792 118 persons carrying that last name were traced in Hamburg. A. Beider, *A Dictionary of Ashkenazic Given Names: Their Origins, Structure, Pronunciation and Migrations* (Bergenfield, NJ: Avotagnu Inc., 2001), p. 362.
30. This family tree is derived from information made available by the Akevoth database, see above, p. 209, n. 21 and by using different wills preserved in the public record office of the National Archives in Kew. The exact references to the wills can be found in the bibliography. An interesting intermarriage pattern is that of the intermarriage between grandchildren of Salomon Norden with children of Elias de Lima Posner Norden, married to Salomon's daughter Rebecca. The adoption of the name Posner refers to the Eastern European origin of the family, probably from around Posen, while the adoption of the name de Lima suggests the desire to gain respectability by using a Portuguese-sounding name. Names of merchants with whom Dormer corresponded are put in a box. Salomon Norden, who died in 1728, was not a correspondent of Dormer but his firm was. The family tree is incomplete for lack of information and desire to keep the figure accessible. Although names on the same horizontal line belong to the same generation, children have not always been put in chronological order, again for the sake of accessibility and due to a lack of information.
31. These firms were also part of the Ashkenazi merchant families that developed a new way of purchasing diamonds after 1750, using a system of respondentia loans. Yogev, *Diamonds and Coral*, p. 154.

32. In October 1744, for example, Samuel Hartog Levy and David Levy received permission to send £2,000 in silver to Fort St George in India for the purchase of diamonds. Court Minute Book 61 E.I.C. (April 1744–April 1746), BL/IOR, B/68. A year earlier, Arthur Isaac Levy and Elias Levy had received a similar permission.
33. Anon., *A Complete Guide to All Persons who have any Trade or Concern with the City of London, and Parts Adjacent* (London: J. Osborn, 1749), pp. 126–59.
34. 'byde van de voornameste Coopluyden onder onse natsie'. With the word 'nation', Levy referred to the Ashkenazi community. 'Ruben Levy & Co. to James Dormer', Amsterdam, 4 April 1746, FAA, IB1708. The exact kinship ties of the Levys and Nordens of Amsterdam with the Levys and Nordens of London remain unclear and deserve a more detailed study.
35. Yogev, *Diamonds and Coral*, p. 154.
36. See also the diaspora communities of the Sephardim and the Huguenots that will be studied in the fifth chapter of this book, pp. 123–48, *passim*.
37. Yogev, *Diamonds and Coral*, p. 285. The partnership between the two brothers is confirmed by a letter in which the firm 'Ruben & Levy' of London is mentioned, 'Salomon Norden & Co. to James Dormer', Amsterdam, 24 June 1746, FAA, IB1721. The will of Ruben Salomons leaves no doubt, since he appointed 'my Brother and copartner Mr Levy [Salomons]' as one of his executors. 'Will of Ruben Salomons', 18 February 1761, BNA/PRO, Prob 11/863.
38. 'Will of Levy Salomons', 1 March 1765, BNA/PRO, Prob 11/907.
39. L. D. Schwarz, 'Income Distribution and Social Structure in London in the Late Eighteenth Century', *Economic History Review*, New Series, 32:2 (May 1979), pp. 250–9, on p. 258.
40. See above, pp. 110–11, 114.
41. 'Henry Salomons Jr to James Dormer', Amsterdam, 4 September 1758, FAA, IB1745.
42. 'Will of Baerent Salomons', 1 October 1755, BNA/PRO, Prob 11/818.
43. Yogev, *Diamonds and Coral*, p. 51.
44. 'Will of Solomon Norden', 7 September 1775, BNA/PRO, Prob 11/1011 and 'Will of Aaron Norden', S.d., BNL/PRO, Prob 11/1135.
45. See above, pp. 110–13.
46. 'Ruben Levy & Co. to James Dormer', Amsterdam, 11 May 1747, FAA, IB1708: 'wij sijnen beesig om deesen Avond onse huijsen te Illuminere 't welk deese gansche stadt Doet ter Eere onse stadhouder De Heere Prince de orange x Nassau etc etc Die Deese middag Alhier glukkig is gearriveert, waer over groote vreugde hier word bedreeven' ('We are busy illuminating our houses this evening, something the whole city does in honour of our stadtholder the Lord Prince of Orange and Nassau etc etc who arrived here luckily this afternoon, which has made everybody happy').
47. 'Ruben Levy & Co. to James Dormer', Amsterdam, 27 July 1747, FAA, IB1708.
48. Endelman, *The Jews of Georgian England 1714–1830*, p. 179 supports this unsettled character of the London Jewish community, but the same can said to be true for the Jews of Amsterdam.
49. 'Ruben Levy & Co. to James Dormer', Amsterdam, 6 August 1744, FAA, IB1707.
50. See de Roover, L'évolution de la Lettre de Change', pp. 50–5, 68–73.
51. 'Ruben Levy & Co. to James Dormer', Amsterdam, 10 November 1746, FAA, IB1708: 'in Handen sijnende bij brave Cooplieden' ('Being in the hands of honest merchants').
52. 'Ruben Levy & Co. to James Dormer', Amsterdam, 25 August 1746, FAA, IB1708. In this letter, Levy mentions the possibility that a bill could come into 'false hands'.

53. 'Ruben Levy & Co. to James Dormer', Amsterdam, 28 January 1746, FAA, IB1708.
54. 'Andries Pels & Sons to James Dormer', Amsterdam, 27 January 1746, FAA, IB1729.
55. 'Andries Pels & Sons to James Dormer', Amsterdam, 28 January 1746, FAA, IB1729.
56. 'Ruben Levy & Co. to James Dormer', Amsterdam, 03 February 1746, FAA, IB1708.
57. 'Ruben Levy & Co. to James Dormer', Amsterdam, 07 February 1746, FAA, IB1708; and 'Andries Pels & Sons to James Dormer', Amsterdam, 3 February 1746; 7 February 1746, FAA, IB1729.
58. 'Andries Pels & Sons to James Dormer', Amsterdam, 03 February 1746, FAA, IB1729: 'Ces gens passent pour etre tres honnetes, nous croyons meme que cette qualité leur fait trouver en general du Credit, outre cela ils paroissent etre fort experte dans leur Commerce'.
59. 'Ruben Levy & Co. to James Dormer', Amsterdam, 3 February 1746, FAA, IB1708.
60. 'Ruben Levy & Co. to James Dormer', Amsterdam, 26 January 1747, FAA, IB1708.
61. 'Ruben Levy & Co. to James Dormer', Amsterdam, 28 March 1743, FAA, IB1708.
62. This table is based on all the letters sent by Ruben Levy & Co. to James Dormer, FAA, IB1707 and IB1708.
63. 'Ruben Levy & Co. to James Dormer', Amsterdam, 3 December 1746, FAA, IB1708.
64. 'Ruben Levy & Co. to James Dormer', Amsterdam, 4 April 1746, FAA, IB1708.
65. 'B. E. van Merlen to James Dormer', Amsterdam, 18 April 1746, FAA, IB1717: 'voerders hebbe vernomen d'heer Levi mede van hier vertrocken is, geloove hij groote klaghten van mij doen sal' ('Further [I] have heard that Mr. Levy has left from here, [I] believe he will make many complaints about me').
66. 'Ruben Levy & Co. to James Dormer', Amsterdam, 4 April 1746; 3 December 1746; 6 December 1746, FAA, IB1708.
67. 'Ruben Levy & Co. to James Dormer', Amsterdam, 06 December 1746, FAA, IB1708: 'tegen alle Coopmans stijl'.
68. 'Ruben Levy & Co. to James Dormer', Amsterdam, 12 December 1746, FAA, IB1708.
69. R. G. Fuks-Mansfeld, 'Enlightenment and Emancipation from c.1750 to 1814', in Blom, Fuks-Mansfeld Schöffer (eds), *The History of the Jews in the Netherlands*, pp. 164–92, on p. 174; J. Israel, 'The Republic of the United Netherlands until about 1750: Demography and Economic Activity', in Blom, Fuks-Mansfeld and Schöffer (eds), *The History of the Jews in the Netherlands*, pp. 85–115, on p. 102 and J. G. Dillen, 'Amsterdam als wereldmarkt der edele metalen in de 17de en 18de eeuw', *De Economist*, 72:1 (December 1923), pp. 717–30, on p. 725.
70. H. I. Bloom, *The Economic Activities of the Jews of Amsterdam in the Seventeenth and Eighteenth Centuries* (Williamsport, Penn.: Bayard Press, 1937), p. 177. It is most likely that Alexander Salomons was in fact Alexander Norden. Other names included Aaron and Joseph Fernandes Nunes, who were relatives of Joseph Salvador, and Abraham van Lopes Suasso.
71. P. Dehing and M. 't Hart, 'Linking the Fortunes: Currency and Banking, 1550–1800', in M. 't Hart, J. Jonker and J. Luiten van Zanden (eds), *A Financial History of The Netherlands* (Cambridge: Cambridge University Press, 1997), pp. 37–63, on pp. 47–9. See also de Vries and van der Woude, *Nederland 1500–1815*, p. 168.
72. A. Attman, *Dutch Enterprise in the World Bullion Trade 1550–1800*, Humaniora, 23 (Göteborg: Kungl. Vetenskaps- och Vitterkets-Samhället, 1983), pp. 35–6.
73. 'Ruben Levy & C° to James Dormer', Amsterdam, 4 April 1746, FAA, IB1708: 'met d:° veel goud x silver ook diamanten same Coopen'.

74. Around 1736, Eastern Jews had outnumbered the Sephardim and there was no longer a separate Sephardic community in Rotterdam. M. A. Shulvass, *From East to West: The Westward Migration of Jews from Eastern Europe during the Seventeenth and Eighteenth Centuries* (Detroit, MI: Wayne State University Press, 1971), pp. 41, 62, 77.
75. 'Ruben Levy & Co. to James Dormer', Amsterdam, 28 August 1744, FAA, IB1707: 'wij staen in voor onse vriend Esechiel Salomons als wij hem voor u goud toe senden wij souden u Intresse in species behartigen' ('We vouch for our friend Ezechiel Salomons if we send him gold for you, we would serve your interest in bullion').
76. 'Ruben Levy & Co. to James Dormer', Amsterdam, 6 August 1744, FAA, IB1707.
77. A network developed by choice was more vulnerable to dissolution than a mono-cultural circuit that was carried by ties of marriage and a social community the members were part of.
78. 'Ruben Levy & Co. to James Dormer', Amsterdam, 6 August 1744, FAA, IB1707.
79. 'Ruben Levy & Co. to James Dormer', Amsterdam, 14 March 1746 and 7 April 1746, FAA, IB1707.
80. 'Ruben Levy & Co. to James Dormer', Amsterdam, 16 August 1746, FAA, IB1708.
81. 'Ruben Levy & Co. to James Dormer', Amsterdam, 26 November 1744, FAA, IB1707: 'Mijn Heer wij hebbe in Eenige tijd d'Eere niet gehad met u wat van Importence te Tenteere, soo is deeses maer Alleen om onse Correspondentie met u niet stil staen te Laeten'.
82. 'Ruben Levy & Co. to James Dormer', Amsterdam, 4 April 1746, FAA, IB1708. It was in the same year that Dormer finally started to make real profits in the diamond trade, setting up the first large transactions between him and Francis Salvador.
83. Bloom, *The Economic Activities of the Jews of Amsterdam*, p. 41.
84. All numerical information regarding diamond transactions between the Ashkenazi firms and James Dormer comes from Dormer's diamond books, Diamond Books N°s 1–4 (1744–62), AdB/DG, nos. 1084–7.
85. See above, Chapter 2, pp. 64–6.
86. 'Ruben Levy & Co. to James Dormer', Amsterdam, 22 August 1746, FAA, IB1708.
87. 'Ruben Levy & Co. to James Dormer', Amsterdam, 14 October 1746, FAA, IB1708.
88. 'Ruben Levy & Co. to James Dormer', Amsterdam, 5 October 1746, FAA, IB1708: '... dat dan de negotie soo sullen Laete x 't gemaekt goet voor ons behouden...' (Translation: 'We shall leave the transaction at that and keep the made goods to ourselves').
89. 'Ruben Levy & Co. to James Dormer', Amsterdam, 8 June 1744, FAA, IB1707. See above, p. 64.
90. One example can be found in Ruben Levy & Co. to James Dormer, Amsterdam, 13 July 1747, FAA, IB1708: 'neemt ons wonder, naerdien 't Rouwe soo schaers is, dat u 't Rouwe nog van ons onder u sijnde niet vercopen Can' ('[you] take our wonder, since the rough [diamonds] are so rare, that you cannot sell the rough still from us with you').
91. 'Ruben Levy & Co. to James Dormer', Amsterdam, 26 June 1747, FAA, IB1708.
92. 'Ruben Levy & Co. to James Dormer', Amsterdam, 28 March 1743; 22 April 1743, FAA, IB1707. See also 'Ruben Levy & Co. to James Dormer', Amsterdam, 19 June 1747, FAA, IB1708.
93. Bloom, *The Economic Activities of the Jews of Amsterdam*, p. 40.
94. See for instance W. J. Fischel, 'The Jewish Merchant-Colony in Madras (Fort St. George) during the 17th and 18th Centuries: A Contribution to the Economic and Social History of the Jews in India', *Journal of the Economic and Social History of the Orient*, 3:1 (April 1960), pp. 78–107 or W. J. Fischel, 'Bombay in Jewish History in the Light of New Documents from the Indian Archive', *Proceedings of the American Academy for Jewish Research*, 38 (1970–1), pp. 119–44.

95. Entry on 10 October 1744 in Court Minute Book 61 E.I.C. (April 1744–April 1746), BL/IOR, B/68, f. 120.
96. Entry on 29 January 1745 in Court Minute Book 61 E.I.C. (April 1744–April 1746), BL/IOR, B/68, f. 425.
97. Entry on 15 November 1749 in Court Minute Book 63 E.I.C. (April 1748–April 1750), BL/IOR, B/70, f. 507.
98. The information is drawn from the Court Minutes preserved at the India Office Records in the British Library: Court Minute Books 60–68 E.I.C. (1742–60), BL/IOR, B/67–B/75. Levy family members were not included, as I have not been able to establish concrete family relations between the Levy family in London and the one in Amsterdam.
99. Francesca Trivellato has analysed cross-cultural networks in which Jewish merchants from Leghorn played an important role. Trivellato, *The Familiarity of Strangers*; and Trivellato, 'Juifs de Livourne, Italiens de Lisbonne, hindous de Goa', pp. 581–603.
100. Although letters have been lost, Dormer's correspondence has remained quite complete. Of Joseph Salomons, only eleven letters remain, one from 1752, the rest from 1758 and 1759 (to Dormer's son). The 1752 letter of the correspondence with Joseph Salomons indicates they were in the middle of a transaction. 'Joseph Salomons to James Dormer', London, 21 August 1752, FAA, IB1745.
101. 'Michael Salomons to James Dormer', London, 19 November 1756, FAA, IB1745.
102. Court Minute Book 66 E.I.C. (April 1754–April 1756), BL/IOR, B/73.
103. Marcus Moses was an eighteenth-century diamond merchant in India who was the son-in-law of Glückel von Hameln, the wife of a jeweller. Her diary gives an excellent insight of the life of an Ashkenazi woman at the end of the seventeenth century. See Hofmeester, 'Diamonds as a Global Luxury Commodity', and G. von Hameln, *The Memoirs of Glückel of Hameln*, transl. M. Lowenthal (New York: Schocken Books, 1977).
104. Anon., *A Complete Guide*, entry on Henry Muilman.
105. 'Will of Joseph Salomons', 7 April 1763, BNA/PRO, Prob 11/886. It was not entirely uncommon for Ashkenazim to include non-Jewish executors in their will, but in almost all cases this was shared by either direct family members of the person making the will or Jewish merchants that were friends.
106. 'Ruben Levy & Co. to James Dormer', Amsterdam, 27 June 1746, FAA, IB1708. Levy continued to inquire about Dormer's health in letters send during the following month.
107. 'Ruben Levy & Co. to James Dormer', Amsterdam, 28 March 1743, FAA, IB1707: 'wij sijn aan u seer verpligt voor de Beleeftheijdt die u aan onse Companion Jacob Elias Levy In sijn Costy weesende getoont heeft'.
108. 'Ruben Levy & Co. to James Dormer', Amsterdam, 24 June 1745, FAA, IB1707.
109. Bloom, *The Economic Activities of the Jews of Amsterdam*, p. 213.
110. M. H. Gans, *Memorbook: History of Dutch Jewry from the Renaissance to 1940* (Baarn: Bosch & Keuning n.v., 1971), p. 167.
111. 'Ruben Levy & Co. to James Dormer', Amsterdam, 2 July 1745; 5 July 1745, FAA, IB1707.
112. See above, pp. 88–94 for an argument regarding the adoption of informal custom in commercial relationships with other merchants by negotiating reputation and credit-worthiness through instruments that became more and more standardized: business letters and bills of exchange.
113. 'Ruben Levy & Co. to James Dormer', Amsterdam, 17 April 1744; 29 June 1744, FAA, IB1707.
114. 'Ruben Levy & Co. to James Dormer', Amsterdam, 19 June 1744, FAA, IB1707: 'als wij Geen oocasie voor gemakd hebe daen is't voor ons niet de pine waerdeg om uyt ons uijs naar Costy te Rijsen' ('If we have no occasion for made [polished] goods, it is not worth it for us to travel there [Antwerp]').

115. 'Ruben Levy & Co. to James Dormer', Amsterdam, 4 July 1746, FAA, IB1708: 'versoeke ons ook te melden of u ons Raeden souden in deese Conjuncture over te Comen, x of er Iets van negocie omgaet' ([We] ask you to let us know whether you recommend us to travel [to Antwerp] in this conjecture, and whether some business is taking palce').
116. 'Francis & Joseph Salvador to James Dormer', London, 10 January 1746, FAA, IB1742.
117. Yogev, *Diamonds and Coral*, p. 152.
118. J. H. Zedler, *Grosses Vollständiges Universal-Lexikon aller Wissenschaften und Künste*, 64 vols (Halle, 1732–50), vol. 16, p. 1806.
119. R. Beachy, *The Soul of Commerce: Credit, Property, and Politics in Leipzig, 1750–1840* (Leiden; Boston: Brill, 2005), pp. 32–7.
120. C. Roth, *History of the Great Synagogue* (London: Edward Goldaton & Son Ltd, 1950).
121. Bloom, *The Economic Activities of the Jews of Amsterdam*, p. 112.
122. 'Ruben Levy & Co. to James Dormer', Amsterdam, 6 April 1744; 26 April 1744; 20 September 1745, FAA, IB1707.
123. Bloom, *The Economic Activities of the Jews of Amsterdam*, p. 111.
124. Ibid., appendix C, vi.
125. 'Jacob Elias Levy to James Dormer', Antwerp, 2 May 1744, FAA, IB1707: 'Ik hebe veel goed geCogt de Leypziger misse is god Loft Redlijk gegaen' ('I have bought many goods, the Leipzig fair has gone reasonably well, thank God').
126. 'Ruben Levy & Co. to James Dormer', Amsterdam, 10 June 1745, FAA, IB1707: 'onse Compagnon heeft die van Lijpsig meede gebragt' (Translation: 'our companion has brought them with him from Leipzig'). See also Attman, *Dutch Enterprise*, p. 10. For the Levy involvement in bullion trade and the role of the Leipzig fair, see above, pp. 107–9.
127. See the first chapter of this monograph for a theoretical analysis, particularly pp. 28–33.
128. 'Ruben Levy & C° to James Dormer', Amsterdam, 6 January 1746, FAA, IB1708.
129. 'Ruben Levy & C° to James Dormer', Amsterdam, 03 February 1746, FAA, IB1708: 'Niet tegenstaende u maer Libre Can seggen, of u ongenoegen in onse Correspondentie neemt sal ons godt loff Egter niet benadele'.
130. See alsoabove, pp. 88–91,, for the importance of reputation and information in commercial society. See also Chapter 1, pp. 31–3.
131. 'u ons niet 't tiende part soo veel kende als nu', 'Ruben Levy & Co. to James Dormer', Amsterdam, 4 April 1746, FAA, IB1708.
132. For the Suasso family and their relationship with the Salvadors, see above, p. 127.
133. 'Abraham van Moses Lopes Suasso Fr. & Companhia to James Dormer', Amsterdam, 27 March 1749, FAA, IB1719.
134. 'Abraham van Moses Lopes Suasso Fr. & Companhia to James Dormer', Amsterdam, 8 May 1749, FAA, IB1719.
135. 'Thomas and Adrian Hope to James Dormer', Amsterdam, 8 May 1749, FAA, IB1701.
136. 'Widow B. E. Van Merlen to James Dormer', Amsterdam, 26 July 1753, FAA, IB1717.
137. 'Thomas and Adrian Hope to James Dormer', Amsterdam, 1 May 1749, FAA, IB1701.
138. 'Francis and Joseph Salvador to James Dormer', London, 30 December 1746, FAA, IB174.
139. 'Ruben Levy & C° to James Dormer', Amsterdam, 26 April 1743, FAA, IB1707: 'aldien In wineg tijt Eene van ons Comp.a a Costy moeg komen soo sulen wij aen Nimand advis van geven' (Translation: 'If shortly someone of our company must come there then we shall keep it unknown to anybody'); also 'Ruben Levy & C° to James Dormer', Amsterdam 3 May 1743, FAA, IB1707: 'onse broeder Mr Jacob Elias Levy Maendag avond

Costi sal sijn 't welk versoeke geheijm te houden' (Translation: 'Our brother Mr. Jacob Elias Levy shall be there Monday evening, which we ask to keep secret').
140. 'Ruben Levy & C° to James Dormer', Amsterdam, 30 December 1743, FAA, IB1707.
141. See above, pp. 58–9.
142. 'Ruben Levy & C° to James Dormer', Amsterdam, 10 July 1744, FAA, IB1707.
143. 'Francis Salvador to James Dormer', London, 10 February 1749; 17 March 1749; 27 March 1749; 30 March 1749, FAA, IB1741.
144. 'the Levy's & other Smous', 'Francis Salvador to James Dormer', London, 17 March 1749, FAA, IB1741.

5 The Embeddedness of Merchants in State and Society

1. M. L. Bush (ed.), *Social Orders and Social Classes in Europe since 1500: Studies in Social Stratification* (London: Longman, 1992) contains essays about both Western and Eastern Europe. For an classic non-European example, see for instance literature on caste systems in India and elsewhere, for instance S. Bayly, *Caste, Society and Politics in India from the Eighteenth Century to the Modern Age* (Cambridge: Cambridge University Press, 1999).
2. This is quoted in N. McKendrick, 'The Commercialization of Fashion', in N. McKendrick, J. H. Plumb and J. Brewer (eds), *The Birth of a Consumer Society: The Commercialization of Eighteenth-Century England* (Bloomington: Indiana University Press, 1982), pp. 34–99, on p. 95.
3. D. Wahrman, *The Making of the Modern Self: Identity and Culture in Eighteenth-Century England* (New Haven: Yale University Press, 2004), p. 205. For different dress codes and their social meaning before the Revolutionary era, see also D. Roche, *The Culture of Clothing: Dress and Fashion in the 'Ancien Régime'* (Cambridge: Cambridge University Press, 1996).
4. See J. G. A. Pocock, *Virtue, Commerce, and History* (Cambridge: Cambridge University Press, 1985). See also the collection of essays in Q. Skinner and M. van Gelderen (eds), *Republicanism: A Shared European Heritage* (Cambridge; New York: Cambridge University Press, 2002), especially vol. 2: *The Values of Republicanism in Early Modern Europe*, part 3: Republicanism and the Rise of Commerce, pp. 177–310.
5. C. Davenant, 'Essay upon the Probable Methods of Making a People Gainers in the Balance of Trade', in C. Davenant, *The Political and Commercial Works of the Celebrated Writer Charles D'Avenant, LL.D. Relating to the Trade and Revenue of England, the Plantation Trade, the East-India Trade, and African Trade* (1771), ed. C. Whitworth, 5 vols (Farnborough: Gregg Press, 1967), vol. 2, pp. 163–382, on p. 275.
6. C. M. Belfanti and F. Giusberti, 'Clothing and Social Inequality in Early Modern Europe: Introductory Remarks', *Continuity and Change*, 15:3 (December 2000), pp. 359–65.
7. A classic example of the pre-revolutionary division of society is for instance G. Duby, *Les Trois Ordres ou l'Imaginaire du féodalisme* (Gallimard: Paris, 1978). For a brief introduction on hierarchy in early modern Europe and the relevance of different models, see P. Burke, 'The Language of Orders in Early Modern Europe', in Bush (ed.), *Social Orders and Social Classes in Europe since 1500*, pp. 1–12. For a more practical and non-European approach, see for instance D. Gupta (ed.), *Social Stratification*, Oxford in India Readings in Sociology and Social Anthropology Series (Oxford: Oxford University Press, 1992), on the caste system in India.

8. See the chapter on Möser entitled 'Justus Möser: The Market as Destroyer of Culture' for a good example of conservative thought on commerce, in J. Z. Muller, *The Mind and the Market: Capitalism in Modern European Thought* (New York: Alfred A. Knopf, 2002), pp. 84–103. See also J. Viner, *Religious Thought and Economic Society: Four Chapters of an Unfinished Work*, ed. J. Melitz and D. Winch (Durham, NC: Duke University Press, 1978), pp. 35–6.
9. A. C. Macintyre, *Whose Justice? Which Rationality?* (London: Duckworth, 1988), pp. 157–62.
10. See for instance the Christian association of Jewish religion and usury. A. Kirschenbaum, 'Jewish and Christian Theories of Usury in the Middle Ages', *Jewish Quarterly Review*, New Series, 75:3 (January 1985), pp. 270–89.
11. For the development of a more positive view towards trade and the theory of individual self-interest leading to the construction of society rather than destroying it, see Hirschman, *The Passions and the Interests* or Force, *Self-Interest before Adam Smith: A Genealogy of Economic Science.*
12. P. Manning, *Migration in World History*, Themes in World History Series (New York: Routledge, 2005), p. 122.
13. Wahrman, *The Making of the Modern Self*, p. 206.
14. See for instance Endelman, *The Jews of Georgian England 1714–1830*, ch. 4, 'Gentlemen Jews: The Acculturation of the Anglo-Jewish Middle Class', pp. 118–65. The connection between the economic success of merchants and their attempts towards integration is not limited to Jewish traders. See for instance Schulte-Beerbühl's work on German merchants in London, and particularly the process of integration in English society in which they participated. Schulte-Beerbühl, *Deutsche Kaufleute in London*, pp. 27–64.
15. L. Sutherland, 'Samson Gideon: Eighteenth Century Jewish Financier', in Sutheralnd, *Politics and Finance in the Eighteenth Century*, pp. 386–98, on p. 389.
16. For the persecution of Jews in Portugal, see M. Newitt, *Portugal in European and World History* (London: Reaktion Books, 2009), pp. 113–18.
17. D. Swetschinski, *Reluctant Cosmopolitans – The Portuguese Jews of Seventeenth-Century Amsterdam* (London; Portland, OR: Littman Library of Jewish Civilization, 2000), pp. 252–7.
18. For information regarding the Jessurun name, see L. Wolf, 'The Jessurun Family', *Jewish Quarterly Review*, 1:4 (July, 1889), pp. 439–41.
19. Wilson, *Anglo-Dutch Commerce and Finance*, pp. 93–4.
20. For the Mendes da Costa family, see above, pp. 136, 167–70.
21. Woolf, 'Joseph Salvador 1716–1786', p. 104.
22. 'Joseph Salvador to James Dormer', London, 18 September 1741, FAA, IB1743.
23. On the links between the Lopes Suasso family and the State, see Israel, *Diasporas within a Diaspora*, pp. 499–502 and Swetschinski, *Reluctant Cosmopolitans*, pp. 135–8. See also D. Swetschinski and L. Schönduve, *The Lopes Suasso Family, Bankers to William III* (Zwolle: Uitgeverij Waanders, 1988).
24. Swetschinski, *Reluctant Cosmopolitans*, p. 138.
25. Wilson, *Anglo-Dutch Commerce and Finance*, pp. 162–3.
26. For a detailed, though somewhat dated, account of his life and his ideas, see J. S. Wijler, *Isaac de Pinto, Sa Vie et Ses Œuvres* (Apeldoorn; C.M.B. Dixon & Co., S.d.). At p. 108, the author published a letter of de Pinto, dated 1759, in which he made Joseph Salvador his 'true and lawfull Attorney'.

27. D. S. Katz, *The Jews in the History of England 1485–1850* (Oxford: Clarendon Press, 1994), pp. 176–7.
28. *Gazetteer and London Daily Advertiser* dated Friday 13 December1765, mentions Abraham de Paiba who was selling a large diamond by auction in Chadwell's coffee house and the *Public Advertiser*, London, Wednesday 21 February 1753, contains an obituary mentioning the death of Isaac de Paiba, 'an eminent diamond broker'. Accessed through BL/BCD.
29. 'Joseph Salvador to James Dormer', London, 18 September 1741, NEHA, Special Collections N°159, 'James Dormer'.
30. Yogev, *Diamonds and Coral*, p. 144.
31. This family tree is based on the wills of different members of the Salvador and Mendes da Costa families preserved in the public record office of the National Archives in Kew. As far as the data collected in this figure goes, the same remarks apply as for Figure 4.1. See p. 208, n. 11.
32. J. Drayton, *Memoirs of the American Revolution, from its Commencement to the Year 1776, Inclusive; As Relating to the State of South-Carolina and Occasionally Refering to the States of North-Carolina and Georgia. In Two Volumes* (Charleston: A .E. Miller, 1831), p. 348.
33. Israel, *Diasporas within a Diaspora*, p. 505.
34. Woolf, 'Joseph Salvador 1716–1786', p. 137.
35. Biographical information found on the website of the Dutch Jewish Historical Museum, online at http://www.jhm.nl/cultuur-en-geschiedenis/personen/s/salvador,+mozes, [accessed 18 March 2011].
36. 'Francis & Joseph Salvador to James Dormer', London, 23 December 1754, FAA, IB1742.
37. Sutherland, 'Samson Gideon', p. 396.
38. Katz, *The Jews in the History of England 1485–1850*), p. 224.
39. Woolf, 'Joseph Salvador 1716–1786', p. 105; and C. Roth, *Anglo-Jewish Letters (1158–1917)* (Edinburgh: R. & R. Clark, Limited, 1938), p. 148.
40. Endelman, *The Jews of Georgian England 1714–1830*, pp. 227–47.
41. Woolf, 'Joseph Salvador 1716–1786', p. 105.
42. As quoted from the diary of Haim David Azulai by David Katz. Katz, *The Jews in the History of England 1485–1850*, p. 272.
43. Ibid., p. 273.
44. Presidents and Secretaries of the Board of Deputies of British Jews, Metropolitan Archives, London, Board of Deputies of British Jews, ACC/3121/B. The first president, between 1760 and 1766, was Benjamin Mendes da Costa, who was succeeded by Joseph Salvador, who was president between 1766 and 1789. After Salvador, an Ashkenazi Jew, Moses Isaac Levy, took over. Presidencies seem to have been divided fairly equal between Sephardim and Ashkenazim.
45. Endelman, *The Jews of Georgian England 1714–1830*, p. 135.
46. 'Joseph Salvador to James Dormer', London, 12 May 1758, FAA, IB1744.
47. Dickson, *The Financial Revolution in England*, p. 288.
48. L. Sutherland, 'London and the Pitt-Devonshire Administration', in Sutherland, *Politics and Finance in the Eighteenth Century*, ed. Newman, pp. 97–111.
49. H. V. Bowen, *The Business of Empire: The East India Company and Imperial Britain, 1756–1833* (Cambridge: Cambridge University Press, 2006), p. 34.
50. Quoted from Woolf, 'Joseph Salvador 1716–1786', p. 106. See also Katz, *The Jews in the History of England 1485–1850*, p. 271. A picture of his house is preserved in the Guild-

hall Library in London. It shows a cricket game taking place with Salvador's house in the background. The picture dates from 1787 and the text under it makes it clear that after Salvador had sold the house in 1757, it was turned into an academy. This back view of Salvadore House Academy, Tooting, Surry Drawn and Engraved by J. Walker, Aquat. by F. Jukes, published April 1787 by R. Wilkinson, Guildhall Library, London, P459236.

51. Woolf, 'Joseph Salvador 1716–1786', p. 108.
52. Katz, *The Jews in the History of England 1485–1850*, pp. 270–71.
53. Endelman, *The Jews of Georgian England 1714–1830*, p. 127.
54. Ibid., p. 126.
55. See above, Chapter 3, p. 87.
56. M. Zell, *Reframing Rembrandt: Jews and the Christian Image in 17th Century Amsterdam* (Berkeley, CA: University of California Press, 2002), p. 31.
57. In some literature it is suggested that Salvador did not only have good personal connections within the East India Company, but also that he was a director. See for instance H. V. Bowen, 'The "Little Parliament": The General Court of the East India Company, 1750–1784', *Historical Journal*, 34:4 (December 1991), pp. 857–72, on p. 866. Salvador's directorship is denied by David Katz. Katz, *The Jews in the History of England 1485–1850*, p. 270. Salvador's directorship indeed seems most unlikely and is not confirmed by concrete evidence. Salvador's possible formal membership of organizations such as the East India Company is not crucial for the general argument of his attachment to certain elite circles that were connected to imperial decision-making. See above, Chapter 6, pp. 172–3.
58. 'I dont frequent the Playhouse much but when I see you on the stage I see you with pleasure', 'Joseph Salvador to C. Macklin', London, 6 February 1761, BL, Egerton Papers, Eg. 2334, f. 3.
59. Endelman, *The Jews of Georgian England 1714–1830*, pp. 128–9.
60. Woolf, 'Joseph Salvador 1716–1786', p. 111.
61. Online at www.sailingnavies.com/show_person.php?nid=1&id=6366 [accessed 18 March 2011]; and www.pbenyon1.plus.com/Nbd/exec/M/Index.html [accessed 18 March 2011].
62. 'Will of Joseph Salvador', 15 January 1788, BNA/PRO, Prob 11/1172. Three additional codicils to the will were only proved on 24 November 1788.
63. See above, Chapter 6, p. 150.
64. Woolf, 'Joseph Salvador 1716–1786', p. 111; and Katz, *The Jews in the History of England 1485–1850*, p. 271.
65. Woolf, 'Joseph Salvador 1716–1786', p. 111.
66. Rudd [née Youngson], Margaret Caroline (b.*c.* 1745, *d.* in or before 1798), *ODNB*.
67. See D. T. Andrew and R. McGowen, *The Perreaus and Mrs. Rudd: Forgery and Betrayal in Eighteenth-Century London* (Berkeley, CA; Los Angeles, CA; London: University of California Press, 2001), in which it is also suggested that Mrs Rudd and the countess de Moriencourt might have been the same person. Mrs Rudd was known to disguise her true identity, and was at one time even pretending to be the sister of John Gore. Andrew and McGowen, *The Perreaus and Mrs. Rudd*, pp. 109, 149. John Gore was involved in the second Brazilian diamond monopoly contract, see above, Chapter 2, pp. 54–5.
68. Andrew and McGowen, *The Perreaus and Mrs. Rudd*, p. 108.
69. Woolf, 'Joseph Salvador 1716–1786', p. 116.
70. For instance, in the *Bath Journal* of 30 March 1775 and the *Middlesex Journal Evening Advertiser* between 13th and 15th July 1775. Salvador admitted he had given Mrs Rudd sums of money. The journal references come from Andrew and McGowen, *The Perreaus and Mrs. Rudd*, p. 300.

71. This is quoted in Andrew and McGowen, *The Perreaus and Mrs. Rudd*, p. 108.
72. For a full account on her career as a celebrated courtesan, as well as an analysis of the art that was devoted to her, from memoirs and poems to portraits and satire, see M. Pointon, 'The Lives of Kitty Fisher', *British Journal for Eighteenth-Century Studies*, 27:1 (Spring 2004), pp. 77–97.
73. Woolf, 'Joseph Salvador 1716–1786', pp. 110–11 and Katz, *The Jews in the History of England 1485–1850*, p. 271.
74. Endelman, *The Jews of Georgian England 1714–1830*, p. 130.
75. Sahlins, *Apologies to Thucydides*, p. 140.
76. A. Dirlik, 'Performing the World: Reality and Representation in the Making of World Histor(ies)', *Journal of World History*, 16:4 (December 2005), pp. 391–410, on p. 396.
77. In this sense, the Salvadors gain historical agency, rather than just being embedded in structural relationships. See also Joseph Salvador's involvement in British imperial policy, above, pp. 172–3.
78. See above, pp. 124–6.
79. The first example of this that comes to mind is the case of Sephardic Jews in both Holland and England. In other civilizations as well, a certain protection was offered to foreign merchants, for instance in the case of pre-colonial Mandé societies in western Africa. J.-L. Amselle, 'L'étranger dans le monde manding et en Grèce ancienne: quelques points de comparaison', *Cahiers d'Études Africaines*, 36:144, Mélanges maliens (1996), pp. 755–61, on pp. 758–9.
80. See for instance I. Hont, *Jealousy of Trade: International Competition and the Nation-State in Historical Perspective* (Cambridge, MA; London: Belknap Press of Harvard University Press, 2005).
81. For the origins of political economy, as well as its international diffusion, see P. Groenewegen, *Eighteenth-Century Economics: Turgot, Beccaria and Smith and their Contemporaries* (London; New York: Routledge, 2002), pp. 32–40.
82. For instance Melon's *A Political Essay upon Commerce* (1738) or James Steuart's *An Inquiry into the Principles of Political Oeconomy* (1767). It can also be observed in the late seventeenth-century development of political arithmetic, stressing the importance of a quantitative approach to study social facts and matters of economy and finance, which were all related to government. L. Desmedt, 'Money in the "Body Politick": The Analysis of Trade and Circulation in the Writings of Seventeenth-Century Political Arithmeticians', *History of Political Economy*, 37:1 (Spring 2005), pp. 79–101.
83. This also includes the position towards freer trade, as it would be the government's duty to ensure it.
84. See for instance W. O'Reilly, 'The Naturalization Act of 1709 and the Settlement of Germans in Britain, Ireland and the Colonies', in C. Littleton and R. Vigne (eds), *From Strangers to Citizens: The integration of Immigrant Communities in Britain, Ireland and Colonial America, 1550–1750* (Brighton; Portland: Sussex Academic Press), pp. 492–502.
85. J. Child, *A New Discourse of Trade: Wherein are Recommended Several Weighty Points ... By Sir Josiah Child, Baronet*, 4th edn (London: J. Hodges; W. Meadows; C. Corbet; J. Jackson; J Stagg; and J. Bevill, [1745]), pp. 150–3.
86. '[Signet Warrant of letters of denization to, 1717]', BL, Egerton Ch. 7458. The Salvador's were intermarried with the Mendes da Costa family, an important family in the Jewish community. See Figure 5.1 on p. 128.

87. L. Luu, 'Natural-Born versus Stranger Born Subjects: Aliens and their Status in Elizabethan London', in N. Goose and L. Luu (eds), *Immigrants in Tudor and early Stuart England* (Brighton: Sussex Academic Press, 2005), pp. 57–75, on p. 59.
88. '[Petition for naturalization ante 1754]', BL/NP, vol. 372, add. 33057, f. 310. Since it deals with the same persons and has similar content to the document in Latin, it seems likely that it was written around the same time. Perhaps this document was a request, while the Latin text granted them the denization.
89. '[Warrant for naturalization]', 11 November 1730 BL, Hardwicke Papers, vol. 781, add. 36129, f. 126.
90. 'Joseph Salvador to James Dormer', London, 20 September 1757, FAA, IB1743.
91. 'Joseph Salvador to Charles Jenkinson, St James's', 25 November 1776, BL/LP, vol. 20, add. 38209, f. 59.
92. See above, Chapter 4, p. 104.
93. Katz, *The Jews in the History of England 1485–1850*, p. 240.
94. Gedalia Yogev and Maurice Woolf were two of them. See Yogev, *Diamonds and Coral*; and Woolf, 'Joseph Salvador 1716–1786'.
95. Philo-Patriae, *Considerations on the Bill to Permit Persons Professing the Jewish Religion to be Naturalized by Parliament* (London: S.n., 1753); and Philo-Patriae, *Further Considerations on the Act to Permit Persons Professing the Jewish Religion, to be Naturalized by Parliament* (London: S.n., 1753).
96. R. Liberles, 'The Jews and their Bill: Motivations in the Controversy of 1753', *Jewish History*, 2:2 (Fall 1987), pp. 29–36, on p. 30.
97. Philo-Patriae, *Further Considerations*, p. 73.
98. E. Samuel, 'The Jews in English Foreign Trade – A Consideration of the 'Philo Patriae' Pamphlets of 1753', in J. M. Shaftesley (ed.), *Remember the Days – Essays on Anglo-Jewish History Presented to Cecil Roth by Members of the Council of the Jewish Historical Society of England* (London: Jewish Historical Society of England, 1966), pp. 123–43, on pp. 126–7.
99. The most complete account of the Jew Bill and the surrounding controversy can be found in T. W. Perry, *Public Opinion, Propaganda and Politics in Eighteenth Century England, A Study of the Jew Bill of 1753* (Harvard, MA: Harvard University Press, 1962).
100. See above, Chapter 6, pp. 159–61.
101. D. Rabin, 'The Jew Bill of 1753: Masculinity, Virility, and the Nation', *Eighteenth-Century Studies*, 39:2 (2006), pp. 157–71, on p. 168.
102. Ibid., p. 168.
103. J. Hanway, *Letters Admonitory and Argumentative, from J. H—y, Merchant, to J. S—r, Merchant in Reply to Particular Passages, and the General Argument, of a Pamphlet, Entitled, Further Considerations on the Bill, &c.* (London: Dodsley, 1753), p. 51.
104. See for instance A. Singer, 'Aliens and Citizens: Jewish and Protestant Naturalization in the Making of the Modern British Nation' (PhD dissertation, University of Missouri, 1999).
105. A. Lièvre, *Histoire des protestants et des églises réformées du Poitou*, 3 vols (Poitiers: Imprimerie de N. Bernard, 1860), vol. 3, pp. 53–4, 83, 284.
106. Reference to him will be made as Paul Berthon the elder, in order not to confuse him with Peter Garnault's partner, who will be referred to as Paul Berthon.
107. 'Will of Paul Berthon', 16 April 1743, BNA/PRO, Prob 11/725.
108. Genealogical information in this part is based on consulted wills, both the Berthon and Garnault family pedigrees that exist in the Huguenot Library, and genealogical data

drawn from the letters sent by Berthon & Garnault to James Dormer. A particularly interesting document that is in the Berthon pedigree is a family tree compiled by John Paul Berthon in 1787. Berthon Family, HLL, Wagner Pedigrees and Garnault Family, HLL, Wagner Pedigrees.

109. 'Will of Martha Berthon formerly Martineau', 21 May 1753, BNA/PRO, Prob 11/801,
110. Edward Lyon Berthon (1813–1899), *ODNB*.
111. 'Berthon Family', HLL, Wagner Pedigrees.
112. 'Will of John Sauret', 28 October 1727, BNA/PRO, Prob 11/618.
113. See above, p. 85.
114. This was also mentioned to the widow of James Dormer, see above. 'Will of Jane Berthon', 10 December 1793, BNA/PRO, Prob 11/1239.
115. 'Will of Michael Berthon', 20 December 1756, BNA/PRO, Prob 11/826.
116. 'Will of Daniel Berthon', 12 May 1795, BNA/PRO, Prob 11/1235.
117. 'Will of Peter Garnault', 1 July 1738, BNA/PRO, Prob 11/690.
118. 'Will of Aymé Garnault', 21 August 1741, BNA/PRO, Prob 11/711; and 'Will of Michael Garnault', 4 December 1749, BNA/PRO, Prob 11/775. For the bill of exchange, see above, pp. 92–3.
119. This information is derived from the online database, http://www.familysearch.org/eng/default.asp, of which CD-ROMs are available for consultation at the British Library.
120. 'Will of Peter Garnault', 4 August 1770, BNA/PRO, Prob 11/959.
121. S. Lachenicht, 'Huguenot Immigrants and the Formation of National Identities, 1548–1787', *Historical Journal*, 50:2 (June 2007), pp. 309–31, on p. 310. J. Butler, *The Huguenots in America: A Refugee People in New World Society* (Cambridge, MA: Harvard University Press, 1983). For the Huguenot diaspora as an international Protestant movement, see also J. F. Bosher, 'Huguenot Merchants and the Protestant International in the Seventeenth Century', *William and Mary Quarterly*, 3rd series, 52:1 (January 1995), pp. 77–102.
122. G. C. Gibbs, 'Huguenot Contributions to England's Intellectual Life, and England's Intellectual Commerce with Europe, c.1680–1720', in I. Scouloudi (ed.), *Huguenots in Britain and their French Background, 1550–1800* (London: Huguenot Society of London, 1985), pp. 20–41, on p. 35. See also R. Eagles, *Francophilia in English Society, 1748–1815* (London: MacMillan Press Ltd, 2000).
123. R. A. Sundstrom, 'French Huguenots and the Civil List, 1696–1727: A Study of Alien Assimilation in England', *Albion: A Quarterly Journal Concerned with British Studies*, 8:3 (Autumn 1976), pp. 219–35.
124. See above, pp. 158–9
125. J. M. Hintermaier, 'The First Modern Refugees? Charity, Entitlement, and Persuasion in the Huguenot Immigration of the 1680s', *Albion: A Quarterly Journal Concerned with British Studies*, 32:3 (Autumn 2000), pp. 429–49.
126. Lachenicht, 'Huguenot Immigrants', p. 312.
127. Ibid., pp. 309–31.
128. 'Will of Aymé Garnault', 21 August 1741, BNA/PRO, Prob 11/711.
129. According to the Treaty, the English were guaranteed 'the same liberties, privileges, and exemptions as the Portuguese in metropolitan and colonial commerce', and it also 'provided for religious toleration and by a secret article prohibited the raising of customs duties on British goods above 23 per cent', as quoted in K. Maxwell, *Conflicts and*

Conspiracies: Brazil and Portugal 1750–1808 (Cambridge; Cambridge University Press, 1973), p. 7.

130. Shaw, *The Anglo-Portuguese Alliance*, p. 18.
131. H. E. S. Fisher, 'Anglo-Portuguese Trade, 1700–1770', *Economic History Review*, New Series, 16:2 (1963), pp. 219–33, on p. 220.
132. For an account of the English trade factory in Lisbon and its activities in the Mediterranean trade, see H. E. S. Fisher, 'Lisbon, its English Merchant Community and the Mediterranean in the Eighteenth Century', in P.L. Cottrell and D.H. Aldcroft (eds), *Shipping, Trade and Commerce: Essays in memory of Ralph Davis* (Leicester: Leicester University Press, 1981), pp. 23–44.
133. R. Lodge, 'The English Factory at Lisbon: Some Chapters in Its History', *Transactions of the Royal Historical* Society, 4th series, 16 (1933), pp. 211–47, on p. 225.
134. See for instance an event concerning the smuggling of bullion involving John Bristow, Salvador's partner in the first diamond monopoly, above, p. 54; D. Francis, *Portugal 1715–1808: Joanine, Pombaline and Rococo Portugal as seen by British Diplomats and Traders* (London: Tamesis Books Limited, 1985), p. 48.
135. A. R. Walford, *The British Factory in Lisbon and its Closing Stages Ensuing upon the Treaty of 1810* (Lisbon: Instituto Britânico em Portugal, 1940), pp. 33–6.
136. Ibid., p. 72.
137. See above, Chapter 3, p. 75.
138. 'Berthon & Garnault to James Dormer', Lisbon, 27 August 1754, FAA, IB1652. The word 'them' refers to Portuguese merchants and traders born in Brazil.
139. See above, pp. 56–7. See also 'Letter of Committee to Lord Tyrawly', Lisbon, 17 April 1752, BL/TP, add. 23634 (1752–7), f. 31.
140. 'Berthon & Garnault to James Dormer', Lisbon, 6 November 1753, FAA, IB1652.
141. 'Berthon & Garnault to James Dormer', Lisbon, 18 June 1754; 9 July 1754, FAA, IB1652.
142. 'Berthon & Garnault to James Dormer', Lisbon, 6 August 1754; 20 August 1754; 27 August 1754, FAA, IB1652.
143. 'Berthon & Garnault to James Dormer', Lisbon, 5 November 1754; 12 November 1754; 17 December 1754, FAA, IB1652. The letter from the 12th confirms that Berthon & Garnault went to the specially appointed judge for English merchants and they referred to him as 'our judge conservator'.
144. 'Berthon & Garnault to James Dormer', Lisbon, 18 March 1755, FAA, IB1652.
145. See above, p. 67.
146. The latter was very common. See Chapter 3, pp. 82–3.
147. 'Letter by Miss Margaret Collier to Samuel Richardson', 31 December 1755, in A. L. Barbauld (ed.), *The Correspondence of Samuel Richardson, Author of Pamela, Clarissa, and Sir Charles Grandison. Selected from the Original Manuscripts, Bequeathed by Him to His Family. To which are Prefixed, a Biographical Account of that Author, and Observations on his Writings*, 6 vols (London: Lewis & Roden, 1804), vol. 2, pp. 90–1.
148. Barbauld, *The Correspondence of Samuel Richardson*, pp. 83, 94.
149. 'Letters of Jane Berthon regarding the Lisbon earthquake' (1755), FLRU/RFP, ms. 279.
150. Henry Fielding, who never recovered and died in 1754, wrote letters to his half brother John from Lisbon. See H. Amory, 'Fielding's Lisbon Letters', *Huntington Library Quarterly*, 35:1 (November 1971), pp. 65–83.
151. Labourdette, *La nation française à Lisbonne de 1669 à 1790*, p. 27.

152. This was one of the prime arguments in the thesis on the firm of James Dormer by Erika Meel. Meel, 'De firma James Dormer tussen traditie en vernieuwing', pp. 533–8.
153. Berthon & Garnault described Portugal as 'ce miserable pays', a country that 'comparée avec celle de Normandie celle cy est en Enfance aupres; et chaque jour cella va de pire en pire Icy', 'Berthon & Garnault to James Dormer', Lisbon, 15 October 1754, FAA, IB1652. The Portuguese were described as 'this unnatural, ingratefull, and unworthy set of People', 'Berthon & Garnault to James Dormer', Lisbon, 16 November 1756, FAA, IB1652.
154. See above, p. 56.
155. Labourdette, *La nation française à Lisbonne de 1669 à 1790*, pp. 672–74.
156. E. Delobette, 'Les mutations du commerce maritime du Havre, 1680–1730 (1ère partie)', *Annales de Normandie*, 51:1 (2001), pp. 3–69, on p. 58.
157. 'Berthon & Garnault to James Dormer', Lisbon, 12 March 1748, FAA, IB1652.
158. For an elaborate study on the French trading nation in Lisbon, see Labourdette, *La nation française à Lisbonne de 1669 à 1790*, particularly the first two chapters: 'Définition et composition de la nation française', pp. 21–44 and 'Les privilèges et les institutions de la nation française', pp. 45–72.
159. Ibid., pp. 36–40, 529.
160. 'Will of Peter Garnault', 6 April 1770, BNA/PRO, Prob 11/959.
161. Labourdette, *La nation française à Lisbonne de 1669 à 1790*, pp. 532–3.
162. These were ambivalent forms of charity, not free of self-interest or prejudice against the Portuguese. 'Berthon & Garnault to James Dormer', Lisbon, 16 March 1756, FAA, IB1652: 'that a Consideration or rather a Charitty would be well placed w.th he poor Man has nothing left him, but the character of the honest man we've experienced in him, its true we always held him as such, mais quelquefois Loccazion fait Le Larron, and finding it but to often so with the generallity of theze People, we praize the Man now, thô in want, for doing us justice'.

6 Trade, Global History and Human Agency

1. Seeman, 'Jews in the Early Modern Atlantic', p. 40.
2. Hancock, *Citizens of the World*, pp. 14–15.
3. P. A. Coclanis, 'Drang Nach Osten: Bernard Bailyn, the World-Island, and the Idea of Atlantic History', *Journal of World History*, 13:1 (March 2002), pp. 169–82, on p. 170.
4. D. Eltis, 'Atlantic History in Global Perspective', *Itinerario*, 23:2 (1999), pp. 141–61, on p. 142.
5. Woolf, 'Joseph Salvador 1716–1786', p. 104.
6. 'Sebastiaó Joze de Carvalho e Mello', London, 21 November 1738, BL, add. 20798 (Cartas diplomaticas de Londres para Lisboa 1738–1739. Cartaz de oficio ao Secretario do Estado e scriptaes por Sebastiaó Joze de Carvalho e Mello desde a cidade de Londres no anno de 1738), f. 15r. He is referred to as 'grande Francisco Salvador, correspondente de Manoel Gomes de Carvalho e Silva nesta cidade [London]'.
7. 'Joseph Salvador to James Dormer', London, 11 November 1740, FAA, IB1743.
8. The request is undated but is included in a letter from the Duke of Newcastle to Lord Tyrawly, ambassador in Lisbon at the time. 'Duke of Newcastle to Lord Tyrawly', Whitehall, 13 December 1737, BL/TP, add. 23629 (1728–41), ff. 46–7.
9. 'Forty-six merchants to Lord Tyrawly', London, 2 October 1752, BL/TP, add. 23634 (1752–7), ff. 126–7.

10. 'Joseph Salvador to James Dormer', 15 December 1755, NEHA, Special Collections N° 159, 'James Dormer'.
11. See above, pp. 159–60.
12. 'Joseph Salvador to James Dormer', London, 11 June 1756, FAA, IB1743.
13. 'Joseph Salvador to James Dormer', London, 17 September 1756, FAA, IB1743.
14. See above, pp. 73–4.
15. Woolf, 'Joseph Salvador 1716–1786', p. 104.
16. 'Francis & Joseph Salvador to James Dormer', London, 20 November 1750, FAA, IB1742.
17. 'Francis & Joseph Salvador to James Dormer', London, 26 July 1751, FAA, IB1742.
18. 'Francis & Joseph Salvador to James Dormer', London, 24 February 1752, FAA, IB1742.
19. 'Francis & Joseph Salvador to James Dormer', London, 21 August 1752, FAA, IB1742.
20. 'Francis & Joseph Salvador to James Dormer', London, 9 February 1752, FAA, IB1742.
21. 'Francis & Joseph Salvador to James Dormer', London, 8 January 1753, FAA, IB1742.
22. 'Francis & Joseph Salvador to James Dormer', London, 23 December 1754, FAA, IB1742.
23. 'Francis & Joseph Salvador to James Dormer', London, 12 February 1753, FAA, IB1742. For the trip and the involvement of other Antwerp merchants, see Degryse, 'Antwerpse fortuinen', pp. 46–7.
24. 'Joseph Salvador to James Dormer', London, 22 November 1757, FAA, IB1743.
25. 'Joseph Salvador to James Dormer', London, 1 October 1756, FAA, IB1743. The regularity of correspondence was crucial, see above, Chapter 3, pp. 84–5.
26. 'Francis & Joseph Salvador to James Dormer', London, 1 April 1751, FAA, IB1742; and 'Joseph Salvador to James Dormer', London, 24 March 1747, FAA, IB1743.
27. 'Mannock & Ryan to James Dormer', Cadiz, 27 November 1753, FAA, IB1716.
28. 'Jacques Brame to James dormer', Gent, 21 March 1752, NEHA, Special Collections N° 159, 'James Dormer'.
29. 'Isaac Faesch Junior & Co. to James Dormer', Curaçåo, 8 March 1751, FAA, IB1680.
30. 'Francis & Joseph Salvador to James Dormer', London, 22 May 1752, FAA, IB1742.
31. 'Joseph Salvador to James Dormer', London, 28 August 1755; 12 September 1755; 10 October 1755; 20 June 1756; 20 June 1757; and 21 February 1758, FAA, IB1743 are a few examples.
32. L. Adriaenssen, 'De plaats van Oisterwijk in het Kempense lakenlandschap', *Textielhistorische Bijdragen*, 41 (2001), pp. 27–48, on p. 40.
33. The registers of the guild from 1734 to 1796 are preserved in the city archive of Turnhout.
34. Meel, 'De firma James Dormer tussen traditie en vernieuwing', pp. 300–4.
35. Of course, insurance had to be paid. This was sometimes done by Berthon & Garnault, in which case they charged Dormer for it on the sales account, or directly by James Dormer himself. 'Berthon & Garnault to James Dormer', Lisbon, 9 March 1751, FAA, IB16523
36. 'Berthon & Garnault to James Dormer', Lisbon, 15 May 1753, FAA, IB1652.
37. 'Berthon & Garnault to James Dormer', 27 August 1754, FAA, IB1652. A similar comment occurs some months later when the Huguenots wrote that 'Franco Joseph Lopes quy destinoit touts ces Coutils pour le Rio de Janeiro', 'Berthon & Garnault to James Dormer', 17 December 1754, FAA, IB1652.
38. One example can be found in 'Berthon & Garnault to James Dormer', Lisbon, 3 April 1753, FAA, IB1652.

39. D. C. Libby, 'Reconsidering Textile Production in Late Colonial Brazil: New Evidence from Minas Gerais', *Latin American Research Review*, 32:1 (1997), pp. 88–108.
40. 'Berthon & Garnault to James Dormer', Lisbon, 7 March 1752, FAA, IB1652.
41. 'Berthon & Garnault to James Dormer', Lisbon, 6 April 1751, FAA, IB1652.
42. 'Berthon & Garnault to James Dormer', Lisbon, 4 May 1756, FAA, IB1652.
43. See above, p. 84.
44. 'Berthon & Garnault to James Dormer', Lisbon, 16 March 1756, FAA, IB1652.
45. 'Berthon & Garnault to James Dormer', Lisbon, 23 March 1756, FAA, IB1652.
46. Meel, 'De firma James Dormer tussen traditie en vernieuwing', p. 701. The Portugal insurances were negotiated by Berthon and Garnault before 1756, and after that by the two separate firms of Paul Berthon and Peter Garnault, see also p. 80.
47. Meel, 'De firma James Dormer tussen traditie en vernieuwing', p. 703.
48. See above, Chapter 2, pp. 41, 47.
49. See above, p. 155 for a contract signed between the E.I.C. and Salvador, Gideon, Pratviel and Bristow regarding silver purchases.
50. 'Francis and Joseph Salvador to James Dormer', London, 22 December 1749, FAA, IB1742.
51. 'Francis & Joseph Salvador to James Dormer', London, 30 July 1750, FAA, IB1742.
52. 'Francis & Joseph Salvador to James Dormer', London, 17 September 1750, FAA, IB1742.
53. 'Francis & Joseph Salvador to James Dormer', London, 2 October 1750, FAA, IB1742.
54. Entry on 21 March 1749 in Court Minute Book 63 E.I.C. (April 1748–April 1750), BL/IOR, B/70ff. 631–3. For John Bristow, whose name appeared regularly in combination with that of Salvador. See above, pp. 54, 155, 172.
55. That this happened is shown in 'Francis & Joseph Salvador to James Dormer', London, 7 September 1751, FAA, IB1742.
56. 'Joseph Salvador to James Dormer', London, 4 May 1756, FAA, IB1743. For members of the de Paiba family and their relationship with the Salvadors, see pp. 127, 155–6.
57. Participation in the exchange trade by sending silver, coral and finished jewellery to India also assured a certain return, although it could not always be predicted beforehand what the trade was to yield.
58. 'Francis & Joseph Salvador to James Dormer', 21 August 1752, FAA, IB1742.
59. 'Diamond Book N°1' (1744–52), AdB/DG, no. 1084, f. 35.
60. One of the largest diamond mines of India was in Golconda. For Chardin, see above, p. 48.
61. Fischel, 'The Jewish Merchant-Colony in Madras'.
62. Samuel, 'Gems from the Orient', p. 354.
63. On the use of different last names by Salvador family members, see pp. 126–7.
64. 'Grootboek van een handelaar in edelstenen', 1675–1685, GAA/PIGA, PA334.858, *passim*. This information checks out with the family tree, see Figure 5.1 on p. 128.
65. Samuel, 'Gems from the Orient', p. 356.
66. Ibid., p. 361.
67. 'Mr Salvador His Account Current with Edward Fenwicke', 23 October1727, in Edward Fenwicke Letterbook, 1723–1728, SCHS, no. 34/577, p. 303.
68. Salvadore, Joseph Burial 12 June 1789, BL/IOR, Biographical Indexes, N/1/4, f. 89r.
69. Fischel, 'The Jewish Merchant-Colony in Madras', p. 195. One of Joseph Salvador's daughters was married to Moses Franco. See above, p. 127 and the Salvador family tree on p. 128.
70. He wrote a text about his voyage, and sent it to Amsterdam for publication. See J. Schorsch, 'Mosseh Pereyra de Paiva: An Amsterdam Portuguese Jewish Merchant Abroad in the Seventeenth Century', in Y. Kaplan (ed.), *The Dutch Intersection: The Jews and the Netherlands in Modern History* (Leiden; Boston: Brill, 2008), pp. 63–85.

71. S. Mentz, *The English Gentleman Merchant at Work: Madras and the City of London 1660–1740* (Copenhagen: Museum Tusculanum Press, 2005), p. 98.
72. A few examples can be found in the following letters: 'Edward Fenwicke to Francis Salvador', London, 28 July 1726, 5 Septemebr 1727, 29 September 1727, 5 October 1727, 23 October 1727; 'Edward Fenwicke to Nathaniel Turner', London, 29 December 1726, 20 December 1727, SCHS, no. 34/577, 'Edward Fenwicke Letterbook', 1723–1728, *passim*.
73. For a detailed account of Jewish involvement in the commerce in ostrich feathers, particularly in the nineteenth century, see S. A. Stein, *Plumes: Ostrich Feathers, Jews, and a Lost World of Global Commerce* (New Haven, CT: Yale University Press, 2008).
74. Court Minute Books 60–68 E.I.C. (1742–1760), BL/IOR, B/67–B/75. These dates have been chosen because they are relevant for the period in which Salvador was in business with Dormer and the cross-cultural network. In the Table 6.1, the row labelled as 'Total value (£)' refers to the sum of amounts of money found in the books with regard to shipping to India, while the last row adds a number of references with regard to silver, which have been noted in the Company's books in weight rather than in financial value.
75. See Chapter 3, *passim*, for the concrete commercial chains that had developed within the cross-cultural diamond trade network.
76. 'Francis & Joseph Salvador to James Dormer', London, 24 November 1747, FAA, IB1743.
77. S. Ville, 'The Growth of Specialization in English Shipowning, 1750–1850', *Economic History Review*, New Series, 46:4 (November, 1993), pp. 702–22, on p. 706.
78. For the Company's reliance on ship owners, see L. Sutherland, *A London Merchant, 1694-1774* (London: Frank Cass & Company, 1962), pp. 82–110.
79. Court Minute Books 60–68 E.I.C. (1742–1760), BL/IOR, B/67–B/75. Nine mentions of the Salvador firm are made with regard to charterparties.
80. This phrase was written in seven out of fifteen occasions, see for instance Court Minute Book 65 E.I.C. (April 1752–April 1754), BL/IOR, B/72, f. 165.
81. Ville, 'The Growth of Specialization in English Shipowning', p. 706.
82. Neal, *Rise of Financial Capitalism*, p. 139.
83. See above, Chapter 4, pp. 96–9 for Ashkenazi immigration and the link that was made between this diaspora, poverty and tolerance.
84. For an overview on Jewish presence in the Americas, see J. Schorsch, *Jews and Blacks in the Early Modern World* (Cambridge; New York: Cambridge University Press, 2004).
85. Endelman, *The Jews of Georgian England 1714–1830*, pp. 168–9. See also C. C. Jones, 'The Settlement of the Jews in Georgia', *American Historical Society, Publications*, 1 (1893), pp. 5–12.
86. Although it is not clear whether he bought land in the Americas because it was easier there, or whether he had become politically active with regard to the Jew Bill because he was interested purchasing in land lying in the British Empire. For Salvador's activities with regard to the Jew Bill, see above, pp. 137–9.
87. 'John Hamilton Esq to Joseph Salvador Esq Lease', 22 August 1766, SCDAH/PRCB, vol. 3F, pp. 133–5. The origin and further developments of the Salvador estate in South Carolina is given in 'Joseph Salvador Esqr By Richard Andrews Rapley his Attorney Abraham Prado Esqr Release in fee simple of 1062 Acres of Land above Ninety Six', 17 January 1774, SCDAH/PRCB, vols 4 E–F 1773–4, pp. 194–9.
88. The Public Register Conveyance Books in South Carolina contain records related to the Salvador estate continue until 1841.
89. For instance 'Michel Duvall to Francis Salvador Release', 5 October 1774, SCDAH/PRCB, vol. 4M, pp. 283–5. Michel Duvall was a planter.
90. See Hancock, *Citizens of the World*. Henry Laurens was one of the commissioners of the American delegation, including Benjamin Franklin and John Adams. Oswald was there on behalf of the British.

91. Letter quoted in G. C. Rogers Jr, D. R. Chesnutt and C. J. Taylor (eds), *The Papers of Henry Laurens*, 16 vols (Columbia, SC: University of South Carolina Press, 1974), vol. 4, pp. 331–9.
92. 'Joseph Salvador to Charles Jenkinson', White Hart Court, 1 November 1763, BL/LP, vol. 11, add. 38201, f. 216.
93. B. A. Elzas, *Joseph Salvador: Jewish Merchant Prince who came to South Carolina* (Charleston: S.n., 1902), pp. 14–17. This is also clear from different records preserved in the Public Conveyance Books in the South Carolina archives, see above,p. 226, nn. 87, 88.
94. Anon., 'Camp 2 miles below Keowee', 4 August 1776, SCDAH, S213089. This letter that tells the story of Francis Salvador's death and was written by an eye witness. The letter is anonymous, but according to another source it was sent by A. Williamson to John Rutledge, president of South Carolina at the time. Drayton, *Memoirs of the American Revolution*, p. 371. More on Salvador's involvement in the American Revolution can be found in L. A. M. Hühner, 'Francis Salvador, a Prominent Patriot of the Revolutionary War', *American Historical Society, Publications*, 9 (1901), pp. 107–22. For his patriotism, Francis Salvador received a commemorating plaque in Charleston, a paper copy of which is preserved. 'Copy of a Plaque Commemorating Francis Salvador 1447–1776 First Jew in South Carolina to hold public office and to die for American Independence', SCHS, Genealogy files 30–4 Salvadore.
95. 'Joseph Salvador to Charles Jenkinson', St James's, 25 November 1776, BL/LP, vol. 20, add. 38209, f. 59.
96. Elzas, *Joseph Salvador*, pp. 6–8.
97. 'Will of Joseph Salvador', 15 January 1788, BNA/PRO, Prob 11/1172.
98. Joseph Salvador to Charles Jenkinson, White Hart Court, 28 October 1768, BL/LP, vol. 17, add. 38206, f. 81. For Salvador's relationship with Jaenkinson, See also p. 172.
99. For Emanuel Mendes da Costa, a scientist and relative to Salvador, see pp. 167–70.
100. 'E. M. da Costa to Joseph Salvador', London, 6 March 1786, BL, add. 28542, ff. 98–9.
101. 'E. M. da Costa to Joseph Salvador', London, 6 March 1786, BL, add. 28542, ff. 98–99.
102. See Chapter 2, p. 59.
103. See Chapter 1, pp. 33–4.
104. Hancock, *Citizens of the World*, pp. 14–15.
105. See above, p. 97.
106. 'Francis Mannock to James Dormer', London, 14 April 1737, FAA, IB1717.
107. 'Francis Mannock to James Dormer', London, 23 August 1737, FAA, IB1717.
108. 'Francis & Jacob Salvador to James Dormer', London, 30 October 1747, FAA, IB1743.
109. 'Berthon & Garnault to James Dormer', Lisbon, 5 August 1755, FAA, IB1652.
110. 'Joseph Salvador to James Dormer', London, 20 June 1757, FAA, IB1743.
111. The first quote is from 'Francis Salvador to James Dormer', London, 28 January 1746, FAA, IB1741 and the second is from 'Francis Salvador to James Dormer', London, 31 January 1746, FAA, IB1741.
112. 'Joseph Salvador to James Dormer', London, 16 August 1757, FAA, IB1743.
113. C. A. Bayly, *The Birth of the Modern World* (Malden, MA; Oxford: Blackwell Publishing, 2004), pp. 9–12. Hodgson, *Rethinking World History*, p. 314.
114. Cooper, *Colonialism in Question*, pp. 153–203.
115. See also pp. 149–50.
116. See for instance Gunder Frank's account of Eurocentrism in methodology. Frank, *ReOrient*, pp. 321–59. See also D. Chakrabarty, *Provincializing Europe: Postcolonial Thought and Historical Difference* (Princeton, NJ: Princeton University Press, 2000).

117. See Chapter 1, pp. 14–15, p. 34 for other reflections in this debate.
118. F. Mauro, 'Merchant Communities, 1350–1750', in Tracy (ed.), *The Rise of Merchant Empires*, pp. 255–86.
119. W. Gungwu, 'Merchants without Empire: The Hokkien Sojourning Communities', in Tracy (ed.), *The Rise of Merchant Empires*, pp. 400–21, on pp. 401–4. An example that shows that similar experiences in different regions allow for a preservation of methodology can be found in K. Mukund, *The Trading World of the Tamil Merchant: Evolution of Merchant Capitalism* (Chennai: Orient Longman, 1999).
120. N. Sohrabi, 'Global Waves, Local Actors: What the Young Turks Knew about Other Revolutions and Why It Mattered', *Comparative Studies in Society and History: An International Quarterly*, 44:1 (January 2002), pp. 45–79.
121. Ibid., p. 72.
122. Jacob, *Strangers Nowhere in the World: The Rise of Cosmopolitanism in Early Modern Europe*, p. 1.
123. Ibid, p. 2.
124. Ibid, p. 69.
125. See Chapter 5 for an analysis of the dialogue that took place between international diaspora and local society.
126. The term was used by Toni Erskine in a twenty-first century context. T. Erskine, *Embedded Cosmopolitanism: Duties to Strangers and Enemies in a World of 'Dislocated Communities'* (Oxford; New York: Oxford University Press, 2008).
127. T. M. Doerflinger, *A Vigorous Spirit of Enterprise: Merchants and Economic Development in Revolutionary Philadelphia* (Williamsburg, NC: University of North Carolina Press, 1986), p. 4.
128. See Chapter 1, pp. 31–3 and Chapter 3, pp. 88–91.
129. Jacob, *Strangers Nowhere in the World*, p. 66.
130. K. A. Appiah, *Cosmopolitanism: Ethics in a world of strangers* (New York: W.W. Norton & Company, 2006), p. xv.
131. See above, pp. 28–33 for a theoretical discourse on trust through reputation and creditworthiness and pp. 181–94 for a case study using business correspondence.
132. J. Hoock, 'Professional Ethics and Commercial Rationality at the Beginning of the Modern Era', in Jacob and Secretan (eds), *The Self-Perception of Early Modern Capitalists* (New York: Palgrave Macmillan, 2008), pp. 149–56.
133. Jacob, *Strangers Nowhere in the World*, p. 2.
134. 'Francis & Joseph Salvador', 10 April 1752, FAA, IB1742.
135. 'Joseph Salvador', RS, EC/1758/14.
136. Katz, *The Jews in the History of England 1485–1850*, p. 270.
137. This has been particularly discussed for the Enlightenment period. T. H. Broman, 'The Habermasian Public Sphere and Eighteenth-Century Historiography: A New Look at "Science in the Enlightenment"', History of Science, 36 (1998), pp. 123-49. See also M. R. Lynn, 'Enlightenment in the Public Sphere: The Musée de Monsieur and Scientific Culture in Late Eighteenth-Century Paris', *Eighteenth-Century Studies*, 32:4 (1999), pp. 463-76; D. Roche, Le *Siècle des Lumières en province: Académies et académiciens provinciaux, 1680-1789*, 2 vols (Paris: Mouton, 1978).
138. The idea of status as a motive should not be discarded, but it is a motive that goes much further than the quest for acceptance by a diaspora merchant. It is much more general, and status is sought by many people.
139. For an account of da Costa's scientific performance, see S. J. Gould, 'The Anatomy Lesson: The Teachings of Naturalist Mendes da Costa, a Sephardi Jew in King George's Court', *Natural History* (December 1995), pp. 12–15, 62–63. For a more psychological account

on the rise and fall of da Costa in the Royal Society, see G. S. Rousseau and D. Haycock, 'The Jew of Crane Court: Emanuel Mendes da Costa (1717–1791), Natural History and Natural Excess', *History of Science*, 37 (2000), pp. 127–70. A biographical account of da Costa's misfortunes combined with an institutional and socio-historical perspective can be found in G. Cantor, 'The Rise and Fall of Emanuel Mendes da Costa: A Severe Case of "The Philosophical Dropsy?"', *English Historical Review*, 116:467 (June 2001), pp. 584–603. For Linnaeus and his acquintance with George Clifford, see above, p. 170.

140. Rousseau and Haycock, 'The Jew of Crane Court', pp. 144, 149–51.
141. See J. Innes, 'The King's Bench Prison in the Later Eighteenth Century', in J. Brewer and J. Styles (eds), *An Ungovernable People: The English and their Law in the Seventeenth and Eighteenth Centuries* (London: Hutchinson, 1980), pp. 251–61.
142. Cantor, 'The Rise and Fall of Emanuel Mendes da Costa', p. 593.
143. For the 1717 warrant, see above, pp. 136–7.
144. Rousseau and Haycock, 'The Jew of Crane Court', pp. 150–1. In the light of the classical paradigm between diaspora and host society, in which two communities exist, the notion of diaspora members interacting socially outside their community but in a public sphere, is an interesting one.
145. 'Joseph Salvador', RS, EC/1758/14.
146. 'E. M. de Costa to Joseph Salvador', London, 26 June 1759, BL, add. 28542, f. 86.
147. 'E. M. de Costa to Joseph Salvador', London, 26 June 1759, BL, add. 28542, f. 86.
148. 'Naphtali Franks', RS, EC/1764/10.
149. Yogev, *Diamonds and Coral*, pp. 65, 153.
150. 'David Riz', RS, EC/1766/10.
151. 'Marie Joseph Louis d'Albert d'Ailly Picquigny', RS, EC/1763/26.
152. 'John Baptist Elie de Beaumont', RS, EC/1765/03.
153. 'William Cracraft', RS, EC/1760/18.
154. For a full account of Lyon's life and scientific merit, see L. B. Glyn, 'Israel Lyons: A Short but Starry Career. The Life of an Eighteenth-Century Jewish Botanist and Astronomer', *Notes and Records of the Royal Society of London*, 56:3 (September 2002), pp. 275–305.
155. Ibid., p. 280.
156. Ibid., p. 282.
157. See above, pp. 96–9 for a critique of the comparative approach.
158. 'Joseph Salvador to E. M. da Costa', Connehal, 22 January 1785, BL, add. 28542, ff. 90–2.
159. 'E. M. da Costa to Joseph Salvador', London, 30 November 1786, BL, add. 28542, ff. 93–4.
160. 'E. M. da Costa to Joseph Salvador', Paris, 17 June 1763, BL, add. 28542, f. 87.
161. J. Bevis, 'Observation of the Eclipse of the Sun, April 1, 1764: In a Letter from Dr. John Bevis, to Joseph Salvador, Esq; F. R. S.', *Philosophical Transactions (1683–1775)*, 54 (1764), pp. 105–8.
162. Three small notes directed to the three clerks are included in Joseph Salvador to E. M. da Costa, Connehal, 22 January 1785, BL, add. 28542, ff. 90–2. On one occasion Salvador refers to the Society of Arts and Manufactures instead of the Society of Arts and Sciences.
163. W. Blunt, *The Complete Naturalist: A Life of Linnaeus* (Princeton, NJ: Princeton University Press, 2001), pp. 99–109, 115–18, 123–7. An online database of Clifford herbarium can be found athttp://www.nhm.ac.uk/research-curation/research/projects/clifford-herbarium/ [accessed 18 March 2011].
164. *London Journal*, CIV (Saturday 22 July1721), accessed through BL/BCD.
165. See Chapter 2, pp. 50–1.
166. 'who amongst those of his Nation was one of the foremost figures in capital, credit and intelligence', 'História Chronológica', f. 49r.

167. 'Sebastiaó Joze de Carvalho e Mello', London, 21 November 1738, BL, add. 20799 ('Cartas diplomaticas de Londres para Lisboa', 1743–1745; 'Extracto das Rellacoes expedidas para a Corte de Lisboa por S.J. de Carvalho e Mello no ministerio de Londres'), f. 126v. 'Sebastiaó Joze de Carvalho e Mello', London, 2 December 1738, BL, add. 20799, ff. 126v–127r. 'Sebastiaó Joze de Carvalho e Mello', London, 15 December 1738, BL, add. 20799, f. 127v.
168. 'Com Francisco Salvador continuey as conversaçoes depois de o conhecer intereçado na Companhia', in 'Sebastiaó Joze de Carvalho e Mello', London, 20 January 1739, BL, add. 20798 ('Cartas diplomaticas de Londres para Lisboa' 1738–1739. 'Cartaz de oficio ao Secretario do Estado e scriptaes por Sebastiaó Joze de Carvalho e Mello desde a cidade de Londres no anno de 1738'), ff. 85–7.
169. 'Discursos sobre o commercio da Azia, emquanto pode servir de meyo para a Coroa de Portugal conservar as illustres porçoes do Estado da India, que ainda lhe restam', 'Sebastiaó Joze de Carvalho e Mello', Vienna, 25 July 1748, BL, add. 20804.
170. 'Cardinal da Motta to Sebastião José de Carvalho e Melo', Lisbon, 19 February 1740, BL, add. 20801 ('Cartas para Londres', 1738–42), ff. 5–7.
171. 'Cardinal da Motta to Sebastião José de Carvalho e Melo', Lisbon, 9 April 1740, BL, add. 20801 ('Cartas para Londres', 1738–42), ff. 12–13.
172. 'Antonio Guedes Pereira and Marco Antonio de Azevedo Coutinho to Sebastião José de Carvalho e Melo', Lisbon, 20 February 1742, BL, add. 20800 ('Cartas diplomaticas de Lisboa para Londres', 1738–1745), ff. 342–3.
173. 'Francisco Caetano to Sebastião Joseph de Carvalho e Melo', London, 30 December 1745; 8 July 1746, BL, add. 20797 ('Cartas de Londres', 1745–7), ff. 83–5 and ff. 162-3.
174. 'Francisco Salvador to Sebastião Joseph de Carvalho e Melo', London, 16 February 1747, BL, add. 20797 ('Cartas de Londres', 1745–7), ff. 257–8.
175. L. Sutherland, 'The City of London and Politics', in Sutherland, *Politics and Finance in the Eighteenth Century*, pp. 37–66, on p. 41. See also Dickson, *The Financial Revolution in England* and Brewer, J., *The Sinews of Power: War, Money and the English State, 1688–1783* (London, Unwin Hyman Ltd, 1989).
176. Bowen, *The Business of Empire*, pp. 27–8.
177. 'Joseph Salvador to the Duke of Newcastle', Lime Street, 13 December 1758, BL/NP, vol. 21, add. 32886, f. 299.
178. 'Joseph Salvador to Charles Jenkinson', St James's, 4 January 1778, BL/LP, vol. 20, add. 38209, f. 216.
179. B. Lenman and P. Lawson, 'Robert Clive, the "Black Jagir", and British Politics', *Historical Journal*, 26:4 (December 1983), pp. 801–29, on pp. 811–2.
180. Ibid., p. 812.
181. Ibid., pp. 816–17.
182. 'Dear Sir, I recievd your favour while in close conference with Mr Amyand, Lord Clive, Mr Rous & Mr Boulton', 'Joseph Salvador to Charles Jenkinson', White Hart Court, 16 March 1764, BL/LP, vol. 13, add. 38202, f. 168.
183. For instance the following quote: '[I] still hope for Mr Grenville's protection', 'Joseph Salvador to Charles Jenkinson', White Hart Court, 16 February 1764, BL/LP, vol. 13, add. 38202, f. 147.
184. Lenman and Lawson, 'Robert Clive, the "Black Jagir", and British Politics', pp. 815–17.
185. 'Joseph Salvador to Charles Jenkinson', Bath, 22 April 1764, BL/LP, vol. 13, add. 38202, f. 248.
186. Lenman and Lawson, 'Robert Clive, the "Black Jagir", and British Politics', p. 819.
187. Ibid., p. 801.
188. Sahlins, *Apologies to Thucydides*, p. 156.
189. Ibid., p. 155.

Conclusion

1. I. Le Long, *De Koophandel van Amsterdam*, 2 vols (Rotterdam: Ph. Losel, 1753), vol. 1, p. 157.
2. 'Jane Berthon to her son', Lisbon, [1755], 'Letters of Jane Berthon regarding the Lisbon earthquake' (1755), FLRU/RFP, ms. 279.
3. Sahlins, *Apologies to Thucydides*, p. 11.
4. Chakrabarty, *Provincializing Europe*, pp. 3–23.

WORKS CITED

Manuscript Sources

Archief De Bergeyck, Deelarchief Goubau, Beveren-Waas, Belgium.

Handelsarchief James Dormer.

'Diamond Book N°1' (1744–52), no. 1084.

'Diamond Book N°2' (1747–50), no. 1085.

'Diamond Book N°3' (1751–3), no. 1086.

'Diamond Book N°4' (1752–62), no. 1087.

'Requête du Sr. James Dormer Contre Les Lapidaires de la ville d'Anvers' (1753), no. 1089.

Perochon, Firth and Gerard to George Clifford and Sons, Lisbon, 1 July 1755, No. 1111 (Bankactiviteiten, Wissels & Secundas).

Archives of the Royal Society, London, UK.

Documents of Admission.

'Joseph Salvador', EC/1758/14.

'Naphtali Franks', EC/1764/10.

'David Riz', EC/1766/10.

'Marie Joseph Louis d'Albert d'Ailly Picquigny', EC/1763/26.

'John Baptist Elie de Beaumont', EC/1765/03.

'William Cracraft', EC/1760/18.

Arquivo Histórico Ultramarino, Lisbon, Portugal.

Conselho Ultramarino Brasil/Minas Gerais.

'Carta do Conde de Sabugosa', 16 January 1733, AHU/CUMG, cx. 23, doc. 4.

'Condicoes para o estabelecimento do commercio dos diamantes', 1734, cx. 28, doc. 71.

'Condicoes para o estabelecimento do commercio dos diamantes', 1734, cx. 28, doc. 73.

'Condicoes para o estabelecimento do commercio dos diamantes', 1734, cx. 28, doc. 74.

Manuscritos Avulsos de Minas Gerais.

'Escritura de sociedade feita entre João Fernandes de Oliveira e Francisco Ferreira Silva, caixas e administradores da companhia de diamantes', 20 June 1739, cx. 41, doc. 55.

'Requerimento de Manuel Nunes da Silva Tojal e José Ferreira de Veiga', 5 May *c.*1751, cx. 58, doc. 3.

'Carta do ouvidor a informar o rei dos excessos cometidos pelo contratador dos diamantes Felisberto Caldeira Brant e das diligencias feitas sobre o assunto', 1752, cx. 58, doc. 110.

'Processo relativo a arremataçao dos contratos dos Diamantes e suas contas', 1751, AHU/MAMG, cx. 58, doc. 111, f. 1v.

'Carta de Sancho de Andrade Castro e Lanções expondo ao Rei os fundamentos da queixa de que formulava contra o contratador Felisberto Caldeira Brant', 5 August 1752, cx. 60, doc. 29.

'Oficio do governador de Minas José Antonio Freire de Andrada para o secretario da marinha e ultramar Diogo de Mendonça Corte Real', 6 September 1752, cx. 60, doc. 56.

Arquivo Nacional da Torre do Tombo, Lisbon, Portugal.

'Decreto Real de 11/08/1753, Col. Leis, Maço 4, N°144'.

'Decreto do estabelecimento da Administração dos Diamantes', 12 July 1771, Livro de Registo Geral da Direcção do Negocio dos Diamantes em Lisboa, f. 1r.

'Recibos dos lapidarias da fabrica de lapidar diamantes do Campo Pequeno, 1806–1807, Núcleos extraídos do conselho da fazenda, junta da direcção geral dos diamantes', livro IV.

Arquivo Público Mineiro, Belo Horizonte, Brazil.

Seção Colonial.

'Condizóes para a extracáo dos Diamantes aprovada pello Senhor General Gomes Freire de Andrada', 20 June 1739, códex 1, Registros de alvarás, cartas patentes, provisões, confirmações de cartas patentes, sesmarias e doações (1609–1799), ff. 173r–7r.

'Matricula dos escravos adventicios e recuperados lojas vendas e officios que pagáo pro racta', códex 51, Registo de escravos, vendas e licenças em Tejuco (1735–84).

Biblioteca Nacional, Lisbon, Portugal.

Códices e Fundo Geral dos Manuscritos.

'História Chronológica dos Contratos da Minerassão dos Diamantes dos Outros Contractos de Extracsão delles dos Cofres de Lisboa para os Paizes Estrangeiros dos Abuzos em que todos laborarão, e das Providencias com que se lhe tem occorrido ate o anno de 1788)', códice 746.

'Ordem Régia ao Ouvidor do Serro do Frio sobre abertura de Devassa contra descaminhos praticados pelo contratador de Diamantes', Felisberto Caldeira Brant, 22 February 1753, mss. 71, no. 8.

Colecção Pombalina.

'Regimento para os administradores do contrato dos diamantes', 1771, cód. 691, ff. 1–11.

'Decreto de 17 de dezembro 1771 autorizando suprimento por empréstimo aos diretores e Caixas da Administração do contrato de diamantes', cód. 691, f. 15.

'Letras sobre o contrato dos Diamantes que há para pagar, e dias dos seus vencimentos', cód. 691, f. 18.

'Deducçaó Compendiosa dos Contractos de Mineraçaó dos diamantes; dos outros contractos da Extracçaó delles; dos cofres de Lisboa para os Payzes Estrangeiros; dos perigos em que todos laboravam e das Providencias, comque a elles occorreo o senhor Rey Dom Jozeph para os conservar', S.d., cód. 695, ff. 306–80.

'Bando do Governador da Capitania, D. Lourenço de Almeida, designando o Dr. Antônio Ferreira do Valle e Mello Ouvidor do Serro do Frio, encarregado do governo de todas a forma minerar diamantes naquela comarca', 24 June 1730, cód. 4530, ff. 280–1.

British Library, London, UK.

'[Signet Warrant of letters of denization to, 1717]', Egerton Ch. 7458.

Add. 20797: 'Cartas de Londres, 1745–1747'.

'Francisco Caetano to Sebastião José de Carvalho e Melo', London, 30 December 1745, ff. 83–5.

'Francisco Caetano to Sebastião José de Carvalho e Melo', London, 8 July 1746, ff. 162–3.

'Francisco Salvador to Sebastião José de Carvalho e Melo', London, 16 February 1747, ff. 257–8.

Add. 20798: 'Cartas diplomaticas de Londres para Lisboa 1738–1739. Cartaz de oficio ao Secretario do Estado e scriptaes por Sebastiaó Joze de Carvalho e Mello desde a cidade de Londres no anno de 1738'.

'Sebastião José de Carvalho e Melo to Antonio Guedes Pereira and Marco Antonio de Azevedo Coutinho', London, 21 November 1738, f. 15r.

'Sebastião José de Carvalho e Melo to Antonio Guedes Pereira and Marco Antonio de Azevedo Coutinho', London, 20 January 1739, ff. 85–7.

Add. 20799: 'Cartas diplomaticas de Londres para Lisboa, 1743–1745. Extracto das Rellacoes expedidas para a Corte de Lisboa por S.J. de Carvalho e Mello no ministerio de Londres.'

'Sebastião José de Carvalho e Melo to Marco Antonio de Azevedo Coutinho', London, 21 November 1738, f. 126v.

'Sebastião José de Carvalho e Melo to Marco Antonio de Azevedo Coutinho', London, 2 December 1738, ff. 126v–127r.

'Sebastião José de Carvalho e Melo to Marco Antonio de Azevedo Coutinho', London, 15 December 1738, f. 127v.

Add. 20800: 'Cartas diplomaticas de Lisboa para Londres, 1738–1745'.

'Antonio Guedes Pereira and Marco Antonio de Azevedo Coutinho to Sebastião José de Carvalho e Melo', Lisbon, 20 February 1742, ff. 342–3.

Add. 20801: 'Cartas para Londres 1738–1742'.

'Cardinal da Motta to Sebastião José de Carvalho e Melo', Lisbon, 19 February 1740, ff. 5–7.

'Cardinal da Motta to Sebastião José de Carvalho e Melo', Lisbon, 9 April 1740, ff. 12–13.

Add. 20804.

'Discursos sobre o commercio da Azia, emquanto pode servir de meyo para a Coroa de Portugal conservar as illustres porçoes do Estado da India, que ainda lhe restam, Sebastião José de Carvalho e Melo', Vienna, 25 July 1748.

Add. 28542: Correspondence E.M. da Costa.

'E. Mendes da Costa to Joseph Salvador', London, 26 June 1759, f. 86.

'E. Mendes da Costa to Joseph Salvador', Paris, 17 June 1763, f. 87.

'Joseph Salvador to E. M. da Costa, Connehal', 22 January 1785, ff. 90–2.

'E. Mendes da Costa to Joseph Salvador', London, 30 November 1786, ff. 93–4.

'E. Mendes da Costa to Joseph Salvador', London, 6 March 1786, ff. 98–9.

Egerton Papers.

'Joseph Salvador to C. Macklin', London, 6 February 1761, Eg. 2334, f. 3.

Hardwicke Papers.

'[Warrant for naturalization]', 11/11/1730, vol. 781, add. 36129, f. 126.

India Office Records

Court Minute Books 60–68 E.I.C. (1742–1760), B/67–B/75.

Salvadore, Joseph Burial 12/06/1789, Biographical Indexes, N/1/4, f. 89r.

Agreement between Sir Robert Nightingale acting for George Drake, and Anthony da Costa acting for Joseph James Osorio, connected with their partnership at Fort St George in the diamond trade, December 1721, L/AG/50/5/5.

Liverpool Papers.

'Joseph Salvador to Charles Jenkinson', White Hart Court, 1 November 1763, vol. 11, add. 38201, f. 216.

'Joseph Salvador to Charles Jenkinson', White Hart Court, 16 February 1764, vol. 13, add. 38202, f. 147.

'Joseph Salvador to Charles Jenkinson', White Hart Court, 16 March 1764, vol. 13, add. 38202, f. 168.

'Joseph Salvador to Charles Jenkinson', Bath, 22 April 1764, vol. 13, add. 38202, f. 248.

'Joseph Salvador to Charles Jenkinson', White Hart Court, 28 October 1768, vol. 17, add. 38206, f. 81.

'Joseph Salvador to Charles Jenkinson', St James's, 25 November 1776, vol. 20, add. 38209, f. 59.

'Joseph Salvador to Charles Jenkinson', St James's, 4 January 1778, vol. 20, add. 38209, f. 216.

Newcastle Papers.

'Joseph Salvador to the Duke of Newcastle', Lime Street, 13 December 1758, vol. 201, add. 32886, f. 299.

'[Petition for naturalisation ante 1754]', vol. 372, add. 33057, f. 310.

Tyrawly Papers.

'Duke of Newcastle to Lord Tyrawly', Whitehall, 13 December 1737, add. 23629 (1728–41), ff. 46–7.

'Letter of Committee to Lord Tyrawly', Lisbon, 17 April 1752, add. 23634 (1752–7), f. 31.

'A narrative of the reasons, which constrained the underwritten Bristow's, Warde & Company to the Committee of the Factory (no minister or consul from His Majesty being then resident here) for their assistance and support in so critical a situation', Lisbon, 22/06/1752, Add. 23634 (Correspondence of Lord Tyrawly when ambassador in Portugal, 1752–7), ff. 86–7.

'Forty-six merchants to Lord Tyrawly', London, 2 October 1752, add. 23634 (1752–7), ff. 126–7.

Burney Collection Electronical Database.

Gazetteer and London Daily Advertiser, Friday 13 December 1765.

London Journal, Saturday July 22, 1721, Issue CIV.

Middlesex Journal or Chronicle of Liberty (London), 276 (Saturday 5 January 1771).

Saturday's Post (London), 2 (6 October 1716).

British National Archives, Kew, UK.

Public Records Office.

'Will of Manuel Levy Duarte', 1 July 1718, Prob 11/564.

'Will of Ribca da Silva', 22 February 1720, Prob 11/573.

'Will of John Sauret', 28 October 1727, Prob 11/618.

'Will of Peter Garnault', 1 July 1738, Prob 11/690.

'Will of Moses Mendes da Costa', 4 March 1739, Prob 11/701.

'Will of Aymé Garnault', 21 August 1741, Prob 11/711.

'Will of Joshua Salvador', 23 October 1741, Prob 11/713.

'Will of Paul Berthon', 16 April 1743, Prob 11/725.

'Will of Isaac Salvador', 22 October 1747, Prob 11/757.

'Will of Jacob Salvador', 2 May 1749, Prob 11/770.

'Will of Michael Garnault', 4 December 1749, Prob 11/775.

'Will of Martha Berthon formerly Martineau', 21 May 1753, Prob 11/801.

'Will of Francis Salvador', 4 November 1754, Prob 11/812.

'Will of Baerent Salomons', 1 October 1755, Prob 11/818.

'Will of Michael Berthon', 20 December 1756, Prob 11/826.

'Will of John Sauret', 3 November 1757, Prob 11/834.

'Will of Rachel Salvador', 1 July 1758, Prob 11/839.

'Will of Moses Lopes Pereira Baron Diego de Aguilar', 20 August 1759, Prob 11/848.

'Will of Ruben Salomons', 18 February 1761, Prob 11/863.

'Will of John otherwise Abraham Mendes da Costa', 7 March 1763, Prob 11/885.

'Will of Joseph Salomons', 7 April 1763, Prob 11/886.

'Will of Salomon Reuben Norden', 2 June 1764, Prob 11/899.

'Will of Levy Salomons', 1 March 1765, Prob 11/907.

'Will of Rachel Fernandes Nunes', 8 October 1766, Prob 11/922.

'Will of Jacob Berthon', 20 May 1767, Prob 11/928.

'Will of Michael Salomons', 27 April 1772, Prob 11/953.

'Will of Peter Garnault', 6 April 1770, Prob 11/959.

'Will of Assur Salomon Norden', 31 August 1771, Prob 11/970.

'Will of Solomon Norden', 7 September 1775, Prob 11/1011.

'Will of Fratje Salomons', 22 December 1775, Prob 11/1014.

'Will of Belah Salomons', 24 July 1776, Prob 11/1022.

'Will of Aaron Norden', S.d., Prob 11/1135.

'Will of Alexander Isaac Keyser', 29 October 1779, Prob 11/1057.

'Will of Joseph Salvador', 15 January, Prob 11/1172.

'Will of Daniel Berthon', 12 May 1795, Prob 11/1235.

'Will of Jane Berthon', 10 December 1793, Prob 11/1239.
'Will of Sarah Salvador', 19 November 1812, Prob 11/1539.
State Papers.
'Lord Tyrawly to the Duke of Newcastle', Lisbon, 2 May 1732, 89/37, ff. 166–8.
Felixarchief Antwerpen, Belgium.
Insolvente Boedelskamer.
Affaytadi.
'Index (1548)', IB1581.
James Dormer.
'Correspondence from Paul Berthon' (Lisbon, 1757–68), IB1651.
'Correspondence from Paul Berthon & Son' (Lisbon, 1761–4), IB1651.
'Correspondence from Paul Berthon & Co.' (London, 1766), IB1651.
'Correspondence from Berthon & Garnault' (Lisbon, 1747–56), IB1652.
'Correspondence from George Clifford & Sons' (Amsterdam, 1746–73), IB1662–1665.
'Correspondence from Isaac Faesch Jr' (Curaçāo, 1751), IB1680.
'Correspondence from Pierre Garnault & Fils' (Lisbonne, 1756–61), IB1690.
'Correspondence from Thomas & Adrian Hope' (Amsterdam, 1747–66), IB1700–1701.
'Correspondence from Jacob Levy' (Antwerp, 1745–8), IB1707.
'Correspondence from Ruben Levy & Co.' (Amsterdam, 1743–52), IB1707–1708.
Correspondence from Francis Mannock (London, Cadiz a.o., 1728–60), IB1710–1714.
'Correspondence from Mannock & Ryan' (Cadiz, 1748–59), IB1716.
'Correspondence from Bernardus van Merlen' (Amsterdam, 1746), IB1717.
'Correspondence from Isabella de Coninck' (Amsterdam, Antwerp, 1750–66), IB1717
'Correspondence from Abraham van Moses Lopes Suasso Frères & Co.' (Amsterdam, 1749–59), IB1719.
'Correspondence from Alexander Norden' (Amsterdam, 1743–7), IB1721.
'Correspondence from Salomon Norden & Co.' (Amsterdam, 1743–58), IB1721.
'Correspondence from Aaron & David Fernandes Nunes' (Amsterdam, 1741–1764), IB1723.
'Correspondence from Joan Osy & Son' (Rotterdam, 1742–67), IB1725–1727.
'Correspondence from Andries Pels & Sons' (Amsterdam, 1736–68), IB1729.
'Correspondence from Francis Salvador' (London, Lille, 1737–49), IB1741.
'Correspondence from Francis & Joseph Salvador' (London, 1749–55), IB1742.
'Correspondence from Jacob Salvador' (London, 1743–8), IB1743.
'Correspondence from Joseph Salvador' (London; Amsterdam; Den Haag; Antwerp; Paris, 1737–57), IB1743.
'Correspondence from Joseph Salvador' (London a.o., 1758–73), IB1744.
'Correspondence from Ezechiel Salomons to James Dormer' (Rotterdam, 1744–52), IB1745.
'Correspondence from Henry Salomons Jr to James Dormer' (Amsterdam, 1758), IB1745.

'Correspondence from Joseph Salomons to James Dormer' (London, 1752–9), IB1745.

'Correspondence from Michael Salomons to James Dormer' (London, 1756–8), IB1745.

'Correspondence from Phineas Serra' (London, 1754–64), IB1747.

'Correspondence from various correspondents', IB1716 and IB1762.

'Akten en Briefwisseling over de Opstart en Liquidatie van de Keizerlijke Assurantiekamer, Compte de Vente', Anvers, 10 March 1756, IB1156.

Wallis-du Jon.

'Ledger Paolo du Jon' (1622–32), IB1737.

Fondren Library Rice University, Houston, Texas, US.

'Letters of Jane Berthon regarding the Lisbon earthquake' (1755), Richardson Family Papers, 1714–1802, ms. 279.

Gemeentearchief Amsterdam,, Amsterdam, the Netherlands.

Archief Clifford Family, no. 236 (1738–1934).

Archief Hope & Co.

'Vander Schroets & Co. to Thomas & Adrian Hope', Constantinople, 2 January 1768, no. 735.111.

'Balance Book Hope & Co.' (1762–1790), no. 735.592.

'Information Booklet' (1778–87), no. 735.1404.

Archief van de Portugees-Israëlitische Gemeente te Amsterdam, the Netherlands.

Grootboek van een handelaar in edelstenen (1675–85), PA334.858.

Guildhall Library, London, UK.

'This back view of Salvadore House Academy', Tooting, Surry Drawn and Engraved by J. Walker, Aquat. by F. Jukes, published April 1787 by R. Wilkinson, P459236.

Huguenot Library, University College London, UK.

Wagner Pedigrees.

'Berthon Family'.

'Garnault Family'.

London Metropolitan Archives, London, UK.

Board of Deputies of British Jews, ACC/3121/B, Presidents and Secretaries of the Board of Deputies of British Jews.

Nationaal Archief, Den Haag, the Netherlands.

Archief Verenigde Oost-Indische Compagnie, 1602–1795 (1811).

'Radicaale Beschrijving van't Eyland Borneo en de Postvatting te Banjermasjing' (1757), Nationaal Archief Den Haag, no. 4885, unnumbered.

Nederlands Economisch-Historisch Archief, Amsterdam, the Netherlands.

Special Collections N°159 'James Dormer'.

'Jacques Brame to James Dormer', Gent, 21 March 1752.

'Joseph Salvador to James Dormer', London, 06 January 1755.

'Joseph Salvador to James Dormer', London, 15 December 1755.

'Joseph Salvador to James Dormer', London, 18 September 1741.

'Phineas Serra to James Dormer, Par Procuration de Monsieur Joseph Salvador', London, 6 January1755.

Special Collections N°188 Firm Joan Osy & Son.

'Letter Copy Book', 1749–1804.

South Carolina Department of Archives & History, Columbia, South Carolina, US.

Anon., 'Camp 2 miles below Keowee', 4 August 1776, S213089.

Public Register Conveyance Books (Charleston Deeds).

'John Hamilton Esq to Joseph Salvador Esq Lease', 22 August 1766, vol. 3F, pp. 133–5.

'Joseph Salvador Esqr By Richard Andrews Rapley his Attorney Abraham Prado Esqr Release in fee simple of 1062 Acres of Land above Ninety Six', 17 January 1774, vols 4 E–F 1773–4, pp. 194–9.

'Michel Duvall to Francis Salvador Release', 05 October 1774, vol. 4M, pp. 283–5.

South Carolina Historical Society, Charleston, South Carolina, US.

'Edward Fenwicke Letterbook', 1723–1728, no. 34/577.

'Copy of a Plaque Commemorating Francis Salvador 1447–1776 First Jew in South Carolina to hold public office and to die for American Independence', Genealogy files 30–4 Salvadore.

Published Sources

Acemoglu, D., S. Johnson and J. A. Robinson, 'The Rise of Europe: Atlantic Trade, Institutional Change, and Economic Growth', *American Economic Review*, 95:3 (June 2005), pp. 546–79.

Adams, J., *The Familial State: Ruling Families and Merchant Capitalism in Early Modern Europe*, Wilder House Series in Politics, History, and Culture (Ithaca, NY: Cornell University Press, 2005).

Adriaenssen, L., 'De plaats van Oisterwijk in het Kempense lakenlandschap', *Textielhistorische Bijdragen*, 41 (2001), pp. 27–48.

Affonso, D. de A., and R. D. T. Valdez, *Livro de oiro da nobreza: apostilas à resenha das famílias titulares do reino de Portugal*, 3 vols (Braga: S.n., 1934), vol. 3.

AKEVOTH (formerly known as the genealogical department of the Center for Research on Dutch Jewry at the Hebrew University of Jerusalem), online at http://shum.huji.ac.il/~dutchjew/genealog/ashkenazi/index.html [accessed 18 March 2011].

Akita, S. (ed.), *Gentlemanly Capitalism, Imperialism, and Global History* (Basingstoke: Macmillan, 2002).

Alexandre, V., *Os sentidos do império* (Porto: Afrondamento, 1993).

Amory, H., 'Fielding's Lisbon Letters', *Huntington Library Quarterly*, 35:1 (November 1971), pp. 65–83.

Amselle, J.-L., 'L'étranger dans le monde manding et en Grèce ancienne: quelques points de comparaison', *Cahiers d'Études Africaines*, 36:144, Mélanges maliens (1996), pp. 755–61.

Andrew, D. T. and R. McGowen, *The Perreaus and Mrs. Rudd: Forgery and Betrayal in Eighteenth-Century London* (Berkeley, CA; Los Angeles, CA; London: University of California Press, 2001).

Angiolini, F., and D. Roche (eds), *Cultures et formations négociantes dans l'Europe moderne* (Paris: Éditions de l'école des hautes études en sciences sociales, 1995).

Anon., *A Complete Guide to All Persons who have any Trade or Concern with the City of London, and Parts Adjacent* (London: J. Osborn, 1749).

Antonil, A. J., *Cultura e Opulência do Brasil* (1711), ed. A.P. Canbrava (São Paulo: Editora Nacional, 1967).

Aslanian, S., 'Social Capital: "Trust" and the Role of Networks in Julfan Trade: Informal and Semi-Formal Institutions at Work', *Journal of Global History*, 1:3 (November, 2006), pp. 383–402.

—, '"The Salt in a Merchant's Letter": The Culture of Julfan Correspondence in the Indian Ocean and the Mediterranean', *Journal of World History*, 19:2 (June 2008), pp. 127–88.

Appiah, K. A., *Cosmopolitanism: Ethics in a world of strangers* (New York: W. W. Norton & Company, 2006).

Attman, A., *Dutch Enterprise in the World Bullion Trade 1550–1800*, Humaniora, 23 (Göteborg: Kungl. Vetenskaps- och Vitterkets-Samhället, 1983).

Austen, R and W. D. Smith, 'Private Tooth Decay as Public Economic Virtue: The Slave-Sugar Triangle, Consumerism, and European Industrialization', in J. E. Imkori and S. Engerman (eds), *The Atlantic Slave Trade* (Durham, NC: Duke University Press, 1992), pp. 183–203.

Bailyn, B., *Atlantic History: Concept and Contours* (Cambridge, MA: Harvard University Press, 2005).

Barbauld, A. L. (ed.), *The Correspondence of Samuel Richardson, Author of Pamela, Clarissa, and Sir Charles Grandison. Selected from the Original Manuscripts, Bequeathed by Him to His Family. To which are Prefixed, a Biographical Account of that Author, and Observations on His Writings*, 6 vols (London: Lewis & Roden, 1804).

Baskind, S., 'Distinguishing the Distinction: Picturing Ashkenazi and Sephardic Jews in Seventeenth- and Eighteenth- Century Amsterdam', *Journal for the Study of Sephardic and Mizrahi Jewry*, 1:1 (February 2007), pp. 1-13.

—, 'Bernard Picart's Etchings of Amsterdam's Jews', *Jewish Social Studies: History, Culture, Society*, 13:2 (Winter 2007), pp. 40–64.

Bayly, C. A., *The Birth of the Modern World* (Malden, MA; and Oxford, UK: Blackwell Publishing, 2004).

Bayly, S., *Caste, Society and Politics in India from the Eighteenth Century to the Modern Age* (Cambridge: Cambridge University Press, 1999).

Baumol, W. J., 'Entrepreneurship: Productive, Unproductive, and Destructive', *Journal of Political Economy*, 98:5, part 1 (October 1990), pp. 893–921.

Beachy, R., *The Soul of Commerce: Credit, Property, and Politics in Leipzig, 1750–1840* (Leiden; Boston: Brill, 2005).

Beider, A., *A Dictionary of Ashkenazic Given Names: Their Origins, Structure, Pronunciation and Migrations* (Bergenfield, NJ: Avotagnu Inc., 2001).

Belfanti, C. M., and Giusberti, F., 'Clothing and Social Inequality in Early Modern Europe: Introductory Remarks', *Continuity and Change*, 15:3 (December 2000), pp. 359–65.

Ben-Amos, I., 'Gifts and Favors: Informal Support in Early Modern England', *Journal of Modern History*, 75 (2000), pp. 295–338.

Bentley, J., 'Cross-Cultural Interaction and Periodization in World History', *American History Review*, 101 (June 1996), pp. 749–70.

Berg, H., 'Thalia and Amsterdam's Ashkenazi Jews in the Late 18th and Early 19th Centuries', in Israel and Salverda (eds), *Dutch Jewry: Its History and Secular Culture*, pp. 191–211.

Bernstein, H., *The Brazilian Diamonds in Contracts, Contraband and Capital*, Atlantic Studies on Society in Change, 54 (Lanham, MD: University Press of America, 1988).

Bernstein, L., 'Opting Out of the Legal System: Extralegal Contractual Relations in the Diamond Industry', *Journal of Legal Studies*, 21 (January 1992), pp. 115–57.

Bernstein, W., *A Splendid Exchange – How Trade Shaped The World* (London: Atlantic Books, 2008).

Bevir, M. and F. Trentmann, 'Markets in Historical Contexts: Ideas, Practices and Governance', in M. Bevir and F. Trentmann (eds), *Markets in Historical Contexts – Ideas and Politics in the Modern World* (Cambridge: Cambridge University Press, 2004), pp. 1–24.

Bevis, J., 'Observation of the Eclipse of the Sun, April 1, 1764: In a Letter from Dr. John Bevis, to Joseph Salvador, Esq; F. R. S.', *Philosophical Transactions (1683–1775)*, 54 (1764), pp. 105–8.

Black, J. *Trade, Empire and British Foreign Policy, 1689–1815: The Politics of a Commercial State* (London: Routledge, 2007).

Blaut, J. M., *Eight Eurocentric Historians* (New York: Guilford Press, 2000).

Blondé, B., 'Conflicting Consumption Models? The Symbolic Meaning of Possessions and Consumption amongst the Antwerp Nobility at the End of the Eighteenth Century', in B. Blondé, N. Coquery, J. Stobart and I. Van Damme (eds), *Fashioning Old and New – Changing Consumer Preferences in Europe (Seventeenth-Nineteenth Centuries)*, Studies in European Urban History (1100–1800) (Turnhout: Brepols Publishers, 2009), pp. 61–79.

Bloom, H. I., *The Economic Activities of the Jews of Amsterdam in the Seventeenth and Eighteenth Centuries* (Williamsport, PA: Bayard Press, 1937).

Blunt, W., *The Complete Naturalist: A Life of Linnaeus* (Princeton, NJ: Princeton University Press, 2001).

Bombelles, Marquis de, *Journal d'un ambassadeur de France au Portugal (1786–1788)*, ed. R. Kann (Paris: Presses Universitaires de France, 1979).

Bonnot, E., *Commerce and Government Considered in their Mutual Relationship* (1776), trans. S. Eltis (Indianapolis: Liberty Fund, 2008).

Bosher, J. F., 'Huguenot Merchants and the Protestant International in the Seventeenth Century', *William and Mary Quarterly*, 3rd series, 52:1 (January 1995), pp. 77–102.

Bossenga, G., 'Protecting Merchants: Guilds and Commercial Capitalism in Eighteenth-Century France', *French Historical Studies*, 15:4 (Autumn 1988), pp. 693–703.

Boulton, J., 'Microhistory in Early Modern London: John Bedford (1601–1667)', *Continuity and Change*, 22:1 (May 2007), pp. 113–41.

Bowen, H. V., 'The "Little Parliament": The General Court of the East India Company, 1750–1784', *Historical Journal*, 34:4 (December 1991), pp. 857–72.

—, *Elites, Enterprise, and the Making of the British Overseas Empire, 1688–1775* (London: Macmillan, 1996).

—, *The Business of Empire: The East India Company and Imperial Britain, 1756–1833* (Cambridge: Cambridge University Press, 2006).

Bowles, S. and H. Gintis, 'The Revenge of Homo Economicus: Contested Exchange and the Revival of Political Economy', *Journal of Economic Perspectives*, 7:1 (Winter 1993), pp. 83–102.

Boxer, C. R., *A Idade de Ouro do Brasil (Dores de Crescimento de uma sociedade Colonial)* (São Paulo: Nova Fronteira, 1963).

Boyajian, J. C., *Portuguese Bankers at the Court of Spain, 1626–1650* (New Brunswick, NJ: Rutgers University Press, 1983).

—, *Portuguese Trade in Asia under the Habsburgs, 1580–1640* (Baltimore, MD: John Hopkins University Press, 2008).

Boyd, A. (ed.), *The Journal of William Beckford in Portugal and Spain 1787–1788* (Stroud: Nonsuch Publishing, 2006).

Brandão, F. de C., *História Diplomática de Portugal, uma cronologia* (Lisbon: Ministério dos Negócios Estrangeiros, 1984).

Brandt, F., *Notice sur la vie de Mr le Baron David de Purry, suivie de son testament et d'un extrait de sa correspondance particulière* (Neuchatel: Imprimerie de C.-H. Wolfrath, 1826).

C. Brasz and Y. Kaplan (eds), *Dutch Jews as Perceived by Themselves and Others*, Proceedings of the Eighth International Symposium on the History of the Jews in the Netherlands (Leiden, Boston; and Köln: Brill, 2001).

Braudel, F., *La méditerranée et le monde méditerranéen à l'époque de Philippe II*, 2 vols (Paris: Armand Colin, 1949).

—, *Civilisation matérielle, économie et capitalisme : XVe–XVIIIe siècle*, 3 vols (Paris: Armand Colin, 1979).

Braun, T. E. and J. B. Radner, *The Lisbon Earthquake of 1755 – Representations and Reactions* (Oxford: Voltaire Foundation, 2005).

Brewer, D., 'Lights in Space', *Eighteenth-Century Studies*, 37:2 (Winter 2004), pp. 171–86.

Brewer, J., *The Sinews of Power: War, Money and the English State, 1688–1783* (London, Unwin Hyman Ltd, 1989).

Broman, T. H., 'The Habermasian Public Sphere and Eighteenth-Century Historiography: A New Look at "Science in the Enlightenment"', *History of Science*, 36 (1998), pp. 123-49.

Buist, M. G., *At spes non fracta: Hope & Co. 1770–1815; Merchant Bankers and Diplomats at Work* (The Hague: M. Nijhoff, 1974).

Burke, E., *Reflections on the Revolution in France, and on the Proceedings in Certain Societies in London Relative to that Event. In a Letter Intended to have been Sent to a Gentleman in Paris. By the Right Honourable Edmund Burke* (London: printed for J. Dodsley, 1793).

Burke, P., 'The Language of Orders in Early Modern Europe', in Bush (ed.), *Social Orders and Social Classes in Europe since 1500*, pp. 1–12.

Bush, M. L. (ed.), *Social Orders and Social Classes in Europe since 1500: Studies in Social Stratification* (London: Longman, 1992).

Butler, J., *The Huguenots in America: A Refugee People in New World Society* (Cambridge, MA: Harvard University Press, 1983).

Cantor, G., 'The Rise and Fall of Emanuel Mendes da Costa: A Severe Case of "The Philosophical Dropsy?"', *English Historical Review*, 116:467 (June 2001), pp. 584–603.

Carrier, J. G., *Exchange and Western Capitalism since 1700* (London; New York: Routledge, 1995).

Carruthers, B. G., 'Homo Economicus and Homo Politicus: Non-Economic Rationality in the Early 18th Century London Stock Market', *Acta Sociologica*, 37:2 (1994), pp. 165–94.

Cesarani, D., *Port Jews – Jewish Communities in Cosmopolitan Maritime Trading Centres, 1550–1950* (London; Portland, OR: Frank Cass, 2002).

Cesarani, D., and G. Romain (eds), *Jews and Port Cities 1590–1990: Commerce, Community, and Cosmopolitanism* (London: Mitchell Vallentine & Co., 2005).

Chakrabarty, D., *Provincializing Europe: Postcolonial Thought and Historical Difference* (Princeton, NJ: Princeton University Press, 2000).

Challe, R., *Journal d'un voyage fait aux Indes Orientales (1690–1691)*(Paris: Mercure de France, 1979).

Chapman, S., *The Rise of Merchant Banking* (London; Boston, MA; Sydney: George Allen & Unwin, 1984).

Chardin, J., *Travels in Persia 1673–1677* (New York: Dover Publications, 1988).

Chartier, R., A. Boureau and C. Dauphin, *Correspondence: Models of Letter-Writing from the Middle Ages to the Nineteenth Century* (Princeton, NJ: Princeton University Press, 1997).

Child, J., *A New Discourse of Trade: Wherein are Recommended Several Weighty Points ... By Sir Josiah Child, Baronet*, 4th edn (London: J. Hodges; W. Meadows; C. Corbet; J. Jackson; J Stagg; and J. Bevill [1745]).

Clark, G., *A Farewell to Alms: A Brief Economic History of the World* (Princeton, NJ; Oxford: Princeton University Press, 2007).

Clifford herbarium, online at http://www.nhm.ac.uk/research-curation/research/projects/clifford-herbarium/ [accessed 18 March 2011].

Coclanis, P. A., 'Drang Nach Osten: Bernard Bailyn, the World-Island, and the Idea of Atlantic History', *Journal of World History*, 13:1 (March 2002), pp. 169–82.

— (ed.), *The Atlantic Economy during the Seventeenth and Eighteenth Centuries: Organization, Operation, Practice, and Personnel* (Columbia, SC: University of South Carolina Press, 2005).

Cohen Albert, P., *The Modernization of French Jewry: Consistory and Community in the Nineteenth Century* (Hanover, NH: Brandeis University Press, 1977).

Coolhaas, W. P., (ed.) *Generale Missiven van Gouverneurs-Generaal en Raden aan Heren XVII der Verenigde Oostindische Compagnie*, Deel I: 1610–1638 (Den Haag: Rijksgeschiedkundige Publicatiën, 1960).

— (ed.),*Generale Missiven van Gouverneurs-Generaal en Raden aan Heren XVII der Verenigde Oostindische Compagnie*, Deel III: 1655-1674 (Den Haag: Rijksgeschiedkundige Publicatiën, 1968).

Cooper, F., *Colonialism in Question: Theory, Knowledge, History* (Berkeley, CA: University of California Press, 2005).

Craswell, R., 'On the Uses of "Trust": Comment on Williamson, "Calculativeness, Trust, and Economic Organization',*Journal of Law & Economics*, 36 (April 1993), pp. 487-500.

Curtin, P. D., *Cross-Cultural Trade in World History* (Cambridge; New York: Cambridge University Press, 1984).

Dahl, G., *Trade, Trust, and Networks: Commercial Culture in Late Medieval Italy* (Lund: Nordic Academic Press, 1998).

Danvers, F. C. (ed.), *Letters Received by the East India Company from its Servants in the East, Transcribed from the 'Original Correspondence' Series of the India Office Records*, vol. 1: 1602–13, (London: Samspon Low, Marston & Company, 1896).

Davenant, C., 'Essay upon the Probable Methods of Making a People Gainers in the Balance of Trade', in C. Davenant, *The Political and Commercial Works of the Celebrated Writer Charles D'Avenant, LL.D. Relating to the Trade and Revenue of England, the Plantation Trade, the East-India Trade, and African Trade* (1771), ed. C. Whitworth, 5 vols (Farnborough: Gregg Press, 1967), vol. 2, pp. 163–382..

David, P. A., 'Why are Institutions the "Carriers of History"?: Path Dependence and the Evolution of Conventions, Organizations and Institutions', *Structural Change and Economic Dynamics*, 5:2 (1994), pp. 205–20.

Degryse, K., 'De Antwerpse fortuinen: kapitaalsaccumulatie, -investering en -rendement te Antwerpen in de 18[de] eeuw', *Bijdragen tot de Geschiedenis*, 88:1–4 (2005).

Dehing, P. and M. 't Hart, 'Linking the Fortunes: Currency and Banking, 1550–1800', in M. 't Hart, J. Jonker and J. Luiten van Zanden (eds), *A Financial History of The Netherlands* (Cambridge: Cambridge University Press, 1997), pp. 37–63.

Denucé, J., 'De Familie Wallis-Du Jon, De Familie van Lamoraal, Graaf van Egmond', *Antwerpsch Archievenblad*, 2:3 (1928), pp. 1–18.

—, 'Het Huis Affaytati', *Antwerpsch Archievenblad*, 2:4 (1929), pp. 218–24.

—, 'James Dormer en de Keizerlijke en Koninklijke Verzekeringskamer te Antwerpen', *Antwerpsch Archievenblad*, 2:4 (1929), pp. 225–62.

de Lima Júnior, A., *História dos Diamantes nas Minas Gerais* (Rio de Janeiro: Dois Mundos, 1945).

Delobette, E., 'Les mutations du commerce maritime du Havre, 1680–1730 (1ère partie)', *Annales de Normandie*, 51:1 (2001), pp. 3–69.

De Roover, R., 'What is Dry Exchange? A Contribution to the Study of English Mercantilism', *Journal of Political Economy*, 52:3 (September 1944), pp. 250–66.

—, *L'évolution de la Lettre de Change XIVe–XVIIIe siècles,* Affaires et gens d'affaires, 4 (Paris: Librairie Armand Colin, 1953).

Desmedt, L., 'Money in the "Body Politick": The Analysis of Trade and Circulation in the Writings of Seventeenth-Century Political Arithmeticians', *History of Political Economy*, 37:1 (Spring 2005), pp. 79–101.

de Souza, T. R., 'Goa-based Portuguese Seaborne Trade in the Early Seventeenth Century', in *Indian Economic & Social History Review*, 12:4 (1975), pp. 433–42.

de Vries, J., 'Connecting Europe and Asia: A Quantitative Analysis of the Cape-Route Trade, 1497–1795', in D.O. Flynn, A. Giráldez and R. Von Glahn (eds), *Global Connections and Monetary History, 1470–1800* (Aldershot: Ashgate, 2003), pp. 35–106.

—, 'The Limits of Globalization in the Early Modern World', *Economic History Review*, 63 (August 2010), pp. 710–33.

de Vries, J. and A. van der Woude, *Nederland 1500–1815: de eerste ronde van moderne economische groei* (Amsterdam: Balans, 1995).

Dickson, P. G. M., *The Financial Revolution in England – A Study in the Development of Public Credit 1688–1756* (Aldershot: Gregg Revivals, 1993).

Dillen, J. G., 'Amsterdam als wereldmarkt der edele metalen in de 17[de] en 18[de] eeuw', *De Economist*, 72:1 (December 1923), pp. 717–30.

—, *Van Rijkdom en Regenten. Handboek tot de economische en sociale geschiedenis van Nederland* ('s Gravenhage: Martinus Nijhoff, 1970).

Dimaggio, P., 'Cultural Aspects of Economic Action and Organization', in N. J. Smelser and R. Swedberg (eds), *Handbook of Economic Sociology* (Princeton, NJ: Princeton University Press, 1994), pp. 22–57.

Dirlik, A., 'Performing the World: Reality and Representation in the Making of World Histor(ies)', *Journal of World History*, 16:4 (December 2005), pp. 391–410.

Doerflinger, T. M., *A Vigorous Spirit of Enterprise: Merchants and Economic Development in Revolutionary Philadelphia* (Williamsburg, NC: University of North Carolina Press, 1986).

dos Santos, J. F., *Memórias do Distrito Diamantino da Comarca do Sêrro Frio* (Rio de Janeiro: Itatiaia, 1956).

Drayton, J., *Memoirs of the American Revolution, from its Commencement to the Year 1776, Inclusive; As Relating to the State of South-Carolina and Occasionally Refering to the States of North-Carolina and Georgia. In Two Volumes* (Charleston: A. E. Miller, 1831).

Duby, G., *Les Trois Ordres ou l'Imaginaire du féodalisme* (Gallimard: Paris, 1978).

Dutch Jewish Historical Museum, online at http://www.jhm.nl/cultuur-en-geschiedenis/personen/s/salvador,+mozes [accessed 18 March 2011].

Eagles, R., *Francophilia in English Society, 1748–1815* (London: MacMillan Press Ltd, 2000).

Elon, A., *The Pity of it All: A History of Jews in Germany, 1743–1933* (New York: Metropolitan Books, 2002).

Eltis, D., 'Atlantic History in Global Perspective', *Itinerario*, 23:2 (1999), pp. 146–61.

Elzas, B. A., *Joseph Salvador: Jewish Merchant Prince who came to South Carolina* (Charleston: S.n., 1902), pp. 14–17.

Endelman, T. M., *The Jews of Georgian England 1714–1830: Tradition and Change in a Liberal Society* (Ann Arbor, MI: University of Michigan Press, 1999).

Erskine, T., *Embedded Cosmopolitanism: Duties to Strangers and Enemies in a World of 'Dislocated Communities'* (Oxford; New York: Oxford University Press, 2008).

Everaert, J., 'Soldaten, diamantairs en jezuïeten – Nederlanders in Portugees-Indië voor 1590', in R. Van Gelder, J. Parmentier and V. Roeper (eds), *Souffrir pour Parvenir – De wereld van Jan Huygen van Linschoten* (Haarlem: Uitgeverij Arcadia, 1998), pp. 80–94, 182–4.

Family Search, online at http://www.familysearch.org/eng/default.asp [accessed 18 March 2011].

Fischel, W. J., 'The Jewish Merchant-Colony in Madras (Fort St. George) during the 17th and 18th Centuries: A Contribution to the Economic and Social History of the Jews in India', *Journal of the Economic and Social History of the Orient*, 3:1 (April 1960), 78–107.

—, 'The Jewish Merchant-Colony in Madras (Fort St. George) during the 17th and 18th Centuries: A Contribution to the Economic and Social History of the Jews in India (Concluded)', *Journal of the Economic and Social History of the Orient*, 3:2 (April 1960), pp. 175–95.

—, 'Bombay in Jewish History in the Light of New Documents from the Indian Archive', *Proceedings of the American Academy for Jewish Research*, 38 (1970–1), pp. 119–44.

Fisher, H. E. S., 'Anglo-Portuguese Trade, 1700–1770', *Economic History Review*, New Series, 16:2 (1963), pp. 219–33.

—, 'Lisbon, its English Merchant Community and the Mediterranean in the Eighteenth Century', in P. L. Cottrell and D. H. Aldcroft (eds), *Shipping, Trade and Commerce: Essays in memory of Ralph Davis* (Leicester: Leicester University Press, 1981), pp. 23–44.

Flynn, D. O. and A. Giraldez, 'Path Dependence, Time Lags, and the Birth of Globalisation: A Critique of O'Rourke and Williamson', *European Review of Economic History*, 8 (2004), pp. 81–108.

Force, P., *Self-Interest before Adam Smith: A Genealogy of Economic Science* (Cambridge: Cambridge University Press, 2003).

Forrest, G. W., 'The Siege of Madras in 1746 and the Action of La Bourdonnais', *Transactions of the Royal Historical Society*, 3rd series, 2 (1908), pp. 189–234.

Francis, D., *Portugal 1715–1808: Joanine, Pombaline and Rococo Portugal as seen by British Diplomats and Traders* (London: Tamesis Books Limited, 1985).

Frank, A. G., *ReOrient: Global Economy in the Asian Age* (Berkeley, CA: University of California Press, 1998).

Frevert, U., *Does Trust Have a History?* Max Weber Lecture Series (European University Institute, MWP – LS 2009/01).

Fuks-Mansfeld, R.G., 'Enlightenment and Emancipation from c.1750 to 1814', in J. C. H. Blom, R. G. Fuks-Mansfeld and I. Schöffer (eds), *The History of the Jews in the Netherlands* (Oxford; Portland: The Littman Library of Jewish Civilization, 2002), pp. 164–92.

Fukuyama, F., *The End of History and the Last Man* (London: Hamilton, 1992).

Furtado, J. F., *O livro da capa verde: o regimento diamantino de 1771 e a vida no Distrito Diamantino no período da real extração* (São Paulo: Annablume, 1996).

—, 'O labirinto da fortuna: ou os revezes na trajetória de um contratador dos diamantes', in E. Nodari, J. M. Pedro et al., *História: fronteiras*, 2 vols (Florianópolis: XX Simpósio Nacional da ANPUH, 1999), vol. 1, pp. 309–20.

—, *Chica da Silva e o contratador dos diamantes: o outro lado do mito* (São Paulo: Companhia das Letras, 2003).

Fusaro, M., *Reti commerciali e traffic globali nell'età moderna* (Bari; Roma: Laterza, 2008).

Gambetta, D. (ed.), *Trust: Making and Breaking Cooperative Relations* (Oxfordp; New York: Basil Blackwell Ltd, 1988).

Games, A. H., 'Atlantic History: Definitions, Challenges, and Opportunities', *American Historical Review*, 111:3 (June, 2006), pp. 741–57.

Gans, M. H., *Memorbook: History of Dutch Jewry from the Renaissance to 1940* (Baarn: Bosch & Keuning n.v., 1971).

Gelpi, R.-M. and F. Julien-Labruyère, *The History of Consumer Credit: Doctrines and Practices* (London: MacMillan, 2000).

Gemici, K., 'Karl Polanyi and the Antinomies of Embeddedness', *Socio-Economic Review*, 6:1 (January 2008), pp. 5–33.

Gibbs, G. C., 'Huguenot Contributions to England's Intellectual Life, and England's Intellectual Commerce with Europe, c.1680–1720', in I. Scouloudi (ed.), *Huguenots in Britain and their French Background, 1550–1800* (London: Huguenot Society of London, 1985), pp. 20–41.

Ginzburg, C. and C. Poni, 'The Name and the Game: Unequal Exchange and the Historiographic Marketplace', in E. Muir and G. Ruggiero (eds), *Microhistory and the Lost Peoples of Europe* (Baltimore, MD: John Hopkins University Press, 1991), pp. 1–10.

Glyn, L. B., 'Israel Lyons: A Short but Starry Career. The Life of an Eighteenth-Century Jewish Botanist and Astronomer', *Notes and Records of the Royal Society of London*, 56:3 (September 2002), pp. 275–305.

Goody, J., *Capitalism and Modernity – The Great Debate* (Cambridge: Polity Press, 2004).

Gould, S. J., 'The Anatomy Lesson: The Teachings of Naturalist Mendes da Costa, a Sephardi Jew in King George's Court', *Natural History* (December 1995), pp. 12–15, 62–3.

Granovetter, M., 'The Strength of Weak Ties', *American Journal of Sociology*, 78:6 (May 1973), pp. 1360–80.

—, 'Economic Action and Social Structure: The Problem of Embeddedness', *American Journal of Sociology*, 91:3 (November 1985), pp. 481–510.

—, *Getting a Job: A Study of Contacts and Careers* (Chicago, IL: University of Chicago Press, 1995).

Grassby, R., *The Idea of Capitalism before the Industrial Revolution* (Oxford: Rowman & Littlefield Publishers, 1999).

Greene, J. P. and P. D. Morgan (eds), *Atlantic History – A Critical Appraisal* (Oxford: Oxford University Press, 2009).

Greif, A., 'Reputation and Coalitions in Medieval Trade: Evidence on the Maghribi Traders', *Journal of Economic History*, 49:4 (December 1989), pp. 857–82.

—, 'Contract Enforceability and Economic Institutions in Early Trade: The Maghribi Traders' Coalition', *American Economic Review*, 83:3 (June 1993), pp. 525–48.

—, 'Institutions, Markets, and Games', in V. Nee and R. Swedberg (eds), *The Economic Sociology of Capitalism* (Princeton, NJ and Oxford: Princeton University Press, 2005), pp. ix–xxxi.

—, *Institutions and the Path to the Modern Economy: Lessons from Medieval Trade* (Cambridge and New York: Cambridge University Press, 2006).

Groenewegen, P., *Eighteenth-Century Economics: Turgot, Beccaria and Smith and their Contemporaries* (London and New York: Routledge, 2002).

Gross, N. (ed.), *Economic History of the Jews* (New York: Schocken Books, 1975).

Grunwald, M., *Hamburgs deutsche Juden bis zur Auflösung der Dreigemeinden 1811* (Hamburg: Alfred Janssen, 1904).

Gudeman, S., *Economics as Culture: Models and Metaphors of Livelihood* (London and Boston, MA: Routledge & Kegan Paul, 1986).

Gungwu, W., 'Merchants without Empire: The Hokkien Sojourning Communities', in Tracy (ed.), *The Rise of Merchant Empires*, pp. 400–21.

Gupta, D. (ed.), *Social Stratification*, Oxford in India Readings in Sociology and Social Anthropology (Oxford: Oxford University Press, 1992).

Hadas, E., *Human Goods, Economic Evils: A Moral Approach to the Dismal Science* (Wilmington, NC: ISI Books, 2007).

Hancock, D., 'L'émergence d'une économie de réseau (1640–1815)', *Annales: Histoire, Sciences sociales*, 58:3 (May–June 2003), pp. 649–72.

—, *Citizens of the World: London Merchants and the Integration of the British Atlantic Community, 1735–1785* (Cambridge: Cambridge University Press, 1995).

Hanway, J., *Letters Admonitory and Argumentative, from J. H—y, Merchant, to J. S—r, Merchant in Reply to Particular Passages, and the General Argument, of a Pamphlet, entitled, Further Considerations on the Bill, &c.* (London: Dodsley, 1753).

Hardin, R., *Trust & Trustworthiness*, Russell Sage Foundation Series on Trust, 4 (New York: Russell Sage Foundation, 2002).

Hatton, T. J., K. H. O'Rourke and A. M. Taylor (eds), *The New Comparative Economic History: Essays in Honor of Jeffrey G. Williamson* (Cambridge, MA; London: MIT Press, 2007).

Hintermaier, J. M., 'The First Modern Refugees? Charity, Entitlement, and Persuasion in the Huguenot Immigration of the 1680s', *Albion: A Quarterly Journal Concerned with British Studies*, 32:3 (Autumn 2000), pp. 429–49.

Hirschman, A. O., *The Passions and the Interests – Political Arguments for Capitalism before its Triumph* (Princeton, NJ: Princeton University Press, 1977).

—, 'Rival Interpretations of Market Society: Civilizing, Destructive, or Feeble?', *Journal of Economic Literature*, 20:4 (1982), pp. 1463–84.

Hodgson, M., *Rethinking World History: Essays on Europe, Islam, and World History*, ed. E. Burke III (Cambridge and New York: Cambridge University Press, 1993).

Hofmeester, K., 'Diamonds as a Global Luxury Commodity', in B.-S. Grewe, *Luxury in Global Perspective: Commodities and Practives, 1600–2000*, International Studies in Social History (New York; Oxford and Berghahn Books, forthcoming).

Holmes, S., *Benjamin Constant and the Making of Modern Liberalism* (New Haven, CT; London: Yale University Press, 1984).

Holton, J. R., *Economy and Society* (Abingdon: Routledge, 1992).

Hont, I., *Jealousy of Trade: International Competition and the Nation-State in Historical Perspective* (Cambridge, MA and London: Belknap Press of Harvard University Press, 2005).

Hoock, J., 'Professional Ethics and Commercial Rationality at the Beginning of the Modern Era', in M. Jacob and C. Secretan (eds), *The Self-Perception of Early Modern Capitalists* (New York: Palgrave Macmillan, 2008), pp. 147–160.

Hoppit, J., 'The Use and Abuse of Credit in Eighteenth-Century England', in D. C. Coleman and N. McKendrick (eds), *Business Life and Public Policy: Essays in Honour of D.C. Coleman* (Cambridge: Cambridge University Press, 1986), pp. 64–78.

Horden, P., and N. Purcell, *The Corrupting Sea – A Study of Mediterranean History* (Oxford: Blackwell, 2000).

—, 'The Mediterranean and "the New Thalassology"', *American Historical Review*, 111:3 (June, 2006), pp. 722–40.

Houtman-De Smedt, H., 'Charles Proli, Antwerps zakenman en bankier, 1723–1786. Een biografische en bedrijfshistorische studie', *Verhandelingen van de Koninklijke Academie voor Wetenschappen, Letteren en Schone Kunsten van België, Klasse der Letteren*, 45:108 (1983).

Hühner, L. A. M., 'Francis Salvador, a Prominent Patriot of the Revolutionary War', *American Historical Society, Publications*, 9 (1901), pp. 107–22.

Ingham, G., 'Some Recent Changes in the Relationship Between Economics and Sociology', *Cambridge Journal of Economics*, 20:2 (March 1996), pp. 243–75.

Innes, J., 'The King's Bench Prison in the Later Eighteenth Century', in J. Brewer and J. Styles (eds), *An Ungovernable People: The English and their Law in the Seventeenth and Eighteenth Centuries* (London: Hutchinson, 1980), pp. 251–61.

Israel, J., *European Jewry in the Age of Mercantilism, 1550–1750* (Oxford: Clarendon Press, 1985).

—, *Dutch Primacy in World Trade, 1585–1740* (Oxford: Oxford University Press, 1989).

—, *The Dutch Republic: Its Rise, Greatness, and Fall 1477–1806* (Oxford: Oxford University Press, 1995).

—, *Diasporas within a Diaspora: Jews, Crypto-Jews and the World Maritime Empires (1540–1740)* (Leiden: Brill, 2002).

—, 'The Republic of the United Netherlands until about 1750: Demography and Economic Activity', in J. C. H. Blom, R. G. Fuks-Mansfeld and I. Schöffer (eds), *The History of the Jews in the Netherlands* (Oxford and Portland, OR: The Littman Library of Jewish Civilization, 2002), pp. 85–115.

Israel, J., and R. Salverda (eds), *Dutch Jewry: Its History and Secular Culture* (Leiden; Boston, MA; Köln: Brill, 2002).

Jacob, M., *Strangers Nowhere in the World: The Rise of Cosmopolitanism in Early Modern Europe* (Philadelphia, PA: University of Pennsylvania Press, 2006).

Jeffries, D., *A Treatise on Diamonds and Pearls* (London: C. & J. Ackers, 1751).

Joseph Salvador Moriencourt, online at

www.sailingnavies.com/show_person.php?nid=1&id=6366 [accessed 18 March 2011]. www.pbenyon1.plus.com/Nbd/exec/M/Index.html

Jones, C. C., 'The Settlement of the Jews in Georgia', *American Historical Society, Publications*, 1 (1893), pp. 5–12.

Jones, E. L., *The European Miracle: Environments, Economies and Geopolitics in the History of Europe and Asia* (Cambridge: Cambridge University Press, 1981).

—, *Cultures Merging – A Historical and Economic Critique of Culture* (Princeton, NJ and Oxford: Princeton University Press, 2006).

Jones, G. and K. E. Sluyterman, 'British and Dutch Business History', in F. Amatori and G. Jones (eds), *Business History around the World* (Cambridge: Cambridge University Press, 2003), pp. 111–45.

Kagan, R. L. and P. D. Morgan (eds), *Atlantic Diasporas: Jews, Conversos, and Crypto-Jews in the Age of Mercantilism, 1500–1800* (Baltimore, MD: The Johns Hopkins University Press, 2009),

Kaplan, Y., 'Amsterdam and Ashkenazic Migration in the Seventeenth Century', in M. P. Beukers and J. J. Cahen (eds), *Proceedings of the 5th International Symposium on the History of the Jews in the Netherlands: The Netherlands and Jewish Migration, the Problem of Migration and Jewish Identity*, Studia Rosenthaliana Special Issue, 23:2 (Fall 1989), pp. 22–44.

—, 'The Jews in the Republic until about 1750: Religious, Cultural, and Social Life', in J. C. H. Blom, R. G. Fuks-Mansfeld and I. Schöffer (eds), *The History of the Jews in the Netherlands* (Oxford; Portland: Littman Library of Jewish Civilization, 2002), pp. 44–163.

Katz, D. S., *The Jews in the History of England 1485–1850* (Oxford: Clarendon Press, 1994).

Kessler, A. D., 'Enforcing Virtue: Social Norms and Self-Interest in an Eighteenth-Century Merchant Court', *Law and History Review*, 22:1 (Spring 2004), pp. 71–118.

—, *A Revolution in Commerce: The Parisian Merchant Court and the Rise of Commercial Society* (New Haven, CT; London: Yale University Press, 2007).

Khalil, E. L., (ed.), *Trust* (Cheltenham; Northampton, MA: Edward Elgar, 2003).

Kindleberger, C. P., *A Financial History of Western Europe* (London: George Allen & Unwin, 1984).

Kirschenbaum, A., 'Jewish and Christian Theories of Usury in the Middle Ages', *Jewish Quarterly Review*, New Series, 75:3 (January 1985), pp. 270–89.

Kooijmans, L., *Vriendschap en de kunst van het overleven in de zeventiende en achttiende eeuw* (Amsterdam: Bert Bakker, 1997).

Labourdette, J.-F., *La nation française à Lisbonne de 1669 à 1790 – Entre Colbertisme et Libéralisme* (Paris: Fondation Calouste Gulbenkian Centre Culturel Portugais, 1988).

Lachenicht, S., 'Huguenot Immigrants and the Formation of National Identities, 1548–1787', *Historical Journal*, 50:2 (June, 2007), pp. 309–31.

Lamoreaux, N., 'Economic History and the Cliometric Revolution', in A. Molho and G.S. Wood (eds), *Imagined Histories: American Historians Interpret the Past* (Princeton, NJ: Princeton University Press, 1998), pp. 59–84.

Lamoreaux, N., D. M. G. Raff and P. Temin, 'Beyond Markets and Hierarchies: Toward a New Synthesis of American Business History', *American Historical Review*, 108:2 (April 2003), pp. 404–33.

Landes, D. S., *The Wealth and Poverty of Nations: Why Some are So Rich and Some So Poor* (New York: W.W. Norton & Company Inc.,1999).

Le Long, I., *De Koophandel van Amsterdam*, 2 vols (Rotterdam: Ph. Losel, 1753).

Lenman, B. and P. Lawson, 'Robert Clive, the "Black Jagir", and British Politics', *Historical Journal*, 26:4 (December 1983), pp. 801–29.

Lenzen, G., *The History of Diamond Production and the Diamond Trade* (New York: Praeger Publishers, 1970).

Lewis, P. and E. Chamlee-Wright, 'Social Embeddedness, Social Capital and the Market Process: An Introduction to the Special Issue on Austrian Economics, Economic Sociology and Social Capital', *Review of Austrian Economics*, 21:2–3 (September 2008), pp. 107–18.

Libby, D. C., 'Reconsidering Textile Production in Late Colonial Brazil: New Evidence from Minas Gerais', *Latin American Research Review*, 32:1 (1997), pp. 88–108.

Liberles, R., 'The Jews and their Bill: Motivations in the Controversy of 1753', *Jewish History*, 2:2 (Fall 1987), pp. 29–36.

Lièvre, A., *Histoire des protestants et des églises réformées du Poitou*, 3 vols (Poitiers: Imprimerie de N. Bernard, 1860).

Lisanti, L. (ed.), *Negócios Coloniais*, 5 vols (Brasília: Ministério da Fazenda; São Paulo: Visão Editorial, 1973).

Litt, S., *Pinkas, Kahal and the Mediene – The Records of Dutch Ashkenazi Communities in the Eighteenth Century as Historical Sources* (Leiden; Boston; Köln: Brill, 2008).

Lodge, R., 'The English Factory at Lisbon: Some Chapters in Its History', *Transactions of the Royal Historical* Society, 4th series, 16 (1933), pp. 211–47.

Luhmann, N., 'Familiarity, Confidence, Trust: Problems and Alternatives', in Gambetta (ed.), *Trust: Making and Breaking Cooperative Relations*, pp. 94–107.

Luu, L., 'Natural-Born versus Stranger Born Subjects: Aliens and their Status in Elizabethan London', in N. Goose and L. Luu (eds), *Immigrants in Tudor and early Stuart England* (Brighton: Sussex Academic Press, 2005), pp. 57–75.

Lynn, M. R., 'Enlightenment in the Public Sphere: The Musée de Monsieur and Scientific Culture in Late Eighteenth-Century Paris', *Eighteenth-Century Studies*, 32:4 (1999), pp. 463-76

Macintyre, A. C., *Whose Justice? Which Rationality?* (London: Duckworth, 1988).

Mahbubani, K., *The New Asian Hemisphere – The Irresistible Shift of Global Power to the East* (New York: Public Affairs Books, 2008).

Maloney, J., 'Marshall, Cunningham, and the Emerging Economics Profession', *Economic History Review*, new series, 29:3 (August 1976), p. 440–51.

Manning, P., *Migration in World History*, Themes in World History Seriers (New York: Routledge, 2005).

Markovits, C., *The Global World of Indian Merchants 1750–1947; Traders of Sind from Bukhara to Panama* (Cambridge: Cambridge University Press, 2000).

Marshall, G., *Presbyteries and Profits: Calvinism and the Development of Capitalism in Scotland: 1560–1707* (Oxford: Oxford University Press, 1971).

—, *In Search of the Spirit of Capitalism: An Essay on Max Weber's Protestant Ethic Thesis* (London: Hutchinson, 1982).

Marshall, P. J., *East India Fortunes: The British in Bengal in the Eighteenth Century* (Oxford: Clarendon Press, 1976).

Mauro, F., 'Merchant Communities, 1350–1750', in Tracy (ed.), *The Rise of Merchant Empires*, pp. 255–86.

Marx, K., 'Das Kapital, Band I: Kritik der politischen Ökonomie', in K. Marx and F. Engels, *Werke*, Band 23 (Berlin: Dietz Verlag, 1962), pp. 11–802.

Matsuda, M. K., 'The Pacific', *American Historical Review*, 111:3 (June, 2006), pp. 758–80.

Mauss, M., *Sociologie et anthropologie* (Paris: Presses Universitaires de France, 1950).

Maxwell, K., 'Pombal and the Nationalization of the Luso-Brazilian Economy', *Hispanic American Historical Review*, 48:4 (November 1968), pp. 608–31.

—, *Conflicts and Conspiracies: Brazil and Portugal 1750–1808* (Cambridge; Cambridge University Press, 1973).

—, *Marquês de Pombal, paradoxo do iluminismo* (São Paulo: Editora Paz e Terra, 1996).

McCabe, I. B., 'Trading Diaspora, State Building and the Idea of National Interest', Presented at Interactions: Regional Studies, Global Processes, and Historical Analysis, Library of Congress, Washington DC, 28 February to 3 March, 2001, online at http://www.historycooperative.org/proceedings/interactions/mccabe.html [accessed 17 June 2009].

McCabe, I. B., G. Harlaftis and I. P. Minoglou (eds), *Diaspora Entrepreneurial Networks – Four Centuries of History* (Oxford and New York: Berg, 2005).

McKendrick, N., 'The Commercialization of Fashion', in N. McKendrick, J. H. Plumb and J. Brewer (eds), *The Birth of a Consumer Society: The Commercialization of Eighteenth-Century England* (Bloomington: Indiana University Press, 1982), pp. 34–99.

Meel, E., 'De firma James Dormer tussen traditie en vernieuwing: een Englishman abroad in het achttiende-eeuwse handelskapitalisme te Antwerpen' (PhD dissertation, Katholieke Universiteit Leuven, 1986).

Mehta, M., *Indian Merchants and Entrepreneurs in Historical Perspective* (Delhi: Academic Foundation, 1991).

Melon, J.-F., *A Political Essay upon Commerce. Written in French by Monsieur M*** Translated, with some Annotations, and Remarks. By David Bindon, Esq* (Dublin: Philip Crampton, 1738).

Mentz, S., 'The Commercial Culture of the Armenian Merchant: Diaspora and Social Behaviour', *Itinerario*, 28:1 (2004), pp. 16–28.

—, *The English Gentleman Merchant at Work: Madras and the City of London 1660–1740* (Copenhagen: Museum Tusculanum Press, 2005).

Michman, J., 'A Decade of Historiography of Dutch Jewry', in *Dutch Jewish History iii* – Proceedings of the Fifth Symposium on the History of the Jews in the Netherlands, Jerusalem, November 25–8, 1991 (Assen:, S.n., 1993), pp. 9–17.

Milgrom, P. R., D. C. North and B. R. Weingast, 'The Role of Institutions in the Revival of Trade: The Law Merchant, Private Judges, and the Champagne Fairs', *Economics & Politics*, 2:1 (March 1990), pp. 1–23.

Misztal, B.A., *Trust in Modern Societies: The Search for the Bases of Social Order* (Cambridge: Polity Press, 1996).

Mizuta, H., 'Moral Philosophy and Civil Society', in A. S. Skinner and T. Wilson (eds), *Essays on Adam Smith* (Oxford: Clarendon Press, 1975), pp. 114–30.

Moglen, E., 'Commercial Arbitration in the Eighteenth Century: Searching for the Transformation of American Law', *Yale Law Journal*, 93:1 (November 1983), pp. 135–52.

Mokyr, J. (ed.), *Oxford Encyclopedia of Economic History*, 5 vols (Oxford: Oxford University Press, 2003), vol. 3.

—, 'The Intellectual Origins of Modern Economic Growth', *Journal of Economic History*, 65:2 (June 2005), pp. 285–351.

Mukund, K., *The Trading World of the Tamil Merchant: Evolution of Merchant Capitalism* (Chennai: Orient Longman, 1999).

Muldrew, C., *The Economy of Obligation: The Culture of Credit and Social Relations in Early Modern England* (Basingstoke: Macmillan, 1998).

Muller, J. Z., *The Mind and the Market: Capitalism in Modern European Thought* (New York: Alfred A. Knopf, 2002).

Neal, L., *Rise of Financial Capitalism: International Capital Markets in the Age of Reason* (Cambridge: Cambridge University Press, 1990).

Newitt, M., *Portugal in European and World History* (London: Reaktion Books, 2009).

North, D., *Institutions, Institutional Change and Economic Performance* (Cambridge, Cambridge University Press, 1990).

—, 'Institutions', *Journal of Economic Perspectives*, 5:1 (Winter 1991), pp. 97–112.

Nozes, J. and M. L. Machado de Sousa, *O Terramoto de 1755 Testemunhos Britânicos – The Lisbon Earthquake of 1755 British Accounts* (Lisbon: British Historical Society of Portugal, 1990).

Nusteling, H. P. H., 'The Jews in the Republic of the United Provinces: Origins, Numbers and Dispersion', in Israel and Salverda (eds), *Dutch Jewry: Its History and Secular Culture*, pp. 43–57.

ODNB, Rudd [née Youngson], Margaret Caroline (*b*.c. 1745, *d.* in or before 1798?),

Offer, A., 'Between the Gift and the Market: The Economy of Regard', *Economic History Review*, New Series, 50:3 (August 1997), pp. 450–76.

O'Reilly, W., 'The Naturalization Act of 1709 and the Settlement of Germans in Britain, Ireland and the Colonies', in C. Littleton and R. Vigne (eds), *From Strangers to Citizens: The integration of Immigrant Communities in Britain, Ireland and Colonial America, 1550–1750* (Brighton; Portland: Sussex Academic Press), pp. 492–502.

Paes Leme, P. T. de A., 'Nobiliarquia Paulistana', *Revista do Instituto Histórico Geográfico Brasileiro*, 34:1 (1871), pp. 203–13.

Perelman, M., 'The Neglected Economics of Trust: The Bentham Paradox and its Implications', *American Journal of Economics and Sociology*, 57:4 (October 1998), pp. 381–89.

Perry, T. W., *Public Opinion, Propaganda and Politics in Eighteenth Century England, A Study of the Jew Bill of 1753* (Harvard, MA: Harvard University Press, 1962).

Phelps, E. S. (ed.), *Altruism, Morality, and Economic Theory* (New York: Russell Sage Foundation, 1975).

Philo-Patriae, *Considerations on the Bill to Permit Persons Professing the Jewish Religion to be Naturalized by Parliament* (London: S.n., 1753).

—, *Further Considerations on the Act to Permit Persons Professing the Jewish Religion, to be Naturalized by Parliament* (London: S.n., 1753).

Pocock, J. G. A., *Virtue, Commerce, and History* (Cambridge: Cambridge University Press, 1985).

Pointon, M., 'Jewellery in Eighteenth-Century England', in M. Berg and H. Clifford (eds), *Consumers and Luxury: Consumer Culture in Europe 1650–1850* (Manchester: Manchester University Press, 1999), pp. 120–46.

—, 'The Lives of Kitty Fisher', *British Journal for Eighteenth-Century Studies*, 27:1 (Spring 2004), pp. 77–97.

—, *Brilliant Effects: A Cultural History of Gem Stones and Jewellery* (New Haven, CT; London: Yale University Press, 2009).

Poirier, J.-P., *Le tremblement de terre de Lisbonne* (Paris: Odile Jacob, 2005).

Poitras, G., *The Early History of Financial Economics, 1478–1776 – From Commercial Arithmetic to Life Annuities and Joint Stocks* (Cheltenham; Northampton: Edward Elgar, 2000).

Pomeranz, K., *The Great Divergence: China, Europe, and the Making of the Modern World Economy* (Princeton, NJ: Princeton University Press, 2000).

Prabha Ray, H. and E. A. Alpers (eds), *Cross Currents and Community Networks: The History of the Indian Ocean World* (Oxford: Oxford University Press, 2007).

Prakash, O., *European Commercial Enterprise in Pre-Colonial India*, The New Cambridge History of India, II.5 (Cambridge: Cambridge University Press, 1998).

Rabello, D., *Os Diamantes do Brasil na rêgencia de Dom João (1792–1816): um estudo de dependência externa* (São Paulo: Editora Arte e Ciência, 1997).

Rabin, D., 'The Jew Bill of 1753: Masculinity, Virility, and the Nation', *Eighteenth-Century Studies*, 39:2 (2006), pp. 157–71.

Rhoden, N. L. (ed.), *English Atlantics Revisited* (Montreal; Kingston; London; Ithaca, NY: McGill-Queen's University Press, 2007).

Richarz, M., *Jewish Social Mobility in Germany during the Time Emancipation 1790–1871*, Leo Baeck Institute Yearbook XX (London: Secker and Warburg, 1975).

Richter, R., 'The New Institutional Economics: Its Start, its Meaning, its Prospects', *European Business Organization Law Review*, 6:2 (June 2005), pp. 161–200.

Richman, B. D., 'How Community Institutions Create Economic Advantage: Jewish Diamond Merchants In New York', *Law & Social Inquiry*, 32:2 (Spring 2006), pp. 383–420.

Robins, N., *The Corporation that Changed the World: How the East India Company Shaped the Modern Multinational* (London: Pluto Press, 2006).

Roche, D., *Le Siècle des Lumières en province: Académies et académiciens provinciaux*, 1680-1789, 2 vols (Paris: Mouton, 1978).

—, *The Culture of Clothing: Dress and Fashion in the 'Ancien Régime'* (Cambridge: Cambridge University Press, 1996).

Rogers, G. C. Jr, D. R. Chesnutt and C. J. Taylor (eds), *The Papers of Henry Laurens*, 16 vols (Columbia, SC: University of South Carolina Press, 1968–2003).

Roth, C., *Anglo-Jewish Letters (1158–1917)* (Edinburgh: R. & R. Clark, Limited, 1938).

—, *History of the Great Synagogue* (London: Edward Goldaton & Son Ltd, 1950).

Rothschild, E., 'An Alarming Commercial Crisis in Eighteenth-Century Angoulême: Sentiments in Economic History', *Economic History Review*, new series, 51:2 (May 1998), pp. 268–93.

—, *Economic Sentiments: Adam Smith, Condorcet, and the Enlightenment* (Cambridge, MA; London: Harvard University Press, 2001).

Rousseau, G. S., and Haycock, D., 'The Jew of Crane Court: Emanuel Mendes da Costa (1717–1791), Natural History and Natural Excess', *History of Science*, 37 (2000), pp. 127–70.

Rozen, M. (ed.), *Homelands and Diasporas: Greeks, Jews and their Migrations* (London and New York: I. B. Tauris & Co, 2008).

Russell-Wood, A. G. R., *Society and Government in Colonial Brazil, 1500–1822* (Aldershot: Ashgate Variorum, 1992).

Sahlins, M., *Stone Age Economics* (London: Tavistock Publications: 1974).

—, *Apologies to Thucydides – Understanding History as Culture and Vice Versa* (London; Chicago, IL: University of Chicago Press, 2004).

Samuel, E., 'The Jews in English Foreign Trade – A Consideration of the "Philo Patriae" Pamphlets of 1753', in J.M. Shaftesley (ed.), *Remember the Days – Essays on Anglo-Jewish History presented to Cecil Roth by members of the Council of The Jewish Historical Society of England* (London: The Jewish Historical Society of England, 1966), pp. 123–43.

—, 'Gems from the Orient: The Activities of Sir John Chardin (1643–1713) as a Diamond Importer and East India merchant', *Proceedings of the Huguenot Society*, 27:3 (2000), pp. 351–68.

Schlugleit, D., 'De Strijd om de Ambachtsregelingen in het Diamantvak te Antwerpen in 1754', *Bijdragen tot de Geschiedenis*, Nieuwe Reeks, 22:9 (1931), pp. 42–9.

Schorsch, J., *Jews and Blacks in the Early Modern World* (Cambridge; New York: Cambridge University Press, 2004).

—, 'Mosseh Pereyra de Paiva: An Amsterdam Portuguese Jewish Merchant Abroad in the Seventeenth Century', in Y. Kaplan (ed.), *The Dutch Intersection: The Jews and the Netherlands in Modern History* (Leiden; Boston: Brill, 2008), pp. 63–85.

Schulte-Beerbühl, M., *Deutsche Kaufleute in London: Welthandel und Einbürgerung (1660–1818)* (München: Oldenbourg, 2007).

Schumpeter, J. A., *Theorie der wirtschaftlichen Entwicklung* (Leipzig: Duncker & Humblot, 1911).

—, *History of Economic Analysis*, ed. E. B. Schumpeter (New York: Oxford University Press, 1954).

Schwarz, L. D., 'Income Distribution and Social Structure in London in the Late Eighteenth Century', *Economic History Review*, New Series, 32:2 (May 1979), pp. 250–9.

Seeman, E. R., 'Jews in the Early Modern Atlantic: Crossing Boundaries, Keeping Faith', in J. Cañizares-Esguerra and E.R. Seeman (eds), *The Atlantic in Global History 1500–2000* (Upper Saddle River, NJ: Pearson Prentice Hall, 2007), pp. 39–59.

Sen, A., *On Ethics and Economics* (Oxford: Blackwell, 1987).

Shaw, L. M. E., *The Anglo-Portuguese Alliance and the English Merchants in Portugal, 1654–1810* (Aldershot; Brookfield, VT: Ashgate, 1998).

Shipman, A., *The Market Revolution and its Limits – A Price for Everything* (London; New York: Routledge, 1999).

Shulvass, M. A., *From East to West: The Westward Migration of Jews from Eastern Europe during the Seventeenth and Eighteenth centuries* (Detroit, MI: Wayne State University Press, 1971).

Silver, A., 'Friendship in Commercial Society: Eighteenth-Century Social Theory and Modern Sociology', *American Journal of Sociology*, 95:6 (May 1990), pp. 1474–1504.

—, '"Two Different Sorts of Commerce" – Friendship and Strangership in Civil Society', in J. Weintraub and K. Kumar (eds), *Public and Private in Thought and Practice* (Chicago, IL: University of Chicago Press, 1998), pp. 43–74.

Simmel, G., *The Philosophy of Money* (London: Routledge & Kegan Paul Ltd, 1978).

Singer, A., 'Aliens and Citizens: Jewish and Protestant Naturalization in the Making of the Modern British Nation' (PhD dissertation, University of Missouri, 1999).

Skinner, Q. and M. van Gelderen (eds), *Republicanism – A Shared European Heritage*, Volume II: *The Values of Republicanism in Early Modern Europe* (Cambridge; New York: Cambridge University Press, 2002).

Slangen, L. H. G., L. A. Loucks and A H. L. Slangen (eds), *Institutional Economics and Economic Organisation Theory* (Wageningen: Wageningen Academic Publishers, 2008).

Slezkine, Y., *The Jewish Century* (Princeton, NJ: Princeton University Press, 2004).

Smail, J., 'Credit, Risk, and Honor in Eighteenth-Century Commerce', *Journal of British Studies*, 44:3 (July 2005), pp. 439–56.

Sohrabi, N., 'Global Waves, Local Actors: What the Young Turks Knew about Other Revolutions and Why It Mattered', *Comparative Studies in Society and History: An International Quarterly*, 44:1 (January 2002), pp. 45–79.

Solow, R. M., 'Economic History and Economics', *American Economic Review*, 75:2, Papers and Proceedings of the Ninety-Seventh Annual Meeting of the American Economic Association (May 1985), pp. 328–31.

Sonnenberg-Stern, K., *Emancipation and Poverty: The Ashkenazi Jews of Amsterdam 1796–1850* (London: Macmillan Press Ltd, 2000).

Spillman, L., 'Enriching Exchange: Cultural Dimensions of Markets', *American Journal of Economics and Sociology*, 58:4 (October 1999), pp. 1056–9.

Stechow, W., 'De Tempel der Kunst of het Kabinet van den Heer Braamcamp', Review Article, *Art Bulletin*, 44:2 (June 1962), pp. 151–2.

Stein, S. A., *Plumes: Ostrich Feathers, Jews, and a Lost World of Global Commerce* (New Haven, CT: Yale University Press, 2008).

Steuart, J., *An Inquiry into the Principles of Political Oeconomy* (London: A. Millar & T. Cadell, 1767).

Subrahmanyam, S. (ed.), *Merchant Networks in the Early Modern World* (Aldershot; Brookfield, VT: Variorum, 1996).

Sundstrom, R. A., 'French Huguenots and the Civil List, 1696–1727: A Study of Alien Assimilation in England', *Albion: A Quarterly Journal Concerned with British Studies*, 8:3 (Autumn 1976), pp. 219–35.

Sutherland, L., *A London merchant, 1695–1774* (London: Frank Cass & Company, 1962).

—, *Politics and Finance in the Eighteenth Century*, ed. Newman (London: The Hambledon Press, 1984).

—, 'The City of London and Politics', in Sutherland, *Politics and Finance in the Eighteenth Century*, pp. 37–66.

—, 'London and the Pitt-Devonshire Administration', in Sutherland, *Politics and Finance in the Eighteenth Century*, pp. 67–113.

—, 'Samson Gideon: Eighteenth Century Jewish Financier', in Sutherland, *Politics and Finance in the Eighteenth Century*, pp. 386–98.

Swedberg, R., *Max Weber and the Idea of Economic Sociology* (Princeton, NJ: Princeton University Press, 1998).

Swetschinski, D. M., 'The Portuguese Jewish Merchants of Seventeenth-Century Amsterdam: A Social Profile' (PhD dissertation, Brandeis University, 1980).

—, *Reluctant Cosmopolitans – The Portuguese Jews of Seventeenth-Century Amsterdam* (London; Portland, OR: Littman Library of Jewish Civilization, 2000).

Swetschinski, D. and L. Schönduve, *The Lopes Suasso Family, Bankers to William III* (Zwolle: Uitgeverij Waanders, 1988).

Tolansky, S., *The History and Use of the Diamond* (London: The Shenval Press, 1962).

Tracy, J. D. (ed.), *The Rise of Merchant Empires: Long-Distance Trade in the Early Modern World 1350–1750* (Cambridge; New York: Cambridge University Press, 1990).

—, *The Political Economy of Merchant Empires: State Power and World Trade 135–1750* (Cambridge; New York: Cambridge University Press, 1991).

Trivellato, F., 'Juifs de Livourne, Italiens de Lisbonne, hindous de Goa. Réseaux marchands et échanges interculturels à l'époque moderne', *Annales: Histoire, Sciences sociales*, 58:3 (May–June 2003), pp. 581–603.

—, 'A Republic of Merchants?', in A. Molho, D. R. Curto and N. Koniordos (eds), *Finding Europe: Discourses on Margins, Communities, Images ca. 13th–18th Centuries* (New York; Oxford: Berghahn Books, 2007), pp. 133–58.

—, 'Merchants' Letters across Geographical and Social Boundaries', in F. Bethencourt and F. Egmond (eds), *Cultural Exchange in Early Modern Europe*, vol. 3: Correspondence and Cultural Exchange in Europe, 1400–1700 (Cambridge: Cambridge University Press, 2007), pp. 80–103.

—, 'Images and Self-Images of Sephardic Merchants in Early Modern Europe and the Mediterranean', in M. Jacob and C. Secretan (eds), *The Self-Perception of Early Modern Capitalists* (New York: Palgrave Macmillan, 2008), pp. 49–74.

—, *The Familiarity of Strangers: The Sephardic Diaspora, Livorno, and Cross-Cultural Trade in the Early Modern Period* (New Haven, CT and London: Yale University Press, 2009).

Turgot, A. R. J., *Mémoires sur le prêt à intérêt et sur le commerce des fers* (Paris: Chez Froullé, 1789).

Valadares, V. M. T., 'Elites mineiras setecentistas: conjugação de dois mundos (1700–1800)', 2 vols (PhD dissertation, Universidade de Lisboa, 2002).

Valenze, D., *The Social Life of Money in the English Past* (Cambridge: Cambridge University Press, 2006).

Van Dam, P., *Beschryvinge van de Oostindische Compagnie*, Tweede Boek, Deel II (Den Haag: F. W. Stapel, 1932).

Van Den Hoek Ostende, J. H., Review of 'Asscher, S., *Diamant, Wonderlijk Kristal* (Bussum: Unieboek, 1975)', *Amstelodamum: Maandblad voor de kennis van Amsterdam*, 63:1 (January–February 1976), p. 24.

Van de Pol, L., 'Amsterdam Jews and Amsterdam Prostitution, 1650–1750', in Brasz and Kaplan (eds), *Dutch Jews as Perceived by Themselves and Others*, pp. 173–85.

Van der Cruysse, D., *Chardin le Persan* (Paris: Fayard, 1998).

Van der Wee, H., 'Monetary, Credit and Banking Systems', in E. E. Rich and C. Wilson (eds), *Cambridge Economic History of Europe*, vol. 5: The Economic Organization of Early Modern Europe (Cambridge: Cambridge University Press, 1977), pp. 290–392.

Van Dijk, L. C. D., *Neerland's vroegste betrekkingen met Borneo, den Solo-Archipel, Cambodja, Siam en Cochin-China* (Amsterdam: J. H. Scheltema, 1862).

Van Leur, J. C., *Indonesian Trade and Society* (Den Haag: W. Van Hoeve, 1955).

Vasconcelos, D. P. R., *Breve descrição geográfica, física e política da capitania de Minas Gerais* (1807), ed. C. M. J. Anastasia (Belo Horizonte: Fundação João Pinheiro, 1994).

Veblen, T., 'Why is Economics Not an Evolutionary Science?', *Quarterly Journal of Economics*, 12 (July 1898), pp. 373–97.

—, *The Vested Interests* (1919; New York: Viking Press, 1964).

Verberckmoes, J. and E. Stols, *Aziatische omzwervingen – het levensverhaal van Jacques de Coutre, een Brugs diamanthandelaar 1591–1627* (Berchem: EPO, 1988).

Ville, S., 'The Growth of Specialization in English Shipowning, 1750–1850', *Economic History Review*, New Series, 46:4 (November, 1993), pp. 702–22.

Viner, J., *Religious Thought and Economic Society: Four Chapters of an Unfinished Work*, ed. J. Melitz and D. Winch (Durham, NC: Duke University Press, 1978).

von Hameln, G., *The Memoirs of Glückel of Hameln*, trans. M. Lowenthal (New York: Schocken Books, 1977).

Wahrman, D., *The Making of the Modern Self: Identity and Culture in Eighteenth-Century England* (New Haven: Yale University Press, 2004).

Walford, A. R., *The British Factory in Lisbon and its Closing Stages Ensuing Upon the Treaty of 1810* (Lisbon: Instituto Britânico em Portugal, 1940).

Ward, K., *Networks of Empire – Forced Migration in the Dutch East India Company* (Cambridge: Cambridge University Press, 2009).

Wegener-Sleeswijk, A., 'La relation problématique entre principal et agent dans la commission: l'exemple de l'exportation des vins vers les Provinces-Unies au XVIIIe siècle', in S. Marzagalli and H. Bonin (eds), *Négoce, Ports et Océans, XVIe–XXe Siècles: Mélanges Offerts à Paul Butel* (Bordeaux: Presses Universitaires de Bordeaux, 2000), pp. 29–60.

Wigen, K., 'AHR Forum – Oceans of History: Introduction', *American Historical Review*, 111:3 (June, 2006), pp. 717–21.

Wijler, J. S., *Isaac de Pinto, Sa Vie et Ses Œuvres* (Apeldoorn; C.M.B. Dixon & Co., S.d.).

Williamson, O. E., *Markets and Hierarchies: Analysis and Antitrust Implications – A Study in the Economics of Internal Organization* (New York: Free Press, 1975).

—, 'Calculativeness, Trust, and Economic Organization', *Journal of Law & Economics*, 36 (April 1993), pp. 453-86.

Wilson, C., *Anglo-Dutch Commerce and Finance in the Eighteenth Century* (Cambridge: Cambridge University Press, 1966).

Wolf, L., 'The Jessurun Family', *Jewish Quarterly Review*, 1:4 (July 1889), pp. 439–41.

Woolf, M., 'Joseph Salvador 1716–1786', *Transactions and Miscellanies of The Jewish Historical Society of England*, 21 (1962–7), pp. 104–37.

Yogev, G., *Diamonds and Coral: Anglo-Dutch Jews and Eighteenth Century Trade* (Leicester: Leicester University Press, 1978).

Zahedieh, N., 'Credit, Risk, and Reputation in Late Seventeenth-Century Colonial Trade', in O. U. Janzen (ed.), *Merchant Organization and Maritime Trade in the North Atlantic, 1660–1815*, Research in Maritime History, 15 (St John's: International Maritime Economic History Association, 1998), pp. 53–74.

Zak, P. J. (ed.), *Moral Markets: The Critical Role of Values in the Economy* (Princeton, NJ; Oxford: Princeton University Press, 2008).

Zedler, J. H., *Grosses Vollständiges Universal-Lexikon aller Wissenschaften und Künste*, 64 vols (Halle, 1732–50).

Zell, M., *Reframing Rembrandt: Jews and the Christian Image in 17th Century Amsterdam* (Berkeley, CA: University of California Press, 2002).

Zemon Davis, N., 'Epilogue', in Kagan and Morgan (eds), *Atlantic Diasporas: Jews, Conversos, and Crypto-Jews in the Age of Mercantilism, 1500–1800*, pp. 213–17.

INDEX

Italics have been used to identify figures and tables.